THE BIBLE STORY

COPYRIGHT, 1906,
COPYRIGHT, 1917,

BY THE KING–RICHARDSON COMPANY,

SPRINGFIELD, MASS.

PREFACE

This volume contains those Old Testament stories of heroic lives, which never lose their charm. No better nor more fascinating stories were ever written than those of Abraham, and Joseph, and Gideon, and Moses. In the ordinary volume, however, they are scattered over many chapters and even books, and the reader has great difficulty in piecing them together. Here they are told as continuous narratives, with illustrations of the famous places, which enhance their charm. We believe that the old heroic figures will come, in this way, before the children, and older people as well, with a vividness and reality never before realized.

CONTENTS

		PAGE
THE PATRIARCHS.		
1	Abraham	21
2	Isaac	49
3	Jacob	60
4	Joseph	91
THE GREAT CAPTAINS.		
1	Moses	137
2	Joshua	277
THE JUDGES.		
1	Ehud	315
2	Gideon	319
3	Abimelech	332
4	Samuel	338
THE GREAT KINGS.		
1	Saul	349
2	David	382
3	Solomon	452
NOTES		485
MEMORY VERSES		503

ON THE WEST OF JERUSALEM, LOOKING TOWARD BETHLEHEM

From a photograph belonging to the Forbes Library, Northampton,
Mass., and used by special permission

PALESTINE

Blest land of Judea! thrice hallowed of song,
Where the holiest of memories pilgrim-like throng;
In the shade of thy palms, by the shores of thy sea,
On the hills of thy beauty, my heart is with thee.

With the eye of a spirit I look on that shore,
Where pilgrim and prophet have lingered before;
With the glide of a spirit I traverse the sod
Made bright by the steps of the angels of God.

Blue sea of the hills!—in my spirit I hear
Thy waters, Gennesaret, chime on my ear;
Where the Lowly and Just with the people sat down,
And thy spray on the dust of His sandals was thrown.

Beyond are Bethulia's mountains of green,
And the desolate hills of the wild Gadarene;
And I pause on the goat-crags of Tabor to see
The gleam of thy waters, O dark Galilee!

Hark, a sound in the valley! where, swollen and strong,
Thy river, O Kishon, is sweeping along;
Where the Canaanite strove with Jehovah in vain,
And thy torrent grew dark with the blood of the slain.

There down from his mountains stern Zebulon came,
And Naphtali's stag, with his eyeballs of flame,
And the chariots of Jabin rolled harmlessly on,
For the arm of the Lord was Abinoam's son!

The Patriarchs

The earliest years of Jewish history are called the Patriarchal Age, and the men who were the leaders of the people were called Patriarchs. It was a very simple age. The people were nomadic, wandering from place to place to find pasturage for their great flocks and herds. They lived in tents. The patriarchs were the sheiks of the tribes, like sheik Ilderim in the story of "Ben-Hur." It must be remembered that they lived at a rude and uncivilized time. They had none of the high moral teaching which we have. They often did things which were evil, but they also sought earnestly after God, and often in the silence of the desert, under the stars of night, found him, and worshiped him as truly as we do. Their story is the common human tale of struggle and defeat and victory, which is repeated under different circumstances in every age.

ABRAHAM

The Story of the First Great Hero of Israel's History. How He Tented with His Flocks on the Upland Pastures of Palestine, and Became the Father of a Great Nation.

THE MIGRATION.

He Leaves His Father's Home and Journeys to a New Country.

There was a man named Abram, who lived in the city of Ur of the Chaldees.

Now the Lord said unto Abram, "Get thee out of thy country, and from thy kindred, and from thy father's house, unto the land that I will show thee: and I will make of thee a great nation, and I will bless thee, and make thy name great; and be thou a blessing: and I will bless them that bless thee, and him that curseth thee will I curse: and in thee shall all the families of the earth be blessed."

So Abram went, as the Lord had spoken unto him; and Lot went with him: and Abram was seventy and five years old when he departed out of Haran. And Abram took Sarai his wife, and Lot his brother's son, and all their substance that they had gathered, and all their families and servants; and they went forth to go into the land of Canaan; and into the land of Canaan they came.

And Abram passed through the land unto the place of

Shechem, unto the oak of Moreh. And the Lord appeared unto Abram, and said, "Unto thy family will I give this land": and there builded he an altar unto the Lord, who appeared unto him.

And he removed from thence unto the mountain on the east of Beth-el, and pitched his tent, having Beth-el on the west, and Ai on the east; and there he builded an altar unto the Lord, and called upon the name of the Lord. And Abram journeyed, going on still toward the South.

ABRAM AND LOT.
The Division of the Land.

And Abram was very rich in cattle, in silver, and in gold. And Lot also, who went with Abram, had flocks, and herds, and tents. And the land was not able to hold them, that they might dwell together: for their substance was great, so that they could not dwell together. And there was a strife between the herdmen of Abram's cattle and the herdmen of Lot's cattle.

And Abram said unto Lot, "Let there be no strife, I pray thee, between me and thee, and between my herdmen and thy herdmen; for we are brethren. Is not the whole land before thee? separate thyself, I pray thee, from me: if thou wilt take the left hand, then I will go to the right; or if thou take the right hand, then I will go to the left."

And Lot lifted up his eyes, and beheld all the Plain of Jordan, that it was well watered everywhere, before the Lord destroyed Sodom and Gomorrah, like the garden of the Lord, like the land of Egypt.

THE TRADITIONAL OAK OF ABRAHAM, NEAR HEBRON
From a photograph belonging to Miss Julia W. Snow
and used by her kind permission

"And Abram passed through the land unto the place of Shechem, unto the Oak of Moreh"

So Lot chose for himself all the Plain of Jordan; and Lot journeyed east: and they separated themselves the one from the other. Abram dwelled in the land of Canaan, and Lot dwelled in the cities of the Plain, and moved his tent as far as Sodom. Now the men of Sodom were wicked and sinners against the Lord exceedingly. And the Lord said unto Abram, after Lot was separated from him, "Lift up now thine eyes, and look from the place where thou art, northward and southward and eastward and westward: for all the land which thou seest, to thee will I give it, and to thy family for ever. And I will make thy family as the dust of the earth: so that if a man can number the dust of the earth, then shall thy family also be numbered. Arise, walk through the land in the length of it and in the breadth of it; for unto thee will I give it."

And Abram moved his tent, and came and dwelt by the oaks of Mamre, which are in Hebron, and built there an altar unto the Lord.

THE FIGHT OF THE FIVE KINGS AGAINST THE FOUR.
The Capture of Lot, and His Rescue by Abram.

And there went out the king of Sodom, and the king of Gomorrah, and the king of Admah, and the king of Zeboiim, and the king of Bela (the same is Zoar); and they set the battle in array against them in the vale of Siddim; against Chedorlaomer, king of Elam, and Tidal, king of Goiim, and Amraphel, king of Shinar, and Arioch, king of Ellasar; four kings against the five.

Now the vale of Siddim was full of pitch pits; and the

kings of Sodom and Gomorrah fled, and they fell there, and they that remained fled to the mountain. And they took all the goods of Sodom and Gomorrah, and all their victuals, and went their way. And they took Lot, Abram's brother's son, who dwelt in Sodom, and his goods, and departed. And there came one that had escaped, and told Abram the Hebrew.

And when Abram heard that his brother was taken captive, he led forth his trained men, born in his house, three hundred and eighteen, and pursued as far as Dan. And he divided himself against them by night, he and his servants, and smote them, and pursued them unto Hobah, which is on the left hand of Damascus. And he brought back all the goods, and also brought again his brother Lot, and his goods, and the women also, and the people.

And the king of Sodom went out to meet him, after his return from the slaughter of Chedorlaomer and the kings that were with him. And Melchizedek, king of Salem, brought forth bread and wine: and he was priest of God Most High. And he blessed him, and said, "Blessed be Abram of God Most High, possessor of heaven and earth: and blessed be God Most High, who hath delivered thine enemies into thy hand." And he gave him a tenth of all.

And the king of Sodom said unto Abram, "Give me the persons and take the goods to thyself." And Abram said to the king of Sodom, "I have lifted up my hand unto the Lord, God Most High, possessor of heaven and earth, that I will not take a thread or a shoelatchet nor aught that is thine, lest thou shouldest say, 'I have made Abram rich':

save only that which the young men have eaten, and the portion of the men which went with me; let them take their portion."

GOD'S PROMISES.
The Making of the Covenant.

After these things the word of the Lord came unto Abram in a vision, saying, "Fear not, Abram: I am thy shield, and thy exceeding great reward."

And Abram said, "O Lord God, what wilt thou give me, seeing I am childless, and he that shall be possessor of my house is my servant, Eliezer of Damascus?"

And Abram said, "Behold, to me thou hast given no child: and, lo, one born in my house is mine heir." And, behold, the word of the Lord came unto him, saying, "This man shall not be thine heir; but he that shall be thine own son shall be thine heir."

And he brought him forth abroad, and said, "Look now toward heaven, and number the stars, if thou be able to number them": and he said unto him, "So shall thy family be."

And he believed in the Lord; and he counted it to him for righteousness. And he said unto him, "I am the Lord who brought thee out of Ur of the Chaldees, to give thee this land to inherit it." And he said, "O Lord God, whereby shall I know that I shall inherit it?"

And he said unto him, "Take me an heifer of three years old, and a she-goat of three years old, and a ram of three years old, and a turtle dove, and a young pigeon."

And he took him all these, and divided them in the

midst, and laid each half over against the other: but the birds divided he not. And the birds of prey came down upon the carcases, and Abram drove them away. And when the sun was going down, a deep sleep fell upon Abram; and, lo, an horror of great darkness fell upon him. And he said unto Abram, "Know of a surety that thy family shall be a stranger in a land that is not theirs, and shall serve them; and they shall afflict them four hundred years; and also that nation, whom they shall serve, will I judge: and afterward shall they come out with great substance. But thou shalt go to thy fathers in peace; thou shalt be buried in a good old age. And in the fourth generation they shall come hither again: for the iniquity of the Amorite is not yet full."

And it came to pass, that, when the sun went down, and it was dark, behold a smoking furnace, and a flaming torch that passed between these pieces. In that day the Lord made a covenant with Abram, saying, "Unto thy family have I given this land, from the river of Egypt unto the great river Euphrates."

THE BIRTH OF ISHMAEL.

Abram Receives a New Name. Visit of the Messengers.

(Now Sarai, Abram's wife, had no children, and, as the custom sometimes was in those days, she gave him her handmaid Hagar, to be his wife. And Hagar had a child, and Abram called the name of the child Ishmael.)

And when Abram was ninety and nine years old, the Lord appeared to Abram, and said unto him, "I am God Almighty; walk before me, and be thou perfect. And I will make my covenant between me and thee, and will multiply thee exceedingly."

And Abram fell on his face: and God talked with him, saying, "As for me, behold, my covenant is with thee, and thou shalt be the father of a multitude of nations. Neither shall thy name any more be called Abram, but thy name shall be Abraham; for the father of a multitude of nations have I made thee. And I will make thee exceeding fruitful, and I will make nations of thee, and kings shall come out of thee. And I will establish my covenant between me and thee and thy family after thee throughout their generations for an everlasting covenant, to be a God unto thee and to thy family after thee. And I will give unto thee, and to thy family after thee, the land of thy sojournings, all the land of Canaan, for an everlasting possession; and I will be their God."

And God said unto Abraham, "And as for thee, thou shalt keep my covenant, thou, and thy family after thee throughout their generations."

And God said unto Abraham, "As for Sarai, thy wife, thou shalt not call her name Sarai, but Sarah shall her name be. And I will bless her, and moreover I will give thee a son of her: yea, I will bless her, and she shall be a mother of nations; she shall bear thee a son; and thou shalt call his name Isaac: and I will establish my covenant with him for an everlasting covenant for his family after him."

And the Lord appeared unto him by the oaks of Mamre, as he sat in the tent door in the heat of the day; and he lifted up his eyes and looked, and, lo, three men stood over against him: and when he saw them, he ran to meet them from the tent door, and bowed himself to the earth and said, "My lord, if now I have found favor in thy sight, pass not away, I pray thee, from thy servant: let now a little water be fetched, and wash your feet, and rest yourselves under the tree: and I will fetch a morsel of bread, and comfort ye your heart; after that ye shall pass on: forasmuch as ye are come to your servant."

And they said, "So do, as thou hast said."

And Abraham hastened into the tent unto Sarah, and said, "Make ready quickly three measures of fine meal, knead it, and make cakes."

And Abraham ran to the herd, and fetched a calf tender and good, and gave it to the servant; and he hasted to dress it. And he took butter, and milk, and the calf which he had dressed, and set it before them; and he stood by them under the tree, and they did eat.

And the men rose up from thence, and looked toward Sodom: and Abraham went with them to bring them on the way. And the Lord said, "Shall I hide from Abraham that which I do; seeing that Abraham shall surely become a great and mighty nation, and all the nations of the earth shall be blessed in him? For I have known him, to the end that he may command his children and his household after him, that they may keep the way of the Lord, to do justice and judgment; to the end that the Lord may bring upon Abraham that which he hath spoken of him."

And the Lord said, "Because the cry of Sodom and Gomorrah is great, and because their sin is very grievous;

I will go down now, and see whether they have done altogether according to the report of it, which is come unto me; and if not, I will know."

And the men turned from thence, and went toward Sodom: but Abraham stood yet before the Lord. And Abraham drew near, and said, "Wilt thou consume the righteous within the city: wilt thou consume and not spare the place for the fifty righteous that are therein? That be far from thee to do after this manner, to slay the righteous with the wicked, that so the righteous should be as the wicked; that be far from thee: shall not the Judge of all the earth do right?"

And the Lord said, "If I find in Sodom fifty righteous within the city, then I will spare all the place for their sake."

And Abraham answered and said, "Behold now, I have taken upon me to speak unto the Lord, who am but dust and ashes: peradventure there shall lack five of the fifty righteous; wilt thou destroy all the city for lack of five?"

And he said, "I will not destroy it, if I find there forty and five."

And he spake unto him yet again, and said, "Peradventure there shall be forty found there."

And he said, "I will not do it for the forty's sake."

And he said, "Oh, let not the Lord be angry, and I will speak: peradventure there shall be thirty found there."

And he said, "I will not do it, if I find thirty there."

And he said, "Behold now, I have taken upon me to speak unto the Lord: peradventure there shall be twenty found there."

And he said, "I will not destroy it for the twenty's sake."

And he said, "Oh, let not the Lord be angry, and I will speak but this once: peradventure ten shall be found there."

And he said, "I will not destroy it for the ten's sake."

And the Lord went his way, as soon as he had done communing with Abraham: and Abraham returned unto his place.

DESTRUCTION OF THE CITIES OF THE PLAIN.
The Fate of Sodom and Gomorrah.

And the two angels came to Sodom at evening; and Lot sat in the gate of Sodom: and Lot saw them and rose up to meet them; and he bowed himself with his face to the earth; and he said, "Behold now, my lords, turn aside, I pray you, into your servant's house, and tarry all night, and wash your feet, and ye shall rise up early, and go on your way."

And they said, "Nay; but we will abide in the street all night."

And he urged them greatly; and they turned in unto him, and entered into his house; and he made them a feast, and baked unleavened bread, and they ate.

And the men said unto Lot, "Hast thou here any besides? son in law, and thy sons, and thy daughters, and whomsoever thou hast in the city; bring them out of the place: for we will destroy this place, because the cry of them has grown great before the Lord; and the Lord hath sent us to destroy it."

And Lot went out, and spoke to his sons in law, which

THE DEAD SEA

The five "Cities of the Plain" are supposed to have been situated to the north of the Dead Sea. The Dead Sea is 47 miles long, with an extreme breadth of about 10 miles. It lies 1290 feet below the sea level and is itself 1300 feet deep in the deepest part. (See note on page 257)

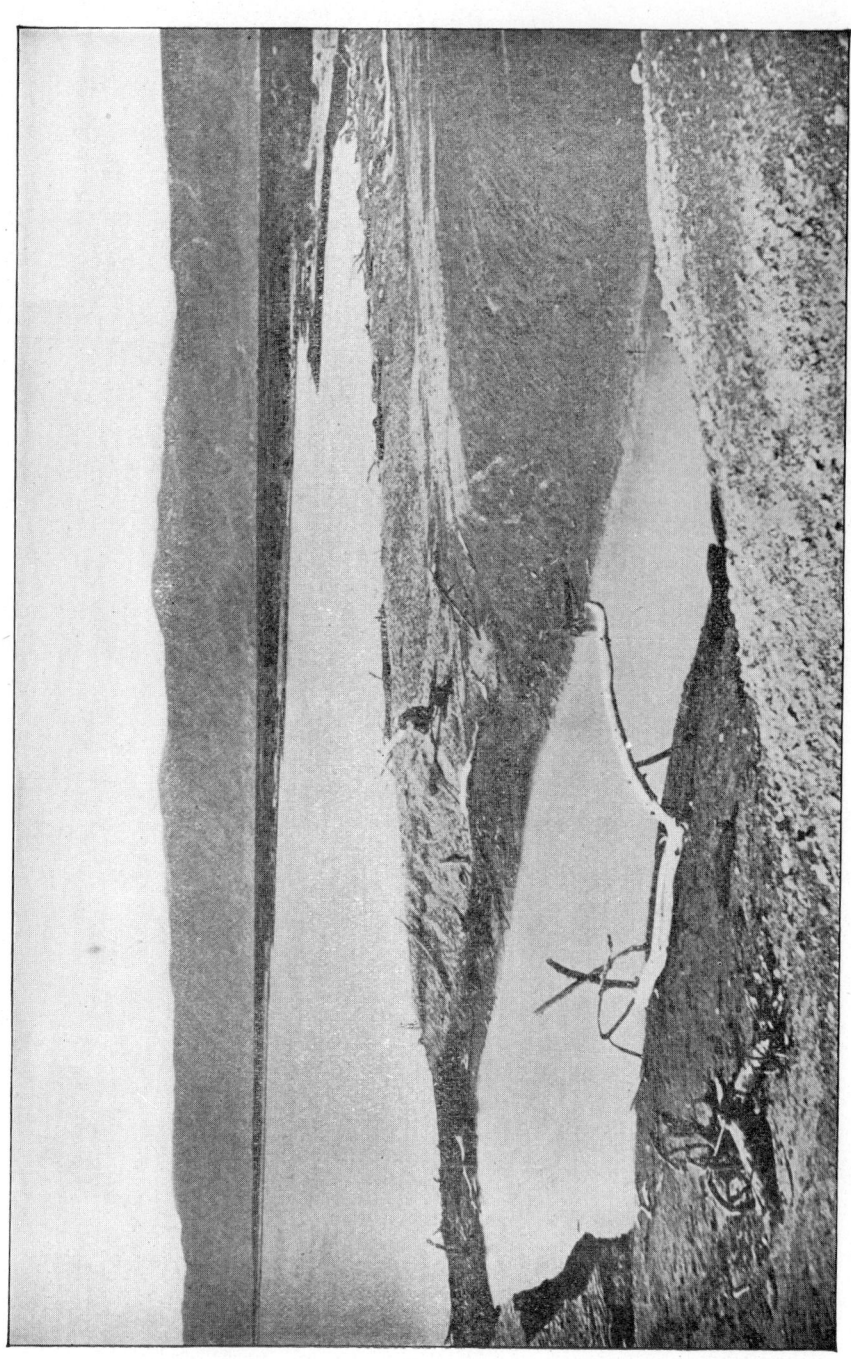

married his daughters, and said, "Up, get you out of this place; for the Lord will destroy the city." But he seemed to his sons in law as one who mocked.

And when the morning came, then the angels hastened Lot, saying, "Arise, take thy wife, and thy two daughters who are here; lest thou be consumed in the iniquity of the city."

But he lingered; and the men laid hold upon his hand, and upon the hand of his wife, and upon the hand of his two daughters; the Lord being merciful unto him: and they brought him forth, and set him without the city.

And it came to pass, when they had brought them forth abroad, that he said, "Escape for thy life; look not behind thee, neither stay thou in all the Plain; escape to the mountain, lest thou be consumed."

And Lot said to them, "Oh, not so, my lord: behold now, thy servant hath found grace in thy sight, and thou hast magnified thy mercy, which thou hast showed unto me in saving my life; and I cannot escape to the mountain, lest evil overtake me, and I die: behold now, this city is near to flee unto, and it is a little one: Oh, let me escape thither (is it not a little one?) and my soul shall live."

And he said unto him, "See, I have accepted thee concerning this thing also, that I will not overthrow the city of which thou hast spoken. Haste thee, escape thither; for I cannot do anything till thou be come thither." Therefore the name of the city was called Zoar, that is, "Little."

The sun was risen upon the earth when Lot came to Zoar. Then the Lord rained upon Sodom and upon Gomorrah brimstone and fire from the Lord out of heaven; and he overthrew those cities, and all the Plain and all the inhabitants of the cities, and that which grew upon the ground. But his wife looked back from behind him, and she became a pillar of salt.

And Abraham got up early in the morning to the place where he had stood before the Lord: and he looked toward Sodom and Gomorrah, and toward all the land of the Plain, and beheld, and, lo, the smoke of the land went up as the smoke of a furnace.

And it came to pass, when God destroyed the cities of the Plain, that God remembered Abraham, and sent Lot out of the midst of the overthrow, when he overthrew the cities in the which Lot dwelt.

BIRTH OF ISAAC.

Hagar and Ishmael Are Cast Out. Treaty with Abimelech.

And a child was born to Sarah, according as the Lord had promised, and Abraham called the name of his son, Isaac. And the child grew, and was weaned: and Abraham made a great feast on the day that Isaac was weaned. And Sarah saw the son of Hagar, the Egyptian, which she had borne unto Abraham, mocking. Wherefore she said unto Abraham, "Cast out this bondwoman and her son: for the son of this bondwoman shall not be heir with my son, even with Isaac."

And the thing was very grievous in Abraham's sight on account of his son. And God said unto Abraham, "Let it not be grievous in thy sight because of the lad, and be-

HAGAR AND ISHMAEL
By Cazin

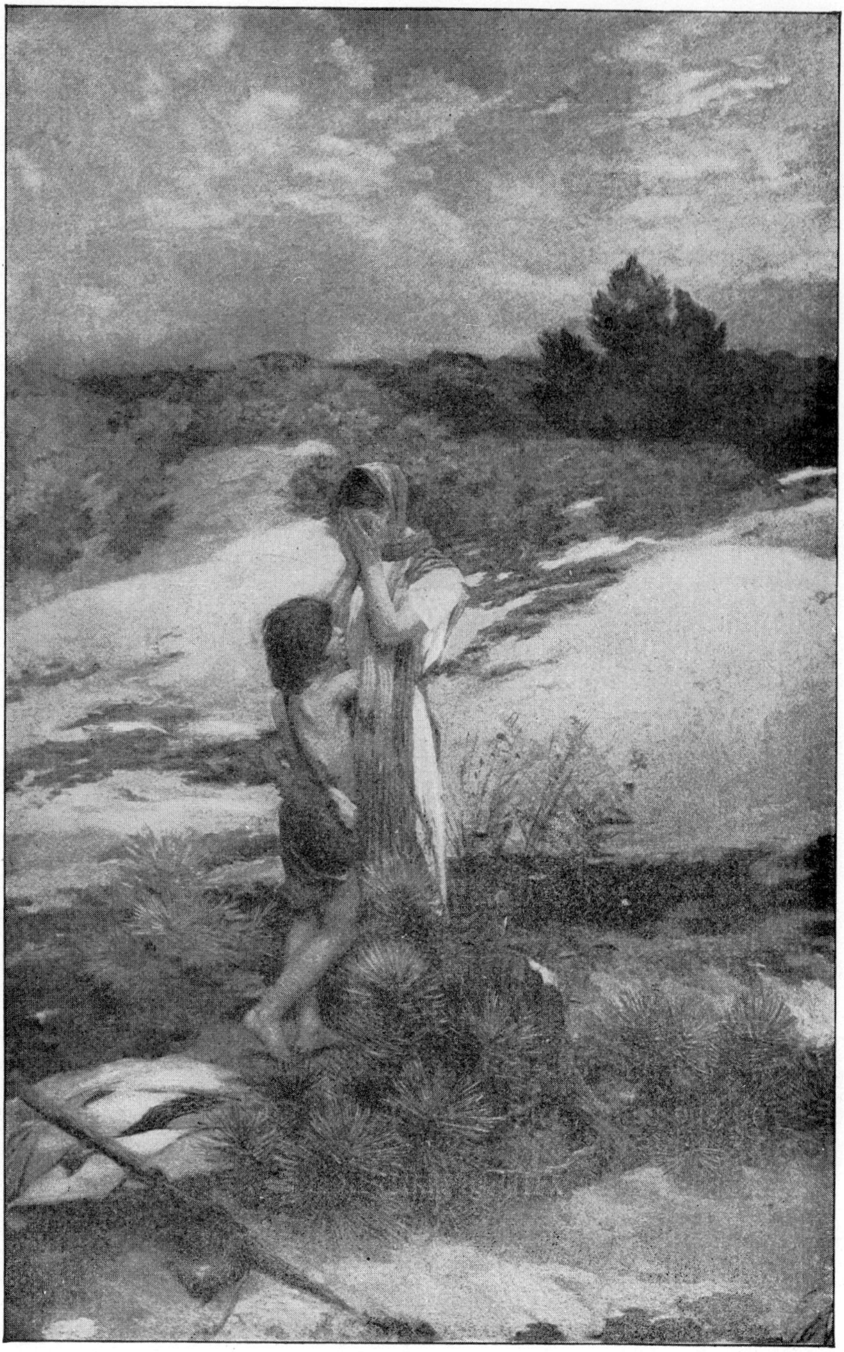

cause of thy bondwoman; in all that Sarah saith unto thee, hearken unto her voice; for in Isaac shall thy family be called. And also of the son of the bondwoman will I make a nation, because he is thy son."

And Abraham rose up early in the morning, and took bread and a bottle of water, and gave it to Hagar, putting it on her shoulder, and the child, and sent her away: and she departed and wandered in the wilderness of Beer-sheba. And the water in the bottle was spent, and she cast the child under one of the shrubs. And she went, and sat her down over against him a good way off, as it were a bow-shot: for she said, "Let me not look upon the death of the child."

And she sat over against him, and lifted up her voice, and wept. And God heard the voice of the lad; and the angel of God called to Hagar out of heaven, and said unto her, "What aileth thee, Hagar? fear not; for God hath heard the voice of the lad where he is. Arise, lift up the lad, and hold him in thine hand; for I will make him a great nation."

And God opened her eyes, and she saw a well of water; and she went, and filled the bottle with water, and gave the lad drink. And God was with the lad, and he grew; and he dwelt in the wilderness, and became an archer. And he dwelt in the wilderness of Paran: and his mother took him a wife out of the land of Egypt.

And it came to pass at that time, that Abimelech and Phicol, the captain of his host, spoke to Abraham, saying, "God is with thee in all that thou doest: now therefore swear unto me here by God that thou wilt not deal falsely with me, nor with my son, nor with my son's son: but according to the kindness that I have done unto thee, thou shalt do unto me, and to the land wherein thou hast sojourned."

And Abraham said, "I will swear."

And Abraham reproved Abimelech because of the well of water, which Abimelech's servants had violently taken away. And Abimelech said, "I know not who hath done this thing: neither didst thou tell me, neither yet heard I of it, but to-day."

And Abraham took sheep and oxen, and gave them unto Abimelech; and they two made a covenant. And Abraham set seven ewe lambs of the flock by themselves. And Abimelech said unto Abraham, "What mean these seven ewe lambs which thou hast set by themselves?"

And he said, "These seven ewe lambs shalt thou take of my hand, that it may be a witness unto me, that I have digged this well."

Wherefore he called that place Beer-sheba; because there they sware both of them. So they made a covenant at Beer-sheba: and Abimelech rose up, and Phicol, the captain of his host, and they returned into the land of the Philistines. And Abraham planted a tamarisk tree in Beer-sheba, and called there on the name of the Lord, the Everlasting God. And Abraham sojourned in the land of the Philistines many days.

THE TESTING OF ABRAHAM.
God Provides the Sacrifice.

And it came to pass after these things, that God proved Abraham, and said to him, "Abraham!"

And he said, "Here am I."

And he said, "Take now thy son, thine only son, whom thou lovest, even Isaac, and get thee into the land of Moriah; and offer him there for a burnt offering upon one of the mountains which I will tell thee of."

And Abraham rose early in the morning, and saddled his ass, and took two of his young men with him, and Isaac his son; and he split the wood for the burnt offering, and rose up, and went unto the place of which God had told him. On the third day Abraham lifted up his eyes, and saw the place afar off. And Abraham said to his young men, "Abide ye here with the ass, and I and the lad will go yonder; and we will worship, and come again to you."

And Abraham took the wood of the burnt offering, and laid it upon Isaac, his son; and he took in his hand the fire and the knife; and they went both of them together. And Isaac spoke unto Abraham, his father, and said, "My father": and he said, "Here am I, my son."

And he said, "Behold, the fire and the wood: but where is the lamb for a burnt offering?"

And Abraham said, "God will himself provide the lamb for a burnt offering, my son": so they went both of them together.

And they came to the place which God had told him of; and Abraham built the altar there, and laid the wood in order, and bound Isaac his son, and laid him on the altar, upon the wood. And Abraham stretched forth his hand, and took the knife to slay his son. And the angel of the Lord called unto him out of heaven, and said, "Abraham, Abraham."

And he said, "Here am I."

And he said, "Lay not thine hand upon the lad, neither do thou anything unto him: for now I know that thou fearest God, seeing thou hast not withheld thy son, thine only son, from me."

And Abraham lifted up his eyes, and looked, and behold, behind him a ram caught in the thicket by his horns; and Abraham went and took the ram, and offered him up for a burnt offering in the place of his son. And Abraham called the name of that place Jehovah-jireh (that is, Jehovah will provide): as it is said to this day, "In the mount of the Lord it shall be provided." And the angel of the Lord called unto Abraham a second time out of heaven, and said, "By myself have I sworn, saith the Lord, because thou hast done this thing, and hast not withheld thy son, thine only son: that I will certainly bless thee, and I will certainly multiply thy family as the stars of the heaven, and as the sand which is upon the sea shore; and thy family shall possess the gate of his enemies; and in thy family shall all the nations of the earth be blessed; because thou hast obeyed my voice."

So Abraham returned unto his young men, and they rose up and went together to Beer-sheba; and Abraham dwelt at Beer-sheba.

HEBRON

Used by special permission of the Palestine Exploration Fund

This is one of the most interesting spots in all the world; for here is the cave of Machpelah, the one ancient burial place which has been handed down from remote antiquity as the genuine site. The spot, as the burial place of Abraham and Sarah, Isaac and Rebekah, Jacob and Leah, has been venerated always by the adherents of the three great religions—Jews, Moslems, and Christians. The space containing the caves is inclosed by a great quadrangle of masonry 197 feet long and 111 feet wide called the Haram. Within this inclosure, directly over the caves, is built a mosque. For six hundred years no European except in disguise was known to have set foot in the sacred precincts. In 1862 the Prince of Wales was given permission, with much reluctance, to visit the inclosure. Since then a few visits have been made, but the cave itself has never been explored. A few visitors have been permitted to look down a shaft in the rock beneath the mosque, but there is no positive information as to what exists below the surface

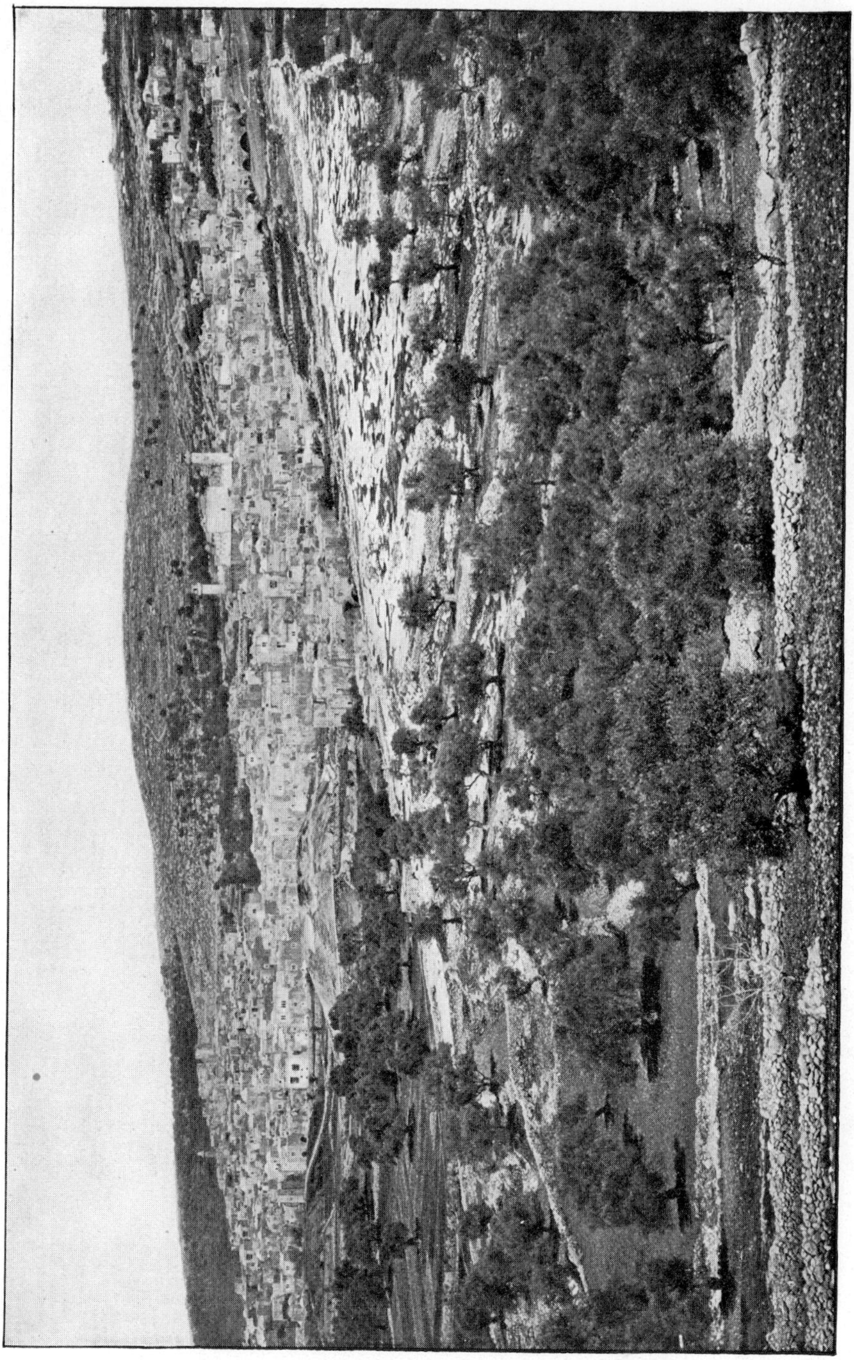

DEATH AND BURIAL OF SARAH.
Abraham Buys a Place to Lay His Dead.

And the life of Sarah was an hundred and seven and twenty years: these were the years of the life of Sarah. And Sarah died in Kiriath-arba (the same is Hebron), in the land of Canaan: and Abraham came to mourn for Sarah, and to weep for her. And Abraham rose up from before his dead, and spoke unto the children of Heth, saying, "I am a stranger and a sojourner with you: give me a possession of a burying place with you, that I may bury my dead out of my sight."

And the children of Heth answered Abraham, saying unto him, "Hear us, my lord: thou art a mighty prince among us: in the choice of our sepulchres bury thy dead; none of us shall withhold from thee his sepulchre, but that thou mayest bury thy dead."

And Abraham rose up and bowed himself to the people of the land, even to the children of Heth. And he communed with them, saying, "If it be your mind that I should bury my dead out of my sight, hear me, and intreat for me to Ephron, the son of Zohar, that he may give me the cave of Machpelah, which he hath, which is in the end of his field; for the full price let him give it to me in the midst of you for a possession of a burying place."

Now Ephron was sitting in the midst of the children of Heth: and Ephron the Hittite answered Abraham in the audience of the children of Heth, even of all that went in at the gate of his city, saying, "Nay, my lord, hear me: the field give I thee, and the cave that is therein, I give it thee; in the presence of the sons of my people give I it thee: bury thy dead."

And Abraham bowed himself down before the people of the land. And he spoke unto Ephron in the audience of the people of the land, saying, "But if thou wilt, I pray thee, hear me: I will give the price of the field; take it of me, and I will bury my dead there."

And Ephron answered Abraham, saying unto him, "My lord, hearken unto me: a piece of land worth four hundred shekels of silver, what is that betwixt me and thee? bury therefore thy dead."

And Abraham hearkened unto Ephron; and Abraham weighed to Ephron the silver, which he had named in the audience of the children of Heth, four hundred shekels of silver, current money with the merchant. So the field of Ephron, which was in Machpelah, which was before Mamre, the field, and the cave which was therein, and all the trees that were in the field, that were in all the border thereof round about, were made sure unto Abraham for a possession in the presence of the children of Heth, before all that went in at the gate of the city.

And after this, Abraham buried Sarah his wife in the cave of the field of Machpelah before Mamre (the same is Hebron), in the land of Canaan. And the field, and the cave that is therein, were made sure unto Abraham for a possession of a burying place by the children of Heth.

REBEKAH AND ELIEZER

From the Sculpture by Thorwaldsen

"And she said, 'Drink, my Lord.' And she hasted and let down her pitcher upon her hand and gave him drink"

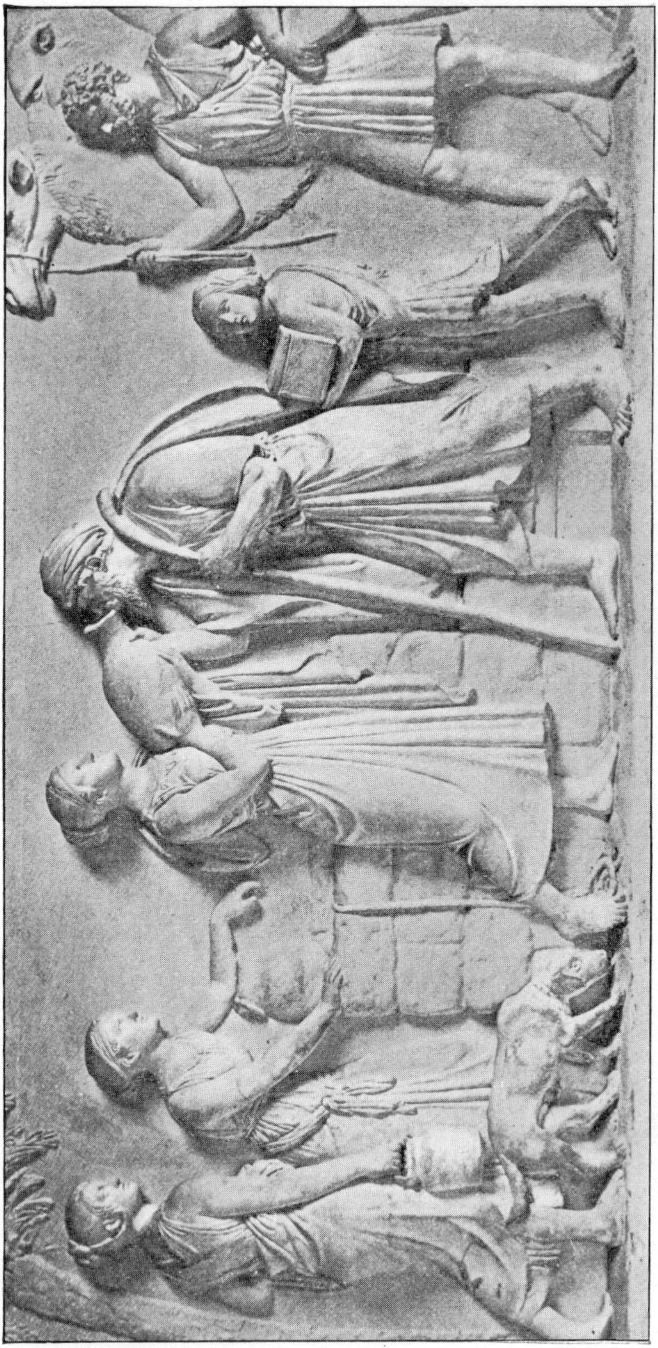

ISAAC

The Story of a Man Who Was Quiet and Gentle in His Nature, Who Lived in Peace with God and Man.

ISAAC AND REBEKAH.

How Abraham Sought a Fair Maiden of Nahor to be His Son's Wife.

And Abraham was old, and the Lord had blessed Abraham in all things.

And Abraham said to his servant, who ruled over all that he had, "Put, I pray thee, thy hand under my thigh: and I will make thee swear by the Lord, the God of heaven and the God of the earth, that thou shalt not take a wife for my son of the daughters of the Canaanites, among whom I dwell: but thou shalt go unto my country, and to my kindred, and take a wife for my son Isaac."

And the servant said unto him, "Peradventure the woman will not be willing to follow me unto this land: must I needs bring thy son again unto the land from whence thou camest?"

And Abraham said to him, "Beware thou that thou bring not my son thither again. The Lord, the God of heaven, who took me from my father's house, and from the land of my nativity, and that spoke unto me, and that swore unto me, saying, 'Unto thy family will I give this land'; he shall send his angel before thee, and thou shalt take a wife for my son from thence. And if the woman be not willing to follow thee, then thou shalt be clear from this my oath; only thou shalt not bring my son thither again."

And the servant put his hand under the thigh of Abraham his master, and swore to him concerning this matter. And the servant took ten camels, of the camels of his master, and departed; having all goodly things of his master's in his hand: and he arose, and went to Mesopotamia, unto the city of Nahor. And he made the camels kneel down outside the city by the well of water at the time of evening, the time that women go out to draw water.

And he said, "O Lord, the God of my master Abraham, send me, I pray thee, good speed this day, and shew kindness unto my master Abraham. Behold, I stand by the fountain of water; and the daughters of the men of the city come out to draw water: and let it come to pass, that the maiden to whom I shall say, 'Let down thy pitcher, I pray thee, that I may drink'; and she shall say, 'Drink, and I will give thy camels drink also': let the same be she that thou hast appointed for thy servant Isaac; and thereby shall I know that thou hast showed kindness unto my master.'"

And it came to pass, before he had done speaking, that, behold, Rebekah came out, who was born to Bethuel, the son of Milcah, the wife of Nahor, Abraham's brother, with her pitcher upon her shoulder. And the maiden was very fair to look upon, and she went down to the fountain, and filled her pitcher, and came up. And the servant ran to meet her, and said, "Give me to drink, I pray thee, a little water out of thy pitcher."

And she said, "Drink, my lord": and she hasted, and let down her pitcher upon her hand, and gave him drink.

And when she had done giving him drink, she said, "I will draw for thy camels also, until they have done drinking."

And she hasted, and emptied her pitcher into the trough, and ran again unto the well to draw, and drew for all his camels. And the man looked steadfastly on her; holding his peace, to know whether the Lord had made his journey prosperous or not.

And it came to pass, as the camels had done drinking, that the man took a golden ring of half a shekel weight, and two bracelets for her hands of ten shekels weight of gold; and said, "Whose daughter art thou? tell me, I pray thee. Is there room in thy father's house for us to lodge in?"

And she said unto him, "I am the daughter of Bethuel, the son of Milcah, which she bare unto Nahor." She said moreover unto him, "We have both straw and provender enough, and room to lodge in."

And the man bowed his head, and worshiped the Lord.

And he said, "Blessed be the Lord, the God of my master Abraham, who hath not forsaken his mercy and his truth toward my master: as for me, the Lord hath led me in the way to the house of my master's brethren."

And the maiden ran, and told her mother's house according to these words. And Rebekah had a brother, and his name was Laban: and Laban ran out unto the man, unto the fountain. And it came to pass, when he saw the ring, and the bracelets upon his sister's hands, and when he heard the words of Rebekah, his sister, saying, "Thus spoke the man unto me"; that he came unto the man; and, behold, he stood by the camels at the fountain.

And he said, "Come in, thou blessed of the Lord; wherefore standest thou without? for I have prepared the house, and room for the camels."

And the man came into the house, and he ungirded the camels; and he gave straw and provender for the camels, and water to wash his feet and the men's feet that were with him.

And there was set food before him to eat: but he said, "I will not eat, until I have told mine errand."

And he said, "Speak on."

And he said, "I am Abraham's servant. And the Lord hath blessed my master greatly; and he is become great: and he hath given him flocks and herds, and silver and gold, and menservants and maidservants, and camels and asses. And Sarah, my master's wife, bore a son to my master when she was old: and unto him hath he given all that he hath. And my master made me swear, saying, 'Thou shalt not take a wife for my son of the daughters of the Canaanites, in whose land I dwell: but thou shalt go unto my father's house, and to my kindred, and take a wife for my son.' And I said unto my master, 'Peradventure the woman will not follow me.' And he said unto me, 'The Lord, before whom I walk, will send his angel with thee, and prosper thy way; and thou shalt take a wife for my son of my kindred, and of my father's house: then shalt

REBEKAH
By Goodall

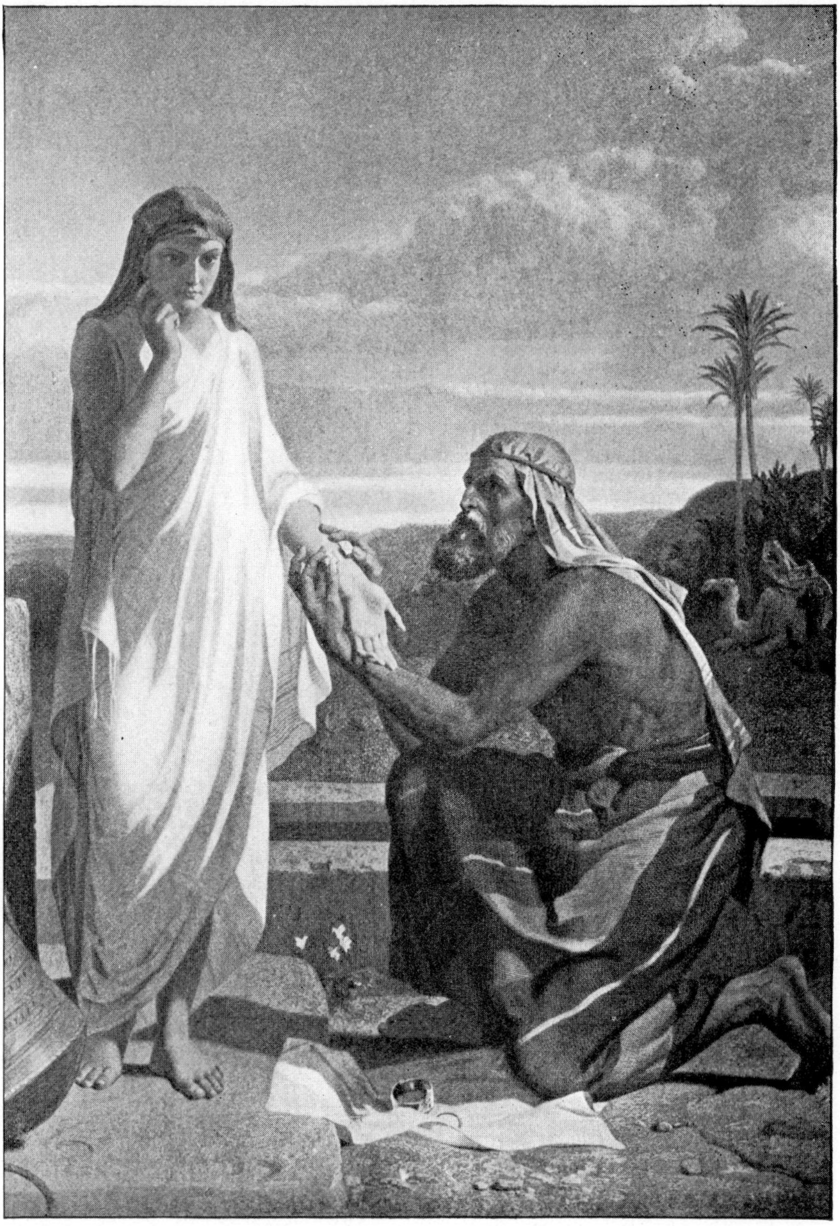

thou be clear from my oath, when thou comest to my kindred; and if they give her not to thee, thou shalt be clear from my oath.'

"And I came this day unto the fountain, and said, 'O Lord, the God of my master Abraham, if now thou do prosper my way which I go: behold, I stand by the fountain of water; and let it come to pass, that the maiden which cometh forth to draw, to whom I shall say, "Give me, I pray thee, a little water out of thy pitcher to drink"; and she shall say to me, "Both drink thou, and I will also draw for thy camels": let the same be the woman whom the Lord hath appointed for my master's son.' And before I had done speaking in mine heart, behold, Rebekah came forth with her pitcher on her shoulder; and she went down unto the fountain, and drew: and I said unto her, 'Let me drink, I pray thee.' And she made haste, and let down her pitcher from her shoulder, and said, 'Drink, and I will give thy camels drink also': so I drank, and she made the camels drink also. And I asked her, and said, 'Whose daughter art thou?' And she said, 'The daughter of Bethuel, Nahor's son, whom Milcah bore unto him': and I put the ring upon her nose, and the bracelets upon her hands. And I bowed my head and worshiped the Lord, and blessed the Lord, the God of my master Abraham, which had led me in the right way to take my master's brother's daughter for his son. And now if ye will deal kindly and truly with my master, tell me: and if not, tell me; that I may turn to the right hand, or to the left."

Then Laban and Bethuel answered and said, "The

thing proceedeth from the Lord: we cannot speak unto thee bad or good. Behold, Rebekah is before thee, take her, and go, and let her be thy master's son's wife, as the Lord hath spoken."

And it came to pass, that, when Abraham's servant heard their words, he bowed himself down to the earth unto the Lord. And the servant brought forth jewels of silver, and jewels of gold, and raiment, and gave them to Rebekah: he gave also to her brother and to her mother precious things.

And they ate and drank, he and the men that were with him, and tarried all night; and they rose up in the morning, and he said, "Send me away unto my master."

And her brother and her mother said, "Let the maiden abide with us a few days, at the least ten; after that she shall go."

And he said unto them, "Hinder me not, seeing the Lord hath prospered my way; send me away that I may go to my master."

And they said, "We will call the maiden, and inquire of her."

And they called Rebekah, and said unto her, "Wilt thou go with this man?"

And she said, "I will go." And they sent away Rebekah their sister, and her nurse, and Abraham's servant, and his men.

And they blessed Rebekah, and said to her, "Our sister, be thou the mother of thousands of ten thousands, and let thy family possess the gate of those who hate them."

A CAMEL RIDER

From a photograph belonging to Miss Clara L. Bodman
and used by her kind permission

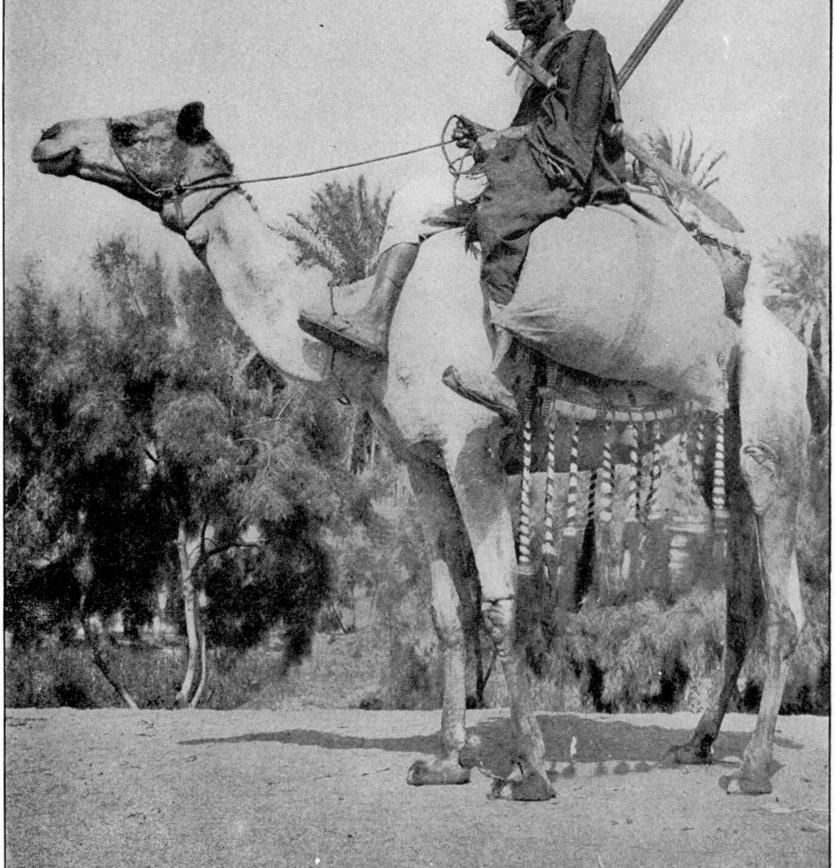

And Rebekah arose, and her maidservants, and they rode upon the camels, and followed the man: and the servant took Rebekah and went his way.

And Isaac came from the way of Beer-lahai-roi; for he dwelt in the land of the South. And Isaac went out to meditate in the field at the eventide: and he lifted up his eyes, and saw, and, behold, there were camels coming.

And Rebekah lifted up her eyes, and when she saw Isaac, she alighted from the camel. And she said unto the servant, "What man is this who walketh in the field to meet us?"

And the servant said, "It is my master": and she took her veil and covered herself. And the servant told Isaac all the things that he had done. And Isaac brought her to his mother Sarah's tent, and took Rebekah, and she became his wife; and he loved her: and Isaac was comforted after his mother's death.

THE DEATH OF ABRAHAM.

And these are the days of the years of Abraham's life which he lived, an hundred threescore and fifteen years. And Abraham died in a good old age, an old man, and full of years; and was gathered to his people. And Isaac and Ishmael his sons buried him in the cave of Machpelah, in the field of Ephron the son of Zohar the Hittite, which is before Mamre; the field which Abraham purchased of the children of Heth: there was Abraham buried, and Sarah, his wife. And it came to pass after the death of Abraham, that God blessed Isaac his son.

JACOB

The Story of the Man Who Struggled Much Between Right and Wrong and Who Suffered Many Things.

THE STRIFE BETWEEN THE BROTHERS.

Esau Sells His Birthright. Jacob Deceives His Father and Receives the Blessing Intended for Esau.

(Isaac, the son of Abraham, and Rebekah, his wife, had twin sons, named Jacob and Esau. Esau was a bold, rough, reckless boy, fond of hunting and adventure. Jacob was more quiet, but also more cunning. The recklessness of Esau and the cunning of Jacob many times cost them dear in later life.)

And the boys grew: and Esau was a cunning hunter, a man of the field; and Jacob was a plain man, dwelling in tents.

Now Isaac loved Esau, because he ate of his venison: and Rebekah loved Jacob. And Jacob boiled pottage: and Esau came in from the field, and he was faint: and Esau said to Jacob, "Feed me, I pray thee, with that same red pottage; for I am faint."

And Jacob said, "Sell me this day thy birthright."

And Esau said, "Behold, I am at the point of death: and what profit shall the birthright be to me?"

And Jacob said, "Swear to me this day"; and he swore unto him: and he sold his birthright to Jacob.

And Jacob gave Esau bread and pottage of lentils; and

he ate and drank, and rose up, and went his way: so Esau despised his birthright.

And it came to pass, that when Isaac was old, and his eyes were dim, so that he could not see, he called Esau his elder son, and said to him, "My son": and he said to him, "Here am I."

And he said, "Behold now, I am old, I know not the day of my death. Now therefore take, I pray thee, thy weapons, thy quiver and thy bow, and go out to the field, and take me venison; and make me savoury meat, such as I love, and bring it to me, that I may eat; that my soul may bless thee before I die."

And Rebekah heard when Isaac spoke to Esau his son. And Esau went to the field to hunt for venison, and to bring it. And Rebekah spoke to Jacob her son, saying, "Behold, I heard thy father speak to Esau thy brother, saying, 'Bring me venison, and make me savoury meat, that I may eat, and bless thee before the Lord before my death.' Now therefore, my son, obey my voice according to that which I command thee. Go now to the flock, and fetch me from thence two good kids of the goats; and I will make them savoury meat for thy father, such as he loveth: and thou shalt bring it to thy father, that he may eat, so that he may bless thee before his death."

And Jacob said to Rebekah his mother, "Behold, Esau my brother is a hairy man, and I am a smooth man. My father peradventure will feel me, and I shall seem to him as a deceiver; and I shall bring a curse upon me, and not a blessing."

And his mother said unto him, "Upon me be thy curse, my son: only obey my voice, and go fetch me them."

And he went, and fetched, and brought them to his mother: and his mother made savoury meat, such as his father loved. And Rebekah took the goodly garments of Esau her elder son, which were with her in the house, and put them upon Jacob her younger son: and she put the skins of the kids of the goats upon his hands, and upon the smooth of his neck: and she gave the savoury meat and the bread, which she had prepared, into the hand of her son Jacob. And he came unto his father, and said, "My father": and he said, "Here am I; who art thou, my son?"

And Jacob said unto his father, "I am Esau thy firstborn; I have done according as thou badest me: arise, I pray thee, sit and eat of my venison, that thy soul may bless me."

And Isaac said unto his son, "How is it that thou hast found it so quickly, my son?"

And he said, "Because the Lord thy God sent me good speed."

And Isaac said unto Jacob, "Come near, I pray thee, that I may feel thee, my son, whether thou be my very son Esau or not."

And Jacob went near unto Isaac his father; and he felt him, and said, "The voice is Jacob's voice, but the hands are the hands of Esau."

And he knew him not, because his hands were hairy, as his brother Esau's hands: so he blessed him.

And he said, "Art thou my very son Esau?"

JACOB'S DREAM
By Murillo

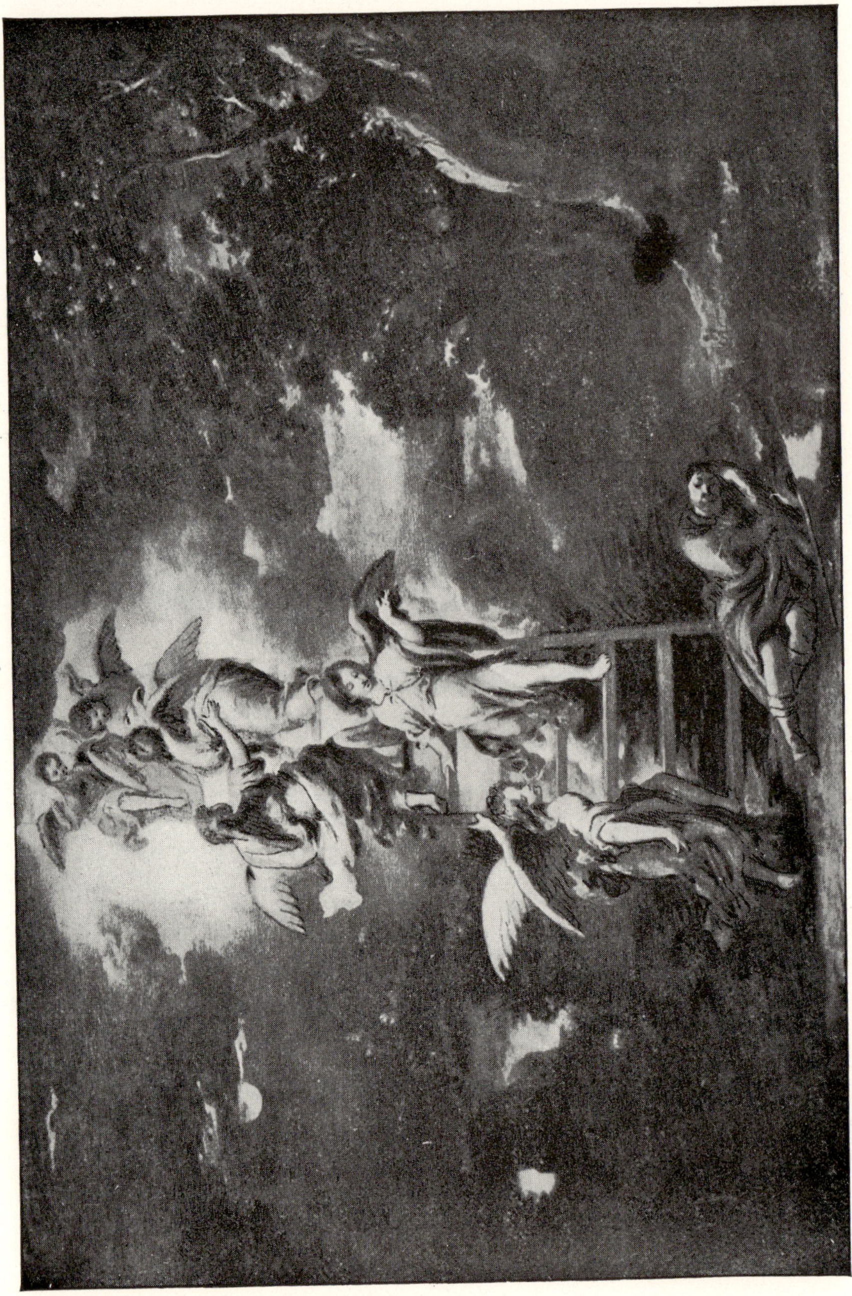

And he said, "I am."

And he said, "Bring it near to me, and I will eat of my son's venison, that my soul may bless thee."

And he brought it near to him, and he ate: and he brought him wine, and he drank. And his father Isaac said unto him, "Come near now, and kiss me, my son." And he came near, and kissed him.

And he smelled the smell of his garment, and blessed him, and said,—

"See, the smell of my son
Is as the smell of a field which the Lord hath blessed:
And God give thee of the dew of heaven,
And of the fatness of the earth,
And plenty of corn and wine:
Let peoples serve thee,
And nations bow down to thee:
Be lord over thy brethren,
And let thy mother's sons bow down to thee:
Cursed be every one that curseth thee,
And blessed be every one that blesseth thee."

And it came to pass, as soon as Isaac had made an end of blessing Jacob, and Jacob was yet scarce gone out from the presence of Isaac his father, that Esau his brother came in from his hunting. And he also made savoury meat, and brought it unto his father; and he said unto his father, "Let my father arise, and eat of his son's venison, that thy soul may bless me."

And Isaac his father said unto him, "Who art thou?"

And he said, "I am thy son, thy firstborn, Esau."

And Isaac trembled very exceedingly, and said, "Who then is he that hath taken venison and brought it to me, and I have eaten of all before thou camest, and have blessed him? yea, and he shall be blessed."

When Esau heard the words of his father, he cried with an exceeding great and bitter cry, and said unto his father, "Bless me, even me also, O my father."

And he said, "Thy brother came with guile, and hath taken away thy blessing."

And he said, "Is not he rightly named Jacob? for he hath supplanted me these two times: he took away my birthright; and, behold, now he hath taken away my blessing."

And he said, "Hast thou not reserved a blessing for me?"

And Isaac answered and said unto Esau, "Behold, I have made him thy lord, and all his brethren have I given to him for servants; and with corn and wine have I sustained him: and what then shall I do for thee, my son?"

And Esau said unto his father, "Hast thou but one blessing, my father? bless me, even me also, O my father."

And Esau lifted up his voice, and wept. And Isaac his father answered and said unto him:—

"Behold, of the fatness of the earth shall be thy dwelling,
And of the dew of heaven from above;
And by thy sword shalt thou live, and thou shalt serve thy brother;

And it shall come to pass when thou shalt break loose,
That thou shalt shake his yoke from off thy neck."

And Esau hated Jacob because of the blessing wherewith his father blessed him: and Esau said in his heart, "The days of mourning for my father are at hand; then will I slay my brother Jacob."

And the words of Esau her elder son were told to Rebekah; and she sent and called Jacob her younger son, and said unto him, "Behold, thy brother Esau comforts himself, purposing to kill thee. Now therefore, my son, obey my voice; and arise, flee thou to Laban my brother to Haran; and tarry with him a few days, until thy brother's fury turn away; until thy brother's anger turn away from thee, and he forget that which thou hast done to him: then I will send, and fetch thee from thence: why should I be bereaved of you both in one day?"

JACOB GOES FORTH FROM HOME.

He Dreams a Dream of a Ladder Reaching to Heaven.

And Isaac called Jacob, and blessed him, and charged him, and said unto him, "Thou shalt not take a wife of the daughters of Canaan. Arise, go to Paddan-aram, to the house of Bethuel thy mother's father; and take thee a wife from thence of the daughters of Laban thy mother's brother. And God Almighty bless thee, and make thee fruitful, and multiply thee, that thou mayest be a company of peoples; and give thee the blessing of Abraham, to thee, and to thy family with thee; that thou mayest inherit the land of thy sojournings, which God gave unto Abraham."

And Isaac sent away Jacob: and he went to Paddan-aram to Laban, son of Bethuel the Syrian, the brother of Rebekah, Jacob's and Esau's mother. Now Esau saw that Isaac had blessed Jacob and sent him away to Paddan-aram, to take him a wife from thence; and that as he blessed him he gave him a charge, saying, "Thou shalt not take a wife of the daughters of Canaan"; and that Jacob obeyed his father and his mother, and was gone to Paddan-aram.

And Jacob went out from Beer-sheba, and went toward Haran. And he came upon a certain place, and tarried there all night, because the sun was set; and he took one of the stones of the place, and put it under his head, and lay down in that place to sleep. And he dreamed, and behold a ladder set up on the earth, and the top of it reached to heaven: and behold the angels of God ascending and descending on it. And, behold, the Lord stood above it, and said, "I am the Lord, the God of Abraham thy father, and the God of Isaac: the land whereon thou liest, to thee will I give it, and to thy family; and thy family shall be as the dust of the earth, and thou shalt spread abroad to the west, and to the east, and to the north, and to the south: and in thee and in thy family shall all the families of the earth be blessed. And, behold, I am with thee, and will keep thee whithersoever thou goest, and will bring thee again into this land; for

I will not leave thee, until I have done that which I have spoken to thee of."

And Jacob awaked out of his sleep, and he said, "Surely the Lord is in this place; and I knew it not."

And he was afraid, and said, "How dreadful is this place! this is none other but the house of God, and this is the gate of heaven."

And Jacob rose up early in the morning, and took the stone that he had put under his head, and set it up for a pillar, and poured oil upon the top of it. And he called the name of that place Beth-el: but the name of the city was Luz at the first.

And Jacob vowed a vow, saying, "If God will be with me, and will keep me in this way that I go, and will give me bread to eat, and raiment to put on, so that I come again to my father's house in peace, then shall the Lord be my God, and this stone, which I have set up for a pillar, shall be God's house: and of all that thou shalt give me I will surely give the tenth unto thee."

JACOB AND RACHEL.
How Jacob Served Seven Years for the Woman He Loved.

Then Jacob went on his journey, and came to the land of the children of the east. And he looked, and behold a well in the field, and, lo, three flocks of sheep lying there by it; for out of that well they watered the flocks: and the stone upon the well's mouth was great. And thither were all the flocks gathered: and they rolled the stone from the well's mouth, and watered the sheep, and put the stone again upon the well's mouth in its place. And Jacob said unto them, "My brethren, whence are ye?" And they said, "Of Haran are we." And he said unto them, "Know ye Laban the son of Nahor?"

And they said, "We know him."

And he said unto them, "Is it well with him?"

And they said, "It is well: and, behold, Rachel his daughter cometh with the sheep."

And he said, "Lo, it is yet high day, neither is it time that the cattle should be gathered together: water ye the sheep, and go and feed them."

And they said, "We cannot, until all the flocks be gathered together, and they roll the stone from the well's mouth; then we water the sheep."

While he yet spoke with them, Rachel came with her father's sheep; for she kept them. And it came to pass, when Jacob saw Rachel the daughter of Laban his mother's brother, and the sheep of Laban his mother's brother, that Jacob went near, and rolled the stone from the well's mouth, and watered the flock of Laban his mother's brother. And Jacob kissed Rachel, and lifted up his voice, and wept. And Jacob told Rachel that he was her father's nephew, and that he was Rebekah's son: and she ran and told her father. And it came to pass, when Laban heard the tidings of Jacob his sister's son, that he ran to meet him, and embraced him, and kissed him, and brought him to his house. And he told Laban all these things.

And Laban said to him, "Surely thou art my bone and my flesh."

And he abode with him the space of a month. And Laban said unto Jacob, "Because thou art my nephew, shouldest thou therefore serve me for nought? tell me, what shall thy wages be?"

And Laban had two daughters: the name of the elder was Leah, and the name of the younger was Rachel. And Leah's eyes were tender; but Rachel was beautiful and well favored. And Jacob loved Rachel; and he said, "I will serve thee seven years for Rachel thy younger daughter."

And Laban said, "It is better that I give her to thee, than that I should give her to another man: abide with me."

And Jacob served seven years for Rachel; and they seemed unto him but a few days, for the love he had to her.

JACOB SETS OUT FOR HIS NATIVE LAND.
He Is Pursued by Laban, but a Covenant of Peace Is Made Between Them.

(Jacob also took Leah to be his wife. After many years of service, in which time many sons and daughters were born to him, Jacob, who increased exceedingly, and had large flocks, and maidservants and menservants, and camels and asses, wished to depart from the household of his father-in-law to his native land. So he went away secretly, with his wives and all his possessions.)

Now Laban was angry, and pursued Jacob, and Laban came up with Jacob. Now Jacob had pitched his tent in the mountain: and Laban with his brethren pitched in the mountain of Gilead. And Laban said to Jacob, "What hast thou done, that thou hast stolen away unawares to me, and carried away my daughters as captives of the sword? Wherefore didst thou flee secretly, and steal away from me; and didst not tell me, that I might have sent thee away with mirth and with songs, with tabret and with harp; and hast not suffered me to kiss my sons and my daughters? now hast thou done foolishly. It is in the power of my hand to do you hurt: but the God of your father spoke unto me yesternight, saying, 'Take heed to thyself that thou speak not to Jacob either good or bad.'"

And Jacob was wroth with Laban: and Jacob answered and said to Laban, "What is my trespass? what is my sin, that thou hast hotly pursued after me? This twenty years have I been with thee. The sheep of the flock which were torn of beasts I brought not unto thee; I bore the loss of them; of my hand didst thou require them, whether stolen by day or stolen by night. Thus I was; in the day the drought consumed me, and the frost by night; and my sleep fled from mine eyes. These twenty years have I been in thy house; I served thee fourteen years for thy two daughters, and six years for thy flock: and thou hast changed my wages ten times. Except the God of my father, the God of Abraham, and the Fear of Isaac, had been with me, surely now hadst thou sent me away empty. God hath seen mine affliction and the labor of my hands, and rebuked thee yesternight."

And Laban answered and said unto Jacob, "The daughters are my daughters, and the children are my children, and the flocks are my flocks, and all that thou seest is mine:

HEBRON

Hebron, famous in Old Testament story, is to-day one of the four sacred cities of the Moslems. It is in a little valley surrounded by hills, which are still covered with vineyards

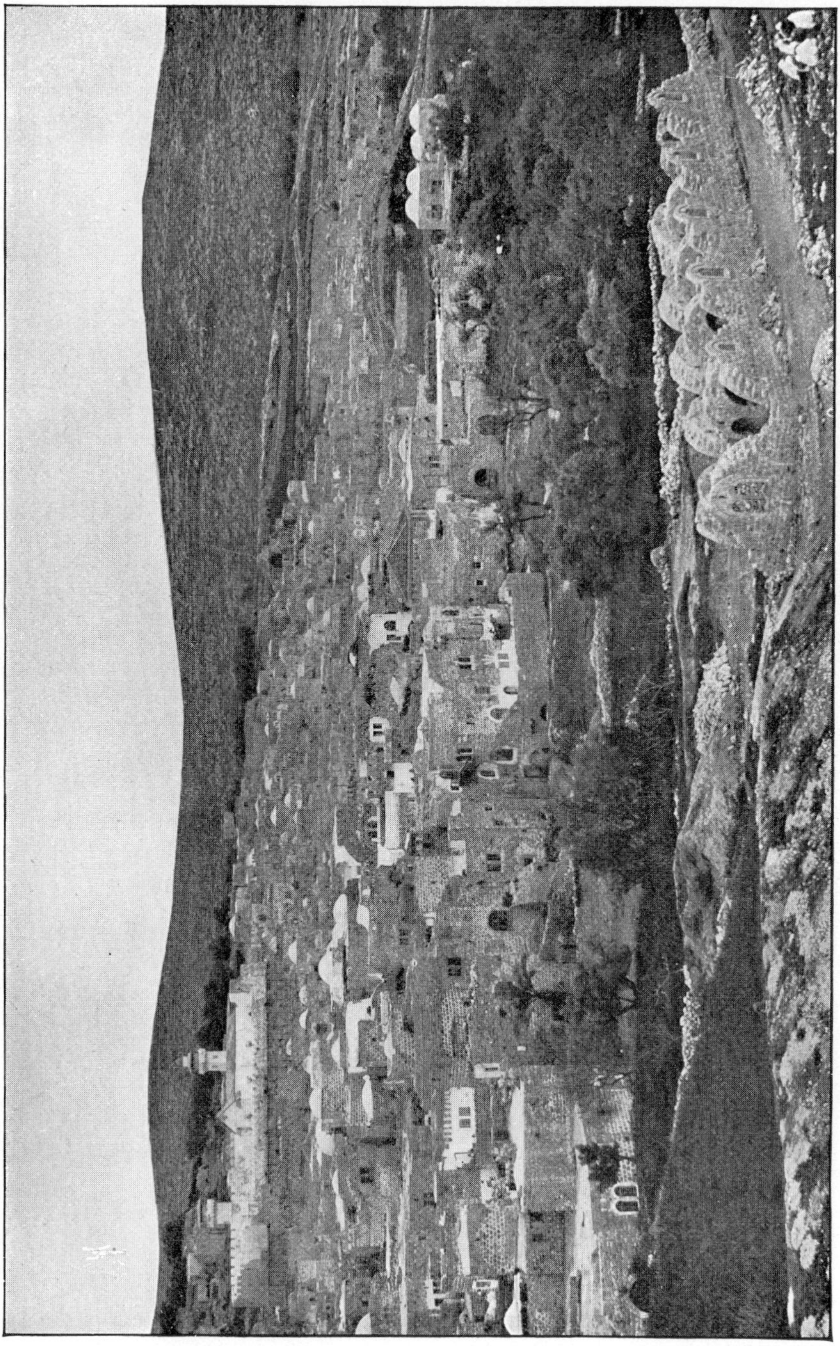

and what can I do this day unto these my daughters, or unto their children which they have borne? And now come, let us make a covenant, I and thou; and let it be for a witness between me and thee."

And Jacob took a stone, and set it up for a pillar. And Jacob said unto his brethren, "Gather stones"; and they took stones, and made an heap: and they ate there by the heap. And Laban called it "Jegar-sahadutha": but Jacob called it Galeed.

And Laban said, "This heap is witness between me and thee this day." Therefore was the name of it called Galeed: and "Mizpah" (that is, watchtower), for he said,

> "The Lord watch between me and thee,
> When we are absent one from another."

"If thou shalt afflict my daughters, and if thou shalt take wives beside my daughters, no man is with us; see, God is witness between me and thee."

And Laban said to Jacob, "Behold this heap, and behold the pillar, which I have set between me and thee. This heap be witness, and the pillar be witness, that I will not pass over this heap to thee, and that thou shalt not pass over this heap and this pillar unto me, for harm.

"The God of Abraham, and the God of Nahor, the God of their father, judge between us."

And Jacob swore by the Fear of his father Isaac. And Jacob offered a sacrifice in the mountain, and called his brethren to eat bread: and they did eat bread, and tarried all night in the mountain. And early in the morning

Laban rose up, and kissed his sons and his daughters, and blessed them: and Laban departed, and returned unto his place.

And Jacob went on his way, and the angels of God met him. And Jacob said when he saw them, "This is God's host": and he called the name of that place Mahanaim (that is, Two Hosts).

JACOB FEARS THE WRATH OF ESAU.
He Wrestles with the Angel. The Brothers Meet and are Reconciled.

And Jacob sent messengers before him to Esau his brother unto the land of Seir, the field of Edom. And he commanded them, saying, "Thus shall ye say unto my lord Esau; 'Thus saith thy servant Jacob, I have sojourned with Laban, and stayed until now: and I have oxen, and asses and flocks, and menservants and maidservants: and I have sent to tell my lord, that I may find grace in thy sight.'"

And the messengers returned to Jacob, saying, "We came to thy brother Esau, and moreover he cometh to meet thee, and four hundred men with him."

Then Jacob was greatly afraid and was distressed: and he divided the people that was with him, and the flocks, and the herds, and the camels, into two companies; and he said, "If Esau come to the one company, and smite it, then the company which is left shall escape."

And Jacob said, "O God of my father Abraham, and God of my father Isaac, O Lord, who saidst unto me,

THE VALLEY OF THE JABBOK

From a photograph taken by Prof. H. G. Mitchell
and used by his kind permission

Over this stream Jacob sent his family and his flock while he remained to wrestle with the angel through the night

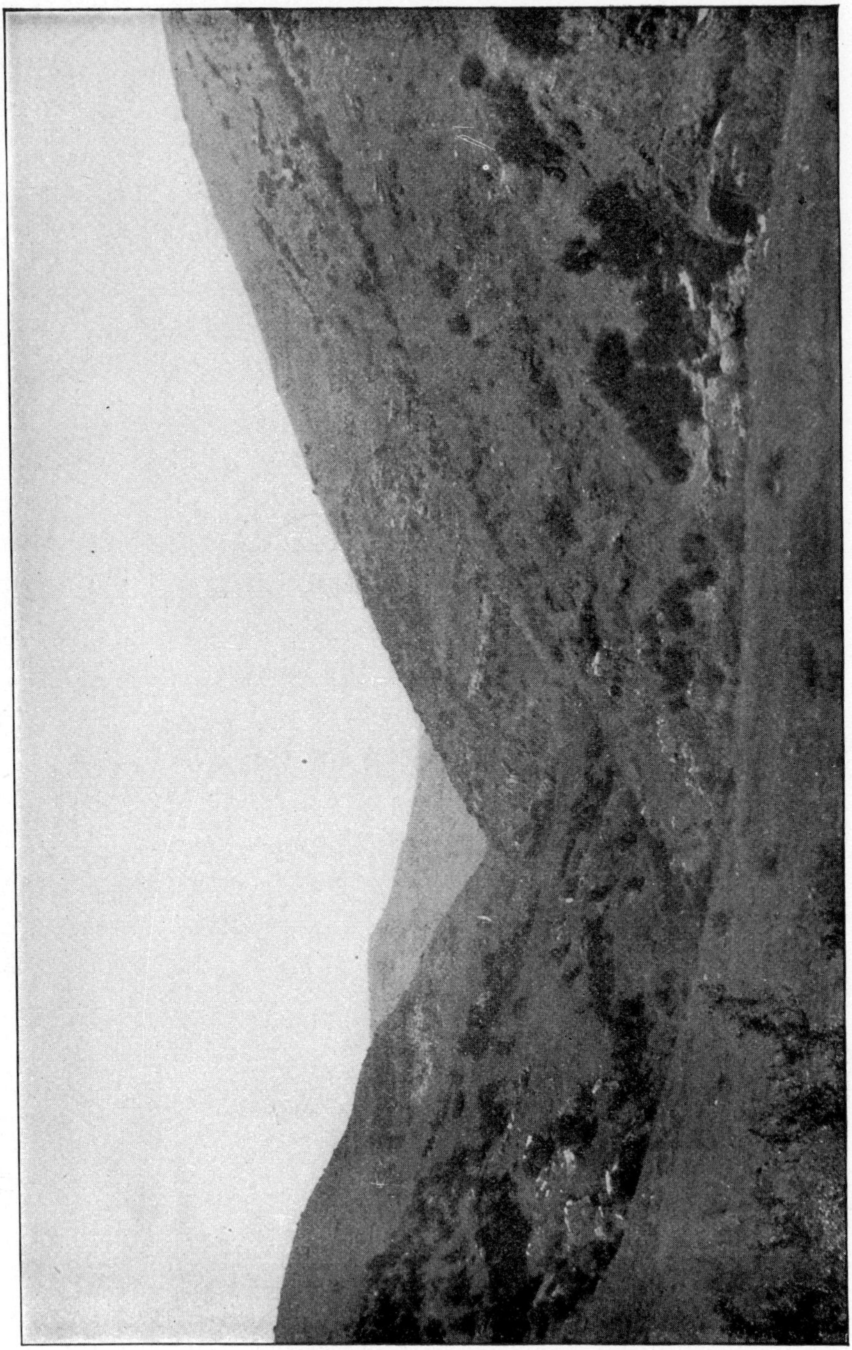

'Return unto thy country, and to thy kindred, and I will do thee good': I am not worthy of the least of all the mercies, and of all the truth, which thou hast showed unto thy servant; for with my staff I passed over this Jordan; and now I am become two companies. Deliver me, I pray thee, from the hand of my brother, from the hand of Esau: for I fear him, lest he come and smite me, the mother with the children. And thou saidst, 'I will surely do thee good, and make thy family as the sand of the sea, which cannot be numbered for multitude.'"

And he lodged there that night; and took of that which he had with him a present for Esau his brother; two hundred she-goats and twenty he-goats, two hundred ewes and twenty rams, thirty milch camels and their colts, forty cows and ten bulls, twenty she-asses and ten foals. And he delivered them into the hand of his servants, every drove by itself; and said unto his servants, "Pass over before me, and put a space between drove and drove."

And he commanded the foremost, saying, "When Esau my brother meeteth thee, and asketh thee, saying, 'Whose art thou? and whither goest thou? and whose are these before thee?' then thou shalt say, 'They are thy servant Jacob's; it is a present sent unto my lord Esau: and, behold, he also is behind us.'"

And he commanded also the second, and the third, and all that followed the droves, saying, "On this manner shall ye speak unto Esau, when ye find him; and ye shall say, 'Moreover, behold, thy servant Jacob is behind us.'"

For he said, "I will appease him with the present that

goeth before me, and afterward I will see his face; peradventure he will accept me."

So the present passed over before him: and he himself lodged that night in the company.

And he rose up that night, and took his two wives, and his two handmaids, and his eleven children, and passed over the ford of Jabbok. And he took them, and sent them over the stream, and sent over that which he had. And Jacob was left alone; and there wrestled a man with him until the breaking of the day. And when he saw that he prevailed not against him, he touched the hollow of his thigh; and the hollow of Jacob's thigh was strained, as he wrestled with him. And he said, "Let me go, for the day breaketh."

And he said, "I will not let thee go, except thou bless me."

And he said unto him, "What is thy name?"

And he said, "Jacob."

And he said, "Thy name shall be called no more Jacob, but Israel: for thou hast striven with God and with men, and hast prevailed."

And Jacob asked him and said, "Tell me, I pray thee, thy name."

And he said, "Wherefore is it that thou dost ask after my name?"

And he blessed him there. And Jacob called the name of the place Penuel: for, said he, "I have seen God face to face, and my life is preserved."

NABLOUS, THE ANCIENT SHECHEM, IN THE VALLEY BETWEEN MOUNTS EBAL AND GERIZIM

Used by special permission of the Detroit Photograph Company

The first camping place of Abraham. Jacob built an altar here, and dug a well, and here Joseph was buried. Joshua set up a great stone "as a witness" here at the end of his life. It was here at "Jacob's well," about a mile and a half from the town, that Jesus met the woman of Samaria

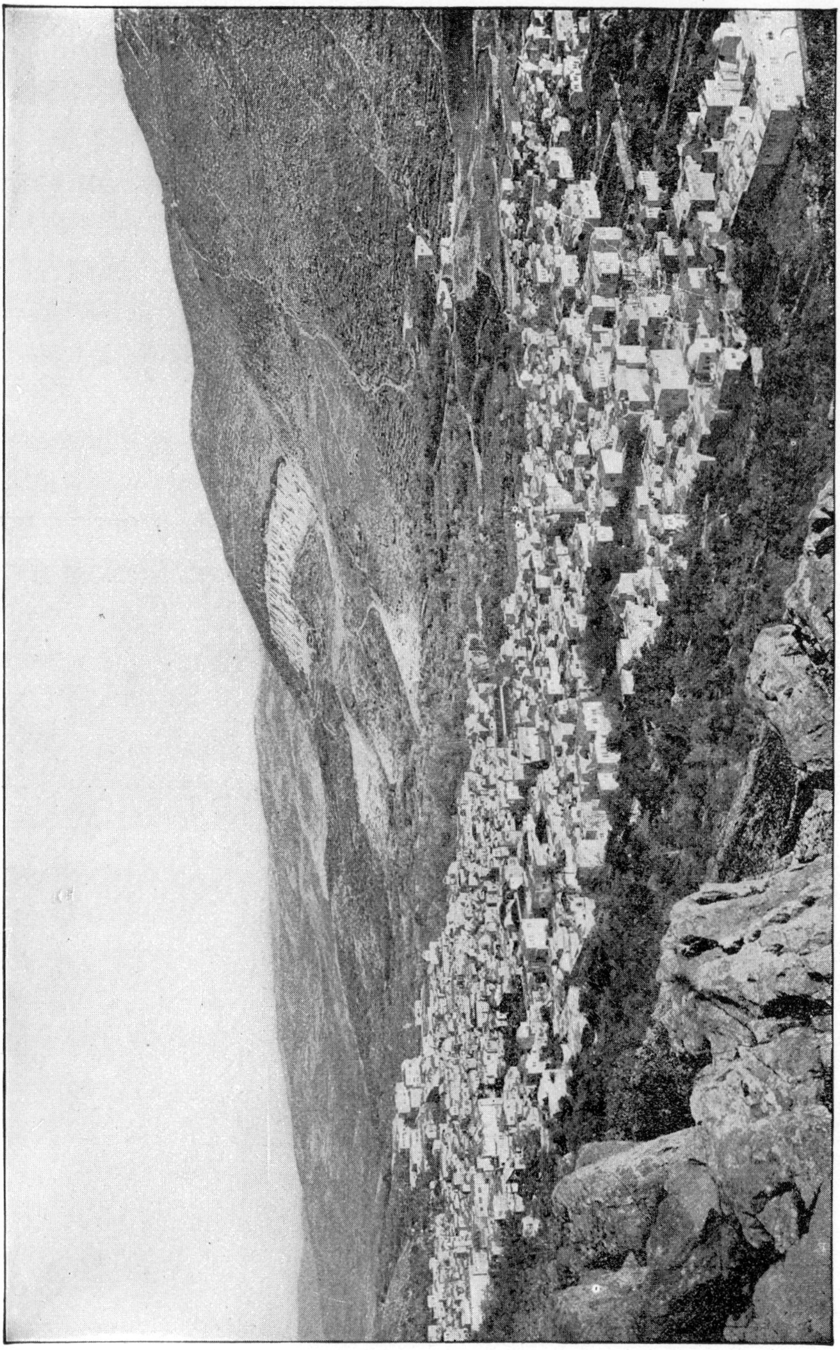

And the sun rose upon him as he passed over Penuel, and he limped upon his thigh.

And Jacob lifted up his eyes, and looked, and, behold, Esau came, and with him four hundred men. And he divided the children unto Leah, and unto Rachel, and unto the two handmaids. And he put the handmaids and their children foremost, and Leah and her children after, and Rachel and Joseph hindermost. And he himself passed over before them, and bowed himself to the ground seven times, until he came near to his brother. And Esau ran to meet him, and embraced him, and fell on his neck, and kissed him: and they wept. And he lifted up his eyes, and saw the women and the children; and said, "Who are these with thee?"

And he said, "The children which God hath graciously given thy servant."

Then the handmaids came near, they and their children, and they bowed themselves. And Leah also and her children came near, and bowed themselves: and after came Joseph near and Rachel, and they bowed themselves. And he said, "What meanest thou by all this company which I met?"

And he said, "To find grace in the sight of my lord."

And Esau said, "I have enough; my brother, let that which thou hast be thine."

And Jacob said, "Nay, I pray thee, if now I have found grace in thy sight, then receive my present at my hand: forasmuch as I have seen thy face, as one seeth the face of God, and thou wast pleased with me. Take, I pray thee, my gift that is brought to thee; because God hath dealt graciously with me, and because I have enough."

And he urged him, and he took it.

And he said, "Let us take our journey, and let us go, and I will go before thee."

And he said unto him, "My lord knoweth that the children are tender, and that the flocks and herds with me have their young: and if they overdrive them one day, all the flocks will die. Let my lord, I pray thee, pass over before his servant: and I will lead on gently, according to the pace of the cattle that are before me and according to the pace of the children, until I come unto my lord unto Seir."

And Esau said, "Let me now leave with thee some of the folk that are with me."

And he said, "What needeth it? let me find grace in the sight of my lord."

So Esau returned that day on his way unto Seir. And Jacob journeyed to Succoth, and built him an house, and made booths for his cattle: therefore the name of the place is called Succoth.

And Jacob came in peace to the city of Shechem, which is in the land of Canaan, when he came from Paddan-aram; and encamped before the city. And he bought the parcel of ground where he had spread his tent, at the hand of the children of Hamor, Shechem's father, for an hundred pieces of money. And he erected there an altar, and called it "God, the God of Israel."

BETHEL

Photograph taken by Mrs. Frank L. Goodspeed, of Springfield, Mass.,
and used by her kind permission

One of Abraham's camping grounds and the place of Jacob's dream

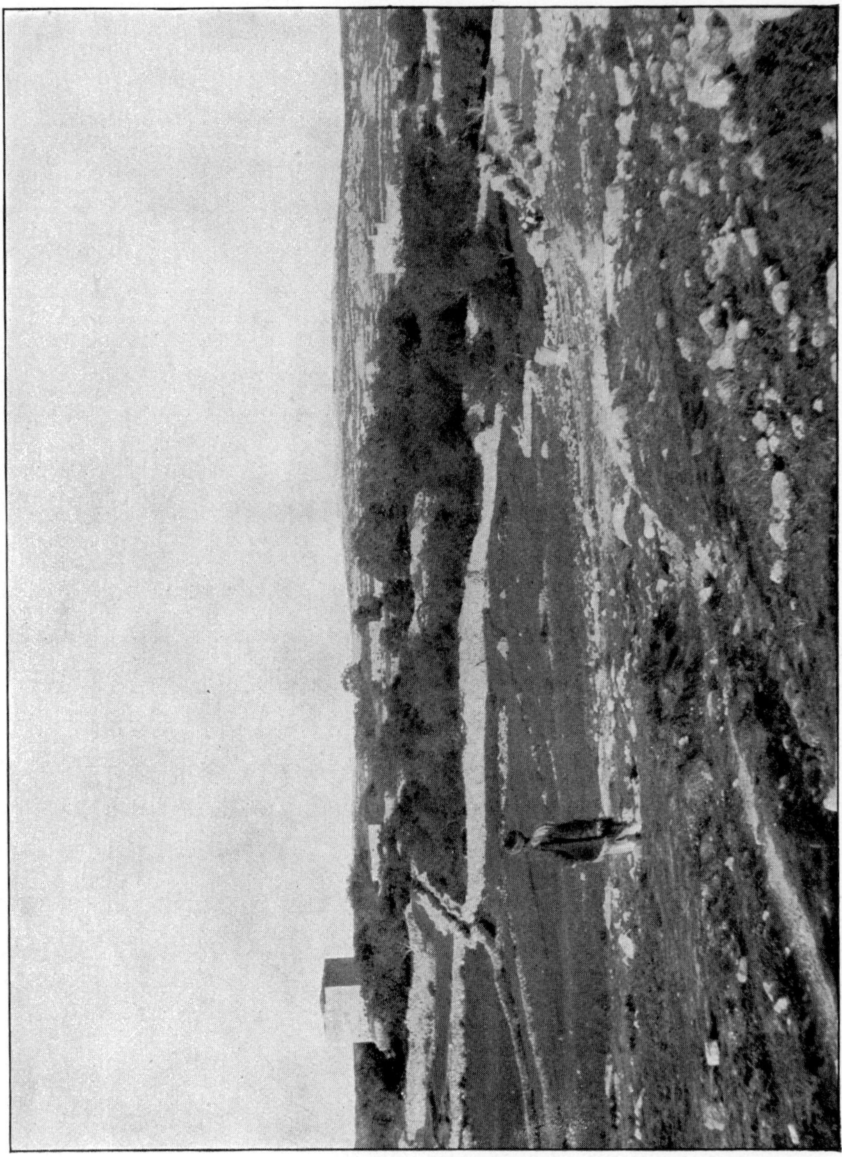

JACOB ERECTS AN ALTAR AT BETH-EL.
He Is Given a New Name. The Death of Rachel.

And God said to Jacob, "Arise, go up to Beth-el, and dwell there: and make there an altar unto God, who appeared unto thee when thou fleddest from the face of Esau thy brother."

Then Jacob said unto his household, and to all that were with him, "Put away the foreign gods that are among you, and purify yourselves, and change your garments: and let us arise, and go up to Beth-el; and I will make there an altar unto God, who answered me in the day of my distress, and was with me in the way which I went."

And they gave to Jacob all the foreign gods which were in their hand, and the rings which were in their ears; and Jacob hid them under the oak which was by Shechem. And they journeyed: and a great terror was upon the cities that were round about them, and they did not pursue after the sons of Jacob. So Jacob came to Luz (the same is Beth-el), he and all the people that were with him. And he built there an altar, and called the place, "The God of Beth-el": because there God was revealed to him, when he fled from the face of his brother. And Deborah Rebekah's nurse died, and she was buried below Beth-el under the oak: and the name of it was called "The Oak of Weeping."

And God appeared to Jacob again, when he came from Paddan-aram, and blessed him. And God said unto him, "Thy name is Jacob: thy name shall not be called any more Jacob, but Israel shall be thy name:" and he called his name Israel.

And God said unto him, "I am God Almighty: be fruitful and multiply; a nation and a company of nations shall be of thee, and kings shall come from thee; and the land which I gave unto Abraham and Isaac, to thee I will give it, and to thy family after thee will I give the land."

And God went up from him in the place where he spoke with him. And Jacob set up a pillar in the place where he spoke with him, a pillar of stone: and he poured out a drink offering thereon, and poured oil thereon. And Jacob called the name of the place where God spoke with him, "Beth-el."

And Rachel died, and was buried in the way to Ephrath (the same is Bethlehem). And Jacob set up a pillar upon her grave: the same is the Pillar of Rachel's grave unto this day.

(In this place Jacob lived for many years; but the sorrow that came to him, and the wonderful things that befell him in his old age, and how he journeyed to Egypt, and died there, are told in the next story, the story of Joseph, his son.)

MOSES

From the frieze of the Prophets, by Sargent, in the Boston Public Library

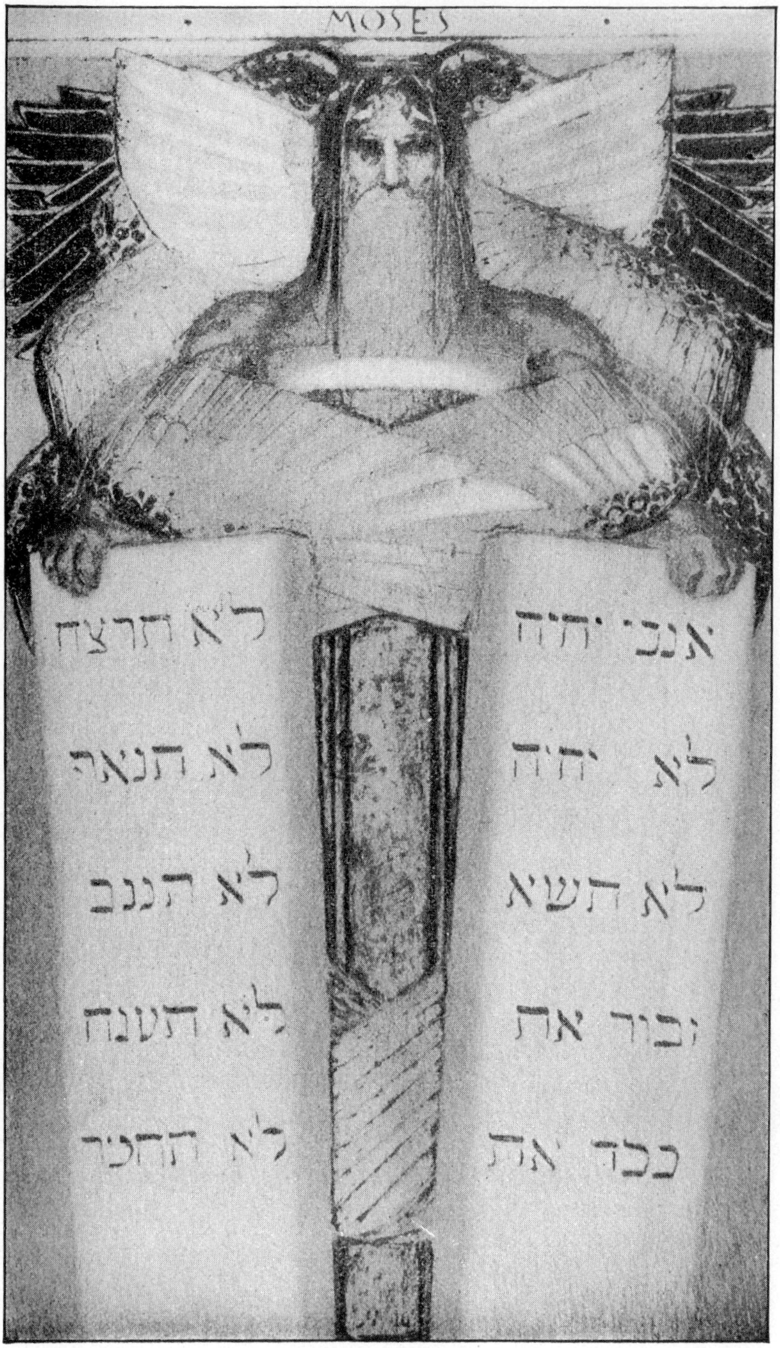
MOSES
אנכי יהוה
לא יהיה
לא תשא
זכור את
כבד את
לא תרצח
לא תנאף
לא תגנב
לא תענה
לא תחמד

JOSEPH

The Story of the Shepherd Boy Who Was Sold into Bondage, and How He Became Ruler in a Great Nation.

A COWARDLY DEED.

Joseph Arouses the Enmity of His Older Brethren, and They Sell Him into Slavery.

(Joseph and Benjamin were the sons of Rachel, Jacob's best loved wife. Their mother died while Joseph was still a little boy and Benjamin was a baby. Their father loved the two motherless boys very much.)

Joseph, when he was seventeen years old, was feeding the flock with his brethren; and he was a lad with the sons of Bilhah, and with the sons of Zilpah, his father's wives: and Joseph brought an evil report of them unto their father. Now Israel loved Joseph more than all his children, because he was the son of his old age: and he made him a coat of many colors. And his brethren saw that their father loved him more than all his brethren; and they hated him, and could not speak peaceably unto him. And Joseph dreamed a dream, and he told it to his brethren: and they hated him yet the more. And he said unto them, "Hear, I pray you, this dream which I have dreamed: for, behold, we were binding sheaves in the field, and, lo, my sheaf arose, and stood upright; and, behold, your sheaves came round about, and bowed down to my sheaf."

And his brethren said to him, "Shalt thou indeed reign over us? or shalt thou indeed have dominion over us?"

And they hated him yet the more for his dreams, and for his words. And he dreamed yet another dream, and told it to his brethren, and said, "Behold, I have dreamed yet a dream; and, behold, the sun and the moon and eleven stars bowed down to me."

And he told it to his father, and to his brethren; and his father rebuked him, and said unto him, "What is this dream that thou hast dreamed? Shall I and thy mother and thy brethren indeed come to bow down ourselves to thee to the earth?"

And his brethren envied him; but his father kept the saying in mind. And his brethren went to feed their father's flock in Shechem. And Israel said unto Joseph, "Do not thy brethren feed the flock in Shechem? come, and I will send thee unto them."

And he said to him, "Here am I."

And he said to him, "Go now, see whether it is well with thy brethren, and well with the flock; and bring me word again."

So he sent him out of the vale of Hebron, and he came to Shechem. And a certain man found him, and, behold, he was wandering in the field: and the man asked him, saying, "What seekest thou?" And he said, "I seek my brethren: tell me, I pray thee, where they are feeding the flock."

A CARAVAN LOADING FOR A JOURNEY

From a photograph in the possession of Dr. W. J. Moulton
and used by his kind permission

AMERICAN COLONY, JERUSALEM.

And the man said, "They are departed hence: for I heard them say, 'Let us go to Dothan.'"

And Joseph went after his brethren, and found them in Dothan. And they saw him afar off, and before he came near unto them, they conspired against him to slay him. And they said one to another, "Behold, this dreamer cometh. Come now therefore, and let us slay him, and cast him into one of the pits, and we will say, 'An evil beast hath devoured him': and we shall see what will become of his dreams."

And Reuben heard it, and delivered him out of their hand; and said, "Let us not take his life."

And Reuben said unto them, "Shed no blood; cast him into this pit that is in the wilderness, but lay no hand upon him": that he might deliver him out of their hand, to restore him to his father.

And it came to pass, when Joseph was come unto his brethren, that they stript Joseph of his coat, the coat of many colors that was on him; and they took him and cast him into the pit: and the pit was empty, there was no water in it. And they sat down to eat bread: and they lifted up their eyes and looked, and, behold, a caravan of Ishmaelites came from Gilead, with their camels bearing spicery and balm and myrrh, going to carry it down to Egypt. And Judah said unto his brethren, "What profit is it if we slay our brother and conceal his blood? Come, and let us sell him to the Ishmaelites, and let not our hand be upon him; for he is our brother, our flesh." And his brethren hearkened unto him.

And they drew and lifted up Joseph out of the pit, and sold Joseph to the Ishmaelites for twenty pieces of silver. And they brought Joseph into Egypt. And Reuben returned unto the pit; and, behold, Joseph was not in the pit; and he rent his clothes. And he returned unto his brethren, and said, "The child is not; and I, whither shall I go?"

And they took Joseph's coat, and killed a he-goat, and dipped the coat in the blood; and they sent the coat of many colors, and they brought it to their father; and said, "This have we found: know now whether it be thy son's coat or not."

And he knew it, and said, "It is my son's coat; an evil beast hath devoured him; Joseph is without doubt torn in pieces."

And Jacob rent his garments, and put sackcloth upon his loins, and mourned for his son many days. And all his sons and all his daughters rose up to comfort him; but he refused to be comforted; and he said, "For I will go down to the grave to my son mourning." And his father wept for him.

JOSEPH IN EGYPT.

Fortunate at First, He is Cast into Prison, but Even There He Finds Favor.

And Joseph was brought down to Egypt; and Potiphar, an officer of Pharaoh's, the captain of the guard, an Egyptian, bought him of the hand of the Ishmaelites, who had brought him down thither. And the Lord was with Joseph, and he was a prosperous man; and he was in

A VIEW OF THE PYRAMIDS AND THE SPHINX

From a photograph belonging to Miss Clara L. Bodman
and used by her kind permission

Egypt is a land of wonder and romance, the seat of one of the oldest civilizations on the face of the globe. Its ancient temples and statues, though in ruins, are among the most beautiful and wonderful in the world. Many of the tombs have been plundered, yet one has only just been opened which contained untouched the priceless memorial of that early time. This is the land over which the Hebrew shepherd lad Joseph ruled and out of which the Hebrew people finally marched to freedom

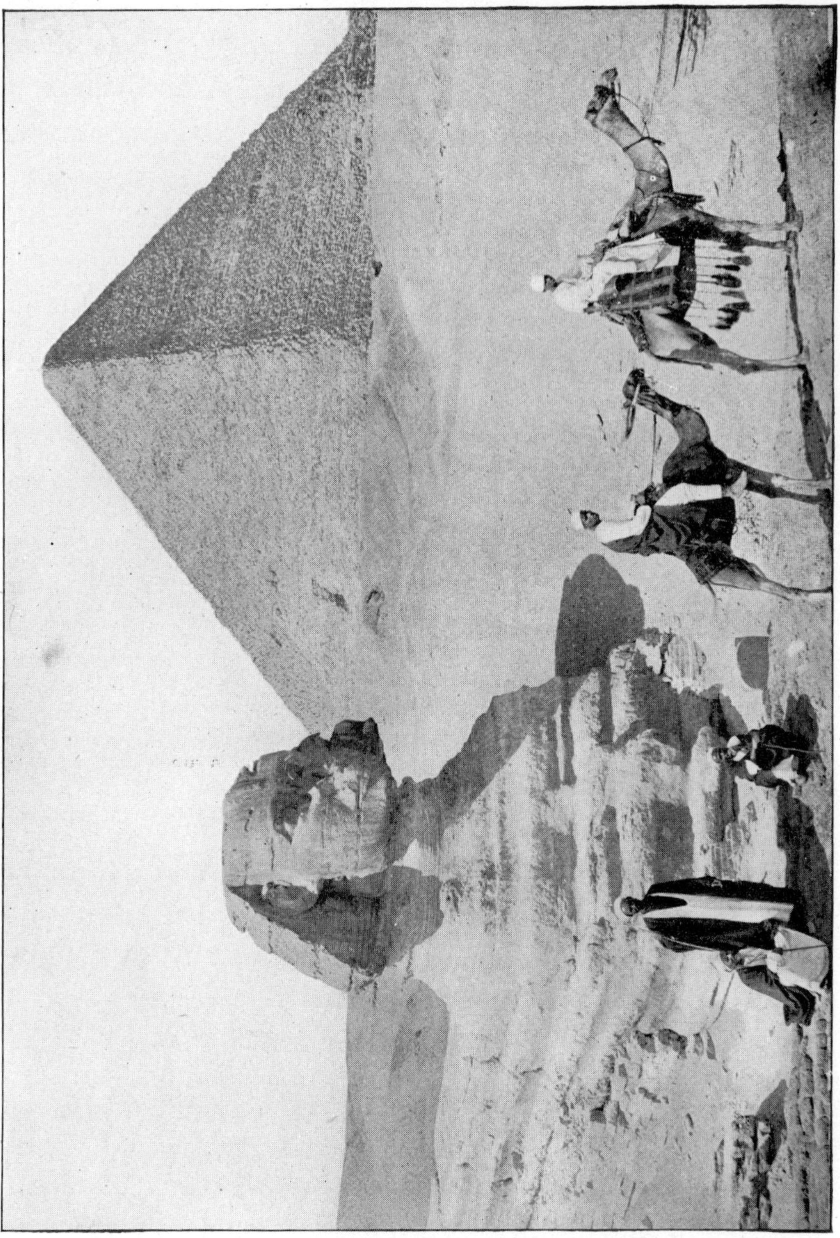

the house of his master the Egyptian. And his master saw that the Lord was with him, and that the Lord made all that he did to prosper in his hand. And Joseph found grace in his sight, and he ministered unto him: and he made him overseer over his house, and all that he had he put into his hand. And it came to pass from the time that he made him overseer in his house, and over all that he had, that the Lord blessed the Egyptian's house for Joseph's sake; and the blessing of the Lord was upon all that he had, in the house and in the field. And he left all that he had in Joseph's hand; and he knew not aught that was with him, save the bread which he did eat.

(But Joseph's mistress was a wicked woman, and, because Joseph would not do wrong, told what was not true about him to his master, so that Joseph's master took him, and put him into the prison, the place where the king's prisoners were bound: and he was there in the prison.)

But the Lord was with Joseph, and showed kindness unto him, and gave him favor in the sight of the keeper of the prison. And the keeper of the prison committed to Joseph's hand all the prisoners that were in the prison; and whatsoever they did there, he was the doer of it. The keeper of the prison looked not to anything that was under his hand, because the Lord was with him; and that which he did, the Lord made it to prosper.

JOSEPH INTERPRETS THE DREAMS OF PHARAOH'S OFFICERS.

The Fate of the Chief Butler and of the Baker of the King.

And it came to pass after these things, that the butler of the king of Egypt and his baker offended their lord the king of Egypt. And Pharaoh was wroth against his two officers, against the chief of the butlers, and against the chief of the bakers. And he put them into the prison, the place where Joseph was bound. And the captain of the guard charged Joseph with them, and he ministered unto them: and they continued a season in prison.

And they dreamed a dream both of them, each man his dream, in one night, the butler and the baker of the king of Egypt, who were bound in the prison. And Joseph came in to them in the morning, and saw them, and, behold, they were sad. And he asked Pharaoh's officers that were with him in prison, saying, "Wherefore look ye so sad to-day?"

And they said unto him, "We have dreamed a dream, and there is none that can interpret it."

And Joseph said unto them, "Do not interpretations belong to God? Tell it me, I pray you."

And the chief butler told his dream to Joseph, and said to him, "In my dream, behold, a vine was before me; and in the vine were three branches: and it was as though it budded, and its blossoms shot forth; and the clusters thereof brought forth ripe grapes: and Pharaoh's cup was in my hand; and I took the grapes, and pressed them into Pharaoh's cup, and I gave the cup into Pharaoh's hand."

And Joseph said unto him, "This is the interpretation of it: the three branches are three days; within yet three days shall Pharaoh lift up thine head, and restore

A GROVE OF DATE PALMS IN EGYPT

From a photograph belonging to Miss Clara L. Bodman
and used by her kind permission

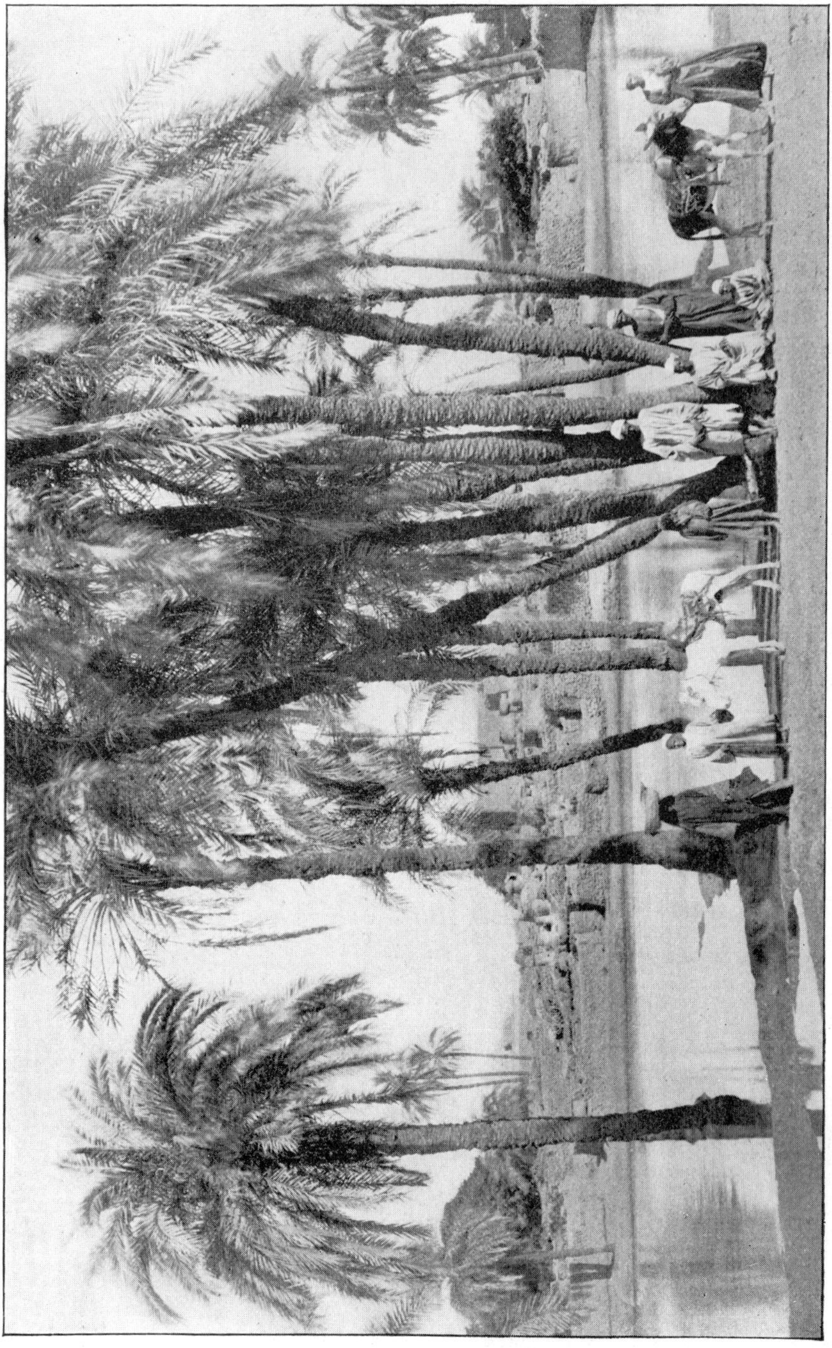

thee unto thine office: and thou shalt give Pharaoh's cup into his hand, after the former manner when thou wast his butler. But have me in thy remembrance when it shall be well with thee, and show kindness, I pray thee, to me, and make mention of me unto Pharaoh, and bring me out of this house: for indeed I was stolen away out of the land of the Hebrews: and here also have I done nothing that they should put me into the dungeon."

When the chief baker saw that the interpretation was good, he said unto Joseph, "I also was in my dream, and, behold, three baskets of white bread were on my head: and in the uppermost basket there was all manner of bakemeats for Pharaoh; and the birds ate them out of the basket upon my head."

And Joseph answered and said, "This is the interpretation thereof: the three baskets are three days; within yet three days shall Pharaoh lift up thy head from off thee, and shall hang thee on a tree; and the birds shall eat thy flesh from off thee."

And it came to pass the third day, which was Pharaoh's birthday, that he made a feast unto all his servants: and he lifted up the head of the chief butler and the head of the chief baker among his servants. And he restored the chief butler unto his butlership again; and he gave the cup into Pharaoh's hand: but he hanged the chief baker: as Joseph had interpreted to them. Yet did not the chief butler remember Joseph, but forgot him.

THE SEVEN FAT KINE AND THE SEVEN LEAN KINE
Which Joseph Told the King Meant Seven Fat Years of Plenty and Seven Lean Years of Want. The Hebrew Boy is Made Chief Ruler of Egypt. The Famine Comes.

And it came to pass at the end of two full years, that Pharaoh dreamed: and, behold, he stood by the river. And, behold, there came up out of the river seven kine, well favored and fatfleshed; and they fed in the reed-grass. And, behold, seven other kine came up after them out of the river, ill favored and leanfleshed; and stood by the other kine upon the brink of the river. And the ill favored and leanfleshed kine did eat up the seven well favored and fat kine. So Pharaoh awoke.

And he slept and dreamed a second time: and, behold, seven ears of corn came up upon one stalk, full and good. And, behold, seven ears, thin and blasted with the east wind, sprung up after them. And the thin ears swallowed up the seven full and good ears. And Pharaoh awoke, and, behold, it was a dream. And it came to pass in the morning that his spirit was troubled; and he sent and called for all the magicians of Egypt, and all the wise men thereof: and Pharaoh told them his dream; but there was none that could interpret them unto Pharaoh.

Then spoke the chief butler unto Pharaoh, saying, "I do remember my faults this day: Pharaoh was wroth with his servants, and put me in prison in the house of the captain of the guard, me and the chief baker: and we dreamed a dream in one night, I and he; we dreamed each man according to the interpretation of his dream. And there was with us there a young man, an Hebrew, servant to the captain of the guard; and we told him, and he interpreted to us our dreams; to each man according to his dream he did interpret. And it came to pass as he interpreted to us, so it was; me he restored unto mine office, and him he hanged."

Then Pharaoh sent and called Joseph, and they brought him hastily out of the dungeon: and he shaved himself, and changed his raiment, and came in to Pharaoh.

And Pharaoh said to Joseph, "I have dreamed a dream, and there is none that can interpret it: and I have heard say of thee, that when thou hearest a dream thou canst interpret it."

And Joseph answered Pharaoh, saying, "It is not in me: God shall give Pharaoh an answer of peace."

And Pharaoh spoke unto Joseph, "In my dream, behold, I stood upon the brink of the river: and, behold, there came up out of the river seven kine, fatfleshed and well favored; and they fed in the reed-grass: and, behold, seven other kine came up after them, poor and very ill favored and leanfleshed, such as I never saw in all the land of Egypt for badness: and the lean and ill favored kine ate up the first seven fat kine: and when they had eaten them up, it could not be known that they had eaten them; but they were still ill favored as at the beginning. So I awoke.

"And I saw in my dream, and, behold, seven ears came up upon one stalk, full and good: and, behold, seven ears, withered, thin, and blasted with the east wind, sprung up after them: and the thin ears swallowed up the seven good ears: and I told it unto the magicians; but there was none that could declare it to me."

And Joseph said unto Pharaoh, "The dream of Pharaoh is one: what God is about to do he hath declared unto Pharaoh. The seven good kine are seven years; and the seven good ears are seven years: the dream is one. And the seven lean and ill favored kine that came up after them are seven years, and also the seven empty ears blasted with the east wind; they shall be seven years of famine. That is the thing which I spoke unto Pharaoh: what God is about to do he hath showed unto Pharaoh. Behold, there come seven years of great plenty throughout all the land of Egypt: and there shall arise after them seven years of famine; and all the plenty shall be forgotten in the land of Egypt; and the famine shall consume the land; and the plenty shall not be known in the land by reason of that famine which followeth; for it shall be very grievous. And the reason that the dream was doubled to Pharaoh is because the thing is established by God, and God will shortly bring it to pass. Now therefore let Pharaoh look out a man discreet and wise, and set him over the land of Egypt. Let Pharaoh do this, and let him appoint overseers over the land, and take up the fifth part of the land of Egypt in the seven plenteous years. And let them gather all the food of these good years that come, and lay up corn under the hand of Pharaoh for food in the cities, and let them keep it. And the food shall be for a store to the land against the seven years of famine, which shall be in the land of Egypt; that the land perish not through the famine."

And the thing was good in the eyes of Pharaoh, and in the eyes of all his servants. And Pharaoh said to his servants, "Can we find such a one as this, a man in whom the spirit of God is?"

And Pharaoh said unto Joseph, "Forasmuch as God hath showed thee all this, there is none so discreet and wise as thou: thou shalt be over my house, and according to thy word shall all my people be ruled: only in the throne will I be greater than thou." And Pharaoh said unto Joseph, "See, I have set thee over all the land of Egypt."

And Pharaoh took off his signet ring from his hand, and put it upon Joseph's hand, and arrayed him in vestures of fine linen, and put a gold chain about his neck; and he made him to ride in the second chariot which he had; and they cried before him, "Bow the knee": and he set him over all the land of Egypt. And Pharaoh said to Joseph, "I am Pharaoh, and without thee shall no man lift up his hand or his foot in all the land of Egypt."

And Pharaoh gave Joseph Asenath the daughter of Poti-phera the priest of On to be his wife. And Joseph went out over the land of Egypt.

And Joseph was thirty years old when he stood before Pharaoh, king of Egypt. And Joseph went out from the presence of Pharaoh, and went throughout all the land of

Egypt. And in the seven plenteous years the earth brought forth by handfuls. And he gathered up all the food of the seven years which were in the land of Egypt, and laid up the food in the cities: the food of the field, which was round about every city, laid he up in the same. And Joseph laid up corn as the sand of the sea, very much, until he left measuring; for it was without measure. And to Joseph were born two sons before the year of famine came, which his wife Asenath the daughter of Poti-phera priest of On bore to him. And Joseph called the name of the firstborn Manasseh: "For," said he, "God hath made me forget all my toil, and all my father's house." And the name of the second called he Ephraim: "For God hath made me fruitful in the land of my affliction."

And the seven years of plenty, that was in the land of Egypt, came to an end. And the seven years of famine began to come, according as Joseph had said: and there was famine in all lands; but in all the land of Egypt there was bread. And when all the land of Egypt was famished, the people cried to Pharaoh for bread: and Pharaoh said unto all the Egyptians, "Go to Joseph; what he saith to you, do."

And the famine was over all the face of the earth: and Joseph opened all the storehouses, and sold unto the Egyptians; and the famine was sore in the land of Egypt. And all countries came into Egypt to Joseph to buy corn; because the famine was sore in all the earth.

A VIEW OF THE PYRAMIDS, WITH A VILLAGE IN THE FOREGROUND

From a photograph belonging to Miss Clara L. Bodman
and used by her kind permission

The pyramids, which are seen in the distance in this picture, were considered one of the "Seven Wonders of the World." There are seventy of them in Egypt and they were built as tombs of the Pharaohs. The "Great Pyramid" is four hundred and eighty feet and nine inches high; it is supposed to have taken one hundred thousand men fifty years to build it, and the date is given as from 3229 to 2123 B. C.

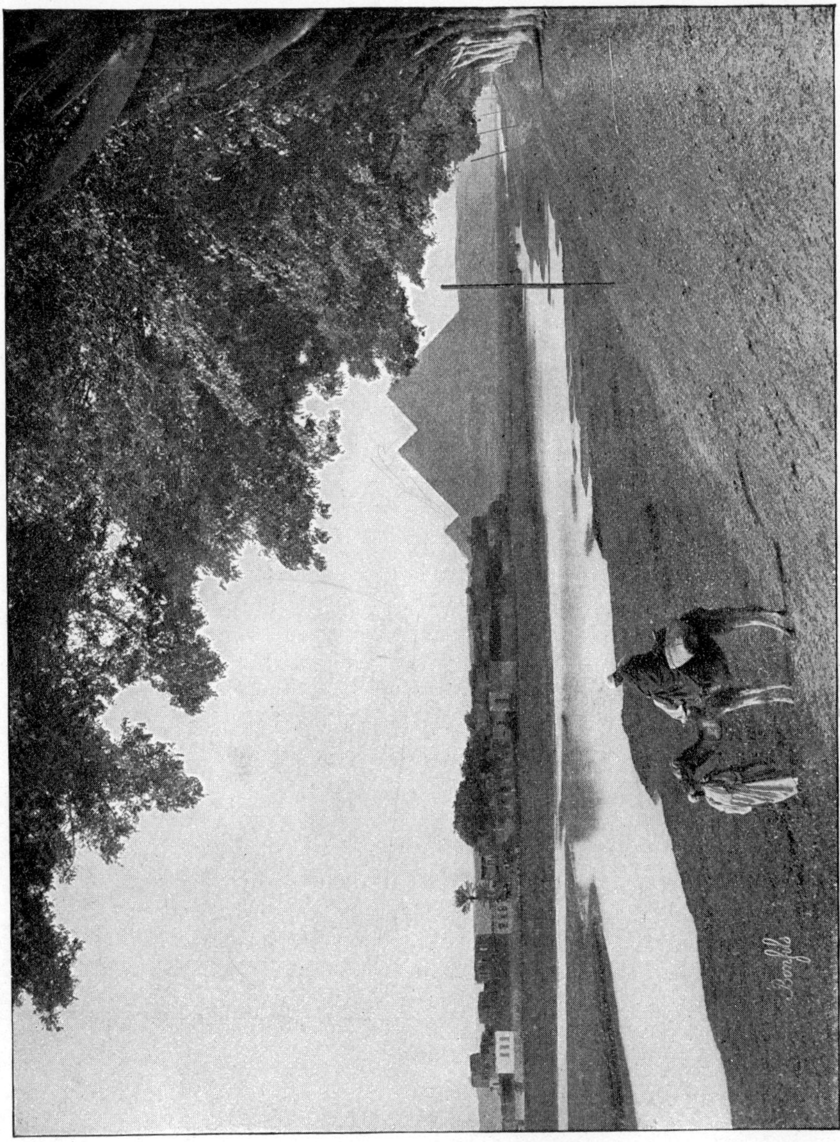
Bonfils

THE SONS OF JACOB COME TO EGYPT TO BUY CORN.
They Do Not Recognize, in the Ruler of the Land, the Brother Whom They Sold. He Commands Them to Bring Their Youngest Brother to Egypt.

Now Jacob saw that there was corn in Egypt, and Jacob said to his sons, "Why do ye look one upon another?"

And he said, "Behold, I have heard that there is corn in Egypt: get you down thither, and buy for us from thence; that we may live, and not die."

And Joseph's ten brethren went down to buy corn from Egypt. But Benjamin, Joseph's brother, Jacob sent not with his brethren; for he said, "Lest peradventure mischief befall him."

And the sons of Israel came to buy among those that came: for the famine was in the land of Canaan. And Joseph was the governor over the land; he it was that sold to all the people of the land: and Joseph's brethren came, and bowed down themselves to him with their faces to the earth. And Joseph saw his brethren, and he knew them, but made himself strange to them, and spoke roughly with them; and he said unto them, "Whence come ye?"

And they said, "From the land of Canaan to buy food."

And Joseph knew his brethren, but they knew not him. And Joseph remembered the dreams which he dreamed of them, and said unto them, "Ye are spies; to see the nakedness of the land ye are come."

And they said unto him, "Nay, my lord, but to buy food are thy servants come. We are all one man's sons; we are true men, thy servants are no spies."

And he said to them, "Nay, but to see the nakedness of the land ye are come."

And they said, "We thy servants are twelve brethren, the sons of one man in the land of Canaan; and, behold, the youngest is this day with our father, and one is not."

And Joseph said unto them, "That is it that I spoke unto you, saying, 'Ye are spies': hereby ye shall be proved: by the life of Pharaoh ye shall not go forth hence, except your youngest brother come hither. Send one of you, and let him fetch your brother, and ye shall be bound, that your words may be proved, whether there be truth in you: or else by the life of Pharaoh surely ye are spies." And he put them all together into prison three days.

And Joseph said unto them the third day, "This do, and live; for I fear God: if ye be true men, let one of your brethren be bound in your prison house; but go ye, carry corn for the famine of your houses: and bring your youngest brother unto me; so shall your words be verified, and ye shall not die."

And they did so. And they said one to another, "We are verily guilty concerning our brother, in that we saw the distress of his soul, when he besought us, and we would not hear; therefore is this distress come upon us."

And Reuben answered them, saying, "Spoke I not unto you, saying, 'Do not sin against the child'; and ye would not hear? therefore also, behold, his blood is required."

And they knew not that Joseph understood them; for there was an interpreter between them.

And he turned himself about from them, and wept;

and he returned to them, and spoke to them, and took Simeon from among them, and bound him before their eyes. Then Joseph commanded to fill their vessels with corn, and to restore every man's money into his sack, and to give them provisions for the way: and thus was it done unto them. And they loaded their asses with their corn, and departed thence. And as one of them opened his sack to feed his ass in the lodging place, he espied his money; and, behold, it was in the mouth of his sack. And he said unto his brethren, "My money is restored; and, lo, it is even in my sack": and their heart failed them, and they turned trembling one to another, saying, "What is this that God hath done unto us?"

And they came to Jacob their father to the land of Canaan, and told him all that had befallen them; saying, "The man, the lord of the land, spoke roughly with us, and took us for spies of the country. And we said to him, 'We are true men; we are no spies: we are twelve brethren, sons of our father; one is not, and the youngest is this day with our father in the land of Canaan.'

"And the man, the lord of the land, said unto us, 'Hereby shall I know that ye are true men; leave one of your brethren with me, and take corn for the famine of your houses, and go your way: and bring your youngest brother unto me: then shall I know that ye are no spies, but that ye are true men: so will I deliver you your brother, and ye shall traffic in the land.' "

And it came to pass as they emptied their sacks, that, behold, every man's bundle of money was in his sack: and when they and their father saw their bundles of money, they were afraid. And Jacob their father said unto them, "Me have ye bereaved of my children: Joseph is not, and Simeon is not, and ye will take Benjamin away: all these things are against me."

And Reuben spoke unto his father, saying, "Slay my two sons, if I bring him not to thee: deliver him into my hand, and I will bring him to thee again." And he said, "My son shall not go down with you; for his brother is dead, and he only is left: if mischief befall him by the way in which ye go, then shall ye bring down my gray hairs with sorrow to the grave."

JOSEPH AND HIS BROTHERS.

Jacob at First Refuses, but at Length Consents, to Let Benjamin Go. Joseph Places the Money in the Sacks. He Threatens the Brothers with Punishment. He tells His Brothers Who He Is, Forgives Them, and Takes Them Into His Favor.

And the famine was sore in the land. And it came to pass, when they had eaten up the corn which they had brought out of Egypt, their father said unto them, "Go again, buy us a little food."

And Judah spoke unto him, saying, "The man did solemnly protest unto us, saying, 'Ye shall not see my face, except your brother be with you.' If thou wilt send our brother with us, we will go down and buy thee food: but if thou wilt not send him, we will not go down: for the man said unto us, 'Ye shall not see my face, except your brother be with you.'"

And Israel said, "Wherefore dealt ye so ill with me, as to tell the man whether ye had yet a brother?"

And they said, "The man asked strictly concerning ourselves, and concerning our kindred, saying, 'Is your father yet alive? have ye another brother?' and we told him according to the nature of these words: could we in any wise know that he would say, 'Bring your brother down'?"

And Judah said unto Israel his father, "Send the lad with me, and we will arise and go; that we may live, and not die, both we, and thou, and also our little ones. I will be surety for him; of my hand shalt thou require him: if I bring him not unto thee, and set him before thee, then let me bear the blame for ever: for except we had lingered, surely we had now returned a second time."

And their father Israel said unto them, "If it be so now, do this; take of the choice fruits of the land in your vessels, and carry down the man a present, a little balm, and a little honey, spicery and myrrh, nuts, and almonds: and take double money in your hand; and the money that was returned in the mouth of your sacks carry again in your hand; peradventure it was an oversight: take also your brother, and arise, go again unto the man: and God Almighty give you mercy before the man, that he may release unto you your other brother and Benjamin. And if I be bereaved of my children, I am bereaved."

And the men took that present, and they took double money in their hand, and Benjamin; and rose up, and went down to Egypt, and stood before Joseph. And when

Joseph saw Benjamin with them, he said to the steward of his house, "Bring the men into the house, and slay, and make ready; for the men shall dine with me at noon."

And the man did as Joseph bade; and the man brought the men into Joseph's house. And the men were afraid, because they were brought into Joseph's house; and they said, "Because of the money that was returned in our sacks at the first time are we brought in; that he may seek occasion against us, and fall upon us, and take us for bondmen, and our asses."

And they came near to the steward of Joseph's house, and they spoke unto him at the door of the house, and said, "Oh my lord, we came indeed down at the first time to buy food: and it came to pass, when we came to the lodging place, that we opened our sacks, and, behold, every man's money was in the mouth of his sack, our money in full weight: and we have brought it again in our hand. And other money have we brought down in our hand to buy food: we know not who put our money in our sacks."

And he said, "Peace be to you, fear not: your God, and the God of your father, hath given you treasure in your sacks: I had your money."

And he brought Simeon out to them. And the man brought the men into Joseph's house, and gave them water, and they washed their feet; and he gave their asses provender. And they made ready the present for Joseph's coming at noon: for they heard that they should eat there.

And when Joseph came home, they brought him the present which was in their hand into the house, and bowed down themselves to him to the earth. And he asked them of their welfare, and said, "Is your father well, the old man of whom ye spoke? Is he yet alive?" and they said, "Thy servant our father is well, he is yet alive." And they bowed the head, and made obeisance.

And he lifted up his eyes and saw Benjamin his brother, his mother's son, and said, "Is this your youngest brother, of whom ye spoke unto me?" And he said, "God be gracious unto thee, my son."

And Joseph made haste; for his heart yearned over his brother: and he sought where to weep; and he entered into his chamber, and wept there. And he washed his face and came out; and he refrained himself, and said, "Set on food."

And they set on for him by himself, and for them by themselves, and for the Egyptians, who ate with him, by themselves: because the Egyptians could not eat with the Hebrews; for that is an abomination to the Egyptians. And they sat before him, the firstborn according to his birthright, and the youngest according to his youth: and the men marveled one with another. And he took of the food and sent portions to them from before him: but Benjamin's portion was five times as much as any of theirs. And they drank, and were merry with him.

And he commanded the steward of his house, saying, "Fill the men's sacks with food, as much as they can carry, and put every man's money in his sack's mouth. And put my cup, the silver cup, in the sack's mouth of the youngest, and his corn money."

And he did according to the word that Joseph had spoken. As soon as the morning was light the men were sent away, they and their asses. And when they were gone out of the city, and were not yet far off, Joseph said to his steward, "Up, follow after the men; and when thou dost overtake them, say to them, 'Wherefore have ye rewarded evil for good? Is not this the cup from which my lord drinketh, and whereby he indeed divineth? ye have done evil in so doing.'"

And he overtook them, and he spoke unto them these words. And they said unto him, "Wherefore speaketh my lord such words as these? God forbid that thy servants should do such a thing. Behold, the money, which we found in our sacks' mouths, we brought again unto thee out of the land of Canaan: how then should we steal out of thy lord's house silver or gold? With whomsoever of thy servants it be found, let him die, and we also will be my lord's bondmen."

And he said, "Now also let it be according unto your words: he with whom it is found shall be my bondman; and ye shall be blameless."

Then they hasted, and took down every man his sack to the ground, and opened every man his sack. And he searched, and began at the eldest, and left off at the youngest: and the cup was found in Benjamin's sack. Then they rent their clothes, and loaded every man his ass, and returned to the city. And Judah and his brethren came to Joseph's house; and he was yet there: and they fell before him on the ground. And Joseph said unto them, "What deed is this that ye have done? know ye not that such a man as I can indeed divine?"

And Judah said, "What shall we say unto my lord? what shall we speak? or how shall we clear ourselves? God hath found out the iniquity of thy servants: behold, we are my lord's bondmen, both we, and he also in whose hand the cup is found."

And he said, "God forbid that I should do so: the man in whose hand the cup is found, he shall be my bondman; but as for you, get you up in peace unto your father."

Then Judah came near unto him, and said, "Oh my lord, let thy servant, I pray thee, speak a word to my lord, and let not thine anger burn against thy servant: for thou art even as Pharaoh. My lord asked his servants, saying, 'Have ye a father, or a brother?' And we said unto my lord, 'We have a father, an old man, and a child of his old age, a little one; and his brother is dead, and he alone is left of his mother, and his father loveth him.' And thou saidst unto thy servants, 'Bring him down unto me, that I may set mine eyes upon him.' And we said to my lord, 'The lad cannot leave his father: for if he should leave his father, his father would die.' And thou saidst unto thy servants, 'Except your youngest brother come down with you, ye shall see my face no more.' And it came to pass when we came up to thy servant my father, we told him the words of my lord. And our father said, 'Go again, buy us a litttle food.' And we said, 'We cannot go down: if our youngest brother be with us, then will we go down: for we may not see the man's face, except our youngest brother be with us.' And thy servant my father said to us, 'Ye know that my wife bore me two sons: and the one went out from me, and I said, "Surely he is torn in pieces"; and I have not seen him since: and if ye take this one also from me, and mischief befall him, ye shall bring down my gray hairs in sorrow to the grave.' Now therefore when I come to thy servant my father, and the lad be not with us; seeing that his life is bound up in the lad's life; it shall come to pass, when he seeth that the lad is not with us, that he will die: and thy servants shall bring down the gray hairs of thy servant our father with sorrow to the grave. For thy servant became surety for the lad unto my father, saying, 'If I bring him not unto thee, then shall I bear the blame to my father for ever.' Now therefore, let thy servant, I pray thee, abide instead of the lad a bondman to my lord; and let the lad go up with his brethren. For how shall I go up to my father, and the lad be not with me? lest I see the evil that shall come on my father."

Then Joseph could not refrain himself before all them that stood by him; and he cried, "Cause every man to go out from me."

And there stood no man with him, while Joseph made himself known to his brethren. And he wept aloud: and the Egyptians heard, and the house of Pharaoh heard. And Joseph said unto his brethren, "I am Joseph; doth my father yet live?"

And his brethren could not answer him; for they were

troubled at his presence. And Joseph said to his brethren, "Come near to me, I pray you."

And they came near. And he said, "I am Joseph your brother, whom ye sold into Egypt. And now be not grieved, nor angry with yourselves, that ye sold me hither: for God did send me before you to preserve life. For these two years hath the famine been in the land: and there are yet five years, in the which there shall be neither plowing nor harvest. And God sent me before you to preserve you a remnant in the earth, and to save you alive by a great deliverance. So now it was not you that sent me hither, but God: and he hath made me a father to Pharaoh, and lord of all his house, and ruler over all the land of Egypt. Haste ye, and go up to my father, and say unto him, 'Thus saith thy son Joseph, God hath made me lord of all Egypt: come down unto me, tarry not: and thou shalt dwell in the land of Goshen, and thou shalt be near unto me, thou, and thy children, and thy children's children, and thy flocks, and thy herds, and all that thou hast: and there will I nourish thee; for there are yet five years of famine; lest thou come to poverty, thou, and thy household, and all that thou hast. And, behold, your eyes see, and the eyes of my brother Benjamin, that it is my mouth that speaketh unto you.' And ye shall tell my father of all my glory in Egypt, and of all that ye have seen; and ye shall haste and bring down my father hither."

And he fell upon his brother Benjamin's neck and wept; and Benjamin wept upon his neck. And he kissed all his brethren, and wept with them: and after that his brethren talked with him.

And the report thereof was heard in Pharaoh's house, saying, "Joseph's brethren are come": and it pleased Pharaoh well, and his servants. And Pharaoh said unto Joseph, "Say unto thy brethren, 'This do ye; load your beasts, and go, get you unto the land of Canaan; and take your father and your households, and come unto me: and I will give you the good of the land of Egypt, and ye shall eat the fat of the land.' Now thou art commanded, this do ye; take you wagons out of the land of Egypt for your little ones, and for your wives, and bring your father, and come. Also regard not your possessions; for the good of all the land of Egypt is yours."

And the sons of Israel did so: and Joseph gave them wagons, according to the commandment of Pharaoh, and gave them provisions for the way. To all of them he gave each man changes of raiment; but to Benjamin he gave three hundred pieces of silver, and five changes of raiment. And to his father he sent after this manner; ten asses laden with the good things of Egypt, and ten she-asses laden with corn and bread and victual for his father by the way.

So he sent his brethren away, and they departed: and he said to them, "See that ye fall not out by the way."

And they went up out of Egypt, and came into the land of Canaan to Jacob their father. And they told him, saying, "Joseph is yet alive, and he is ruler over all the land of Egypt." And his heart fainted, for he believed them not. And they told him all the words of Joseph, which he had said unto them: and when he saw the wagons which Joseph had sent to carry him, the spirit of Jacob their father revived: and Israel said, "It is enough; Joseph my son is yet alive: I will go and see him before I die."

JACOB IN EGYPT.
The Famine Wastes the Land. Death of Jacob. Death of Joseph.

And Israel took his journey with all that he had, and came to Beer-sheba, and offered sacrifices to the God of his father Isaac. And God spoke unto Israel in the visions of the night, and said, "Jacob, Jacob."

And he said, "Here am I."

And he said, "I am God, the God of thy father: fear not to go down into Egypt; for I will there make of thee a great nation: I will go down with thee into Egypt; and I will also surely bring thee up again: and Joseph shall put his hand upon thine eyes."

And Jacob rose up from Beer-sheba: and the sons of Israel carried Jacob their father, and their little ones, and their wives, in the wagons which Pharaoh had sent to carry him. And they took their cattle and their goods, which they had gotten in the land of Canaan, and came into Egypt, Jacob, and all his family with him: his sons, and his sons' sons with him, his daughters, and his sons' daughters, and all his family brought he with him into Egypt.

And he sent Judah before him unto Joseph, to show the way before him unto Goshen; and they came into the land of Goshen. And Joseph made ready his chariot, and went up to meet Israel his father, to Goshen; and he presented himself to him, and fell on his neck, and wept on his neck a good while. And Israel said unto Joseph, "Now let me die, since I have seen thy face, and know that thou art yet alive."

And Joseph said to his brethren, and to his father's house, "I will go up, and tell Pharaoh, and will say unto him, 'My brethren, and my father's house, which were in the land of Canaan, are come unto me; and the men are shepherds, for they have been keepers of cattle; and they have brought their flocks, and their herds, and all that they have.' And it shall come to pass, when Pharaoh shall call you, and shall say, 'What is your occupation?' that ye shall say, 'Thy servants have been keepers of cattle from our youth even until now, both we, and our fathers': that ye may dwell in the land of Goshen; for every shepherd is an abomination unto the Egyptians."

Then Joseph went in and told Pharaoh, and said, "My father and my brethren, and their flocks, and their herds, and all that they have, are come out of the land of Canaan; and, behold, they are in the land of Goshen."

And from among his brethren he took five men, and presented them to Pharaoh. And Pharaoh said to his brethren, "What is your occupation?"

And they said to Pharaoh, "Thy servants are shepherds, both we, and our fathers."

And they said to Pharaoh, "To sojourn in the land are we come; for there is no pasture for thy servants' flocks; for the famine is sore in the land of Canaan: now therefore, we pray thee, let thy servants dwell in the land of Goshen."

And Pharaoh spoke unto Joseph, saying, "Thy father and thy brethren are come to thee: the land of Egypt is before thee; in the best of the land make thy father and thy brethren to dwell; in the land of Goshen let them dwell: and if thou knowest any able men among them, then make them rulers over my cattle."

And Joseph brought in Jacob his father, and set him before Pharaoh: and Jacob blessed Pharaoh. And Pharaoh said unto Jacob, "How many are the days of the years of thy life?"

And Jacob said unto Pharaoh, "The days of the years of my pilgrimage are an hundred and thirty years: few and evil have been the days of the years of my life, and they have not attained unto the days of the years of the life of my fathers in the days of their pilgrimage."

And Jacob blessed Pharaoh, and went out from the presence of Pharaoh. And Joseph placed his father and his brethren, and gave them a possession in the land of Egypt, in the best of the land, in the land of Rameses, as Pharaoh had commanded. And Joseph nourished his father, and his brethren, and all his father's household, with food, according to their families.

And there was no food in all the land; for the famine was very sore, so that the land of Egypt and the land of Canaan fainted by reason of the famine. And Joseph gathered up all the money that was found in the land of

Egypt, and in the land of Canaan, for the corn which they bought: and Joseph brought the money into Pharaoh's house. And when the money was all spent in the land of Egypt, and in the land of Canaan, all the Egyptians came to Joseph, and said, "Give us bread: for why should we die in thy presence? for our money faileth."

And Joseph said, "Give your cattle; and I will give you for your cattle if money fail."

And they brought their cattle unto Joseph: and Joseph gave them food in exchange for the horses, and for the flocks, and for the herds, and for the asses: and he fed them with food in exchange for all their cattle for that year. And when that year was ended, they came to him the second year, and said to him, "We will not hide from my lord, how that our money is all spent; and the herds of cattle are my lord's; there is nought left in the sight of my lord, but our bodies, and our lands: wherefore should we die before thine eyes, both we and our land? buy us and our land for food, and we and our land will be servants unto Pharaoh: and give us seed, that we may live, and not die, and that the land be not desolate."

So Joseph bought all the land of Egypt for Pharaoh; for the Egyptians sold every man his field, because the famine was sore upon them: and the land became Pharaoh's. And as for the people, he removed them to the cities from one end of the border of Egypt even to the other end thereof.

Only the land of the priests bought he not: for the priests had a portion from Pharaoh, and did eat their

A VIEW IN LUXOR

From a photograph belonging to Miss Clara L. Bodman
and used by her kind permission

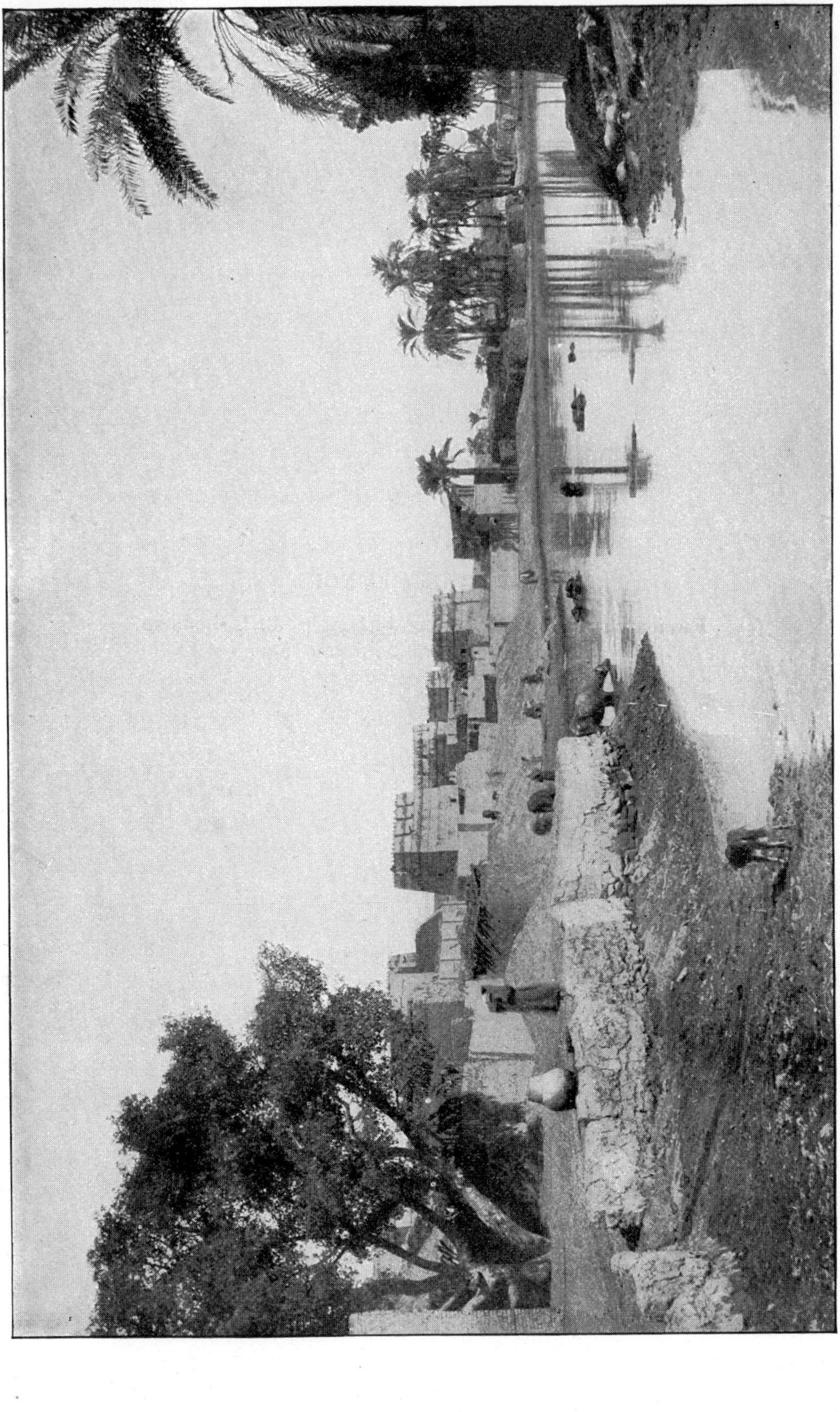

portion which Pharaoh gave them; wherefore they sold not their land. Then Joseph said unto the people, "Behold, I have bought you this day and your land for Pharaoh: lo, here is seed for you, and ye shall sow the land. And it shall come to pass at the ingatherings, that ye shall give a fifth to Pharaoh, and four parts shall be your own, for seed of the field, and for your food, and for them of your households, and for food for your little ones."

And they said, "Thou hast saved our lives: let us find grace in the sight of my lord, and we will be Pharaoh's servants."

And Joseph made it a statute concerning the land of Egypt unto this day, that Pharaoh should have the fifth; only the land of the priests alone became not Pharaoh's. And Israel dwelt in the land of Egypt, in the land of Goshen; and they got them possessions therein, and were fruitful, and multiplied exceedingly.

And Jacob lived in the land of Egypt seventeen years: so the days of Jacob, the years of his life, were an hundred forty and seven years. And the time drew near that Israel must die: and he called his son Joseph, and said unto him, "If now I have found grace in thy sight, put, I pray thee, thy hand under my thigh, and deal kindly and truly with me; bury me not, I pray thee, in Egypt: bury me with my fathers in the cave that is in the field of Ephron the Hittite, in the cave that is in the field of Machpelah, which is before Mamre, in the land of Canaan, which Abraham bought with the field from Ephron the Hittite for a possession of a buryingplace: there they buried Abraham and Sarah his wife; there they buried Isaac and Rebekah his wife; and there I buried Leah: the field and the cave that is therein, which was purchased from the children of Heth."

And when Jacob made an end of charging his sons, he laid himself down upon his bed and died. And Joseph fell upon his father's face, and wept upon him, and kissed him. And Joseph commanded his servants the physicians to embalm his father: and the physicians embalmed Israel. And forty days were fulfilled for him; for so are fulfilled the days of embalming: and the Egyptians wept for him threescore and ten days.

And when the days of weeping for him were past, Joseph spoke unto the house of Pharaoh, saying, "If now I have found grace in your eyes, speak, I pray you, in the ears of Pharaoh, saying, 'My father made me swear, saying, Lo, I die: in my grave which I have digged for me in the land of Canaan, there shalt thou bury me. Now therefore let me go up, I pray thee, and bury my father, and I will come again.'"

And Pharaoh said, "Go up, and bury thy father, according as he made thee swear." And Joseph went up to bury his father: and with him went up all the servants of Pharaoh, the elders of his house, and all the elders of the land of Egypt, and all the house of Joseph, and his brethren, and his father's house: only their little ones, and their flocks and their herds, they left in the land of Goshen. And there went up with him both chariots and horsemen: and it was a very great company. And they came to the threshing-floor of Atad, which is beyond Jordan, and there they lamented with a very great and sore lamentation: and he made a mourning for his father seven days. And when the inhabitants of the land, the Canaanites, saw the mourning in the floor of Atad, they said, "This is a grievous mourning to the Egyptians": wherefore the name of it was called "The Mourning of Egypt," which is beyond Jordan. And his sons did unto him according as he commanded them: for his sons carried him into the land of Canaan, and buried him in the cave of the field of Machpelah, which Abraham bought with the field, for a possession of a buryingplace, of Ephron the Hittite, before Mamre.

And Joseph returned into Egypt, he, and his brethren, and all that went up with him to bury his father, after he had buried his father. And when Joseph's brethren saw that their father was dead, they said, "It may be that Joseph will hate us, and will fully requite us all the evil which we did unto him." And they sent a message unto Joseph, saying, "Thy father did command before he died, saying, 'So shall ye say unto Joseph, Forgive, I pray thee now, the transgression of thy brethren, and their sin, in that they did unto thee evil': and now, we pray thee, forgive the transgression of the servants of the God of thy father."

And Joseph wept when they spoke unto him. And his brethren also went and fell down before his face; and they said, "Behold, we are thy servants." And Joseph said unto them, "Fear not: for am I in the place of God? And as for you, ye meant evil against me; but God meant it for good, to bring to pass, as it is this day, to save much people alive. Now therefore fear ye not: I will nourish you, and your little ones." And he comforted them, and spoke kindly unto them.

And Joseph dwelt in Egypt, he, and his father's house: and Joseph lived an hundred and ten years. And Joseph saw Ephraim's children of the third generation. And Joseph said unto his brethren, "I die: but God will surely visit you, and bring you up out of this land unto the land which he swore to Abraham, to Isaac, and to Jacob."

And Joseph took an oath of the children of Israel, saying, "God will surely visit you, and ye shall carry up my bones from hence."

So Joseph died, being an hundred and ten years old: and they embalmed him, and he was put in a coffin in Egypt.

The Great Captains

The word "captain," following the use in the Bible and all literature down to the present day, is not the particular term, designating the commander of a small company of soldiers, but the general term, standing for leadership in the largest sense. Moses, according to this meaning of the word, was one of the greatest of the world's captains, for he took a cowardly, unorganized mob of slaves and led them through the most appalling difficulties and dangers, to freedom, and to a position where national existence was possible. While there was little actual fighting in the journey from Egypt to Palestine, yet there was necessity, every step of the way, for the highest qualities of leadership.

Joshua was a great captain in the more strictly military sense of the word. He found the force organized and disciplined by the leadership of Moses, and he used it as a skillful swordsman uses a keen and tempered blade. In his campaigns he displayed the abilities of the great military genius.

THE FINDING OF MOSES

Slow glides the Nile: amid the margin flags,
Closed in a bulrush ark, the babe is left,—
Left by a mother's hand. His sister waits
Far off; and pale, 'tween hope and fear, beholds
The royal maid, surrounded by her train,
Approach the river bank,—approach the spot
Where sleeps the innocent: she sees them stoop
With meeting plumes; the rushy lid is oped,
And wakes the infant, smiling in his tears,
As when along a little mountain lake
The summer south-wind breathes, with gentle sigh,
And parts the reeds, unveiling, as they bend,
A water-lily floating on the wave.

VIEW FROM RAMAH, THE TRADITIONAL HOME OF SAMUEL

Copyright by Underwood & Underwood
and used by special permission

"We know not with certainty the situation of Ramah. Of Samuel as of Moses it may be said, 'No man knoweth of his sepulchre unto this day.' But the lofty peak above Gibeon, which has long borne his name, has this feature (in common, to a certain extent, with any high place which can have been the scene of his life and death), that it overlooks the whole of that broad table-land, on which the fortunes of the Jewish monarchy were afterwards unrolled. Its towering eminence, from which the pilgrims first obtained their view of Jerusalem, is no unfit likeness of the solitary grandeur of the prophet Samuel, who lived and died in the very midst of the future glory of his country"

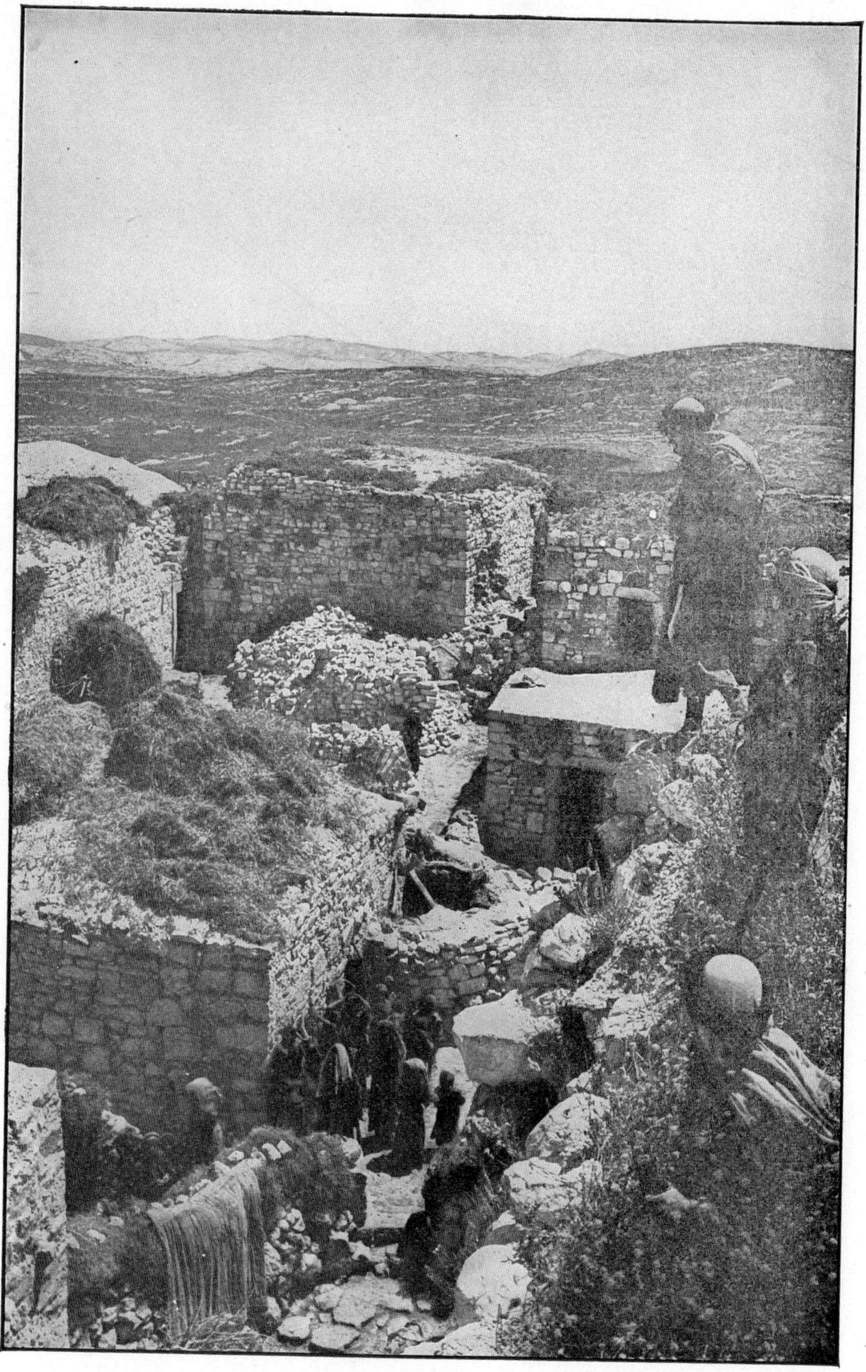

MOSES

The Story of the Man Who Led a Race of Slaves Out of Bondage, and Became the Emancipator of a Great Nation.

THE ISRAELITES ARE ENSLAVED IN EGYPT.

The Slave Who Was Brought Up in a King's Palace. Moses Kills One of the Egyptian Taskmasters and Flees from the Country.

Now there arose a new king over Egypt, who knew not Joseph. And he said to his people, "Behold, the people of the children of Israel are more and mightier than we: come, let us deal wisely with them; lest they multiply, and it come to pass, that, when there falleth out any war, they also join themselves unto our enemies, and fight against us, and get them up out of the land."

Therefore they set over them taskmasters to afflict them with their burdens. And they built for Pharaoh store cities, Pithom and Raamses. But the more they afflicted them, the more they multiplied and the more they spread abroad. And they were grieved because of the children of Israel. And the Egyptians made the children of Israel to serve with rigor: and they made their lives bitter with hard service, in mortar and in brick, and in all manner of service in the field, all their service, wherein they made them serve with rigor.

And Pharaoh charged all his people, saying, "Every son that is born to the Hebrews ye shall cast into the river, and every daughter ye shall save alive."

And there went a man of the house of Levi, and took for his wife a daughter of Levi. And the woman had a son: and when she saw that he was a goodly child, she hid him three months. And when she could not longer hide him, she took for him an ark of bulrushes, and daubed it with pitch; and she put the child therein, and laid it in the flags by the river's brink. And his sister stood afar off, to know what would be done to him. And the daughter of Pharaoh came down to bathe at the river; and her maidens walked along by the river side; and she saw the ark among the flags, and sent her handmaid to fetch it. And she opened it and saw the child: and, behold, the babe wept. And she had compassion on him, and said, "This is one of the Hebrews' children."

Then said his sister to Pharaoh's daughter, "Shall I go and call thee a nurse of the Hebrew women, that she may nurse the child for thee?"

And Pharaoh's daughter said to her, "Go."

And the maid went and called the child's mother. And Pharaoh's daughter said to her, "Take this child away, and nurse it for me, and I will give thee thy wages."

And the woman took the child, and nursed it. And the child grew, and she brought him to Pharaoh's daughter, and he became her son. And she called his name Moses, and said, "Because I drew him out of the water."

And it came to pass in those days, when Moses was

THE SPHINX

From a photograph in the possession of Mr. S. E. Bridgman
and used by his kind permission

The Great Sphinx at Gizeh is a colossal figure carved out of the solid rock. It perhaps represents the reigning monarch as a conqueror. The age of the Great Sphinx is thought to be about the same as that of the pyramids

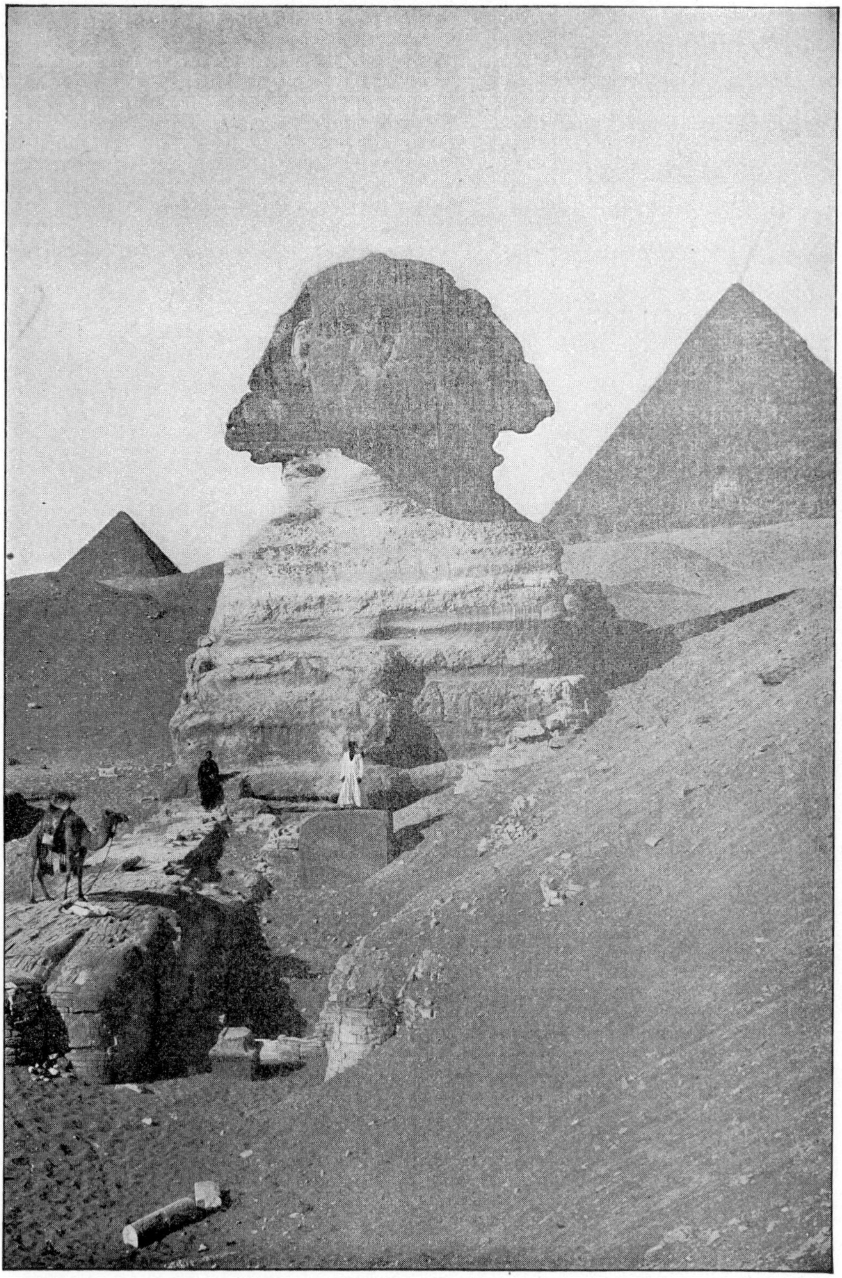

grown up, that he went out to his brethren, and looked on their burdens: and he saw an Egyptian smiting an Hebrew, one of his brethren. And he looked this way and that way, and when he saw that there was no man, he smote the Egyptian, and hid him in the sand. And he went out the second day, and, behold, two men of the Hebrews strove together: and he said to him that did the wrong, "Wherefore smitest thou thy fellow?"

And he said, "Who made thee a prince and a judge over us? thinkest thou to kill me, as thou killedst the Egyptian?"

And Moses feared, and said, "Surely the thing is known."

Now when Pharaoh heard this thing, he sought to slay Moses. But Moses fled from the face of Pharaoh, and dwelt in the land of Midian: and he sat down by a well. Now the priest of Midian had seven daughters: and they came and drew water, and filled the troughs to water their father's flock. And the shepherds came and drove them away: but Moses stood up and helped them, and watered their flock. And when they came to Reuel their father, he said, "How is it that ye are come so soon to-day?"

And they said, "An Egyptian delivered us out of the hand of the shepherds, and moreover he drew water for us, and watered the flock." And he said to his daughters, "And where is he? why is it that ye have left the man? call him, that he may eat bread."

And Moses was content to dwell with the man: and he gave Moses Zipporah his daughter. And she had a

And God said moreover to Moses, "Thus shalt thou say to the children of Israel, 'The Lord, the God of your fathers, the God of Abraham, the God of Isaac, and the God of Jacob, hath sent me to you': this is my name for ever, and this is my memorial to all generations. Go, and gather the elders of Israel together, and say unto them, 'The Lord, the God of your fathers, the God of Abraham, of Isaac, and of Jacob, hath appeared to me, saying, I have surely visited you, and seen that which is done to you in Egypt: and I have said, I will bring you up out of the affliction of Egypt, to a land flowing with milk and honey.' And they shall hearken to thy voice: and thou shalt come, thou and the elders of Israel, to the king of Egypt, and ye shall say to him, 'The Lord, the God of the Hebrews, hath met with us: and now let us go, we pray thee, three days' journey into the wilderness, that we may sacrifice to the Lord our God.' And I know that the king of Egypt will not give you leave to go, no, not by a mighty hand. And I will put forth my hand, and smite Egypt with all my wonders which I will do in the midst thereof: and after that he will let you go. And I will give this people favor in the sight of the Egyptians: and it shall come to pass, that, when ye go, ye shall not go empty: but every woman shall ask of her neighbor, and of her that sojourneth in her house, jewels of silver, and jewels of gold, and raiment: and ye shall put them upon your sons, and upon your daughters; and ye shall spoil the Egyptians."

And Moses answered and said, "But, behold, they will

not believe me, nor hearken unto my voice: for they will say, 'The Lord hath not appeared to thee.'"

And the Lord said unto him, "What is that in thine hand?"

And he said, "A rod."

And he said, "Cast it on the ground."

And he cast it on the ground, and it became a serpent; and Moses fled from before it. And the Lord said unto Moses, "Put forth thine hand, and take it by the tail." And he put forth his hand, and laid hold of it, and it became a rod in his hand.

And the Lord said furthermore to him, "Put now thine hand into thy bosom."

And he put his hand into his bosom: and when he took it out, behold, his hand was leprous, as white as snow. And he said, "Put thine hand into thy bosom again." And he put his hand into his bosom again; and when he took it out of his bosom, behold, it was turned again as his other flesh.

The Lord said, "It shall come to pass, if they will not believe thee, neither hearken to the voice of the first sign, that they will believe the voice of the latter sign. And it shall come to pass, if they will not believe even these two signs, neither hearken to thy voice, that thou shalt take of the water of the river, and pour it upon the dry land: and the water which thou takest out of the river shall become blood upon the dry land."

And Moses said unto the Lord, "Oh Lord, I am not eloquent, neither heretofore, nor since thou hast spoken unto thy servant: for I am slow of speech, and of a slow tongue."

And the Lord said unto him, "Who hath made man's mouth? or who maketh a man dumb, or deaf, or seeing, or blind? is it not I, the Lord? Now therefore go, and I will be with thy mouth, and teach thee what thou shalt speak."

And he said, "Oh Lord, send, I pray thee, by the hand of him whom thou wilt send."

And the anger of the Lord was kindled against Moses, and he said, "Is there not Aaron thy brother the Levite? I know that he can speak well. And also, behold, he cometh forth to meet thee: and when he seeth thee, he will be glad in his heart. And thou shalt speak to him, and put the words in his mouth: and I will be with thy mouth, and with his mouth, and will teach you what ye shall do. And he shall be thy spokesman unto the people: and it shall come to pass, that he shall be to thee a mouth, and thou shalt be to him as God. And thou shalt take in thine hand this rod, wherewith thou shalt do the signs."

And Moses went and returned to Jethro his father-in-law, and said unto him, "Let me go, I pray thee, and return to my brethren which are in Egypt, and see whether they be yet alive."

And Jethro said to Moses, "Go in peace."

And the Lord said to Moses in Midian, "Go, return into Egypt: for all the men are dead which sought thy life."

And Moses took his wife and his sons, and set them upon an ass, and he returned to the land of Egypt: and

THE BANKS OF THE NILE NEAR CAIRO

From a photograph owned by Mr. S. E. Bridgman
and used by his kind permission

The Nile was the life and glory of Egypt. It afforded a magnificent waterway for commerce, and the annual overflow gave the greatest fertility to the soil

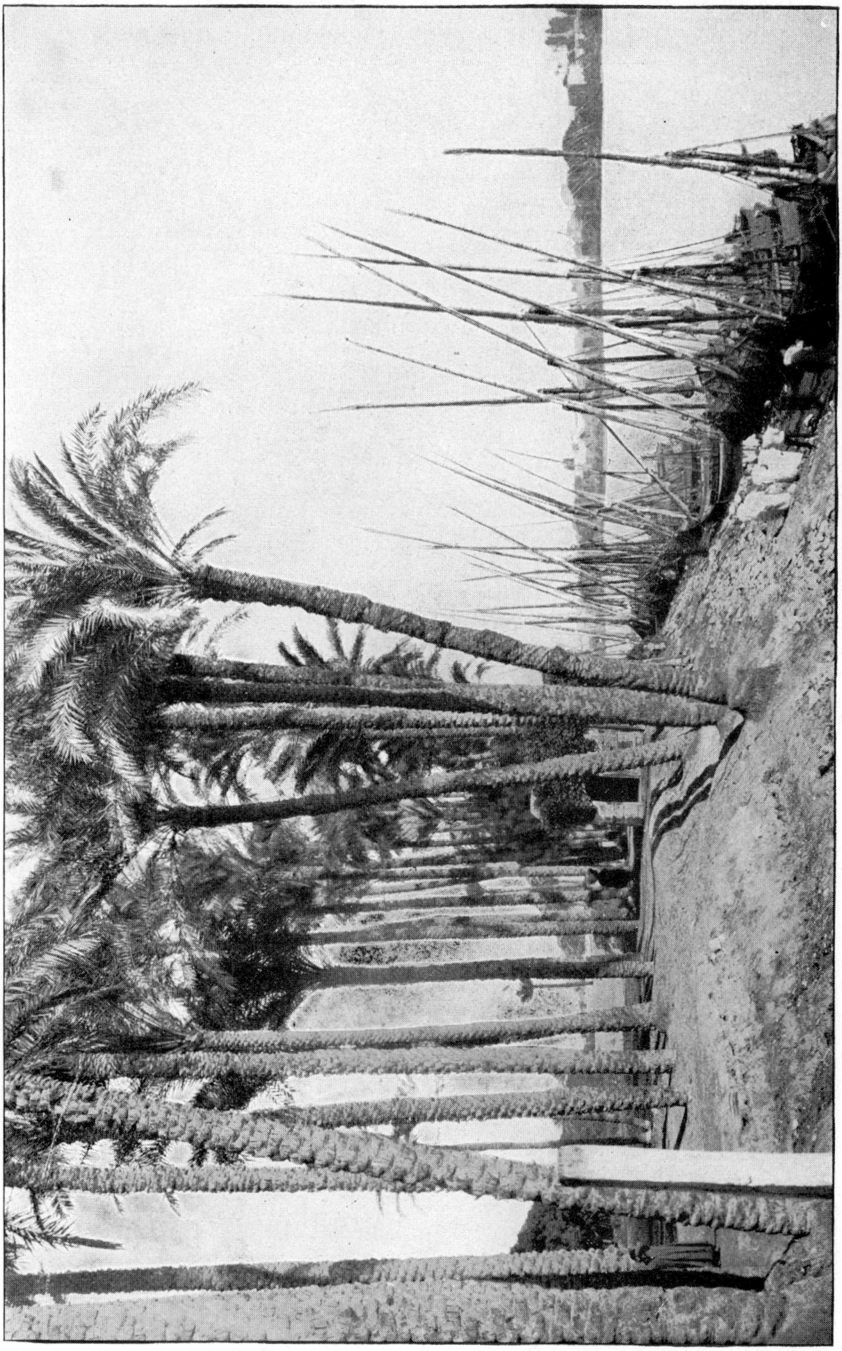

Moses took the rod of God in his hand. And the Lord said to Moses, "When thou goest back into Egypt, see that thou do before Pharaoh all the wonders which I have put in thine hand: but I will harden his heart, and he will not let the people go. And thou shalt say to Pharaoh, 'Thus saith the Lord, Israel is my son, my firstborn: and I have said to thee, Let my son go, that he may serve me; and thou hast refused to let him go: behold I will slay thy son, thy firstborn.'"

And the Lord said to Aaron, "Go into the wilderness to meet Moses." And he went, and met him in the mountain of God, and kissed him. And Moses told Aaron all the words of the Lord wherewith he had sent him, and all the signs wherewith he had charged him. And Moses and Aaron went and gathered together all the elders of the children of Israel: and Aaron spoke all the words which the Lord had spoken to Moses, and did the signs in the sight of the people. And the people believed.

"LET MY PEOPLE GO."
Moses and Aaron Demand the Release of the Israelites. Pharaoh Refuses.

And afterward Moses and Aaron came, and said to Pharaoh, "Thus saith the Lord, the God of Israel, 'Let my people go, that they may hold a feast unto me in the wilderness.'"

And Pharaoh said, "Who is the Lord, that I should hearken to his voice to let Israel go? I know not the Lord, and moreover I will not let Israel go."

And they said, "The God of the Hebrews hath met with us: let us go, we pray thee, three days' journey into the wilderness, and sacrifice to the Lord our God; lest he fall upon us with pestilence, or with the sword."

And the king of Egypt said to them, "Wherefore do ye, Moses and Aaron, loose the people from their works? get you to your burdens." And Pharaoh said, "Behold, the people of the land are now many, and ye make them rest from their burdens."

And the same day Pharaoh commanded the taskmasters of the people, and their officers, saying, "Ye shall no more give the people straw to make brick, as heretofore: let them go and gather straw for themselves. And the number of the bricks, which they did make heretofore, ye shall lay upon them; ye shall not diminish aught thereof: for they are idle; therefore they cry, saying, 'Let us go and sacrifice to our God.' Let heavier work be laid upon the men, that they may labor therein; and let them not regard lying words."

And the taskmasters of the people went out, and their officers, and they spoke to the people, saying, "Thus saith Pharaoh, I will not give you straw. Go yourselves, get you straw where ye can find it: for naught of your work shall be diminished."

So the people were scattered abroad throughout all the land of Egypt to gather stubble for straw. And the taskmasters were urgent, saying, "Fulfill your works, your daily tasks, as when there was straw."

And the officers of the children of Israel, which Pharaoh's taskmasters had set over them, were beaten, and demanded, "Wherefore have ye not fulfilled your task both yesterday and to-day, in making brick as heretofore?"

Then the officers of the children of Israel came and cried to Pharaoh, saying, "Wherefore dealest thou thus with thy servants? There is no straw given unto thy servants, and they say to us, 'Make brick': and, behold, thy servants are beaten; but the fault is in thine own people."

But he said, "Ye are idle, ye are idle: therefore ye say, 'Let us go and sacrifice to the Lord.' Go therefore now, and work; for there shall no straw be given you, yet shall ye deliver the number of bricks."

And the officers of the children of Israel saw that they were in deep trouble when it was said, "Ye shall not diminish aught from your bricks, your daily tasks."

And they met Moses and Aaron, who stood in the way, as they came forth from Pharaoh: and they said to them, "The Lord look upon you, and judge; because ye have made us to be abhorred in the eyes of Pharaoh, and in the eyes of his servants, to put a sword in their hand to slay us."

And the Lord said unto Moses, "Now shalt thou see what I will do to Pharaoh: for by a strong hand shall he let them go, and by a strong hand shall he drive them out of his land."

And it came to pass on the day when the Lord spoke unto Moses in the land of Egypt, that the Lord spoke to Moses, saying, "I am the Lord: speak thou to Pharaoh king of Egypt all that I speak to thee."

And Moses said before the Lord, "Behold, I am slow of speech and of a slow tongue, and how shall Pharaoh hearken unto me?"

And the Lord said unto Moses, "See, I have made thee a god to Pharaoh: and Aaron thy brother shall be thy spokesman. Thou shalt speak all that I command thee: and Aaron thy brother shall speak unto Pharaoh, that he let the children of Israel go out of his land. And I will harden Pharaoh's heart, and multiply my signs and my wonders in the land of Egypt. But Pharaoh will not hearken unto you, and I will lay my hand upon Egypt, and bring forth my hosts, my people the children of Israel, out of the land of Egypt by great judgments. And the Egyptians shall know that I am the Lord, when I stretch forth mine hand upon Egypt, and bring out the children of Israel from among them."

And Moses and Aaron did so; as the Lord commanded them, so did they.

And the Lord spoke to Moses and to Aaron, saying, "When Pharaoh shall speak to you, saying, 'Show a wonder for you:' then thou shalt say unto Aaron, 'Take thy rod, and cast it down before Pharaoh, that it become a serpent.'"

And Moses and Aaron went in unto Pharaoh, and they did so, as the Lord had commanded: and Aaron cast down his rod before Pharaoh and before his servants, and it became a serpent. Then Pharaoh also called for the wise men and the magicians: and they also did in like manner with their enchantments. For they cast down

THE RIVER NILE

From a photograph belonging to Miss Clara L. Bodman
and used by her kind permission

"And all the waters that were in the river were turned to blood"

This picture shows the broad Nile with one of the boats now in use called a "dahabiyeh." There has been built recently on the upper Nile an immense dam which will be used to regulate the flow of water and bring great agricultural prosperity to Egypt

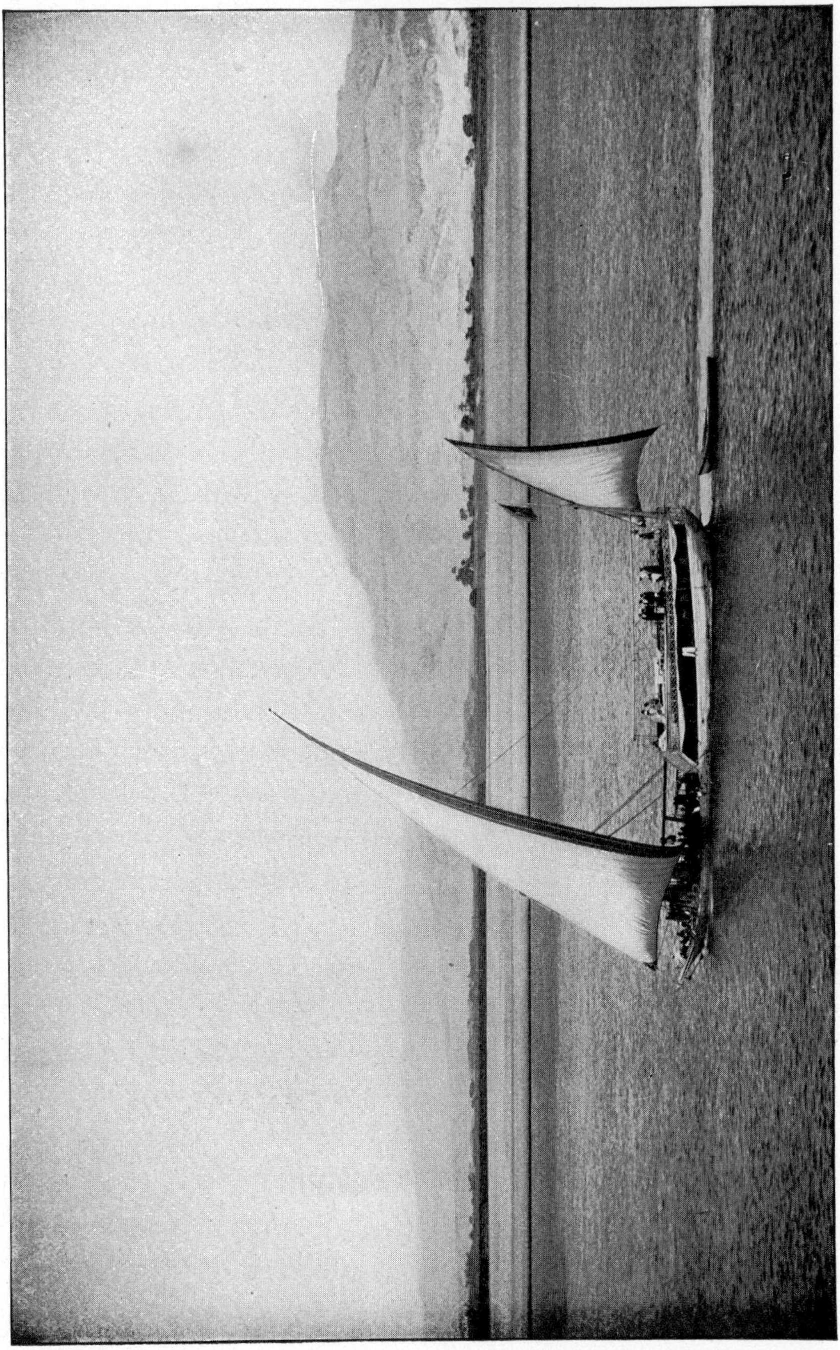

every man his rod, and they became serpents: but Aaron's rod swallowed up their rods. And Pharaoh's heart was hardened, and he hearkened not unto them; as the Lord had spoken.

THE PLAGUES OF EGYPT.
1. The Plague of Blood.

And the Lord said unto Moses, "Pharaoh's heart is stubborn, he refuseth to let the people go. Get thee to Pharaoh in the morning; lo, he goeth out unto the water; and thou shalt stand by the river's brink to meet him; and the rod which was turned to a serpent shalt thou take in thine hand. And thou shalt say unto him, 'The Lord, the God of the Hebrews, hath sent me to thee, saying, Let my people go, that they may serve me in the wilderness: and, behold, hitherto thou hast not hearkened. Thus saith the Lord, In this thou shalt know that I am the Lord: behold, I will smite with the rod that is in mine hand upon the waters which are in the river, and they shall be turned to blood. And the fish that are in the river shall die, and the river shall stink; and the Egyptians shall loathe to drink water from the river.'"

And the Lord said to Moses, "Say unto Aaron, 'Take thy rod, and stretch out thine hand over the waters of Egypt, over their rivers, over their streams, and over their pools, and over all their ponds of water, that they may become blood; and there shall be blood throughout all the land of Egypt, both in vessels of wood and in vessels of stone.'"

And Moses and Aaron did so, as the Lord commanded; and he lifted up the rod, and smote the waters that were in the river, in the sight of Pharaoh, and in the sight of his servants; and all the waters that were in the river were turned to blood. And the fish that were in the river died; and the river stank, and the Egyptians could not drink water from the river; and the blood was throughout all the land of Egypt.

And the magicians of Egypt did in like manner with their enchantments: and Pharaoh's heart was hardened, and he hearkened not unto them; as the Lord had spoken. And Pharaoh turned and went into his house, neither did he lay even this to heart. And all the Egyptians digged round about the river for water to drink; for they could not drink of the water of the river. And seven days were fulfilled, after the Lord had smitten the river.

2. The Plague of Frogs.

And the Lord spoke to Moses, "Go in unto Pharaoh, and say unto him, 'Thus saith the Lord, Let my people go, that they may serve me. And if thou refuse to let them go, behold, I will smite all thy borders with frogs: and the river shall swarm with frogs, which shall go up and come into thine house, and into thy bedchamber, and upon thy bed, and into the house of thy servants, and upon thy people, and into thine ovens, and into thy kneading-troughs: and the frogs shall come up both upon thee, and upon thy people, and upon all thy servants.'"

And the Lord said to Moses, "Say to Aaron, 'Stretch

forth thine hand with thy rod over the rivers, over the streams, and over the pools, and cause frogs to come up upon the land of Egypt.'"

And Aaron stretched out his hand over the waters of Egypt; and the frogs came up, and covered the land of Egypt. And the magicians did in like manner with their enchantments, and brought up frogs upon the land of Egypt.

Then Pharaoh called for Moses and Aaron, and said, "Intreat the Lord, that he take away the frogs from me, and from my people; and I will let the people go, that they may sacrifice unto the Lord."

And Moses said to Pharaoh, "For what time shall I intreat for thee, and for thy servants, and for thy people, that the frogs be destroyed from thee and thy houses, and remain in the river only?"

And he said, "For to-morrow."

And he said, "Be it according to thy word: that thou mayest know that there is none like unto the Lord our God. And the frogs shall depart from thee, and from thy houses, and from thy servants, and from thy people; they shall remain in the river only."

And Moses and Aaron went out from Pharaoh: and Moses cried unto the Lord concerning the frogs which he had brought upon Pharaoh. And the Lord did according to the word of Moses; and the frogs died out of the houses, out of the courts, and out of the fields. And they gathered them together in heaps: and the land stank. But when Pharaoh saw that there was relief, he hardened his heart, and hearkened not unto them; as the Lord had spoken.

3. The Plague of Lice.

And the Lord said unto Moses, "Say unto Aaron, 'Stretch out thy rod, and smite the dust of the earth, that it may become lice throughout all the land of Egypt.'"

And they did so; and Aaron stretched out his hand with his rod, and smote the dust of the earth, and there were lice upon man, and upon beast; all the dust of the earth became lice throughout all the land of Egypt. And the magicians did so with their enchantments to bring forth lice, but they could not: and there were lice upon man, and upon beast.

Then the magicians said to Pharaoh, "This is the finger of God": and Pharaoh's heart was hardened, and he hearkened not to them; as the Lord had spoken.

4. The Plague of Flies.

And the Lord said to Moses, "Rise up early in the morning, and stand before Pharaoh; lo, he cometh forth to the water; and say to him, 'Thus saith the Lord, Let my people go, that they may serve me. Else, if thou wilt not let my people go, behold, I will send swarms of flies upon thee, and upon thy servants, and upon thy people, and into thy houses: and the houses of the Egyptians shall be full of swarms of flies, and also the ground whereon they are. And I will set apart in that day the land of Goshen, in which my people dwell, that no swarms of flies shall be there; to the end thou mayest know that I am the

Lord in the midst of the earth. And I will put a division between my people and thy people: by to-morrow shall this sign be.'"

And the Lord did so; and there came grievous swarms of flies into the house of Pharaoh, and into his servants' houses: and in all the land of Egypt the land was corrupted by reason of the swarms of flies. And Pharaoh called for Moses and for Aaron, and said, "Go ye, sacrifice to your God in the land."

And Moses said, "It is not right so to do; for we shall sacrifice the holy things of the Egyptians to the Lord our God: lo, shall we sacrifice the holy things of the Egyptians before their eyes, and will they not stone us? We will go three days' journey into the wilderness, and sacrifice to the Lord our God, as he shall command us."

And Pharaoh said, "I will let you go, that ye may sacrifice to the Lord your God in the wilderness; only ye shall not go very far away: intreat for me."

And Moses said, "Behold, I go out from thee, and I will intreat the Lord that the swarms of flies may depart from Pharaoh, from his servants, and from his people, to-morrow: only let not Pharaoh deal deceitfully any more in not letting the people go to sacrifice to the Lord."

And Moses went out from Pharaoh and intreated the Lord. And the Lord did according to the word of Moses; and he removed the swarms of flies from Pharaoh, from his servants, and from his people; there remained not one. And Pharaoh hardened his heart this time also, and he did not let the people go.

5. The Plague of Cattle Disease.

Then the Lord said unto Moses, "Go in to Pharaoh, and tell him, 'Thus saith the Lord, the God of the Hebrews, Let my people go that they may serve me. For if thou refuse to let them go, and wilt hold them still, behold, the hand of the Lord is upon thy cattle which are in the field, upon the horses, upon the asses, upon the camels, upon the herds, and upon the flocks: there shall be a very grievous distemper. And the Lord shall distinguish between the cattle of Israel and the cattle of Egypt: and there shall nothing die of all that belongeth to the children of Israel.'"

And the Lord appointed a set time, saying, "To-morrow the Lord shall do this thing in the land."

And the Lord did that thing on the morrow, and all the cattle of Egypt died: but of the cattle of the children of Israel died not one. And Pharaoh sent, and, behold, there was not so much as one of the cattle of the Israelites dead. But the heart of Pharaoh was stubborn, and he did not let the people go.

6. The Plague of Boils.

And the Lord said unto Moses and unto Aaron, "Take to you handfuls of ashes, and let Moses sprinkle it toward the heaven in the sight of Pharaoh. And it shall become small dust over all the land of Egypt, and shall be a boil breaking forth upon man and upon beast, throughout all the land of Egypt."

And they took ashes, and stood before Pharaoh; and Moses sprinkled it up toward heaven; and it became a boil breaking forth upon man and upon beast.

And the magicians could not stand before Moses because of the boils; for the boils were upon the magicians, and upon all the Egyptians. And the Lord hardened the heart of Pharaoh, and he hearkened not to them; as the Lord had spoken to Moses.

And the Lord said to Moses, "Rise up early in the morning, and stand before Pharaoh, and say to him, 'Thus saith the Lord, the God of the Hebrews, Let my people go, that they may serve me. For I will this time send all my plagues upon thine heart, and upon thy servants, and upon thy people; that thou mayest know that there is none like me in all the earth. For now I had put forth my hand, and smitten thee and thy people with pestilence, and thou hadst been cut off from the earth: but for this very cause have I made thee to stand, in order to show thee my power, that my name may be declared throughout all the earth. Exaltest thou thyself still against my people, that thou wilt not let them go? Behold, to-morrow about this time I will cause a very grievous hail, such as hath not been in Egypt since the day it was founded even until now. Now therefore send, hasten in thy cattle and all that thou hast in the field; for every man and beast which shall be found in the field, and shall not be brought home, the hail shall come down upon them, and they shall die.'"

He that feared the word of the Lord among the servants of Pharaoh made his servants and his cattle flee into the houses: and he that regarded not the word of the Lord left his servants and his cattle in the field.

THE SEVENTH PLAGUE OF EGYPT

I.

'T was morn,—the rising splendor rolled
On marble towers and roofs of gold;
Hall, court, and gallery, below,
Were crowded with a living flow;
Egyptian, Arab, Nubian, there,—
The bearers of the bow and spear,
The hoary priest, the Chaldee sage,
The slave, the gemmed and glittering page,—
Helm, turban, and tiara, shone
A dazzling ring round Pharaoh's throne.

II.

There came a man:—the human tide
Shrank backward from his stately stride:
His cheek with storm and time was tanned;
A shepherd's staff was in his hand;
A shudder of instinctive fear
Told the dark king what step was near;
On through the host the stranger came,
It parted round his form like flame.

III.

He stooped not at the footstool stone,
He clasped not sandal, kissed not throne;
Erect he stood amid the ring,
His only words, "Be just, O king!"
On Pharaoh's cheek the blood flushed high,
A fire was in his sullen eye;

Yet on the chief of Israel
No arrow of his thousands fell;
All mute and moveless as the grave
Stood chilled the satrap and the slave.

IV.

"Thou'rt come," at length the monarch spoke;
(Haughty and high the words outbroke;)
"Is Israel weary of its lair,
The forehead peeled, the shoulder bare?
Take back the answer to your band:
Go, reap the wind! go, plow the sand!
Go, vilest of the living vile,
To build the never-ending pile,
Till, darkest of the nameless dead,
The vulture on their flesh is fed!
What better asks the howling slave
Than the base life our bounty gave?"

V.

Shouted in pride the turbaned peers,
Upclashed to heaven the golden spears.—
"King! thou and thine are doomed!—Behold!"
The prophet spoke,—the thunder rolled!
Along the pathway of the sun
Sailed vapory mountains, wild and dun.
"Yet there is time," the prophet said:
He raised his staff,—the storm was stayed:
"King! be the word of freedom given:
What art thou, man, to war with Heaven?"

VI.

There came no word.—The thunder broke!—
Like a huge city's final smoke,
Thick, lurid, stifling, mixed with flame,
Through court and hall the vapors came.
Loose as the stubble in the field,

Wide flew the men of spear and shield;
Scattered like foam along the wave,
Flew the proud pageant, prince and slave;
Or in the chains of terror bound,
Lay, corpse-like, on the smouldering ground.
"Speak, king!—the wrath is but begun!—
Still dumb?—then, Heaven, thy will be done!"

VII.

Echoed from earth a hollow roar
Like ocean on the midnight shore!
A sheet of lightning o'er them wheeled,
The solid ground beneath them reeled;
In dust sank roof and battlement;
Like webs the giant walls were rent;
Red, broad, before his startled gaze
The monarch saw his Egypt blaze.
Still swelled the plague,—the flame grew pale,
Burst from the clouds the charge of hail:
With arrowy keenness, iron weight,
Down poured the ministers of fate;
Till man and cattle, crushed, congealed,
Covered with death the boundless field.

VIII.

Still swelled the plague,—uprose the blast,
The avenger, fit to be the last:
On ocean, river, forest, vale,
Thundered at once the mighty gale.
Before the whirlwind flew the tree,
Beneath the whirlwind roared the sea;
A thousand ships were on the wave—
Where are they?—ask that foaming grave!
Down go the hope, the pride of years,
Down go the myriad mariners;
The riches of earth's richest zone,
Gone! like a flash of lightning, gone!

IX.

And, lo! that first fierce triumph o'er,
Swells ocean on the shrinking shore;
Still onward, onward, dark and wide,
Engulfs the land the furious tide.—
Then bowed thy spirit, stubborn king,
Thou serpent, reft of fang and sting;
Humbled before the prophet's knee,
He groaned, "Be injured Israel free!"

X.

To heaven the sage upraised his hand;
Back rolled the deluge from the land;
Back to its caverns sank the gale;
Fled from the moon the vapors pale;
Broad burned again the joyous sun:
The hour of wrath and death was done.

—*Croly.*

7. The Plague of Hail.

And the Lord said to Moses, "Stretch forth thine hand toward heaven, that there may be hail in all the land of Egypt, upon man, and upon beast, and upon every herb of the field, throughout the land of Egypt."

And Moses stretched forth his rod toward heaven: and the Lord sent thunder and hail, and lightning; and the Lord sent hail upon the land of Egypt. So there was hail, and lightning mingled with the hail, very grievous, such as had not been in all the land of Egypt since it became a nation. And the hail smote throughout all the land of Egypt all that was in the field, both man and beast; and the hail smote every herb of the field, and broke every tree of the field. Only in the land of Goshen, where the children of Israel were, was there no hail. And Pharaoh sent, and called for Moses and Aaron, and said to them, "I have sinned this time: the Lord is righteous, and I and my people are wicked. Intreat the Lord; for there hath been enough of these mighty thunderings and hail; and I will let you go, and ye shall stay no longer."

And Moses said unto him, "As soon as I am gone out of the city, I will spread abroad my hands to the Lord; the thunders shall cease, neither shall there be any more hail; that thou mayest know that the earth is the Lord's. But as for thee and thy servants, I know that ye will not yet fear the Lord God."

And Moses went out of the city from Pharaoh, and

spread abroad his hands unto the Lord: and the thunders and hail ceased, and the rain was not poured upon the earth. And when Pharaoh saw that the rain and the hail and the thunders were ceased, he sinned yet more, and hardened his heart, he and his servants. And the heart of Pharaoh was hardened, and he did not let the children of Israel go; as the Lord had spoken by Moses.

And the Lord said unto Moses, "Go in to Pharaoh: for I have hardened his heart, and the heart of his servants, that I might shew these my signs in the midst of them: and that thou mayest tell to thy son, and to thy son's son, what things I have wrought upon Egypt, and my signs which I have done among them; that ye may know that I am the Lord."

And Moses and Aaron went in unto Pharaoh, and said to him, "Thus saith the Lord, the God of the Hebrews, 'How long wilt thou refuse to humble thyself before me? let my people go, that they may serve me. Else, if thou refuse to let my people go, behold, to-morrow will I bring locusts into thy border: and they shall cover the face of the earth, that one shall not be able to see the earth: and they shall eat what remaineth unto you from the hail, and shall eat every tree which groweth for you out of the field: and thy houses shall be filled, and the houses of all thy servants, and the houses of all the Egyptians; as neither thy fathers nor thy fathers' fathers have seen, since the day that they were upon the earth to this day.'" And he turned, and went out from Pharaoh.

And Pharaoh's servants said unto him, "How long

shall this man be a snare unto us? let the men go, that they may serve the Lord their God: knowest thou not yet that Egypt is destroyed?"

And Moses and Aaron were brought again to Pharaoh: and he said unto them, "Go, serve the Lord your God: but who are they that shall go?" And Moses said, "We will go with our young and with our old, with our sons and with our daughters, with our flocks and with our herds will we go; for we must hold a feast unto the Lord."

And he said unto them, "No, I will not let you go with your little ones. Not so. But go now ye that are men, and serve the Lord; for that is what ye desire."

And they were driven out from Pharaoh's presence.

8. The Plague of Locusts.

And the Lord said to Moses, "Stretch out thine hand over the land of Egypt for the locusts, that they may come up upon the land of Egypt, and eat every herb of the land, even all that the hail hath left."

And Moses stretched forth his rod over the land of Egypt, and the Lord brought an east wind upon the land all that day, and all the night; and when it was morning, the east wind brought the locusts. And the locusts went up over all the land of Egypt, and rested in all the borders of Egypt; very grievous were they; before them there were no such locusts as they, neither after them shall be such. For they covered the face of the whole earth, so that the land was darkened; and they ate every herb of the land, and all the fruit of the trees which the hail had

CLIFFS NEAR LUXOR.   TEMPLE OF DAR EL BAHARI
From a photograph belonging to Miss Clara L. Bodman
and used by her kind permission

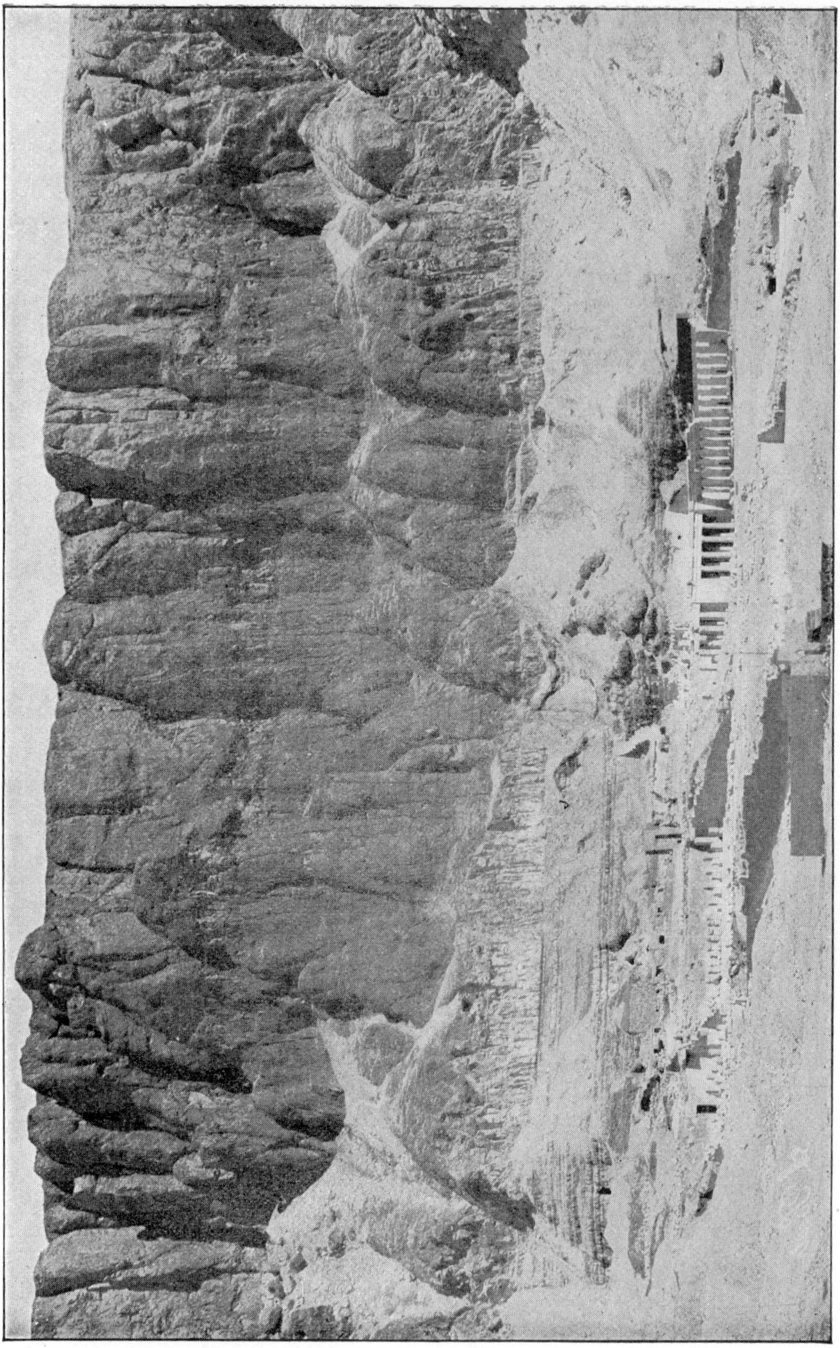

left: and there remained not any green thing, either tree or herb of the field, through all the land of Egypt.

Then Pharaoh called for Moses and Aaron in haste; and he said, "I have sinned against the Lord your God, and against you. Now therefore forgive, I pray thee, my sin only this once, and intreat the Lord your God, that he may take away from me this death only."

And he went out from Pharaoh, and intreated the Lord. And the Lord turned an exceeding strong west wind, which took up the locusts, and drove them into the Red Sea; there remained not one locust in all the border of Egypt. But the Lord hardened Pharaoh's heart, and he did not let the children of Israel go.

9. The Plague of Darkness.

And the Lord said to Moses, "Stretch out thine hand toward heaven, that there may be darkness over the land of Egypt, even darkness which may be felt."

And Moses stretched forth his hand toward heaven; and there was a thick darkness in all the land of Egypt three days; they saw not one another, neither rose any from his place for three days: but all the children of Israel had light in their dwellings.

And Pharaoh called to Moses, and said, "Go ye, serve the Lord; only let your flocks and your herds be stayed: let your little ones also go with you."

And Moses said, "Thou must also give into our hand sacrifices and burnt offerings, that we may sacrifice unto the Lord our God. Our cattle also shall go with us; there shall not an hoof be left behind; for thereof must we take to serve the Lord our God; and we know not with what we must serve the Lord, until we come thither."

But the Lord hardened Pharaoh's heart, and he would not let them go.

And Pharaoh said to him, "Get thee from me, take heed to thyself, see my face no more; for in the day thou seest my face thou shalt die."

And Moses said, "Thou hast spoken well; I will see thy face again no more."

And the Lord said to Moses, "Yet one plague more will I bring upon Pharaoh, and upon Egypt; afterwards he will let you go hence: when he shall let you go, he shall surely thrust you out hence altogether. Speak now to the people, and let them ask every man of his neighbor, and every woman of her neighbor, jewels of silver, and jewels of gold."

And the Lord gave the people favor in the sight of the Egyptians. Moreover the man Moses was very great in the land of Egypt, in the sight of Pharaoh's servants, and in the sight of the people.

And Moses said, "Thus saith the Lord, 'About midnight will I go out into the midst of Egypt: and all the firstborn in the land of Egypt shall die, from the firstborn of Pharaoh that sitteth upon his throne, even to the firstborn of the maidservant who grinds at the mill; and all the firstborn of cattle. And there shall be a great cry throughout all the land of Egypt, such as there hath been none like it, nor shall be like it any more. But against any of the children of Israel shall not a dog move his tongue, against man or beast: that ye may know how that the Lord doth put a difference between the Egyptians and Israel.' And all these thy servants shall come down unto me, and bow down themselves unto me, saying, 'Get thee out, and all the people that follow thee: and after that I will go out.'" And he went out from Pharaoh in hot anger.

And the Lord said unto Moses, "Pharaoh will not hearken unto you: that my wonders may be multiplied in the land of Egypt."

And Moses and Aaron did all these wonders before Pharaoh: and the Lord hardened Pharaoh's heart, and he did not let the children of Israel go out of his land.

(After the ninth plague, the plague of darkness, came a tenth plague, the very worst of all, the description of which is given in another place.)

THE FEAST OF THE PASSOVER.
The Israelites Make Ready for the March.

And the Lord spoke to Moses and Aaron in the land of Egypt, saying, "This month shall be unto you the beginning of months: it shall be the first month of the year to you. Speak ye to all the congregation of Israel, saying, 'In the tenth day of this month they shall take to them every man a lamb, according to their fathers' houses, a lamb for an household: and if the household be too little for a lamb, then shall he and his neighbor next unto his house take one according to the number of the souls.

Your lamb shall be without blemish, a male of the first year: ye shall take it from the sheep, or from the goats: and ye shall keep it up until the fourteenth day of the same month: and the whole assembly of the congregation of Israel shall kill it at even. And they shall take of the blood, and put it on the two side posts and on the lintel, upon the houses wherein they shall eat it. And they shall eat the flesh in that night, roasted with fire, and unleavened bread; with bitter herbs they shall eat it. Eat not of it raw, nor boiled with water, but roast with fire; its head with its legs and with the inwards thereof. And ye shall let nothing of it remain until the morning; but that which remaineth of it until the morning ye shall burn with fire.

" 'And thus shall ye eat it; with your loins girded, your shoes on your feet, and your staff in your hand: and ye shall eat it in haste: it is the Lord's passover. For I will go through the land of Egypt in that night, and will smite all the firstborn in the land of Egypt, both man and beast; and against all the gods of Egypt I will execute judgments: I am the Lord. And the blood shall be to you for a token upon the houses where ye are: and when I see the blood, I will pass over you, and there shall no plague be upon you to destroy you, when I smite the land of Egypt.' "

Then Moses called for all the elders of Israel, and said unto them, "Draw out, and take you lambs according to your families, and kill the passover. And ye shall take a bunch of hyssop, and dip it in the blood that is in the

THE VALLEY OF THE TOMBS OF THE KINGS, AT THEBES

Here the steep ramparts were divided by a tortuous cleft, which wound back with many cross fissures deep into the desert. The ravine was simply a chasm with perpendicular sides of naked rock. This was the valley of the Tombs of the Kings
—"The Yoke"

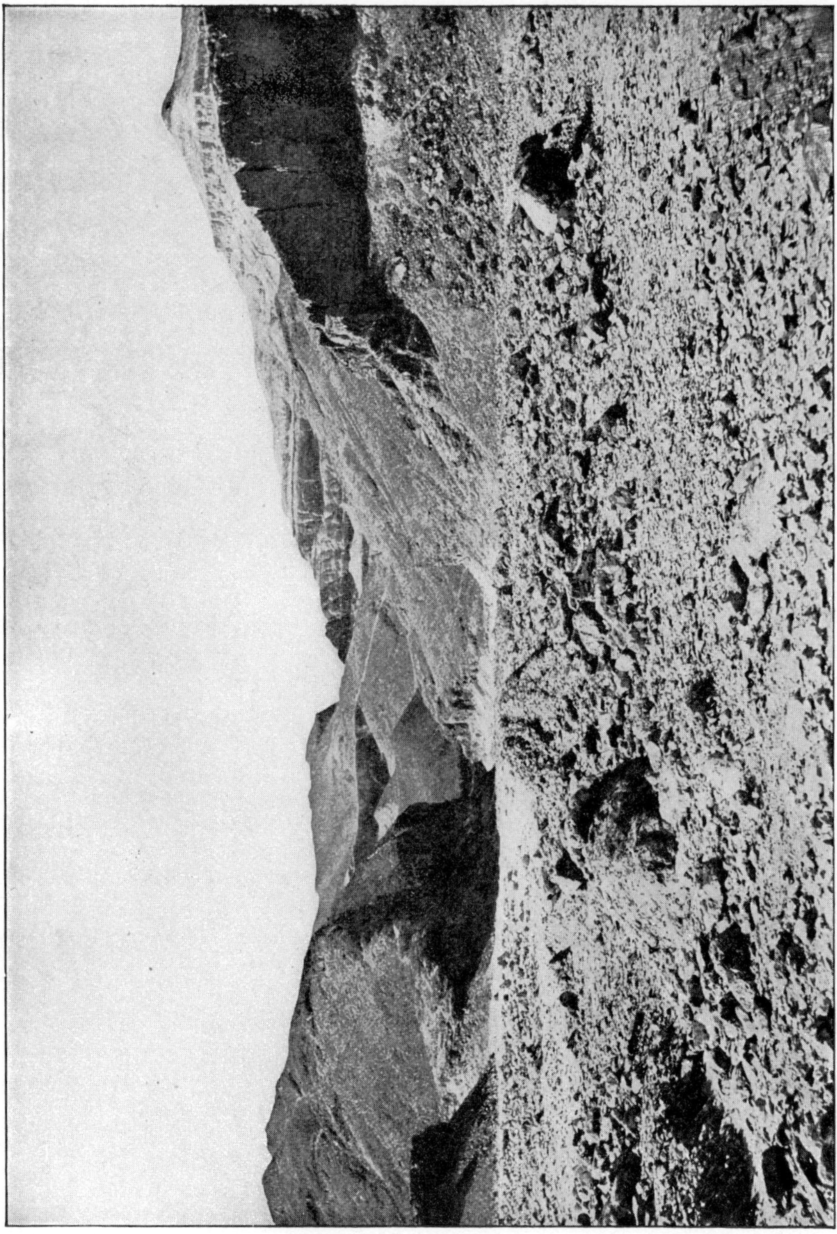

basin, and strike the lintel and the two side posts with the blood that is in the basin; and none of you shall go out of the door of his house until the morning. For the Lord will pass through to smite the Egyptians; and when he seeth the blood upon the lintel, and on the two side posts, the Lord will pass over the door, and will not suffer the destroyer to come in unto your houses to smite you. And ye shall observe this thing for an ordinance to thee and to thy sons for ever. And it shall come to pass, when ye be come to the land which the Lord will give you, according as he hath promised, that ye shall keep this service. And it shall come to pass, when your children shall say unto you, 'What mean ye by this service?' that ye shall say, 'It is the sacrifice of the Lord's passover, who passed over the houses of the children of Israel in Egypt, when he smote the Egyptians, and delivered our houses.'"

And the people bowed the head and worshiped. And the children of Israel went and did so; as the Lord had commanded Moses and Aaron, so did they.

10. THE PLAGUE OF THE DEATH OF THE FIRSTBORN.

And it came to pass at midnight, that the Lord smote all the firstborn in the land of Egypt, from the firstborn of Pharaoh that sat on his throne to the firstborn of the captive that was in the dungeon; and all the firstborn of cattle.

And Pharaoh rose up in the night, he, and all his servants, and all the Egyptians; and there was a great cry in Egypt; for there was not a house where there was not one dead. And he called for Moses and Aaron by night, and said, "Rise up, get you forth from among my people, both ye and the children of Israel; and go, serve the Lord, as ye have said. Take both your flocks and your herds, as ye have said, and be gone; and bless me also."

And the Egyptians were urgent upon the people, to send them out of the land in haste; for they said, "We be all dead men."

And the people took their dough before it was leavened, their kneading troughs being bound up in their clothes upon their shoulders. And the children of Israel did according to the word of Moses; and they asked of the Egyptians jewels of silver, and jewels of gold, and raiment: and the Lord gave the people favor in the sight of the Egyptians, so that they let them have what they asked. And they took the spoil of the Egyptians.

OUT OF BONDAGE.
On the Road to Freedom.

And the children of Israel journeyed from Rameses to Succoth, about six hundred thousand men on foot, beside children. And a mixed multitude went up also with them; and flocks, and herds, even very much cattle. And they baked unleavened cakes of the dough which they brought forth out of Egypt, for it was not leavened; because they were thrust out of Egypt, and could not tarry, neither had they prepared for themselves any food. Now the sojourning of the children of Israel, which they sojourned in Egypt, was four hundred and thirty years. And it came to pass at the end of four hundred and thirty years. even the selfsame day it came to pass, that all the hosts of the Lord went out from the land of Egypt. It is a night to be much observed unto the Lord for bringing them out from the land of Egypt.

And it came to pass, when Pharaoh had let the people go, that God led them not by the way of the land of the Philistines, although that was near; for God said, "Lest peradventure the people repent when they see war, and they return to Egypt."

But God led the people about, by the way of the wilderness by the Red Sea: and the children of Israel went up armed out of the land of Egypt. And Moses took the bones of Joseph with him: for he had strictly charged the children of Israel, saying, "God will surely visit you; and ye shall carry up my bones away hence with you."

And they took their journey from Succoth, and encamped in Etham, in the edge of the wilderness. And the Lord went before them by day in a pillar of cloud, to lead them the way; and by night in a pillar of fire, to give them light; that they might go by day and by night: the pillar of cloud by day, and the pillar of fire by night.

"THE HORSE AND HIS RIDER HATH HE THROWN INTO THE SEA."

Pursuit of the Egyptians. The Host of Pharaoh Is Drowned in the Red Sea.

And the Lord spoke unto Moses, saying, "Speak unto the children of Israel, that they turn back and encamp by the sea. And Pharaoh will say of the children of Israel, 'They are entangled in the land, the wilderness hath shut them in.' And I will harden Pharaoh's heart, and he shall follow after them; and I will get me honor upon Pharaoh, and upon all his host; and the Egyptians shall know that I am the Lord." And they did so.

And it was told the king of Egypt that the people were fled: and the heart of Pharaoh and of his servants was changed towards the people, and they said, "What is this we have done, that we have let Israel go from serving us?"

And he made ready his chariot, and took his people with him: and he took six hundred chosen chariots, and all the chariots of Egypt, and captains over all of them. And the Lord hardened the heart of Pharaoh king of Egypt, and he pursued after the children of Israel: for the children of Israel went out with an high hand.

And the Egyptians pursued after them, all the horses and chariots of Pharaoh, and his horsemen, and his army, and overtook them encamping by the sea. And when Pharaoh drew nigh, the children of Israel lifted up their eyes, and, behold, the Egyptians marched after them; and they were sore afraid: and the children of Israel cried out unto the Lord.

THE VALLEY OF THE TOMBS OF THE KINGS AT THEBES
(A view nearer the entrance)

From a photograph in the possession of the Springfield Public Library
and used by permission

"There is nothing in the whole valley of the Nile which is more grandly characteristic of old Egypt than the Tombs of the Kings at Thebes. The entire course of the ravine presents a spectacle of desolate grandeur which is to the highest degree impressive"

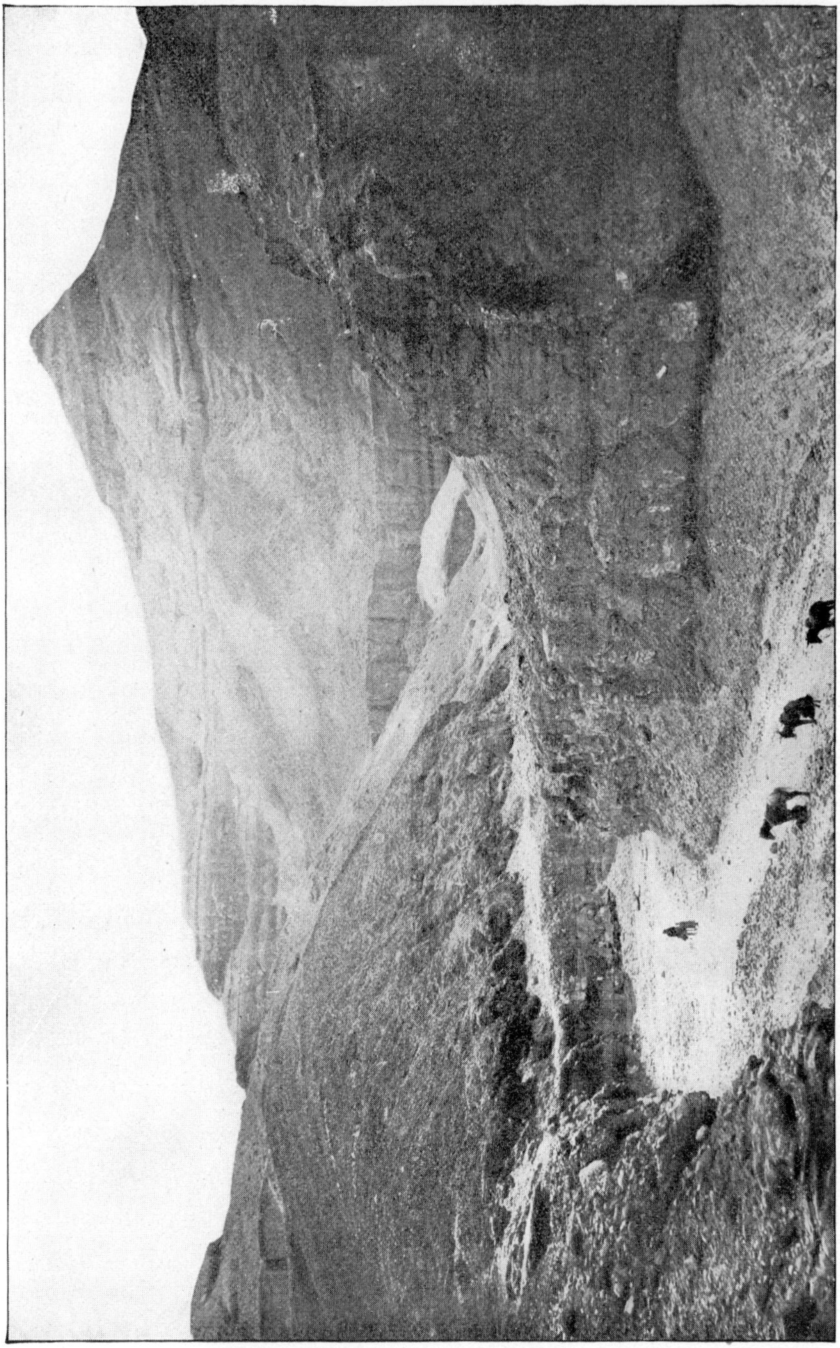

And they said unto Moses, "Because there were no graves in Egypt, hast thou taken us away to die in the wilderness? wherefore hast thou dealt thus with us, to bring us forth out of Egypt? Is not this the word that we spoke unto thee in Egypt, saying, 'Let us alone, that we may serve the Egyptians?' For it were better for us to serve the Egyptians, than that we should die in the wilderness."

And Moses said unto the people, "Fear ye not, stand still, and see the salvation of the Lord, which he will work for you to-day: for the Egyptians whom ye have seen to-day, ye shall see them again no more for ever. The Lord shall fight for you, and ye shall hold your peace."

And the Lord said unto Moses, "Wherefore criest thou unto me? speak to the children of Israel, that they go forward. And lift thou up thy rod, and stretch out thine hand over the sea, and divide it: and the children of Israel shall go into the midst of the sea on dry ground. And I, behold, I will harden the hearts of the Egyptians, and they shall go in after them: and I will get me honor upon Pharaoh, and upon all his host, upon his chariots, and upon his horsemen. And the Egyptians shall know that I am the Lord, when I have gotten me honor upon Pharaoh, upon his chariots, and upon his horsemen."

And the angel of God, which went before the camp of Israel, removed and went behind them; and the pillar of cloud removed from before them, and stood behind them: and it came between the camp of Egypt and the camp of Israel; and there was the cloud and the darkness, yet gave it light by night: and the one came not near the other all the night. And Moses stretched out his hand over the sea; and the Lord caused the sea to go back by a strong east wind all the night, and made the sea dry land, and the waters were divided. And the children of Israel went into the midst of the sea upon the dry ground: and the waters were a wall to them on their right hand, and on their left.

And the Egyptians pursued, and went in after them into the midst of the sea, all Pharaoh's horses, his chariots, and his horsemen. And it came to pass in the morning watch, that the Lord looked forth upon the host of the Egyptians through the pillar of fire and of cloud, and discomfited the host of the Egyptians. And he took off their chariot wheels, that they drove them heavily: so that the Egyptians said, "Let us flee from the face of Israel; for the Lord fighteth for them against the Egyptians."

And the Lord said to Moses, "Stretch out thine hand over the sea, that the waters may come again upon the Egyptians, upon their chariots, and upon their horsemen."

And Moses stretched forth his hand over the sea, and the sea returned to its strength when the morning appeared; and the Egyptians fled against it; and the Lord overthrew the Egyptians in the midst of the sea. And the waters returned, and covered the chariots, and the horsemen, even all the host of Pharaoh that went in after them into the sea; there remained not so much as one of them.

But the children of Israel walked upon dry land in

LOOKING ACROSS THE RED SEA FROM SINAI TOWARD EGYPT
Copyright by Underwood & Underwood
and used by special permission

"The Israelites were encamped on the western shore of the Red Sea, when suddenly a cry of alarm ran through the vast multitude. Over the ridges of the desert hills were seen the well-known horses, the terrible chariots of the Egyptian host: Pharaoh pursued after the children of Israel, and they were sore afraid

"They were sore afraid; and in that terror and perplexity the sun went down behind the huge mountain range which rose on their rear, and cut off their return to Egypt; and the dark night fell over the waters of the sea which rolled before them, and cut off their advance into the desert. So closed in upon them that evening; where were they when the morning broke over the hills of Arabia? Where were they, and where were their enemies?

"They stood in safety on the further shore; and the chariots, and the horsemen, and the host of Pharaoh had vanished in the waters"

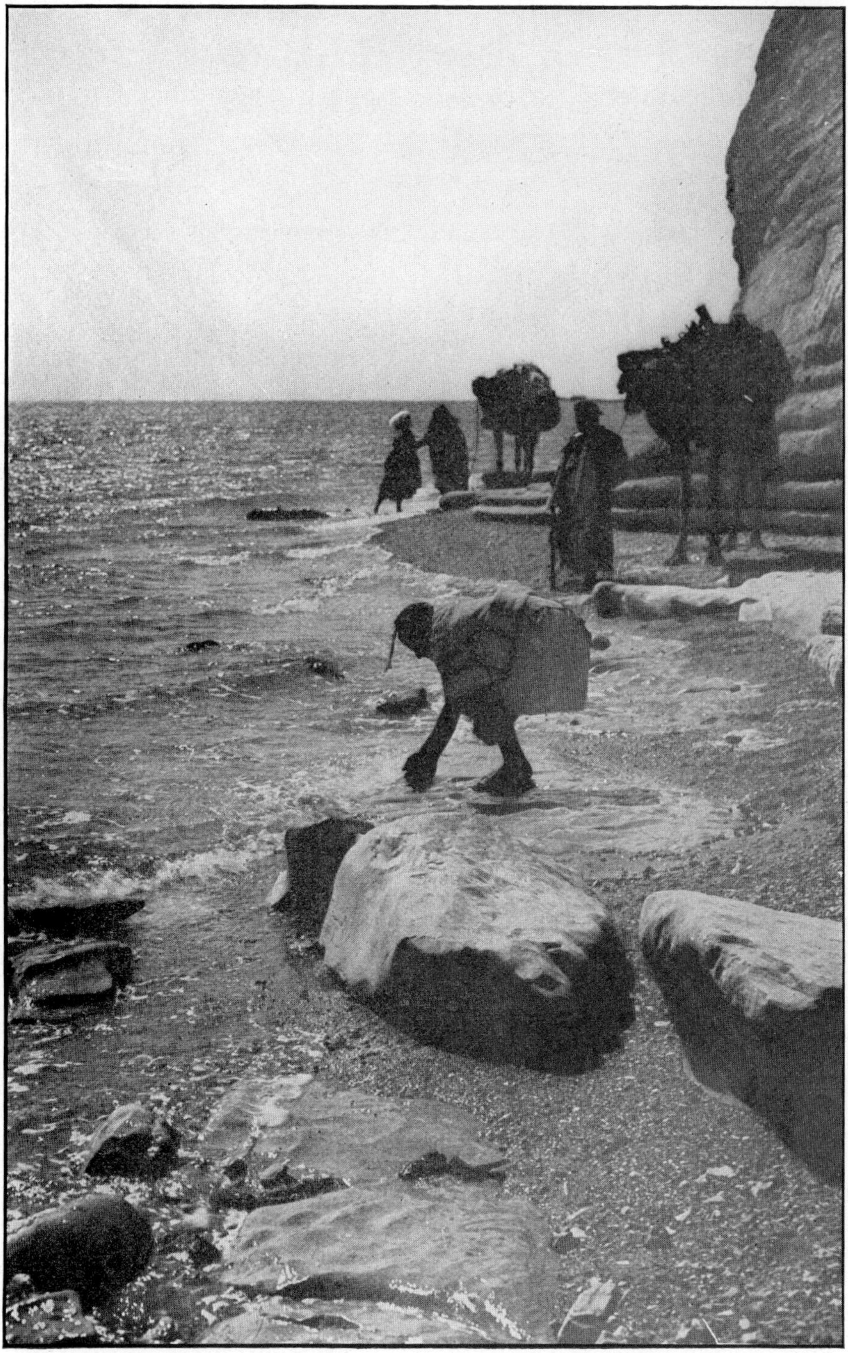

the midst of the sea; and the waters were a wall to them on their right hand, and on their left.

Thus the Lord saved Israel that day out of the hand of the Egyptians; and Israel saw the Egyptians dead upon the sea shore. And Israel saw the great work which the Lord did upon the Egyptians, and the people feared the Lord: and they believed in the Lord, and in his servant Moses.

For the horses of Pharaoh went in with his chariots and with his horsemen into the sea, and the Lord brought again the waters of the sea upon them; but the children of Israel walked on dry land in the midst of the sea. And Miriam the prophetess, the sister of Aaron, took a timbrel in her hand; and all the women went out after her with timbrels and with dances.

And Miriam sang:—

The Song of Victory.

Sing ye to the Lord, for he hath triumphed gloriously;
The horse and his rider hath he thrown into the sea.
Thy right hand, O Lord, dasheth in pieces the enemy.
And in the greatness of thine excellency thou overthrowest them that rise up against thee:
Thou sendest forth thy wrath, it consumeth them as stubble.
And with the blast of thy nostrils the waters were piled up,
The floods stood upright as an heap;
The deeps were congealed in the heart of the sea.
The enemy said,
"I will pursue, I will overtake, I will divide the spoil:

My desire shall be satisfied upon them;
I will draw my sword, my hand shall destroy them."
Thou didst blow with thy wind, the sea covered them:
They sank as lead in the mighty waters.
Who is like unto thee, O Lord, among the gods?
Who is like thee, glorious in holiness,
Fearful in praises, doing wonders?
Thou stretchedst out thy right hand,
The earth swallowed them.
Thou in thy mercy hast led the people which thou hast redeemed:
Thou hast guided them in thy strength to thy holy habitation.
The peoples have heard, they tremble:
Pangs have taken hold on the inhabitants of Philistia.
Then were the dukes of Edom amazed;
The mighty men of Moab, trembling taketh hold upon them:
All the inhabitants of Canaan are melted away.
Terror and dread falleth upon them;
By the greatness of thine arm they are as still as a stone;
Till thy people pass over, O Lord,
Till the people pass over which thou hast purchased.
Thou shalt bring them in, and plant them in the mountain of thine inheritance,
The place, O Lord, which thou hast made for thee to dwell in,
The sanctuary, O Lord, which thy hands have established.
The Lord shall reign for ever and ever.

SHEPHERD WITH HIS FLOCK NEAR TEKOA

Copyright by Underwood & Underwood
and used by special permission

Two of the great prophets of Israel lived in this region, Amos at Tekoa and Jeremiah at Anathoth. It is a wild and desolate region

"The wilderness of Judea played a great part in her history as the refuge of political fugitives and religious solitaries—a part which it still continues. The story of Saul's hunt after David and of David's narrow escapes becomes very vivid among those tossed and broken hills, where the valleys are all alike and large bodies of men may camp near each other without knowing it. Ambushes are everywhere possible and alarms pass rapidly across the bare and silent hills. You may travel for hours and feel as solitary as at sea without a sail in sight; but if you are in search of any one, your guide's signal will make men leap from slopes that did not seem to shelter a rabbit, and if you are suspected, your passage may be stopped by a dozen men as though they had sprung from the earth"

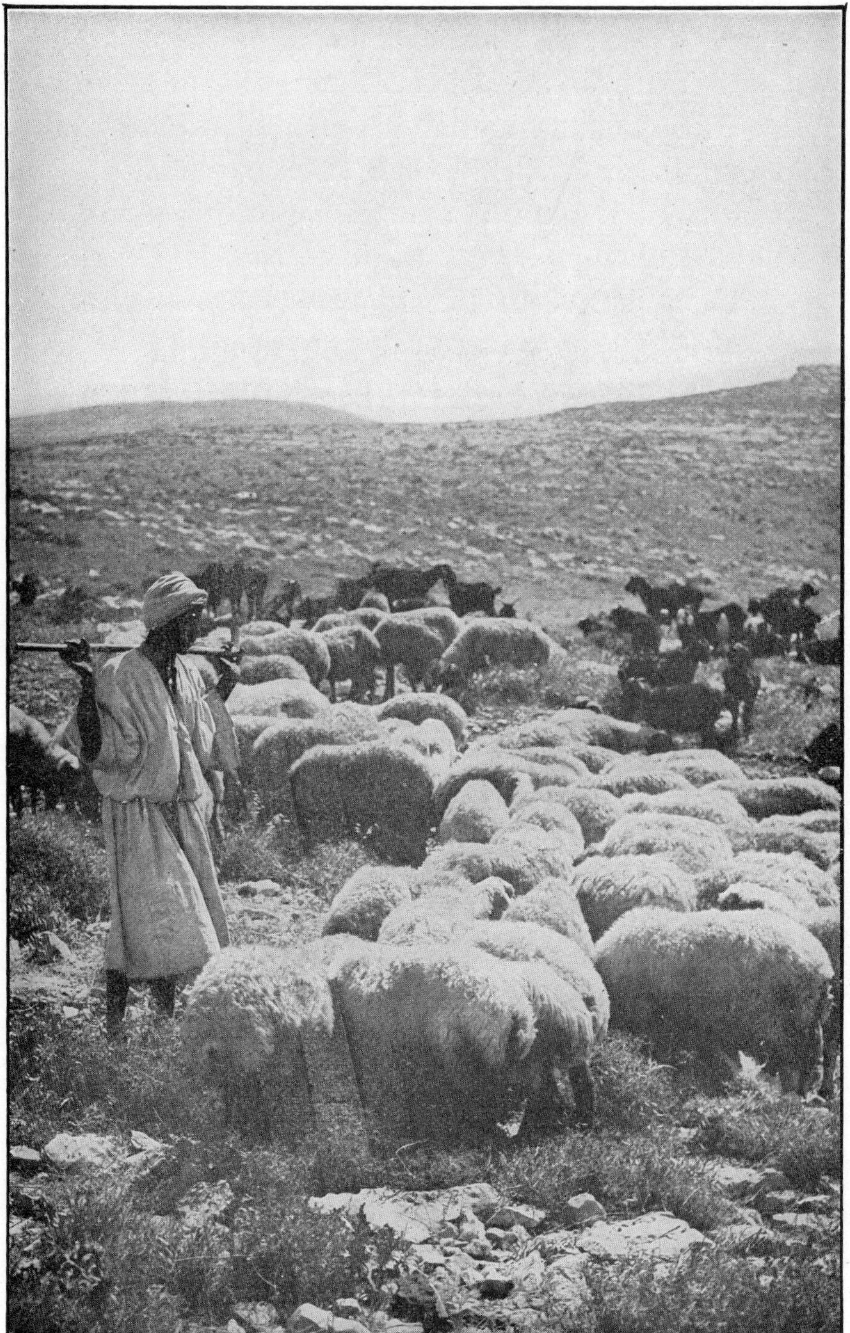

THE WANDERINGS IN THE WILDERNESS

THE RED SEA IS LEFT BEHIND AND THE MARCH TO CANAAN IS BEGUN.

The Bitter Water of Marah.

And Moses led Israel onward from the Red Sea, and they went out into the wilderness of Shur; and they went three days in the wilderness, and found no water. And when they came to Marah, they could not drink of the waters of Marah, for they were bitter: therefore the name of it was called "Marah," that is, bitter.

And the people murmured against Moses, saying, "What shall we drink?"

And he cried to the Lord; and the Lord showed him a tree, and he cast it into the waters, and the waters were made sweet. There he made for them a statute and an ordinance, and there he proved them; and he said, "If thou wilt diligently hearken to the voice of the Lord thy God, and wilt do that which is right in his eyes, and wilt give ear to his commandments, and keep all his statutes, I will put none of the diseases upon thee, which I have put upon the Egyptians: for I am the Lord that healeth thee."

And they came to Elim, where were twelve springs of water, and threescore and ten palm trees: and they encamped there by the waters.

And they took their journey from Elim, and all the

congregation of the children of Israel came unto the wilderness of Sin, which is between Elim and Sinai, on the fifteenth day of the second month after their departing out of the land of Egypt. And the whole congregation of the children of Israel murmured against Moses and against Aaron in the wilderness: and the children of Israel said unto them, "Would that we had died by the hand of the Lord in the land of Egypt, when we sat by the flesh pots, when we did eat bread to the full; for ye have brought us forth into this wilderness, to kill this whole multitude with hunger."

The Quails and the Manna.

Then said the Lord unto Moses, "Behold, I will rain bread from heaven for you; and the people shall go out and gather a day's portion every day, that I may prove them, whether they will walk in my law, or not. And it shall come to pass on the sixth day, that they shall prepare that which they bring in, and it shall be twice as much as they gather daily."

And Moses and Aaron said to all the children of Israel, "At even, then ye shall know that the Lord hath brought you out from the land of Egypt: and in the morning, then ye shall see the glory of the Lord; for that he heareth your murmurings against the Lord: and what are we, that ye murmur against us?"

And Moses said unto Aaron, "Say to all the congregation of the children of Israel, 'Come near before the Lord: for he hath heard your murmurings.'"

And it came to pass, as Aaron spoke unto the whole con-

RESTING PLACE UNDER THE PALMS AT THE "SPRING OF MOSES" IN THE WILDERNESS OF SINAI

Copyright by Underwood & Underwood
and used by special permission

This brackish pool of water with palms growing about it is supposed to be the place of the "bitter waters of Marah" which Moses sweetened for the weary Israelites in their flight, the first stopping place after escaping from Egypt. This place is not far from Suez

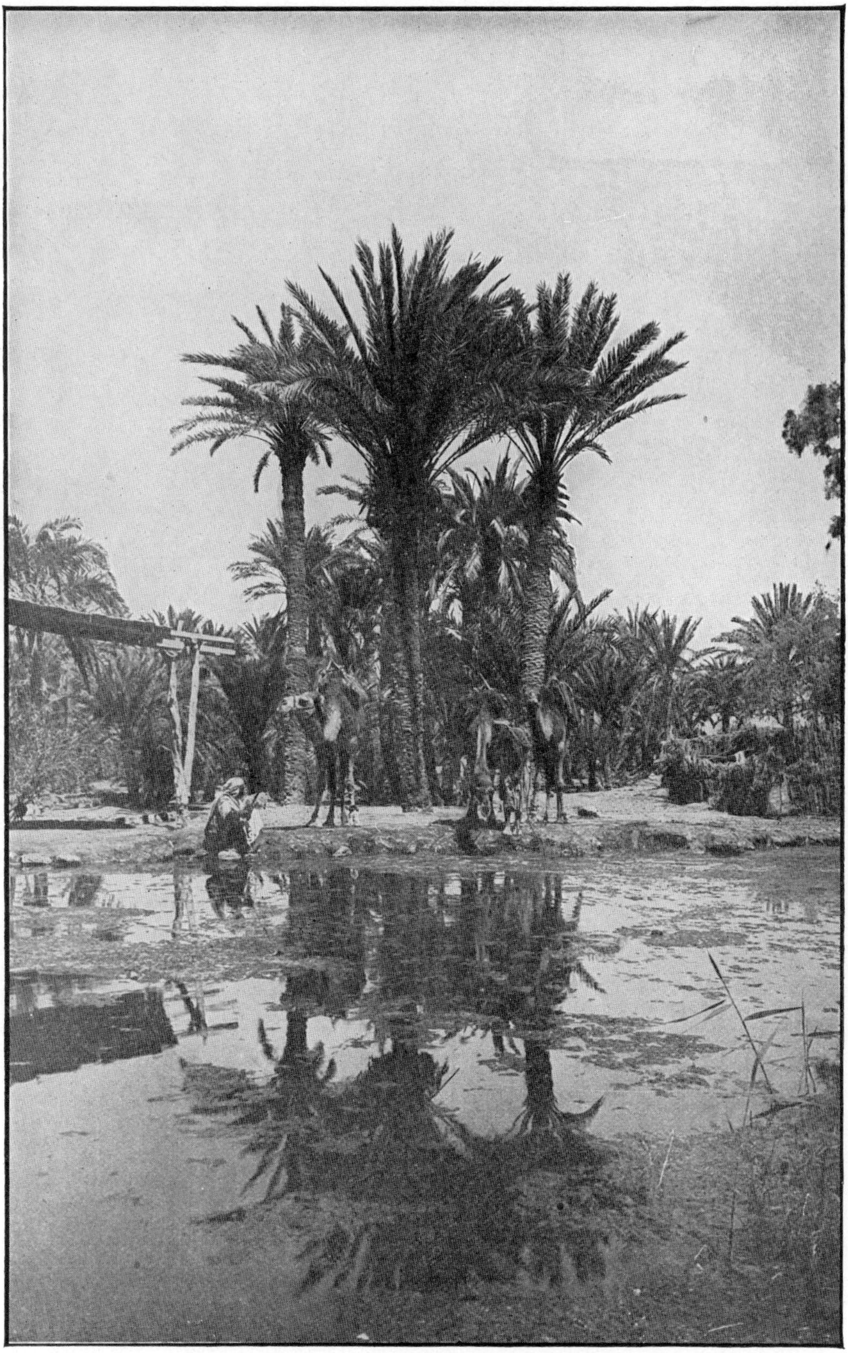

gregation of the children of Israel, that they looked toward the wilderness, and, behold, the glory of the Lord appeared in the cloud. And the Lord spoke to Moses, saying, "I have heard the murmurings of the children of Israel: speak unto them, saying, 'At even ye shall eat flesh, and in the morning ye shall be filled with bread; and ye shall know that I am the Lord your God.'"

And it came to pass at even, that the quails came up, and covered the camp: and in the morning the dew lay round about the camp. And when the dew that lay was gone up, behold, upon the face of the wilderness a small round thing, small as the hoar frost on the ground. And when the children of Israel saw it, they said one to another, "What is it?" for they knew not what it was.

And Moses said to them, "It is the bread which the Lord hath given you to eat. This is the thing which the Lord hath commanded, 'Gather ye of it every man according to his eating; an omer a head, according to the number of your persons, shall ye take it, every man for them which are in his tent.'"

And the children of Israel did so, and gathered some more, some less. And Moses said unto them, "Let no man leave of it till the morning."

Notwithstanding they hearkened not unto Moses; but some of them left of it until the morning, and it bred worms, and stank: and Moses was wroth with them. And they gathered it morning by morning, every man according to his eating: and when the sun grew hot, it melted. And it came to pass, that on the sixth day they gathered twice as much bread, two omers for each one: and all the rulers of the congregation came and told Moses. And he said to them, "This is that which the Lord hath spoken, 'To-morrow is a solemn rest, a holy sabbath unto the Lord: bake that which ye will bake, and boil that which ye will boil; and all that remaineth over lay up for you to be kept until the morning.'"

And they laid it up till the morning, as Moses bade: and it did not stink, neither was there any worm therein. And Moses said, "Eat that to-day; for to-day is a sabbath unto the Lord: to-day ye shall not find it in the field. Six days ye shall gather it; but on the seventh day is the sabbath, in it there shall be none."

And it came to pass on the seventh day, that there went out some of the people to gather, and they found none.

And the Lord said unto Moses, "How long refuse ye to keep my commandments and my laws? See, because the Lord hath given you the sabbath, therefore he giveth you on the sixth day the bread of two days; abide ye every man in his place, let no man go out of his place on the seventh day."

So the people rested on the seventh day. And the house of Israel called the name thereof "Manna": and it was like coriander seed, white; and the taste of it was like wafers made with honey.

And Moses said, "This is the thing which the Lord hath commanded, 'Let an omerful of it be kept for your generations; that they may see the bread wherewith I fed you in the wilderness, when I brought you forth from the land of Egypt.'"

And Moses said unto Aaron, "Take a pot, and put an omerful of manna therein, and lay it up before the Lord, to be kept for your generations."

As the Lord commanded Moses, so Aaron did. And the children of Israel ate the manna forty years, until they came to a land inhabited; they ate the manna, until they came to the borders of the land of Canaan.

The Battle with Amalek at Rephidim.

Then came Amalek, and fought with Israel in Rephidim. And Moses said to Joshua, "Choose us out men, and go out, fight with Amalek: to-morrow I will stand on the top of the hill with the rod of God in mine hand."

So Joshua did as Moses had said to him, and fought with Amalek: and Moses, Aaron, and Hur went up to the top of the hill. And it came to pass, when Moses held up his hand, that Israel prevailed: and when he let down his hand, Amalek prevailed. But Moses' hands were heavy; and they took a stone, and put it under him, and he sat thereon; and Aaron and Hur stayed up his hands, the one on the one side, and the other on the other side; and his hands were steady until the going down of the sun. And Joshua discomfited Amalek and his people with the edge of the sword.

And Moses built an altar, and called the name of it Jehovah my Banner: and he said, "The Lord hath sworn: the Lord will have war with Amalek from generation to generation."

THE SONG OF THE MANNA GATHERERS

Comrades, haste! the tent's tall shading
  Lies along the level sand,
Far and faint: the stars are fading
  Over the gleaming western strand,
    Airs of morning
  Freshen the bleak burning land.

Haste, or e'er the third hour glowing
  With its eager thirst prevail
O'er the moist pearls, now bestrowing
  Thymy slope and rushy vale.

. . . . . .

Comrades—what our sires have told us,
  Watch and wait, for it will come.

. . . . . .

Not by manna show'rs at morning
  Shall our board be then supplied,
But a strange pale gold, adorning
  Many a tufted mountain's side,
    Yearly feed us,
  Year by year our murmurings chide.

There, no prophet's touch awaiting,
  From each cool deep cavern start
Rills, that since their first creating
  Ne'er have ceased to sing their part;
    Oft we hear them
  In our dreams, with thirsty heart.

—John Keble.

IN THE WILDERNESS OF SINAI

From a photograph belonging to the Forbes Library, Northampton, Mass.,
and used by special permission

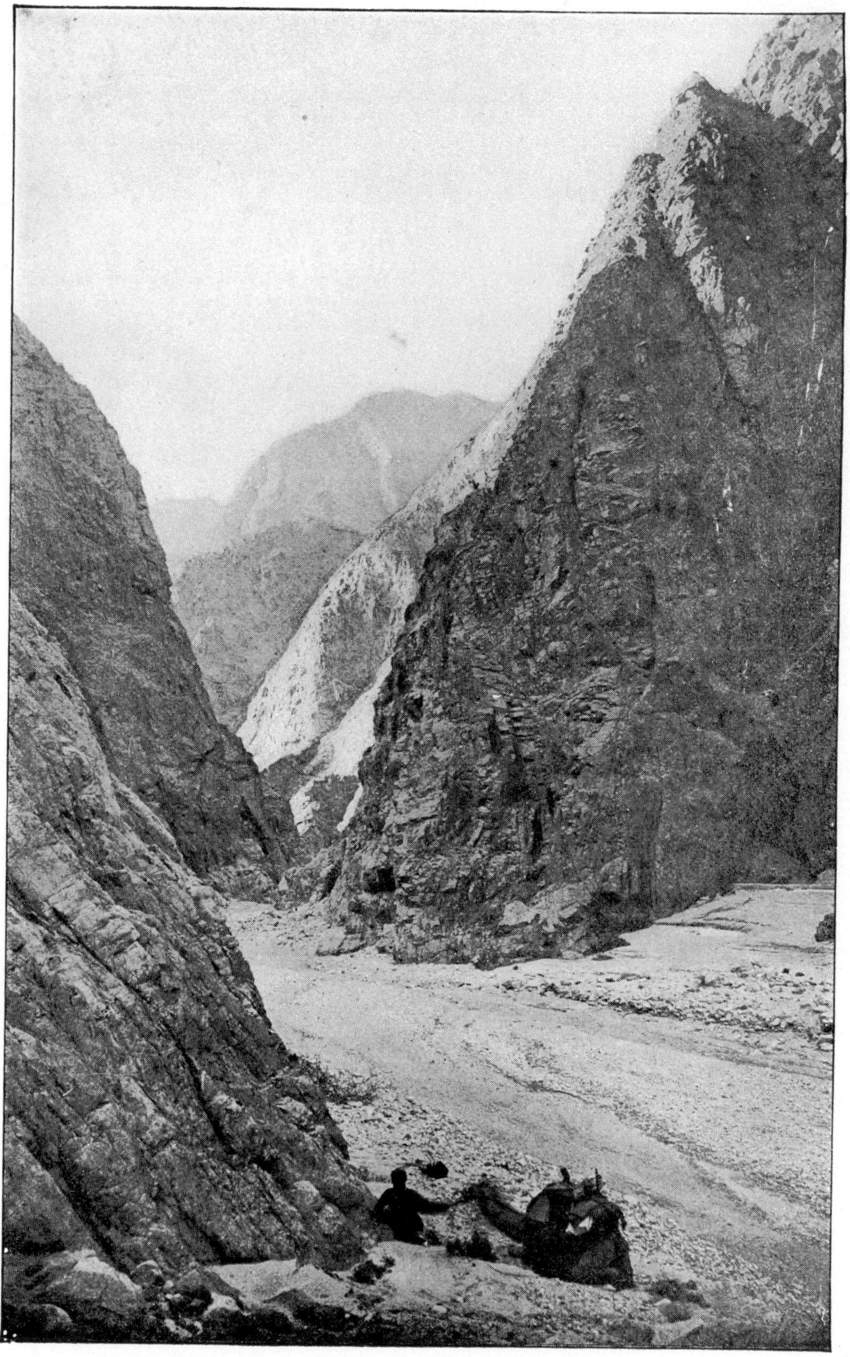

MOSES CLIMBS MOUNT SINAI TO TALK WITH GOD.
The Giving of the Commandments.

In the third month after the children of Israel had gone forth out of the land of Egypt, the same day came they into the wilderness of Sinai. And when they were departed from Rephidim, and were come to the wilderness of Sinai, they camped in the wilderness; and there Israel camped before the mount. And Moses went up to God, and the Lord called to him out of the mountain, saying, "Thus shalt thou say to the house of Jacob, and tell the children of Israel; 'Ye have seen what I did unto the Egyptians, and how I bore you on eagles' wings, and brought you unto myself. Now therefore, if ye will obey my voice indeed, and keep my covenant, then ye shall be a peculiar treasure to me from among all peoples: for all the earth is mine: and ye shall be to me a kingdom of priests, and an holy nation.' These are words which thou shalt speak unto the children of Israel."

And Moses came and called for the elders of the people, and set before them all these words which the Lord commanded him. And all the people answered together, and said, "All that the Lord hath spoken we will do."

And Moses brought forth the people out of the camp to meet God; and they stood at the foot of the mount. And all Mount Sinai smoked, because the Lord descended upon it in fire: and the smoke thereof ascended as the smoke of a furnace, and the whole mount quaked greatly. And when the voice of the trumpet grew louder and louder, Moses spoke, and God answered him by a voice. And the

Lord came down upon Mount Sinai, to the top of the mount: and the Lord called Moses to the top of the mount; and Moses went up.

And God spoke all these words, saying,—

THE COMMANDMENTS.

"I am the Lord thy God, which brought thee out of the land of Egypt, out of the house of bondage.

I.

"Thou shalt have none other gods before me.

II.

"Thou shalt not make unto thee a graven image, nor the likeness of any form that is in heaven above, or that is in the earth beneath, or that is in the water under the earth: thou shalt not bow down thyself unto them, nor serve them: for I the Lord thy God am a jealous God, visiting the iniquity of the fathers upon the children, upon the third and upon the fourth generation of them that hate me; and shewing mercy unto thousands, of them that love me and keep my commandments.

III.

"Thou shalt not take the name of the Lord thy God in vain; for the Lord will not hold him guiltless that taketh his name in vain.

IV.

"Remember the sabbath day, to keep it holy. Six days shalt thou labor, and do all thy work: but the seventh day is a sabbath unto the Lord thy God: in it thou shalt not do any work, thou, nor thy son, nor thy daughter, thy manservant, nor thy maidservant, nor thy cattle, nor thy stranger that is within thy gates: for in six days the Lord made heaven and earth, the sea, and all that in them is, and rested the seventh day: wherefore the Lord blessed the sabbath day, and hallowed it.

V.

"Honor thy father and thy mother: that thy days may be long upon the land which the Lord thy God giveth thee.

VI.

"Thou shalt not kill.

VII.

"Thou shalt not commit adultery.

VIII.

"Thou shalt not steal.

IX.

"Thou shalt not bear false witness against thy neighbor.

X.

"Thou shalt not covet thy neighbor's house, thou shalt not covet thy neighbor's wife, nor his manservant, nor his maidservant, nor his ox, nor his ass, nor any thing that is thy neighbor's."

And all the people saw the thunderings, and the lightnings, and the voice of the trumpet, and the mountain smoking: and when the people saw it, they trembled, and stood afar off. And they said to Moses, "Speak thou with us, and we will hear: but let not God speak with us, lest we die."

And Moses said to the people, "Fear not: for God is come to prove you, and that his fear may be before you, that ye sin not."

And the people stood afar off, and Moses drew near to the thick darkness where God was.

THE GOLDEN CALF.

Israel Sins Grievously and Is Severely Punished.

And when the people saw that Moses delayed to come down from the mount, the people gathered themselves together about Aaron, and said to him, "Up, make us gods, which shall go before us; for as for this Moses, the man that brought us up out of the land of Egypt, we know not what is become of him."

And Aaron said to them, "Break off the golden rings, which are in the ears of your wives, of your sons, and of your daughters, and bring them to me."

And all the people broke off the golden rings which were in their ears, and brought them unto Aaron. And he received the gold at their hand, and fashioned it with a graving tool, and made it a molten calf: and they said, "These are thy gods, O Israel, which brought thee up out of the land of Egypt."

And when Aaron saw this, he built an altar before it; and Aaron made proclamation, and said, "To-morrow shall be a feast to the Lord."

And they rose up early on the morrow, and offered burnt offerings, and brought peace offerings; and the people sat down to eat and to drink, and rose up to play.

And the Lord spoke unto Moses, "Go, get thee down; for thy people, which thou broughtest up out of the land

HILL OF THE GOLDEN CALF (JEBEL AARON) AND ITS MOSLEM TOWER BELOW THE RIDGE OF SINAI

Copyright by Underwood & Underwood
and used by special permission

A traveler writes: "We started to descend by the gorge on the northeast side of the mountain (Jethro's Path), by which possibly Moses may have descended when he heard the sounds of the camp before he could see what was taking place there. We were completely shut in by the sides of the gorge until just as we emerged near the bottom. There was no sound below for us to hear, but we could readily accept Mr. Palmeston's statement that he had distinctly heard the sounds of his own camp at the foot of the mountain which was entirely hidden from view. If the worship of the golden calf be supposed to have taken place anywhere in the neighborhood of the hill of Aaron this circumstance would be in striking conformity with the several other facts which singularly adapt this place to be the scene of the lawgiving"

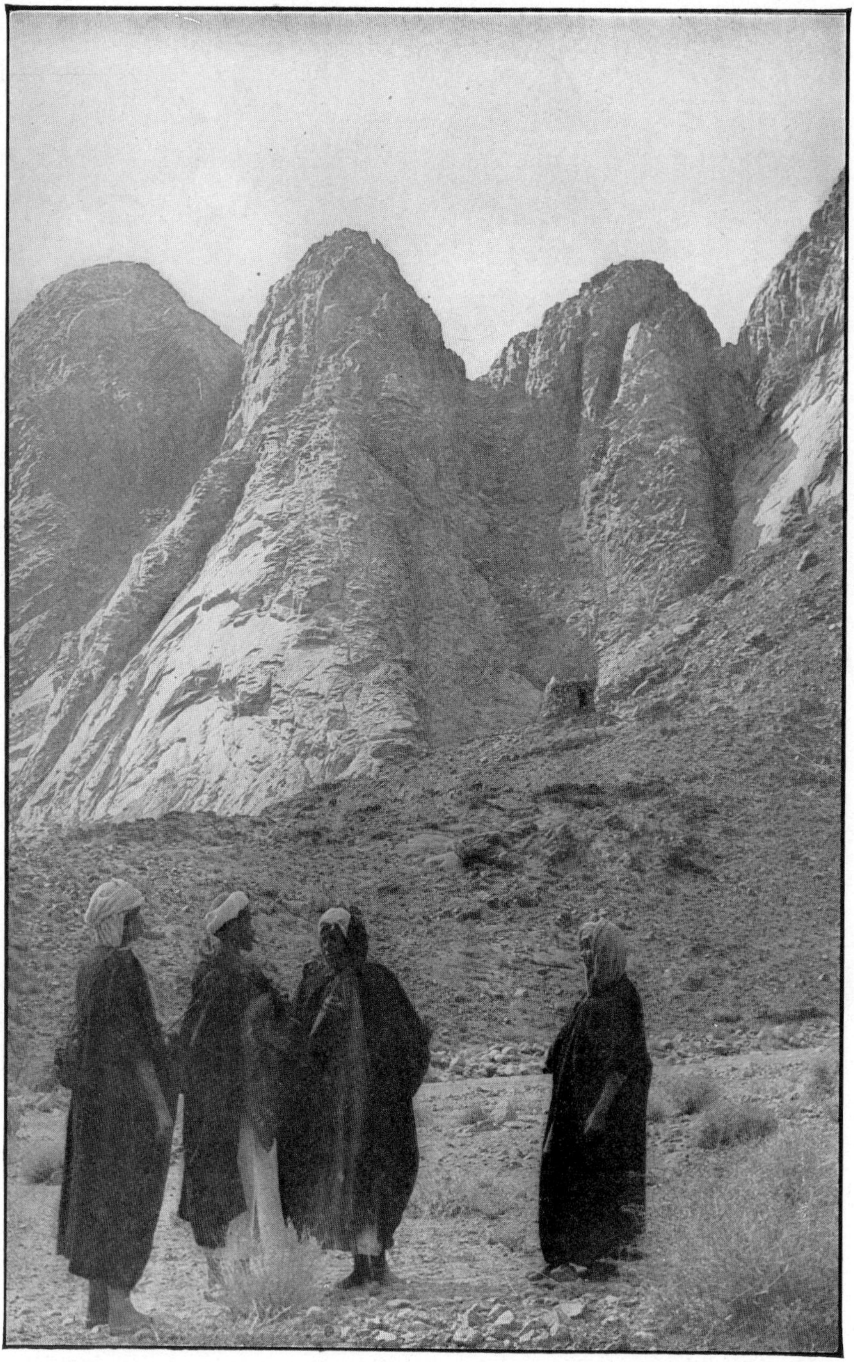

of Egypt, have corrupted themselves: they have turned aside quickly out of the way which I commanded them: they have made them a molten calf, and have worshiped it, and have sacrificed unto it, and said, 'These are thy gods, O Israel, which brought thee up out of the land of Egypt.'"

And the Lord said to Moses, "I have seen this people, and, behold, it is a stiffnecked people: now therefore let me alone, that my wrath may grow hot against them, and that I may consume them: and I will make of thee a great nation."

And Moses besought the Lord his God, and said, "Lord, why doth thy wrath grow hot against thy people, which thou hast brought forth out of the land of Egypt with great power and with a mighty hand? Wherefore should the Egyptians speak, saying, 'For evil did he bring them forth, to slay them in the mountains, and to consume them from the face of the earth'? Turn from thy fierce wrath, and repent of this evil against thy people. Remember Abraham, Isaac, and Israel, thy servants, to whom thou swarest by thine own self, and saidst unto them, 'I will multiply your family as the stars of heaven, and all this land that I have spoken of will I give unto your family, and they shall inherit it for ever.'"

And the Lord repented of the evil which he said he would do unto his people.

And Moses turned, and went down from the mount, with the two tables of the testimony in his hand; tables that were written on both sides; on the one side and on the other were they written. And the tables were the work of God, and the writing was the writing of God, graven upon the tables.

And when Joshua heard the noise of the people as they shouted, he said to Moses, "There is a noise of war in the camp."

And he said, "It is not the voice of them that shout for mastery, neither is it the voice of them that cry for being overcome: but the noise of them that sing do I hear."

And it came to pass, as soon as he came nigh unto the camp, that he saw the calf and the dancing: and Moses' anger grew hot, and he cast the tables out of his hands, and broke them beneath the mount.

And he took the calf which they had made, and burnt it with fire, and ground it to powder, and strewed it upon the water, and made the children of Israel drink of it. And Moses said to Aaron, "What did this people unto thee, that thou hast brought a great sin upon them?"

And Aaron said, "Let not the anger of my lord grow hot: thou knowest the people, that they are set on evil. For they said to me, 'Make us gods, which shall go before us: for as for this Moses, the man that brought us up out of the land of Egypt, we know not what is become of him.' And I said to them, 'Whosoever hath any gold, let them break it off'; so they gave it me: and I cast it into the fire, and there came out this calf."

And when Moses saw that the people were broken loose; for Aaron had let them loose for a derision among their enemies: then Moses stood in the gate of the camp,

FAMOUS MONASTERY OF SAINT CATHERINE IN THE SHADOW OF MOUNT SINAI

Copyright by Underwood & Underwood
and used by special permission

It was in this monastery that Prof. C. Tischendorf discovered one of the oldest and most valuable manuscripts of the Bible in existence. Tischendorf made three visits to the monastery, in 1844, 1853, and 1859. On the first visit he found forty-three leaves of the manuscript in a wastebasket. Later he found the entire manuscript with the exception of a few pages. It was published by Czar Alexander II in celebration of the first millennium of the Russian Empire. A traveler says, "When on a visit to Mount Sinai in March, 1877, I saw a copy of the magnificent four volume edition in the convent library and mentioned the name of Tischendorf, the sub-prior kindled up in indignation and called him a thief, who had stolen their greatest treasure on the pretext of a temporary loan; and when I reminded him of the large reward of the Emperor of Russia, who had furnished a new silver shrine for the coffin of Saint Catherine, he admitted it reluctantly, but remarked that they did not want the silver, but the manuscript—the manuscript which their monks could not read and were about to throw into the fire"

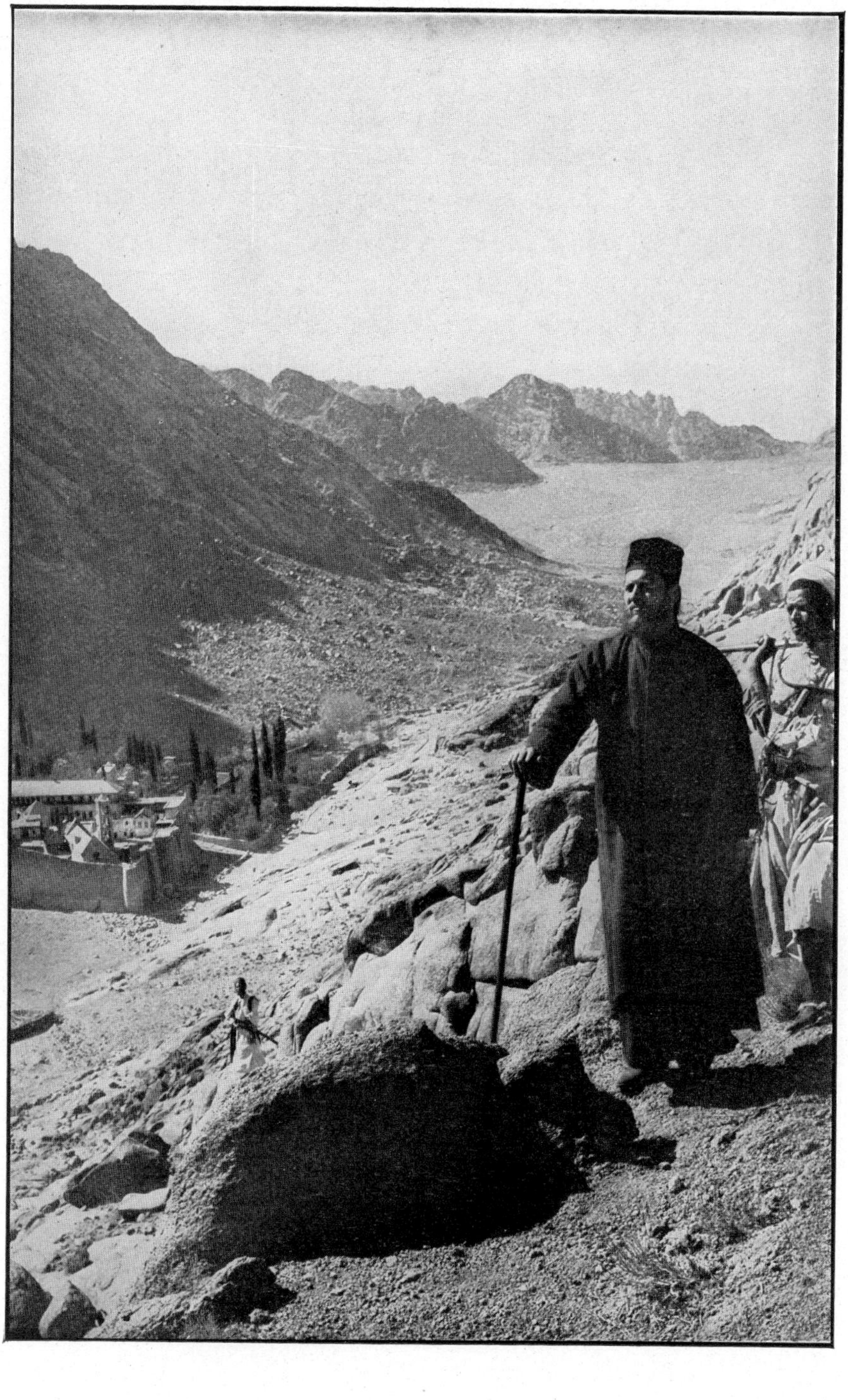

and said, "Whoso is on the Lord's side, let him come unto me."

And all the sons of Levi gathered themselves together unto him. And he said unto them, "Thus saith the Lord, the God of Israel, 'Put ye every man his sword upon his thigh, and go to and fro from gate to gate throughout the camp, and slay every man his brother, and every man his companion, and every man his neighbor.'"

And the sons of Levi did according to the word of Moses: and there fell of the people that day about three thousand men. And Moses said, "Consecrate yourselves to-day to the Lord, yea, every man against his son, and against his brother; that he may bestow upon you a blessing this day."

And it came to pass on the morrow, that Moses said unto the people, "Ye have sinned a great sin: and now I will go up unto the Lord; peradventure I shall make atonement for your sin."

And Moses returned unto the Lord, and said, "Oh, this people have sinned a great sin, and have made them gods of gold. Yet now, if thou wilt forgive their sin—; and if not, blot me, I pray thee, out of thy book which thou hast written."

And the Lord said to Moses, "Whosover hath sinned against me, him will I blot out of my book. And now go, lead the people unto the place of which I have spoken unto thee: behold, mine angel shall go before thee: nevertheless in the day when I punish, I will punish them for their sins."

And the Lord smote the people, because they made the calf, which Aaron made.

THE NEW TABLES OF STONE.
How the Tables Which Had Been Broken Were Replaced.

And the Lord said unto Moses, "Hew thee two tables of stone like unto the first: and I will write upon the tables the words that were on the first tables, which thou brokest.

"And be ready by the morning, and come up in the morning unto Mount Sinai, and present thyself there to me on the top of the mount.

"And no man shall come up with thee; neither let any man be seen throughout all the mount; neither let the flocks nor herds feed before that mount."

And he hewed two tables of stone like unto the first; and Moses rose up early in the morning, and went up unto Mount Sinai, as the Lord had commanded him, and took in his hand two tables of stone.

And the Lord descended in the cloud, and stood with him there, and proclaimed the name of the Lord.

And the Lord passed by before him, and a voice said, "The Lord, the Lord, a God merciful and gracious, slow to anger, and abundant in loving kindness and truth; keeping loving kindness for thousands, forgiving iniquity and transgression and sin; who will by no means clear the guilty."

And Moses made haste, and bowed his head toward the earth, and worshiped.

And he said, "If now I have found favor in thy sight,

O Lord, let the Lord, I pray thee, go in the midst of us; and pardon our iniquity and our sin, and take us for thine inheritance."

And he was there with the Lord forty days and forty nights; he did neither eat bread, nor drink water. And he wrote upon the tables the words of the covenant, the ten commandments.

And Moses came down from Mount Sinai with the two tables of the testimony in his hand.

THE TABERNACLE IN THE WILDERNESS
THE PEOPLE GIVE A FREE-WILL OFFERING TO THE LORD.

And Moses assembled all the congregation of the children of Israel, and said unto them, "These are the words which the Lord hath commanded, that ye should do them. 'Six days shall work be done, but on the seventh day there shall be to you an holy day, a sabbath of solemn rest to the Lord: whosoever doeth any work therein shall be put to death. Ye shall kindle no fire throughout your habitations upon the sabbath day.'"

And Moses spoke unto all the congregation of the children of Israel, saying, "This is the thing which the Lord commanded, saying, 'Take ye from among you an offering unto the Lord: whosoever is of a willing heart, let him bring it, the Lord's offering; gold, and silver, and brass; and blue, and purple, and scarlet, and fine linen, and goats' hair; and rams' skins dyed red, and sealskins, and acacia wood; and oil for the light, and spices for the anointing oil, and for the sweet incense; and onyx stones, and stones to be set, for the ephod, and for the breastplate.

"'And let every skilled workman among you come, and make all that the Lord hath commanded; the tabernacle, its tent, and its covering, its clasps, and its boards, its bars, its pillars, and its sockets; the ark, and the staves thereof, the mercy-seat, and the veil of the screen; the table, and its staves, and all its vessels, and the shewbread; the candlestick also for the light, and its vessels, and its lamps, and the oil for the light; and the altar of incense, and its staves, and the anointing oil, and the sweet incense, and the screen for the door, at the door of the tabernacle; the altar of burnt offering, with its grating of brass, its staves, and all its vessels, the laver and its base; the hangings of the court, the pillars thereof, and their sockets, and the screen for the gate of the court; the pins of the tabernacle, and the pins of the court, and their cords; the finely wrought garments, for ministering in the holy place, the holy garments for Aaron the priest, and the garments of his sons, to minister in the priest's office.' "

And all the congregation of the children of Israel departed from the presence of Moses.

And they came, every one whose heart stirred him up, and every one whom his spirit made willing, and brought the Lord's offering, for the work of the tent of meeting, and for all the service thereof, and for the holy garments.

And they came, both men and women, as many as were willing hearted, and brought brooches, and earrings, and signet-rings, and armlets, all jewels of gold; even every man that offered an offering of gold unto the Lord.

And every man, who had blue, and purple, and scarlet, and fine linen, and goats' hair, and rams' skins dyed red, and sealskins, brought them. Every one that offered an offering of silver and brass brought the Lord's offering:

and every man, who had acacia wood for any work of the service, brought it.

And all the women that were skillful spun with their hands, and brought that which they had spun, the blue, and the purple, the scarlet, and the fine linen.

And all the women who were skillful spun the goats' hair.

And the rulers brought the onyx stones, and the stones to be set, for the ephod, and for the breastplate; and the spice, and the oil; for the light, and for the anointing oil, and for the sweet incense.

The children of Israel brought a freewill offering unto the Lord; every man and woman, whose heart made them willing to bring for all the work, which the Lord had commanded to be made by the hand of Moses.

And Moses said unto the children of Israel, "See, the Lord hath called by name Bezalel, the son of Uri, the son of Hur, of the tribe of Judah; and he hath filled him with the spirit of God, in wisdom, in understanding, and in knowledge, and in all manner of workmanship; and to devise cunning works, to work in gold, and in silver, and in brass, and in cutting of stones for setting, and in carving of wood, to work in all manner of cunning workmanship. And he hath put in his heart that he may teach, both he, and Oholiab, the son of Ahisamach, of the tribe of Dan. Them hath he filled with wisdom of heart, to work all manner of workmanship, of the engraver, and of the cunning workman, and of the embroiderer, in blue, and in purple, in scarlet, and in fine linen, and of the weaver, even of them that do any workmanship, and of those that devise cunning works."

THE TABERNACLE AND ITS FURNISHINGS.
The Tent.

And every skillful man among them that wrought the work made the tabernacle with ten curtains; of fine linen, and blue, and purple, and scarlet, with cherubim the work of the cunning workman made he them. The length of each curtain was eight and twenty cubits, and the breadth of each curtain four cubits: all the curtains had one measure. And he coupled five curtains one to another: and the other five curtains he coupled one to another. And he made loops of blue upon the edge of the one curtain from the selvedge in the coupling: likewise he made in the edge of the curtain that was outmost in the second coupling. Fifty loops made he in the one curtain, and fifty loops made he in the edge of the curtain that was in the second coupling: the loops were opposite one to another. And he made fifty clasps of gold, and coupled the curtains one to another with the clasps: so the tabernacle was one. And he made curtains of goats' hair for a tent over the tabernacle: eleven curtains he made. The length of each curtain was thirty cubits, and four cubits the breadth of each curtain: the eleven curtains had one measure. And he coupled five curtains by themselves, and six curtains by themselves. And he made fifty loops on the edge of the curtain that was outmost in the coupling, and fifty loops made he upon the edge of the curtain which was outmost in the second coupling. And he made fifty clasps of brass to couple the tent together, that it might be one. And he made a covering for the tent of rams' skins dyed red, and a covering of sealskins above.

And he made the boards for the tabernacle of acacia wood, standing up. Ten cubits was the length of a board, and a cubit and a half the breadth of each board. Each board had two tenons, joined one to another: thus did he make for all the boards of the tabernacle. And he made the boards for the tabernacle; twenty boards for the south side southward; and he made forty sockets of silver under the twenty boards; two sockets under one board for its two tenons, and two sockets under another board for its two tenons. And for the second side of the tabernacle, on the north side, he made twenty boards, and their forty sockets of silver; two sockets under one board, and two sockets under another board. And for the hinder part of the tabernacle westward he made six boards. And two boards made he for the corners of the tabernacle in the hinder part. And there were eight boards, and their sockets of silver, sixteen sockets; under every board two sockets. And he made bars of acacia wood; five for the boards of the one side of the tabernacle, and five bars for the boards of the other side of the tabernacle, and five bars for the boards of the tabernacle for the hinder part westward. And he made the middle bar to pass through in the midst of the boards from the one end to the other. And he overlaid the boards with gold, and made their rings of gold for places for the bars, and overlaid the bars with gold.

And he made the veil of blue, and purple, and scarlet, and fine twined linen: with cherubim the work of the cunning workman made he it. And he made thereunto four pillars of acacia, and overlaid them with gold: their hooks were of gold; and he cast for them four sockets of silver. And he made a screen for the door of the Tent, of blue, and purple, and scarlet, and fine linen, the work of the embroiderer; and the five pillars of it with their hooks: and he overlaid their capitals and their fillets with gold: and their five sockets were of brass.

The Workmen Are Chosen.

"And Bezalel and Oholiab shall work, and every skillful man, in whom the Lord hath put wisdom and understanding to know how to work all the work for the service of the sanctuary, according to all that the Lord hath commanded."

And Moses called Bezalel and Oholiab, and every skillful man, in whose heart the Lord had put wisdom, even every one whose heart stirred him up to come unto the work to do it: and they received of Moses all the offering, which the children of Israel had brought for the work of the service of the sanctuary, to make it. And they brought yet unto him freewill offerings every morning. And all the wise men, that wrought all the work of the sanctuary, came every man from his work which they wrought; and they spoke unto Moses, saying, "The people bring much more than enough for the service of the work, which the Lord commanded to make."

And Moses gave commandment, and they caused it to be proclaimed throughout the camp, saying,—

"Let neither man nor woman make any more work for the offering of the sanctuary." So the people were restrained from bringing. For the stuff they had was sufficient for all the work to make it, and too much.

The Ark.

And Bezalel made the ark of acacia wood: two cubits and a half was the length of it, and a cubit and a half the breadth of it, and a cubit and a half the height of it: and he overlaid it with pure gold within and without, and made a rim of gold to it round about. And he cast for it four rings of gold, in the four feet thereof; two rings on the one side of it, and two rings on the other side of it. And he made staves of acacia wood, and overlaid them with gold. And he put the staves into the rings on the sides of the ark, to bear the ark. And he made a mercy seat of pure gold: two cubits and a half was the length thereof, and a cubit and a half the breadth thereof. And he made two cherubim of gold; of beaten work made he them, at the two ends of the mercy seat; one cherub at the one end, and one cherub at the other end: of one piece with the mercy seat made he the cherubim at the two ends thereof. And the cherubim spread out their wings on high, covering the mercy seat with their wings, with their faces one to another; toward the mercy seat were the faces of the cherubim.

The Table.

And he made the table of acacia wood: two cubits was the length thereof, and a cubit the breadth thereof, and a cubit and a half the height thereof: and he overlaid it with pure gold, and made thereto a rim of gold round about. And he made for it a border of an handbreadth round about, and made a golden rim to the border thereof round about. And he cast for it four rings of gold, and put the rings in the four corners that were on the four feet thereof. Close by the border were the rings, the places for the staves to bear the table. And he made the staves of acacia wood, and overlaid them with gold, to bear the table. And he made the vessels which were upon the table, the dishes thereof, and the spoons thereof, and the bowls thereof, and the flagons thereof, to pour out of, pure gold.

The Candlestick.

And he made the candlestick of pure gold: of beaten work made he the candlestick, even its base, and its shaft; its cups, its knobs, and its flowers, were of one piece with it: and there were six branches going out of the sides thereof; three branches of the candlestick out of the one side thereof, and three branches of the candlestick out of the other side thereof: three cups made like almond blossoms in one branch, a knob and a flower; and three cups made like almond blossoms in the other branch, a knob and a flower: so for the six branches going out of the candlestick. And in the candlestick were four cups made like almond blossoms, the knobs thereof, and the flowers thereof: and a knob under two branches of one piece with it, and a knob under two branches of one piece with it, and a knob under two branches of one piece with it, for the six branches going out of it. Their knobs and their branches were of one piece with it: the whole of it was one beaten work of pure gold. And he made the lamps thereof, seven, and the tongs thereof, and the snuff-dishes thereof, of pure gold. Of a talent of pure gold made he it, and all the vessels thereof.

The Altar of Incense.

And he made the altar of incense of acacia wood: a cubit was the length thereof, and a cubit the breadth thereof, foursquare; and two cubits was the height thereof; the horns thereof were of one piece with it. And he overlaid it with pure gold, the top thereof, and the sides thereof round about, and the horns of it: and he made unto it a rim of gold round about. And he made for it two golden rings under the rim thereof, upon the two ribs thereof, upon the two sides of it, for places for staves to bear it withal. And he made the staves of acacia wood, and overlaid them with gold. And he made the holy anointing oil, and the pure incense of sweet spices, after the art of the perfumer.

The Altar of Burnt Offering.

And he made the altar of burnt offering of acacia wood: five cubits was the length thereof, and five cubits the breadth thereof, foursquare; and three cubits the height

THE TRADITIONAL SPOT ON WHICH MOSES READ THE TEN COMMANDMENTS

Copyright by Underwood & Underwood
and used by special permission

The traditional Sinai is bounded on the north by the great plain Er-Rahab out of which it rises precipitately. The northernmost peak is called the "Head of the Willow," probably from a willow tree growing in one of the gullies, and is commonly taken as the place of the giving of the Law. The height of the peak is 6,937 feet. "Now the whole prospect is before us. The vast plain of Er-Rahab, flecked with a few camels and black Arab tents, and capable of holding millions of people all in view of the Mount, gradually slopes away from the eminences where we are"

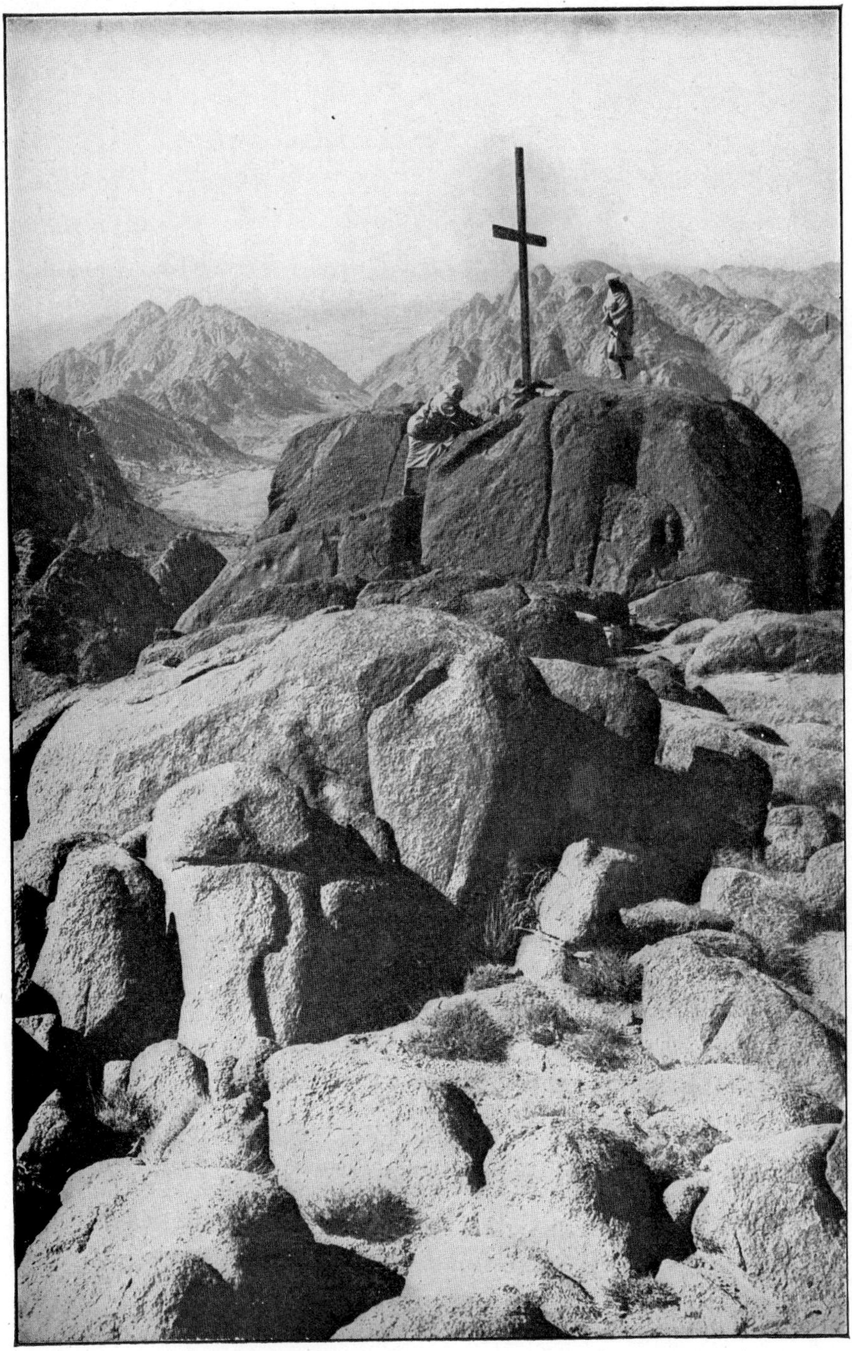

thereof. And he made the horns thereof upon the four corners of it; the horns thereof were of one piece with it: and he overlaid it with brass. And he made all the vessels of the altar, the pots, and the shovels, and the basins, the fleshhooks, and the firepans: all the vessels thereof made he of brass. And he made for the altar a grating of network of brass, under the ledge round it beneath, reaching halfway up. And he cast four rings for the four ends of the grating of brass, to be places for the staves. And he made the staves of acacia wood, and overlaid them with brass. And he put the staves into the rings on the sides of the altar, to bear it withal; he made it hollow with planks.

And he made the laver of brass, and the base thereof of brass, of the mirrors of the serving women which served at the door of the tent of meeting.

The Court.

And he made the court: for the south side southward the hangings of the court were of fine linen, an hundred cubits: their pillars were twenty, and their sockets twenty, of brass; the hooks of the pillars and their fillets were of silver. And for the north side an hundred cubits, their pillars twenty, and their sockets twenty, of brass; the hooks of the pillars and their fillets of silver. And for the west side were hangings of fifty cubits, their pillars ten, and their sockets ten; the hooks of the pillars and their fillets of silver. And for the east side eastward fifty cubits. The hangings for the one side of the gate were fifteen cubits; their pillars three, and their sockets three; and so for the other side: on this hand and that hand by the gate of the court were hangings of fifteen cubits; their pillars three, and their sockets three. All the hangings of the court round about were of fine linen. And the sockets for the pillars were of brass; the hooks of the pillars and their fillets of silver; and the overlaying of their capitals of silver; and all the pillars of the court were filleted with silver. And the screen for the gate of the court was the work of the embroiderer, of blue, and purple, and scarlet, and fine twined linen: and twenty cubits was the length, and the height in the breadth was five cubits, corresponding to the hangings of the court. And their pillars were four, and their sockets four, of brass; their hooks of silver, and the overlaying of their capitals and their fillets of silver. And all the pins of the tabernacle, and of the court round about, were of brass.

The Workmen and the Materials.

This is the sum of the things for the tabernacle, even the tabernacle of the testimony, as they were counted, according to the commandment of Moses, for the service of the Levites, by the hand of Ithamar, the son of Aaron the priest. And Bezalel the son of Uri, the son of Hur, of the tribe of Judah, made all that the Lord commanded Moses. And with him was Oholiab, the son of Ahisamach, of the tribe of Dan, an engraver, and a cunning workman, and an embroiderer in blue, and in purple, and in scarlet, and fine linen.

All the gold that was used for the work in all the work of the sanctuary, even the gold of the offering, was twenty and nine talents, and seven hundred and thirty shekels, after the shekel of the sanctuary. And the silver of them that were numbered of the congregation was an hundred talents, and a thousand seven hundred and threescore and fifteen shekels, after the shekel of the sanctuary. And the hundred talents of silver were for casting the sockets of the sanctuary, and the sockets of the veil; an hundred sockets for the hundred talents, a talent for a socket. And of the thousand seven hundred seventy and five shekels he made hooks for the pillars, and overlaid their capitals, and made fillets for them. And the brass of the offering was seventy talents, and two thousand and four hundred shekels. And therewith he made the sockets to the door of the tent of meeting, and the brazen altar, and the brazen grating for it, and all the vessels of the altar, and the sockets of the court round about, and the sockets of the gate of the court, and all the pins of the tabernacle, and all the pins of the court round about.

The Garments of the Priests.

And of the blue, and purple, and scarlet, they made finely wrought garments, for ministering in the holy place, and made the holy garments for Aaron; as the Lord commanded Moses.

And he made the ephod of gold, blue, and purple, and scarlet, and fine linen. And they beat the gold into thin plates, and cut it into wires, to work it in the blue, and in the purple, and in the scarlet, and in the fine linen, the work of the cunning workman. They made shoulderpieces for it, joined together: at the two ends was it joined together. And the cunningly woven band, that was upon it, to gird it on withal, was of the same piece and like the work thereof; of gold, of blue, and purple, and scarlet, and fine twined linen; as the Lord commanded Moses.

And they wrought the onyx stones, inclosed in clasps of gold, graven with the engravings of a signet, according to the names of the children of Israel. And he put them on the shoulderpieces of the ephod, to be stones of memorial for the children of Israel; as the Lord commanded Moses.

And he made the breastplate, the work of the cunning workman, like the work of the ephod; of gold, of blue, and purple, and scarlet, and fine linen. It was foursquare; they made the breastplate double: a span was the length thereof, and a span the breadth thereof, being double. And they set in it four rows of stones: a row of sardius, topaz, and carbuncle was the first row. And the second row, an emerald, a sapphire, and a diamond. And the third row, a jacinth, an agate, and an amethyst. And the fourth row, a beryl, an onyx, and a jasper: they were inclosed in clasps of gold in their settings. And the stones were according to the names of the children of Israel, twelve, according to their names; like the engravings of a signet, every one according to his name, for the twelve tribes.

And he made the robe of the ephod of woven work, all

VIEW FROM MOUNT HOR
From an old engraving

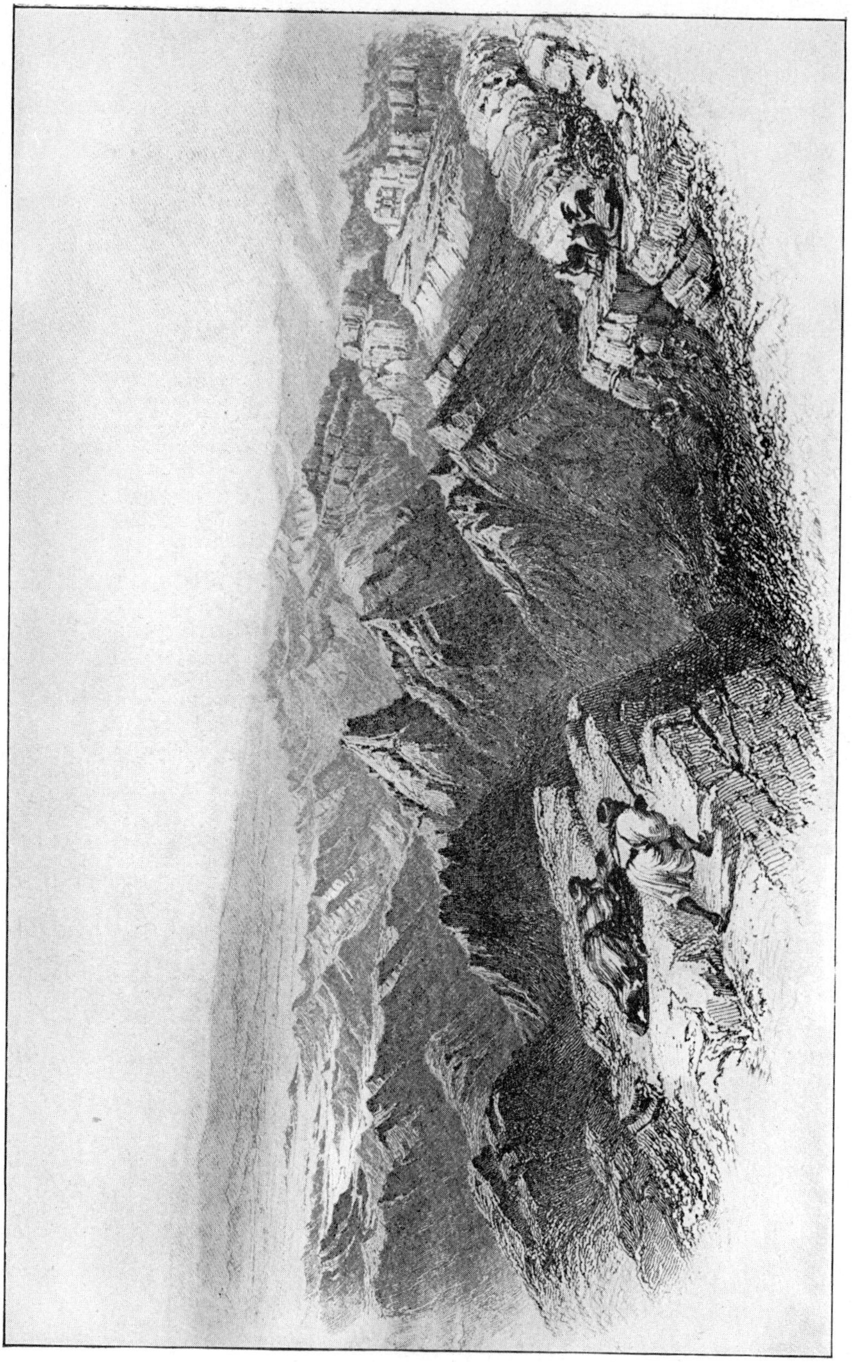

of blue; and the hole of the robe in the midst thereof, as the hole of a coat of mail, with a binding round about the hole of it, that it should not be rent. And they made upon the skirts of the robe pomegranates of blue, and purple, and scarlet, and linen. And they made bells of pure gold, and put the bells between the pomegranates upon the skirts of the robe round about, between the pomegranates; a bell and a pomegranate, a bell and a pomegranate, upon the skirts of the robe round about, to minister in; as the Lord commanded Moses.

And they made the coats of fine linen of woven work for Aaron, and for his sons, and the miter of fine linen, and the goodly turbans of fine linen, and the linen breeches of fine linen, and the girdle of fine twined linen, and blue, and purple, and scarlet, the work of the embroiderer; as the Lord commanded Moses.

And they made the plate of the holy crown of pure gold, and wrote upon it a writing, like the engravings of a signet, "Holy to the Lord." And they tied unto it a lace of blue, to fasten it upon the miter above; as the Lord commanded Moses.

Thus was finished all the work of the tabernacle of the tent of meeting: and the children of Israel did according to all that the Lord commanded Moses, so did they.

The Work Is Approved.

And they brought the tabernacle to Moses, the Tent, and all its furniture, its clasps, its boards, its bars, and its pillars, and its sockets; and the covering of rams' skins dyed red, and the covering of sealskins, and the veil of the screen; the ark of the testimony, and the staves thereof, and the mercy seat; the table, all the vessels thereof, and the shewbread; the pure candlestick, the lamps thereof, even the lamps to be set in order, and all the vessels thereof, and the oil for the light; and the golden altar, and the anointing oil, and the sweet incense, and the screen for the door of the Tent; the brazen altar, and its grating of brass, its staves, and all its vessels, the laver and its base; the hangings of the court, its pillars, and its sockets, and the screen for the gate of the court, the cords thereof, and the pins thereof, and all the instruments of the service of the tabernacle, for the tent of meeting; the finely wrought garments for ministering in the holy place, and the holy garments for Aaron the priest, and the garments of his sons, to minister in the priest's office. According to all that the Lord commanded Moses, so the children of Israel did all the work. And Moses saw all the work, and, behold, they had done it; as the Lord had commanded, even so had they done it: and Moses blessed them.

The Tabernacle Is Set Up.

And the Lord spoke unto Moses, saying, "On the first day of the first month shalt thou set up the tabernacle of the tent of meeting. And thou shalt put therein the ark of the testimony, and thou shalt screen the ark with the veil. And thou shalt bring in the table, and set in order the things that are upon it; and thou shalt bring in the

FOUR THOUSAND YEARS UNCHANGED PATRIARCHAL LIFE IN PALESTINE TO-DAY

Copyright by Underwood & Underwood
and used by special permission

The unchanged habits of the East render it in this respect a kind of living Pompeii. The outward appearances, which in the case of the Greeks and Romans we know only through art and writing, through marble, fresco, and parchment, in the case of Jewish history we know through the forms of actual men, living and moving before us, wearing almost the same garb, speaking in almost the same language, and certainly with the same general turns of speech and tone and manners. Such as we see them now, starting on a pilgrimage, or a journey, were Abraham and his brother's son, when they "went forth" to go into the land of Canaan. All their substance that they had "gathered" is heaped high on the backs of their kneeling camels. The slaves that they "had bought in Haran" run along by their sides. Round about them are their flocks of sheep and goats, and the asses moving underneath the towering forms of the camels. The chief is there, amidst the stir of movement, or resting at noon within his black tent, marked out from the rest by his cloak of brilliant scarlet, by the fillet of rope which binds the loose handkerchief round his head, by the spear which he holds in his hand to guide the march, and to fix the encampment. The chief's wife, the princess of the tribe, is there in her own tent, to make the cakes and prepare the usual meal of milk and butter; the slave or the child is ready to bring in the red lentil soup for the weary hunter, or to kill the calf for the unexpected guest

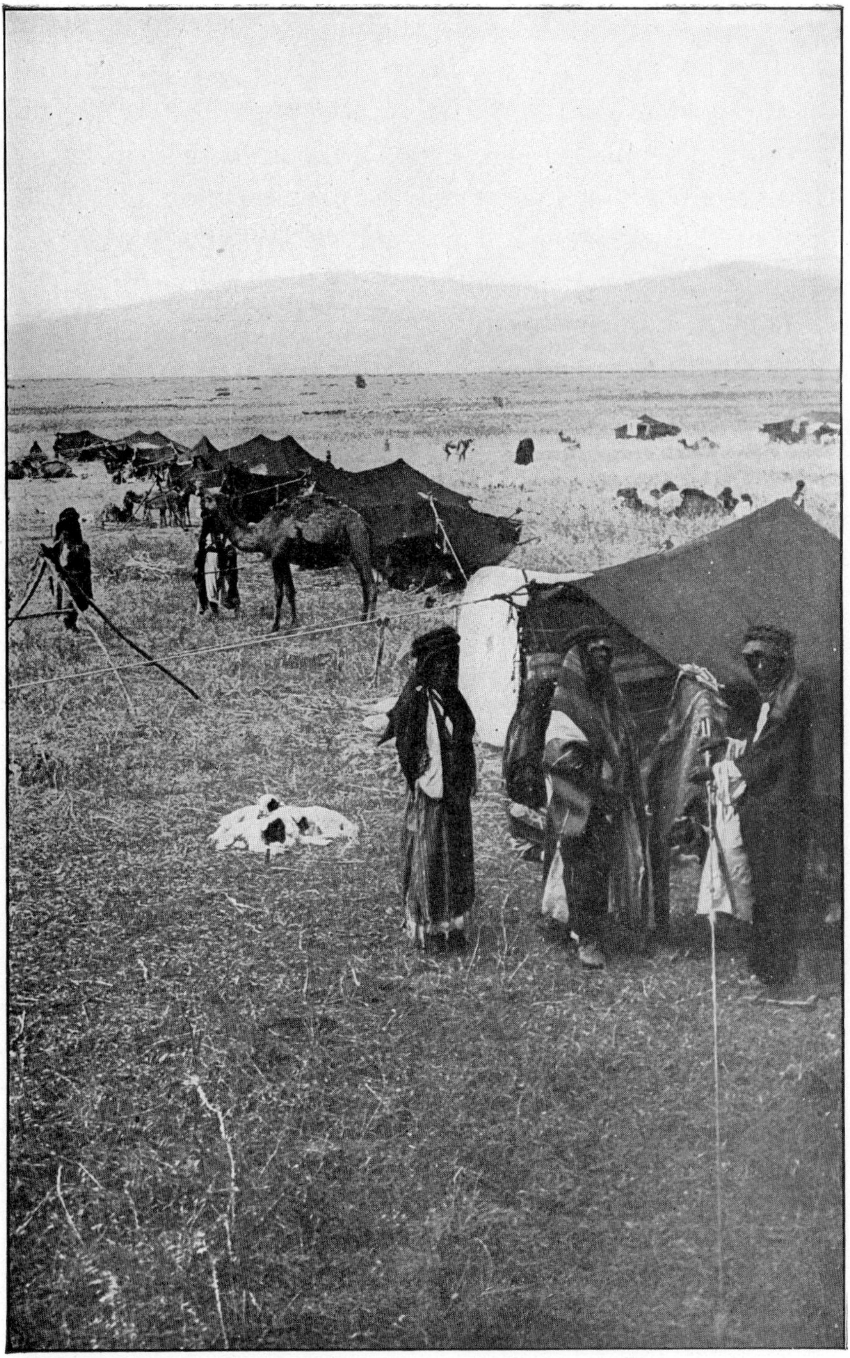

candlestick, and light the lamps thereof. And thou shalt set the golden altar for incense before the ark of the testimony, and put the screen of the door to the tabernacle. And thou shalt set the altar of burnt offering before the door of the tabernacle of the tent of meeting. And thou shalt set the laver between the tent of meeting and the altar, and shalt put water therein. And thou shalt set up the court round about, and hang up the screen of the gate of the court. And thou shalt take the anointing oil, and anoint the tabernacle, and all that is therein, and shalt hallow it, and all the furniture thereof: and it shall be holy. And thou shalt anoint the altar of burnt offering, and all its vessels, and sanctify the altar: and the altar shall be most holy. And thou shalt anoint the laver and its base, and sanctify it. And thou shalt bring Aaron and his sons unto the door of the tent of meeting, and thou shalt wash them with water. And thou shalt put upon Aaron the holy garments; and thou shalt anoint him, and sanctify him, that he may minister unto me in the priest's office. And thou shalt bring his sons, and put coats upon them: and thou shalt anoint them, as thou didst anoint their father, that they may minister unto me in the priest's office: and their anointing shall be to them for an everlasting priesthood throughout their generations." Thus did Moses: according to all that the Lord commanded him, so did he.

And it came to pass in the first month in the second year, on the first day of the month, that the tabernacle was reared up. And Moses set up the tabernacle, and laid its sockets, and set up the boards thereof, and put in the bars thereof, and set up its pillars. And he spread the tent over the tabernacle, and put the covering of the tent above upon it; as the Lord commanded Moses. And he put the testimony into the ark, and set the staves on the ark, and put the mercy seat above upon the ark: and he brought the ark into the tabernacle, and set up the veil of the screen, and screened the ark of the testimony; as the Lord commanded Moses. And he put the table in the tent of meeting, upon the side of the tabernacle northward, without the veil. And he set the bread in order upon it before the Lord; as the Lord commanded Moses. And he put the candlestick in the tent of meeting, over against the table, on the side of the tabernacle southward. And he lighted the lamps before the Lord; as the Lord commanded Moses. And he put the golden altar in the tent of meeting before the veil: and he burnt therein incense of sweet spices; as the Lord commanded Moses. And he put the screen of the door to the tabernacle. And he set the altar of burnt offering at the door of the tabernacle of the tent of meeting, and offered upon it the burnt offering and the meal offering; as the Lord commanded Moses. And he set the laver between the tent of meeting and the altar, and put water therein, to wash withal. And Moses and Aaron and his sons washed their hands and their feet thereat; when they went into the tent of meeting, and when they came near unto the altar, they washed: as the Lord commanded Moses. And he reared up the court round about the tabernacle and the altar, and set up the screen of the gate of the court. So Moses finished the work.

The Cloud of the Glory of God in the Tent.

Then the cloud covered the tent of meeting, and the glory of the Lord filled the tabernacle. And Moses was not able to enter into the tent of meeting, because the cloud abode thereon, and the glory of the Lord filled the tabernacle. And when the cloud was taken up from over the tabernacle, the children of Israel went onward, throughout all their journeys: but if the cloud was not taken up, then they journeyed not till the day that it was taken up. For the cloud of the Lord was upon the tabernacle by day, and there was fire therein by night, in the sight of all the house of Israel, throughout all their journeys.

LEAD ME ON

Traveling to the better land,
O'er the desert's scorching sand,
Father! let me grasp thy hand;
    Lead me on, lead me on!

When at Marah, parched with heat,
I the sparkling fountain greet,
Make the bitter water sweet;
    Lead me on!

When the wilderness is drear,
Show me Elim's palm-grove near,
And her wells, as crystal clear:
    Lead me on!

Through the water, through the fire,
Never let me fall or tire,
Every step brings Canaan nigher:
    Lead me on!

Bid me stand on Nebo's height,
Gaze upon the land of light,
Then, transported with the sight,
    Lead me on!

When I stand on Jordan's brink,
Never let me fear or shrink;
Hold me, Father, lest I sink:
    Lead me on!

When the victory is won,
And eternal life begun,
Up to glory lead me on!
    Lead me on, lead me on!

MOUNT HOREB

From a photograph in the possession of the Forbes Library
and used by permission

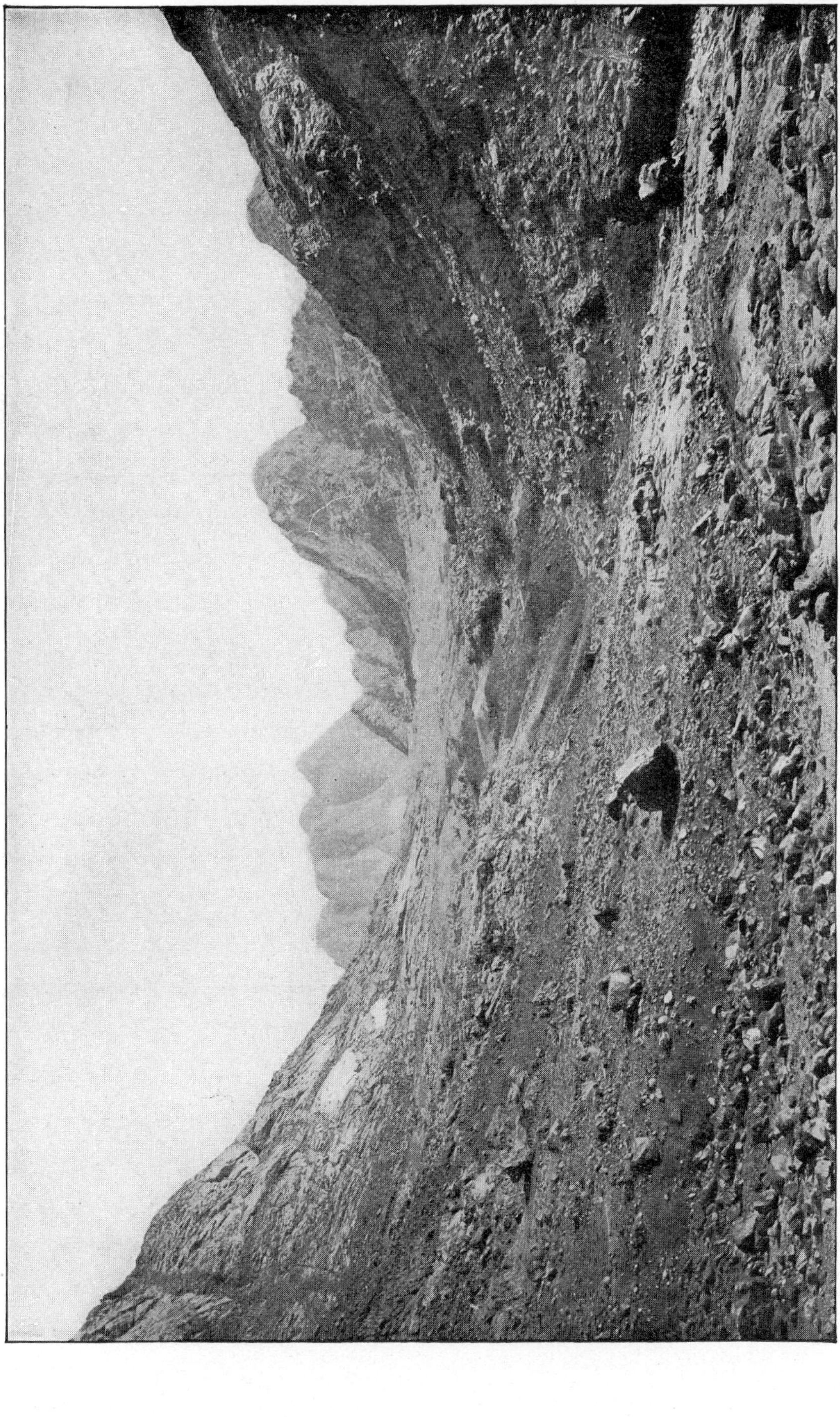

THE MARCH TO THE PROMISED LAND

THE PILLAR OF FIRE AND THE CLOUD OF SMOKE.

And on the day that the tabernacle was set up the cloud covered the tabernacle, even the tent of the testimony: and at even it was upon the tabernacle as it were the appearance of fire, until morning. So it was always: the cloud covered it, and the appearance of fire by night. And whenever the cloud was taken up from over the Tent, then after that the children of Israel journeyed: and in the place where the cloud abode, there the children of Israel encamped. At the commandment of the Lord the children of Israel journeyed, and at the commandment of the Lord they encamped: as long as the cloud abode upon the tabernacle they remained encamped. And when the cloud tarried upon the tabernacle many days, then the children of Israel kept the charge of the Lord, and journeyed not. And sometimes the cloud was a few days upon the tabernacle; then according to the commandment of the Lord they remained encamped, and according to the commandment of the Lord they journeyed. And sometimes the cloud was from evening until morning; and when the cloud was taken up in the morning, they journeyed: or if it continued by day and by night, when the cloud was taken up, they journeyed.

Whether it were two days, or a month, or a year, that the cloud tarried upon the tabernacle, abiding thereon, the children of Israel remained encamped, and journeyed not: but when it was taken up, they journeyed. At the commandment of the Lord they encamped, and at the commandment of the Lord they journeyed: they kept the charge of the Lord, at the commandment of the Lord by the hand of Moses.

The Long Journey from Sinai Begins.

And it came to pass in the second year, in the second month, on the twentieth day of the month, that the cloud was taken up from over the tabernacle of the testimony. And the children of Israel set forward according to their journeys out of the wilderness of Sinai; and the cloud abode in the wilderness of Paran. And they first took their journey according to the commandment of the Lord by the hand of Moses.

And they set forward from the mount of the Lord three days' journey; and the ark of the covenant of the Lord went before them three days' journey, to seek out a resting place for them. And the cloud of the Lord was over them by day, when they set forward from the camp.

And it came to pass, when the ark set forward, that Moses said,—

"Rise up, O Lord, and let thine enemies be scattered;
And let them that hate thee flee before thee."

And when it rested he said,—

"Return, O Lord,
Unto the ten thousands of the thousands of Israel."

THE SENDING OUT OF THE SPIES.
They Report "a Land Flowing with Milk and Honey."

And the Lord spoke to Moses, saying, "Send thou men, that they may spy out the land of Canaan, which I give unto the children of Israel: of every tribe of their fathers shall ye send a man, every one a prince among them."

And Moses sent them from the wilderness of Paran according to the commandment of the Lord: all of them men who were heads of the children of Israel.

And Moses sent them to spy out the land of Canaan, and said to them, "Get you up this way by the south, and go up into the mountains: and see the land, what it is; and the people that dwelleth therein, whether they are strong or weak, whether they are few or many; and what the land is that they dwell in, whether it is good or bad; and what cities they are that they dwell in, whether in camps, or in strong holds; and what the land is, whether it be fat or lean, whether there be wood therein, or not. And be ye of good courage, and bring of the fruit of the land."

Now the time was the time of the first ripe grapes. So they went up, and spied out the land from the wilderness of Zin unto Rehob, to the entering in of Hamath. And they went up by the south, and came to Hebron; and the children of Anak were there.

And they came unto the valley of Eshcol, and cut down from thence a branch with one cluster of grapes, and they bore it upon a staff between two; they brought also of the pomegranates, and of the figs. That place was called the valley of Eshcol (that is, "cluster"). And they returned from spying out the land at the end of forty days. And they went and came to Moses, and to Aaron, and to all the congregation of the children of Israel, to the wilderness of Paran, to Kadesh; and brought back word unto them, and to all the congregation, and showed them the fruit of the land. And they told him, and said, "We came unto the land whither thou sentest us, and surely it floweth with milk and honey; and this is the fruit of it. Howbeit the people that dwell in the land are strong, and the cities are fortified and very great: and moreover we saw the children of Anak there. Amalek dwelleth in the land of the south: and the Hittite, and the Jebusite, and the Amorite, dwell in the mountains: and the Canaanite dwelleth by the sea, and along by the side of Jordan."

And Caleb stilled the people before Moses, and said, "Let us go up at once, and possess it; for we are well able to overcome it."

But the men that went up with him said, "We are not able to go up against the people; for they are stronger than we."

And they brought up an evil report of the land which they had spied out unto the children of Israel, saying, "The land, through which we have gone to spy it out, is a land that eateth up the inhabitants thereof; and all the people that we saw in it are men of great stature. And there we saw the giants, the sons of Anak: and we were in our own sight as grasshoppers, and so we were in their sight."

And all the congregation lifted up their voice, and

MOSES SMITING THE ROCK
By Murillo

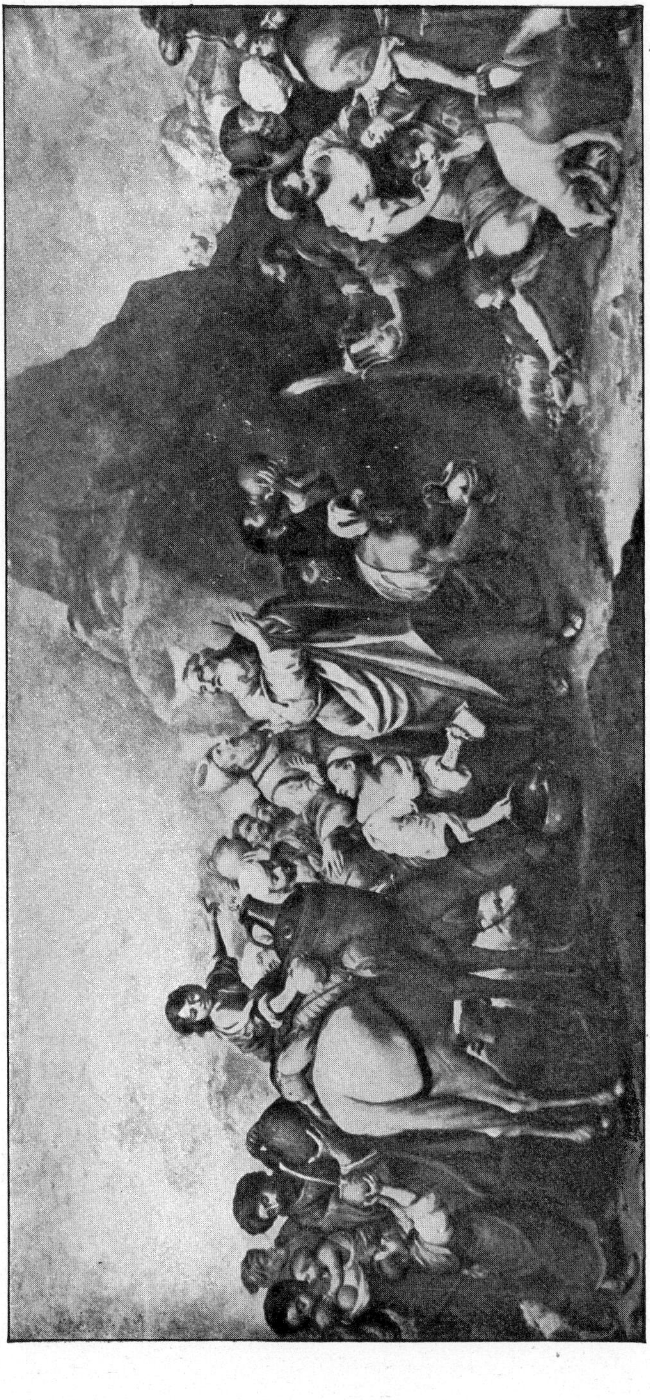

cried; and the people wept that night. And all the children of Israel murmured against Moses and against Aaron: and the whole congregation said unto them, "Would God that we had died in the land of Egypt! or would God we had died in this wilderness! And wherefore doth the Lord bring us unto this land, to fall by the sword? Our wives and our little ones shall be a prey: were it not better for us to return into Egypt?"

And they said one to another, "Let us make a captain, and let us return into Egypt."

Then Moses and Aaron fell on their faces before all the assembly of the congregation of the children of Israel. And Joshua the son of Nun and Caleb the son of Jephunneh, which were of them that spied out the land, rent their clothes: and they spoke unto all the congregation of the children of Israel, saying, "The land, which we passed through to spy it out, is an exceeding good land. If the Lord delight in us, then he will bring us into this land, and give it to us; a land which floweth with milk and honey. Only rebel not against the Lord, neither fear ye the people of the land; for they are bread for us: their defense is removed from over them, and the Lord is with us: fear them not."

WATER FROM THE ROCK.
Passage Through Edom Refused.

(The people refused to believe the report of the courageous spies, and their wanderings continued.)

And the children of Israel, even the whole multitude,

came into the wilderness of Zin in the first month: and the people abode in Kadesh; and Miriam died there, and was buried there. And there was no water for the multitude: and they assembled themselves together against Moses and against Aaron.

And the people strove with Moses, and spoke, saying, "Would God that we had died when our brethren died before the Lord! And why have ye brought the people of the Lord into this wilderness, that we should die there, we and our cattle? And wherefore have ye made us to come up out of Egypt, to bring us unto this evil place? it is no place of seed, or of figs, or of vines, or of pomegranates; neither is there any water to drink."

And Moses and Aaron went from the presence of the people to the door of the tent of meeting, and fell upon their faces: and the glory of the Lord appeared to them. And the Lord spoke to Moses, saying, "Take the rod, and assemble the multitude, thou, and Aaron thy brother, and speak ye to the rock before their eyes, that it give forth its water; and thou shalt bring forth to them water out of the rock: so thou shalt give the multitude and their cattle drink."

And Moses took the rod from before the Lord, as he commanded him. And Moses and Aaron gathered the people together before the rock, and he said unto them, "Hear now, ye rebels; shall we bring you forth water out of this rock?"

And Moses lifted up his hand, and smote the rock with his rod twice: and water came forth abundantly, and the multitude drank, and their cattle. And the Lord said to Moses and Aaron, "Because ye believed not in me, to sanctify me in the eyes of the children of Israel, therefore ye shall not bring this people into the land which I have given them." These are the waters of Meribah (that is, strife); because the children of Israel strove with the Lord, and he was sanctified in them.

And Moses sent messengers from Kadesh to the king of Edom, "Thus saith thy brother Israel, 'Thou knowest all the trouble that hath befallen us: how our fathers went down into Egypt, and we dwelt in Egypt a long time: and the Egyptians oppressed us, and our fathers: and when we cried to the Lord, he heard our voice, and sent an angel, and brought us forth out of Egypt: and, behold, we are in Kadesh, a city in the uttermost of thy border: let us pass, I pray thee, through thy land: we will not pass through field or through vineyard, neither will we drink of the water of the wells: we will go along the king's highway, we will not turn aside to the right hand nor to the left, until we have passed thy border.'"

And Edom said unto him, "Thou shalt not pass through my land, lest I come out with the sword against thee."

And the children of Israel said unto him, "We will go up by the highway: and if we drink of thy water, I and my cattle, then will I give the price thereof: let me only, without doing anything else, pass through on my feet."

And he said, "Thou shalt not pass through."

And Edom came out against him with much people, and with a strong hand. Thus Edom refused to give

Israel passage through his border: wherefore Israel turned away from him.

And they journeyed from Kadesh: and the children of Israel, even the whole multitude, came unto Mount Hor. And the Lord spoke unto Moses and Aaron in Mount Hor, by the border of the land of Edom, saying, "Aaron shall be gathered to his people: for he shall not enter into the land which I have given to the children of Israel, because ye rebelled against my word at the waters of Meribah. Take Aaron and Eleazar his son, and bring them up unto Mount Hor: and strip Aaron of his priestly garments, and put them upon Eleazar his son: and Aaron shall be gathered to his people, and shall die there."

And Moses did as the Lord commanded: and they went up into Mount Hor in the sight of all the multitude. And Moses stripped Aaron of his priestly garments, and put them upon Eleazar his son; and Aaron died there in the top of the mount: and Moses and Eleazar came down from the mount. And when all the multitude saw that Aaron was dead, they wept for Aaron thirty days, even all the house of Israel.

THE BRAZEN SERPENT.

And they journeyed from Mount Hor by the way to the Red Sea, to go around the land of Edom: and the soul of the people was much discouraged because of the difficulties. And the people spoke against God, and against Moses, "Wherefore have ye brought us up out of Egypt to die in the wilderness? for there is no bread, and there is no water; and our soul loatheth this bread of manna."

ROCK TEMPLE IN PETRA, IN THE LAND OF EDOM

From a photograph belonging to the Forbes Library, Northampton, Mass., and used by special permission

Hidden away in the rocky gorges of Edom, Petra is one of the strangest and most marvelous cities of the world. Even yet it has not been fully explored. Its temples and tombs are carved out of the solid rock

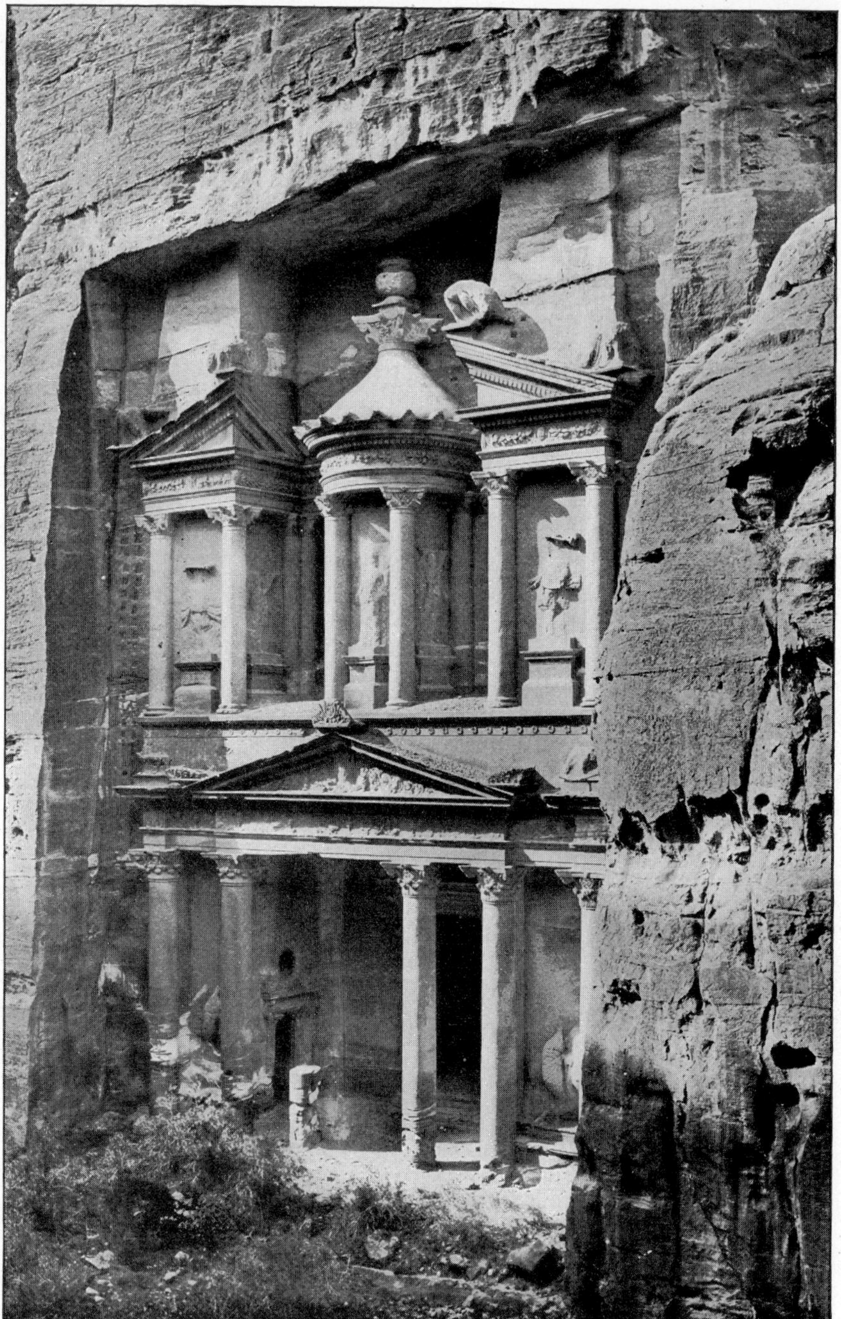

And the Lord sent fiery serpents among the people, and they bit the people; and many people of Israel died. And the people came to Moses, and said, "We have sinned, because we have spoken against the Lord, and against thee; pray unto the Lord, that he take away the serpents from us."

And Moses prayed for the people. And the Lord said unto Moses, "Make thee a fiery serpent, and set it upon a standard: and it shall come to pass, that every one who is bitten, when he seeth it, shall live."

And Moses made a serpent of brass, and set it upon the standard: and it came to pass, that if a serpent had bitten any man, when he looked unto the serpent of brass, he lived.

Battles by the Way.

And from thence they journeyed to Beer: that is the well whereof the Lord said unto Moses, "Gather the people together, and I will give them water."

Then sang Israel this song:—

The Song of the Well.

"Spring up, O well; sing ye unto it:
The well, which the princes digged,
Which the nobles of the people delved,
With the scepter, and with their staves."

And from the wilderness they journeyed past many places, to the top of Pisgah, which looketh down upon the desert.

And Israel sent messengers unto Sihon king of the

Amorites, saying, "Let me pass through thy land: we will not turn aside into field, or into vineyard; we will not drink of the water of the wells: we will go by the king's highway, until we have passed thy border." And Sihon would not suffer Israel to pass through his border: but Sihon gathered all his people together, and went out against Israel into the wilderness, and came to Jahaz: and he fought against Israel. And Israel smote him with the edge of the sword, and possessed his land from Arnon unto Jabbok, even unto the children of Ammon: for the border of the children of Ammon was strong.

And Israel took all these cities: and Israel dwelt in all the cities of the Amorites, in Heshbon, and in all the towns thereof. For Heshbon was the city of Sihon the king of the Amorites, who had fought against the former king of Moab, and taken all his land out of his hand, even to Arnon. Wherefore they that speak in proverbs say,—

"Come ye to Heshbon,
Let the city of Sihon be built and established:
For a fire is gone out of Heshbon,
A flame from the city of Sihon.
It hath devoured Ar of Moab,
The lords of the high places of Arnon.
Woe to thee, Moab!
Thou art undone, O people of Chemosh:
He hath given his sons as fugitives,
And his daughters into captivity,
Unto Sihon king of the Amorites.

We have shot at them; Heshbon is perished even unto
  Dibon,
And we have laid waste even unto Nophah,
Which reacheth unto Medeba."

Thus Israel dwelt in the land of the Amorites. And Moses sent to spy out Jazer, and they took the towns thereof, and drove out the Amorites that were there.

And they turned and went up by the way of Bashan: and Og the king of Bashan went out against them, he and all his people, to battle at Edrei. And the Lord said to Moses, "Fear him not: for I have delivered him into thy hand, and all his people, and his land; and thou shalt do to him as thou didst to Sihon king of the Amorites, which dwelt at Heshbon."

So they smote him, and his sons, and all his people, until there was none left him remaining: and they possessed his land.

BALAAM AND BALAK.

The Story of the Prophet Who Was Tempted by a Bribe and of the Ass Which Knew More Than His Master.

And the children of Israel journeyed, and encamped in the plains of Moab beyond the Jordan at Jericho.

And Balak the son of Zippor saw all that Israel had done to the Amorites. And Moab was sore afraid of the people, because they were many: and Moab was distressed because of the children of Israel. And Moab said unto the elders of Midian, "Now shall this multitude lick up all that is round about us, as the ox licketh up the grass of the field."

And Balak the son of Zippor was king of Moab at that time. And he sent messengers unto Balaam the son of Beor, to Pethor, which is by the River, to the land of the children of his people, to call him, saying, "Behold, there is a people come out from Egypt: behold, they cover the face of the earth, and they abide over against me: come now therefore, I pray thee, curse me this people; for they are too mighty for me: peradventure I shall prevail, that we may smite them, and that I may drive them out of the land: for I know that he whom thou blessest is blessed, and he whom thou cursest is cursed."

And the elders of Moab and the elders of Midian departed with bribes in their hands; and they came unto Balaam, and spoke unto him the words of Balak.

And he said unto them, "Lodge here this night, and I will bring you word again, as the Lord shall speak unto me."

And the princes of Moab abode with Balaam. And God came unto Balaam, and said, "What men are these with thee?"

And Balaam said unto God, "Balak the son of Zippor, king of Moab, hath sent unto me, saying, 'Behold, the people that is come out of Egypt, it covereth the face of the earth: now, come curse me them; peradventure I shall be able to fight against them, and shall drive them out.'"

And God said unto Balaam, "Thou shalt not go with them; thou shalt not curse the people: for they are blessed."

VIEW OF THE DEAD SEA

From a photograph taken by Mr. Louis L. Tribus, Consulting Engineer and Commissioner of Public Works of the Borough of Richmond, City of New York

An interesting fact in connection with this picture of the Dead Sea concerns the boat which is floating upon it. The owner succeeded in securing a concession from the Turkish Government to put a steamboat upon the Dead Sea. When he started to run it he was advised that the concession had not included the operation of the boat and a considerable further sum of money was desired by the officials. This being beyond the power of the man to raise, the boat has not been operated and remains as the picture shows it.

The water of the Dead Sea contains about 25 per cent. of solid substances. There are common salt, chloride of calcium, chloride of magnesium, and other ingredients, and it is not to be wondered at that the human body floats easily on the surface.

The area of the sea is 360 square miles. Its length is 47½ miles; its greatest width, 10 miles. The surface is about 1295 feet below sea level.

Scientific observation justifies the estimate that a daily average of 6,500,000 tons of water is received into the Dead Sea from the Jordan and other sources during the year. During the rainy season the amount is very much greater; during the dry season it is, of course, very much less, but this average will be maintained year after year.

There is no outlet, and the level is kept down by evaporation only, which is very rapid because of the intense heat, the dry atmosphere and the dry winds which are constantly blowing down the gorges between the mountains.

The waters of the Jordan, when they reach the sea, are as brown as the earth through which they flow—a thick solution of mud—but the instant they mingle with the salt water of the lake the particles of soil are precipitated and they become as clear as crystal, with an intensely green tint.

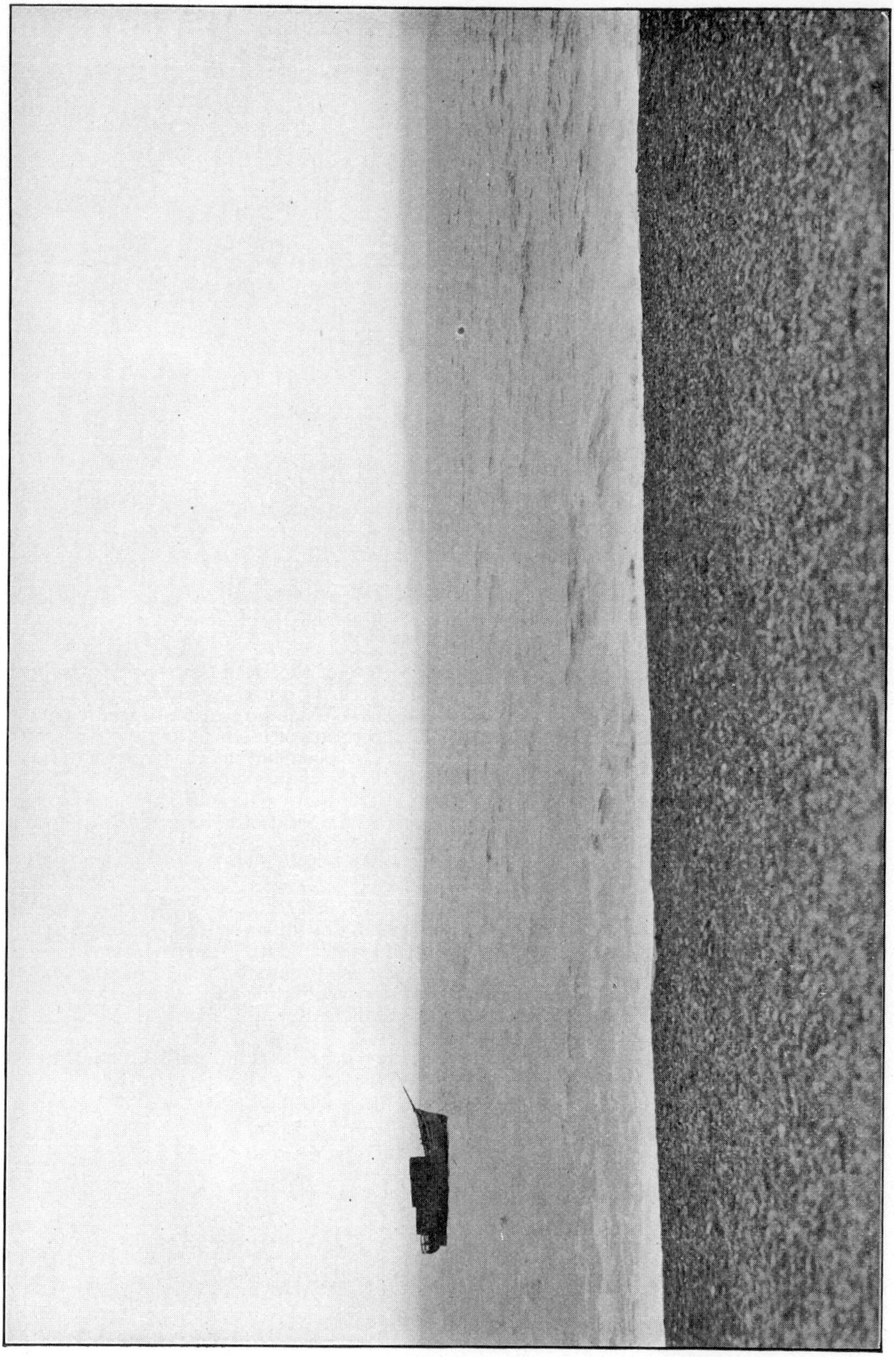

And Balaam rose up in the morning, and said unto the princes of Balak, "Get you into your land: for the Lord refuseth to give me leave to go with you."

And the princes of Moab rose up, and they went unto Balak, and said, "Balaam refuseth to come with us."

And Balak sent yet again princes, more, and more honorable than they. And they came to Balaam, and said to him, "Thus saith Balak the son of Zippor, 'Let nothing, I pray thee, hinder thee from coming unto me: for I will promote thee unto very great honor, and whatsoever thou sayest unto me I will do: come therefore, I pray thee, curse me this people.'"

And Balaam answered and said unto the servants of Balak, "If Balak would give me his house full of silver and gold, I cannot go beyond the word of the Lord my God, to do less or more. Now therefore, I pray you, tarry ye also here this night, that I may know what the Lord will speak unto me more."

And God came unto Balaam at night, and said unto him, "If the men be come to call thee, rise up, go with them; but only the word which I speak unto thee, that shalt thou do."

And Balaam rose up in the morning, and saddled his ass, and went with the princes of Moab. And God's anger was kindled because he went: and the angel of the Lord placed himself in the way for an adversary against him. Now he was riding upon his ass, and his two servants were with him. And the ass saw the angel of the Lord standing in the way, with his sword drawn in his hand:

and the ass turned aside out of the way, and went into the field: and Balaam smote the ass, to turn her into the way.

Then the angel of the Lord stood in a hollow place between the vineyards, a fence being on this side, and a fence on that side. And the ass saw the angel of the Lord, and she thrust herself unto the wall, and crushed Balaam's foot against the wall: and he smote her again.

And the angel of the Lord went further, and stood in a narrow place, where was no way to turn either to the right hand or to the left.

And the ass saw the angel of the Lord, and she lay down under Balaam: and Balaam's anger was kindled, and he smote the ass with his staff.

And the Lord opened the mouth of the ass, and she said unto Balaam, "What have I done unto thee, that thou hast smitten me these three times?"

And Balaam said unto the ass, "Because thou hast mocked me: I would there were a sword in mine hand, for now I had killed thee."

And the ass said unto Balaam, "Am not I thine ass, upon which thou hast ridden all thy life long unto this day? was I ever wont to do so unto thee?"

And he said, "No."

Then the Lord opened the eyes of Balaam, and he saw the angel of the Lord standing in the way, with his sword drawn in his hand: and he bowed his head, and fell on his face.

And the angel of the Lord said unto him, "Wherefore

hast thou smitten thine ass these three times? behold, I am come forth for an adversary, because thy way is perverse before me: and the ass saw me, and turned aside before me these three times: unless she had turned aside from me, surely now I had even slain thee, and saved her alive."

And Balaam said unto the angel of the Lord, "I have sinned; for I knew not that thou stoodest in the way against me: now therefore, if it displease thee, I will get me back again."

And the angel of the Lord said unto Balaam, "Go with the men: but only the word that I shall speak unto thee, that thou shalt speak."

So Balaam went with the princes of Balak. And when Balak heard that Balaam was come, he went out to meet him unto the city of Moab, which is on the border of Arnon.

And Balak said unto Balaam, "Did I not earnestly send unto thee to call thee? wherefore camest thou not unto me? am I not able indeed to promote thee to honor?"

And Balaam said unto Balak, "Lo, I am come unto thee: have I now any power at all to speak anything? the word that God putteth in my mouth, that shall I speak."

And Balaam went with Balak, and they came unto Kiriath-huzoth. And Balak sacrificed oxen and sheep, and sent to Balaam, and to the princes that were with him. And it came to pass in the morning, that Balak took Balaam, and brought him up into the high places of

Baal, and he saw from thence the utmost part of the people.

And Balaam said unto Balak, "Build me here seven altars, and prepare me here seven bullocks and seven rams."

And Balak did as Balaam had spoken; and Balak and Balaam offered on every altar a bullock and a ram.

And Balaam said unto Balak, "Stand by thy burnt offering, and I will go; peradventure the Lord will come to meet me: and whatsoever he showeth me I will tell thee." And he went to a bare summit.

And God met Balaam: and he said unto him, "I have prepared the seven altars, and I have offered up a bullock and a ram on every altar."

And the Lord put a word in Balaam's mouth, and said, "Return unto Balak, and thus thou shalt speak."

And he returned unto him, and, lo, he stood by his burnt offering, he, and all the princes of Moab. And Balaam said,—

"From Aram hath Balak brought me,
The king of Moab from the mountains of the East:
'Come, curse me Jacob,
And come, defy Israel.'
How shall I curse, whom God hath not cursed?
And how shall I defy, whom the Lord hath not defied?
For from the top of the rocks I see him,
And from the hills I behold him:
Lo, it is a people that dwell alone,
And shall not be reckoned among the nations.

Who can count the dust of Jacob,
Or number the fourth part of Israel?
Let me die the death of the righteous,
And let my last end be like his!"

And Balak said unto Balaam, "What hast thou done unto me? I took thee to curse mine enemies, and, behold, thou hast blessed them altogether."

And he answered and said, "Must I not take heed to speak that which the Lord putteth in my mouth?"

And Balak said unto him, "Come, I pray thee, with me unto another place, from whence thou mayest see them; thou shalt see but the utmost part of them, and shalt not see them all: and curse me them from thence."

And he took him into the field of Zophim, to the top of Pisgah, and built seven altars, and offered up a bullock and a ram on every altar.

And he said unto Balak, "Stand here by thy burnt offering, while I meet the Lord yonder."

And the Lord met Balaam, and put a word in his mouth, and said, "Return unto Balak, and thus shalt thou speak."

And he came to him, and, lo, he stood by his burnt offering, and the princes of Moab with him. And Balak said unto him, "What hath the Lord spoken?" And he said,—

"Rise up, Balak, and hear;
Hearken unto me, thou son of Zippor:
God is not a man, that he should lie;
Neither the son of man, that he should repent:

Hath he said, and shall he not do it?
Or hath he spoken, and shall he not make it good?
Behold, I have received commandment to bless:
And he hath blessed, and I cannot reverse it.
He hath not beheld iniquity in Jacob,
Neither hath he seen perverseness in Israel:
The Lord his God is with him,
And the shout of a king is among them.
God bringeth them forth out of Egypt;
He hath as it were the strength of the wild ox.
Surely there is no enchantment with Jacob,
Neither is there any divination with Israel:
Now shall it be said of Jacob and of Israel,
'What hath God wrought!'
Behold, the people riseth up as a lioness,
And as a lion doth he lift himself up:
He shall not lie down until he eat of the prey,
And drink the blood of the slain."

And Balak said unto Balaam, "Neither curse them at all, nor bless them at all." But Balaam answered and said unto Balak, "Told not I thee, saying, 'All that the Lord speaketh, that I must do'?"

And Balak said unto Balaam, "Come now, I will take thee unto another place; peradventure it will please God that thou mayest curse me them from thence."

And Balak took Balaam unto the top of Peor, that looketh down upon the desert.

And Balaam said unto Balak, "Build me here seven altars, and prepare me here seven bullocks and seven rams."

And Balak did as Balaam had said, and offered up a bullock and a ram on every altar.

And when Balaam saw that it pleased the Lord to bless Israel, he set his face toward the wilderness. And Balaam lifted up his eyes, and he saw Israel dwelling according to their tribes; and the spirit of God came upon him. And he said,—

"Balaam the son of Beor saith,
And the man whose eye was closed saith:
He saith, who heareth the words of God,
Who seeth the vision of the Almighty,
Falling down, and having his eyes open:
How goodly are thy tents, O Jacob,
Thy tabernacles, O Israel!
As valleys are they spread forth,
As gardens by the river side,
As aloes which the Lord hath planted,
As cedar trees beside the waters.
Water shall flow from his buckets,
And his family shall be in many waters,
And his king shall be higher than Agag,
And his kingdom shall be exalted.
God bringeth him forth out of Egypt;
He hath as it were the strength of the wild ox:
He shall eat up the nations his adversaries,
And shall break their bones in pieces,
And smite them through with his arrows.
He couched, he lay down as a lion,
And as a lioness; who shall rouse him up?
Blessed be every one that blesseth thee,
And cursed be every one that curseth thee."

And Balak's anger was kindled against Balaam, and he smote his hands together: and Balak said unto Balaam, "I called thee to curse mine enemies, and, behold, thou hast altogether blessed them these three times. Therefore now flee thou to thy place: I thought to promote thee unto great honor; but, lo, the Lord hath kept thee back from honor."

And Balaam said unto Balak, "Spoke I not also to thy messengers which thou sentest unto me, saying, 'If Balak would give me his house full of silver and gold, I cannot go beyond the word of the Lord, to do either good or bad of mine own mind; what the Lord speaketh, that will I speak'?

"And now, behold, I go unto my people: come, and I will announce to thee what this people shall do to thy people in the latter days." And he said,—

"Balaam the son of Beor saith,
And the man whose eye was closed saith:
He saith, who heareth the words of God,
And knoweth the knowledge of the Most High,
Who seeth the vision of the Almighty,
Falling down, and having his eyes open:
I see him, but not now:
I behold him, but not nigh:
There shall come forth a star out of Jacob,
And a scepter shall rise out of Israel,
And shall smite through the corners of Moab,
And break down all the sons of tumult.
And Edom shall be a possession,
Seir also shall be a possession, which were his enemies;

While Israel doeth valiantly.
And out of Jacob shall one have dominion,
And shall destroy the remnant from the city."

And he looked on Amalek, and said,—
"Amalek was the first of the nations;
But his latter end shall come to destruction."

And he looked on the Kenite, and said,—
"Strong is thy dwelling place,
And thy nest is set in the rock.
Nevertheless Kain shall be wasted,
Until Asshur shall carry thee away captive."

And he said, —
"Alas, who shall live when God doeth this?
But ships shall come from the coast of Kittim,
And they shall afflict Asshur, and shall afflict Eber,
And he also shall come to destruction."

And Balaam rose up, and went and returned to his place: and Balak also went his way.

THE DEATH OF MOSES.

He Sees but Cannot Enter the Promised Land.

(After the Israelites had wandered for many years in the desert, they approached at last the river Jordan, on the borders of the promised land. Moses, their great hero and leader, was not permitted to cross the river, but, after giving the people his last words of advice, climbed the rugged slopes of Mount Nebo, and was never again seen by the eye of man.)

And Moses went and spoke these words unto all Israel. And he said to them, "I am an hundred and twenty years old this day; I can no more go out and come in: and the Lord hath said to me, 'Thou shalt not go over this Jordan.' The Lord thy God, he will go over before thee; he will destroy these nations from before thee, and thou shalt possess them: and Joshua, he shall go over before thee, as the Lord hath spoken. And the Lord shall do unto them as he did to Sihon and to Og, the kings of the Amorites, and unto their land; whom he destroyed. And the Lord shall deliver them up before you, and ye shall do to them according unto all the commandment which I have commanded you. Be strong and of a good courage, fear not, nor be affrighted at them: for the Lord thy God, he it is that doth go with thee; he will not fail thee, nor forsake thee."

And Moses called to Joshua, and said to him in the sight of all Israel, "Be strong and of a good courage: for thou shalt go with this people into the land which the Lord hath sworn unto their fathers to give them; and thou shalt cause them to inherit it. And the Lord, he it

MOSES ON MOUNT NEBO

Thomas Nast

This picture by the famous cartoonist Nast, represents Moses from the summit of Nebo gazing into the land which he was never to enter

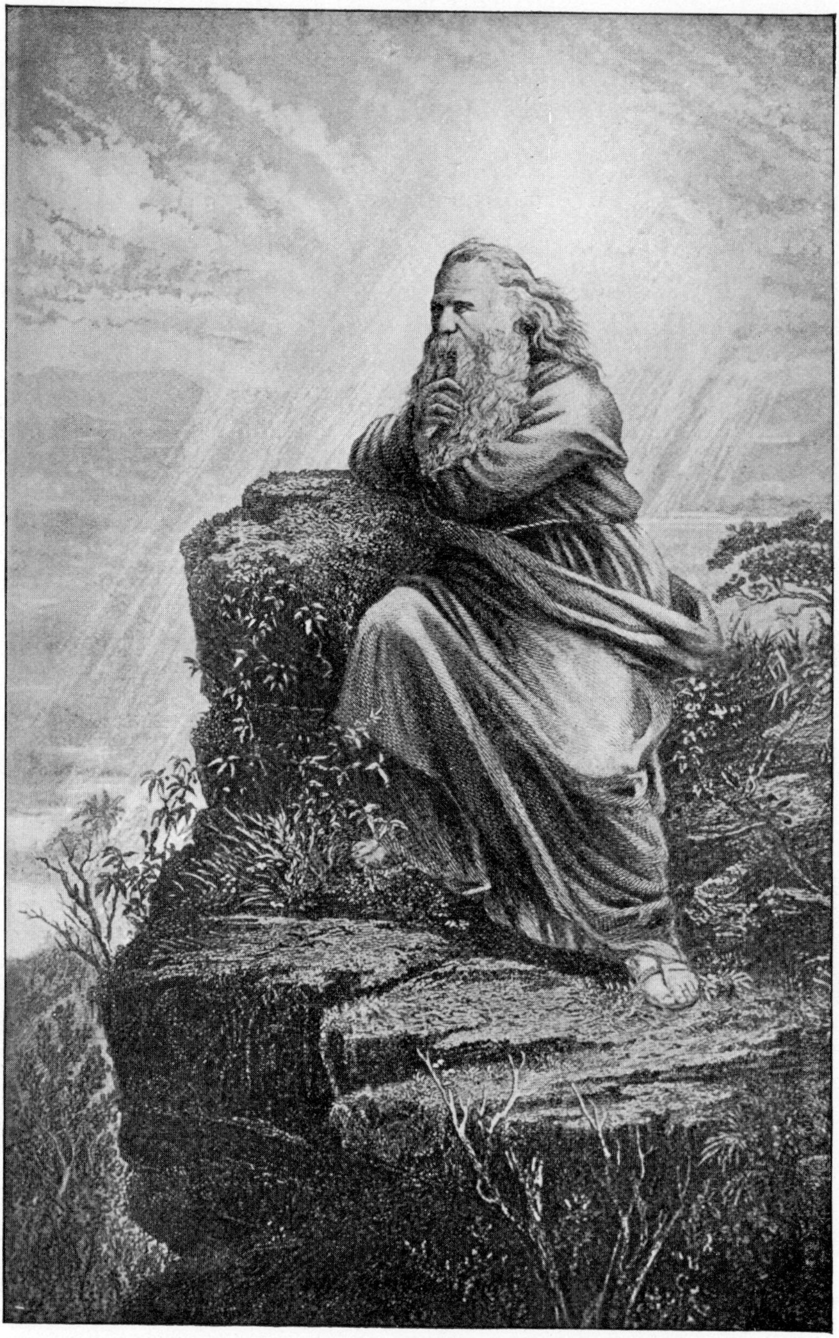

is that doth go before thee; he will be with thee, he will not fail thee, neither forsake thee: fear not, neither be dismayed.

"For this commandment which I command thee this day, it is not too hard for thee, neither is it far off. It is not in heaven, that thou shouldest say, 'Who shall go up for us to heaven, and bring it unto us, and make us to hear it, that we may do it?' Neither is it beyond the sea, that thou shouldest say, 'Who shall go over the sea for us, and bring it unto us, and make us to hear it, that we may do it?' But the word is very nigh unto thee, in thy mouth, and in thy heart, that thou mayest do it.

"See, I have set before thee this day life and good, and death and evil; in that I command thee this day to love the Lord thy God, to walk in his ways, and to keep his commandments and his statutes and his judgments, that thou mayest live and multiply, and that the Lord thy God may bless thee in the land whither thou goest in to possess it. But if thine heart turn away, and thou wilt not hear, but shalt be drawn away, and worship other gods, and serve them; I announce to you this day, that ye shall surely perish; ye shall not prolong your days upon the land, whither thou passest over Jordan to go in to possess it. I call heaven and earth to witness against you this day, that I have set before thee life and death, the blessing and the curse: therefore choose life, that thou mayest live, thou and thy families: to love the Lord thy God, to obey his voice, and to cleave unto him: for he is thy life, and the length of thy days: that thou mayest dwell in the land which the Lord swore unto thy fathers, to Abraham, to Isaac, and to Jacob, to give them."

And Moses made an end of speaking all these words to all Israel: and he said to them, "Set your heart to all the words which I testify to you this day; which ye shall command your children, to observe to do all the words of this law. For it is no vain thing for you; because it is your life, and through this thing ye shall prolong your days upon the land, whither ye go over Jordan to possess it."

And the Lord spoke to Moses that selfsame day, saying, "Get thee up into this mountain of Abarim, unto Mount Nebo, which is in the land of Moab, that is over against Jericho; and behold the land of Canaan, which I give unto the children of Israel for a possession: and die in the mount whither thou goest up; as Aaron thy brother died in Mount Hor: because ye trespassed against me in the midst of the children of Israel at the waters of Meribah of Kadesh, in the wilderness of Zin; because ye sanctified me not in the midst of the children of Israel. For thou shalt see the land before thee; but thou shalt not go thither into the land which I give the children of Israel."

And Moses went up from the plains of Moab to Mount Nebo, to the top of Pisgah, that is over against Jericho. And the Lord showed him all the land of Gilead, as far as Dan; and all Naphtali, and the land of Ephraim and Manasseh, and all the land of Judah, to the western sea; and the South, and the Plain of the valley of Jericho the city of palm trees, as far as Zoar. And the Lord said to him, "This is the land which I swore unto Abraham, unto Isaac, and unto Jacob, saying, 'I will give it unto thy family': I have caused thee to see it with thine eyes, but thou shalt not go over thither."

So Moses the servant of the Lord died there in the land of Moab, according to the word of the Lord. And He buried him in the valley in the land of Moab over against Beth-peor: but no man knoweth of his sepulcher unto this day.

And Moses was an hundred and twenty years old when he died: his eye was not dim, nor his natural force abated. And the children of Israel wept for Moses in the plains of Moab thirty days: so the days of weeping in the mourning for Moses were ended.

And there hath not arisen a prophet since in Israel like unto Moses, whom the Lord knew face to face; in all the signs and the wonders, which the Lord sent him to do in the land of Egypt, to Pharaoh, and to all his servants, and to all his land; and in all the mighty hand, and in all the great terror, which Moses wrought in the sight of all Israel.

THE BURIAL OF MOSES

By Nebo's lonely mountain,
On this side Jordan's wave,
In a vale in the land of Moab,
There lies a lonely grave.
And no man knows that sepulcher,
And no man saw it e'er,
For the angels of God upturned the sod,
And laid the dead man there.

That was the grandest funeral
That ever passed on earth;
But no man heard the trampling,
Or saw the train go forth:
Noiselessly as the daylight
Comes back when night is done,
And the crimson streak on ocean's cheek
Grows into the great sun;

Noiselessly as the spring-time
Her crown of verdure weaves,
And all the trees on all the hills
Open their thousand leaves;
So without sound of music
Or voice of them that wept,
Silently down from the mountain's crown
The great procession swept.

Perchance that bald old eagle
On gray Beth-Peor's height,
Out of his lonely eyrie
Looked on the wondrous sight:

THE GREAT CAPTAINS

Perchance the lion, stalking,
Stills shuns that hallowed spot,
For beast and bird have seen and heard
That which man knoweth not.

But when the warrior dieth,
His comrades in the war,
With arms reversed and muffled drum,
Follow his funeral car;
They show the banners taken,
They tell his battles won,
And after him lead his masterless steed,
While peals the minute-gun.

Amid the noblest of the land
We lay the sage to rest,
And give the bard an honored place,
With costly marble drest,
In the great minster transept
Where lights like glories fall,
And the organ rings and the sweet choir sings
Along the emblazoned wall.

This was the truest warrior
That ever buckled sword,
This the most gifted poet
That ever breathed a word;
And never earth's philosopher
Traced with his golden pen,
On the deathless page, truths half so sage
As he wrote down for men.

And had he not high honor,—
The hillside for a pall,
To lie in state while angels wait,
With stars for tapers tall,

And the dark rock-pines like tossing plumes
Over his bier to wave,
And God's own hand, in that lonely land,
To lay him in the grave?

In that strange grave without a name,
Whence his uncoffined clay
Shall break again, O wondrous thought!
Before the judgment day,
And stand with glory wrapt around
On the hills he never trod,
And speak of the strife that won our life
With the Incarnate Son of God.

O, lonely grave in Moab's land!
O, dark Beth-Peor's hill!
Speak to these curious hearts of ours,
And teach them to be still.
God hath his mysteries of grace,
Ways that we cannot tell;
He hides them deep, like the hidden sleep
Of him he loved so well.

—*Cecil Frances Alexander.*

JOSHUA

The Story of the Hero Whose Genius as a Warrior Won the Land of Canaan for Israel.

(The Israelites found the land of Canaan occupied by a fierce and warlike people with whom they fought many battles and waged long campaigns. The story of this warfare is filled with deeds of cruelty and violence, yet it is no more terrible than war has always been. We cannot understand why God has permitted so much suffering, but we know that in some cases at least the world has advanced in freedom through the loss and sacrifice of war. Even in war men have grown less cruel, and we may hope for the time when all war shall cease and men shall live together as brethren.)

JOSHUA IS MADE CAPTAIN OF THE HOST.

Spies Are Sent to Jericho.

Now it came to pass after the death of Moses the servant of the Lord, that the Lord spoke to Joshua the son of Nun, saying, "Moses my servant is dead; now therefore arise, go over this Jordan, thou, and all this people, to the land which I give to them, even to the children of Israel. Every place that the sole of your foot shall tread upon, to you have I given it, as I spoke to Moses. From the wilderness, and this Lebanon, even unto the great river, the river Euphrates, all the land of the Hittites, and to the great sea to the going down of the sun, shall be your border. There shall not any man be able to stand before thee all the days of thy life: as I was with Moses, so I will be with thee: I will not fail thee, nor forsake thee. Be strong and of a good courage: for thou shalt cause this people to inherit the land which I swore unto their fathers to give them. Only be strong and very courageous, to observe to do according to all the law, which Moses my servant commanded thee: turn not from it to the right hand or to the left, that thou mayest have good success whithersoever thou goest. This book of the law shall not depart out of thy mouth, but thou shalt meditate therein day and night, that thou mayest observe to do according to all that is written therein: for then thou shalt make thy way prosperous, and then thou shalt have good success. Have not I commanded thee? Be strong and of a good courage; be not affrighted, neither be thou dismayed: for the Lord thy God is with thee whithersoever thou goest."

Then Joshua commanded the officers of the people, saying, "Pass through the midst of the camp, and command the people, saying, 'Prepare you victuals; for within three days ye are to pass over this Jordan, to go in to possess the land, which the Lord your God giveth you to possess it.'"

And Joshua the son of Nun sent out of Shittim two men as spies secretly, saying, "Go view the land, and Jericho." And they went, and came into the house of a woman whose name was Rahab, and lay there. And it was told the king of Jericho, saying, "Behold, there came

MOUNDS MARKING THE SITE OF OLD JERICHO

From the road from Jerusalem to Jericho

From a photograph taken by Prof. D. G. Lyon
and used by his kind permission

Jericho, "the city of palm trees," was the only important place in the Jordan valley. In Bible times it was a beautiful and prosperous city, but now it is only a waste. Its palm trees are gone and the site is desolate. It was often conquered by the armies which passed through Palestine. After its walls fell down before Joshua's hosts, "no great man was born in Jericho ; no heroic deed was ever done in her. She never stood a siege and her inhabitants were always running away." — *Smith*

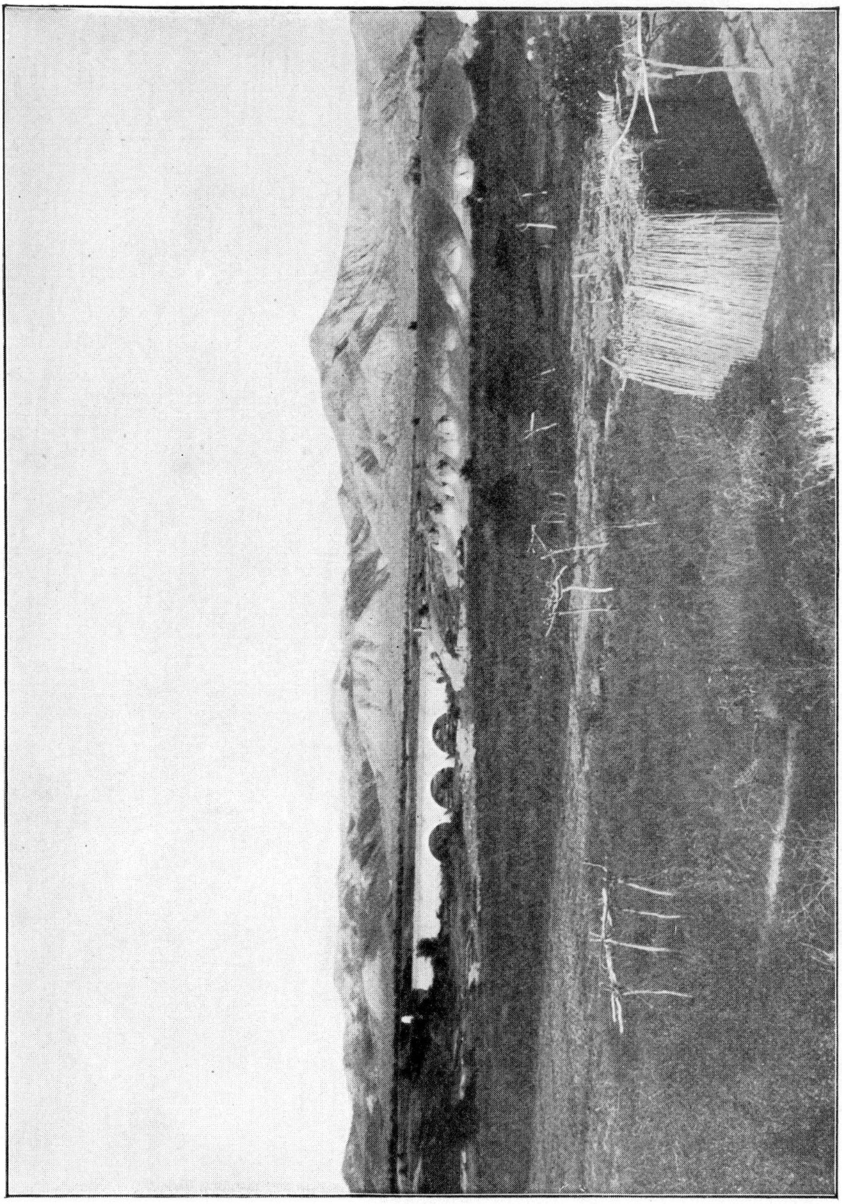

men in hither to-night of the children of Israel to search out the land."

And the king of Jericho sent to Rahab, saying, "Bring forth the men that are come to thee, which are entered into thine house: for they are come to search out all the land."

And the woman took the two men, and hid them; and she said, "Yea, the men came unto me, but I knew not whence they were: and it came to pass about the time of the shutting of the gate, when it was dark, that the men went out: whither the men went I know not: pursue after them quickly; for ye shall overtake them."

But she had brought them up to the roof, and hid them with the stalks of flax, which she had laid in order upon the roof. And the men pursued after them along the way to Jordan to the fords: and as soon as those who pursued after them were gone out, they shut the gate. And before they were laid down, she came up to them upon the roof; and she said to the men, "I know that the Lord hath given you the land, and that the fear of you is fallen upon us, and that all the inhabitants of the land melt away before you. For we have heard how the Lord dried up the water of the Red Sea before you, when ye came out of Egypt; and what ye did unto the two kings of the Amorites, that were beyond Jordan, unto Sihon and to Og, whom ye utterly destroyed. And as soon as we had heard it, our hearts melted, neither did there remain any more spirit in any man, because of you: for the Lord your God, he is God in heaven above, and on earth beneath. Now therefore, I pray you, swear unto me by the Lord, since I have dealt kindly with you, that ye also will deal kindly with my father's house, and give me a true token: and that ye will save alive my father, and my mother, and my brethren, and my sisters, and all that they have, and will deliver our lives from death."

And the men said to her, "Our life for yours, if ye speak not of this our business; and it shall be, when the Lord giveth us the land, that we will deal kindly and truly with thee."

Then she let them down by a cord through the window: for her house was upon the town wall, and she dwelt upon the wall. And she said to them, "Get you to the mountain, lest the pursuers find you; and hide yourselves there three days, until the pursuers have returned: and afterward may ye go your way."

And the men said unto her, "We will be guiltless of this thine oath which thou hast made us to swear, unless, when we come into the land, thou shalt bind this line of scarlet thread in the window which thou didst let us down by: and thou shalt gather into the house thy father, and thy mother, and thy brethren, and all thy father's household. And it shall be, that whosoever shall go out of the doors of thy house into the street, his blood shall be upon his head, and we will be guiltless: and whosoever shall be with thee in the house, his blood shall be on our head, if any hand be upon him. But if thou speak of this our business, then we will be guiltless of thine oath which thou hast made us to swear."

LOWER FORDS OF THE JORDAN

From a photograph in the possession of Rev. Louis F. Giroux
of the International College, Springfield, Mass.,
and used by his kind permission

Jordan river is a narrow, winding stream flowing down on the eastern border of the "Promised Land." When not in flood its width does not average over two hundred feet and it is rarely over five feet deep at such times; in flood it becomes in places a mile broad. It is so winding that in sixty-five miles direct course it covers a distance of two hundred miles. There are some fifty fords across the river, and in Roman times it was spanned by bridges. This picture shows the "lower fords." At this point, or near here, the Israelites crossed. "There are hundreds of other streams more large, more useful, or more beautiful; there is none which has been more spoken about by mankind"

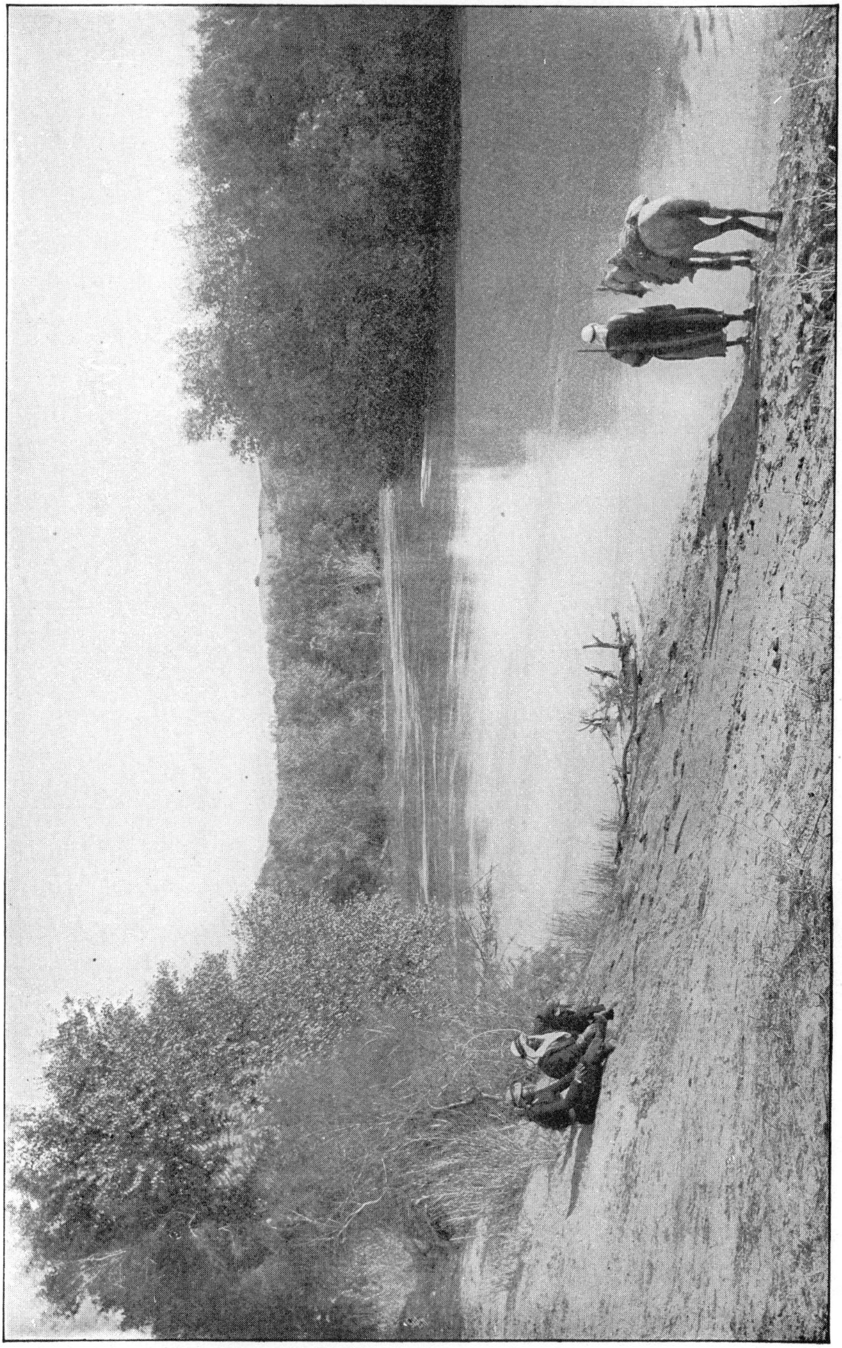

And she said, "According to your words, so be it." And she sent them away, and they departed: and she bound the scarlet line in the window.

And they went, and came to the mountain, and hid there three days, until the pursuers were returned: and the pursuers sought them throughout all the way, but found them not. Then the two men returned, and descended from the mountain, and passed over, and came to Joshua the son of Nun; and they told him all that had befallen them. And they said unto Joshua, "Truly the Lord hath delivered into our hands all the land; and moreover all the inhabitants of the land do melt away before us."

THE PASSAGE OF THE JORDAN.

The Israelites Leave the Jordan Behind Them as **They Left** *the Red Sea.*

And Joshua rose up early in the morning, and they marched from Shittim, and came to Jordan, he and all the children of Israel; and they lodged there before they passed over. And it came to pass after three days, that the officers went through the midst of the camp; and they commanded the people, saying, "When ye see the ark of the covenant of the Lord your God, and the priests the Levites bearing it, then ye shall advance from your place, and go after it. Yet there shall be a space between you and it, about two thousand cubits by measure: come not near unto it, that ye may know the way by which ye must go; for ye have not passed this way heretofore."

And Joshua said to the people, "Sanctify yourselves: for to-morrow the Lord will do wonders among you."

And Joshua spoke to the priests, saying, "Take up the ark of the covenant, and pass over before the people." And they took up the ark of the covenant, and went before the people.

And the Lord said to Joshua, "This day will I begin to magnify thee in the sight of all Israel, that they may know that, as I was with Moses, so I will be with thee. And thou shalt command the priests that bear the ark of the covenant, saying, 'When ye are come to the brink of the waters of Jordan, ye shall stand still in Jordan.'"

And Joshua said unto the children of Israel, "Come hither, and hear the words of the Lord your God."

And Joshua said, "Hereby ye shall know that the living God is among you, and that he will without fail drive out from before you the Canaanite, and all the people of the land. Behold, the ark of the covenant of the Lord of all the earth passeth over before you into Jordan. Now therefore take you twelve men out of the tribes of Israel, for every tribe a man. And it shall come to pass, when the soles of the feet of the priests that bear the ark of the Lord, the Lord of all the earth, shall rest in the waters of Jordan, that the waters of Jordan shall be cut off, even the waters that come down from above; and they shall stand in one heap."

And it came to pass, when the people removed from their tents, to pass over Jordan, the priests that bore the ark of the covenant being before the people; and when they that bore the ark were come to Jordan, and the feet of the priests that bore the ark were dipped in the brink of the water (for Jordan overfloweth all its banks all the time of harvest), that the waters which came down from above stood, and rose up in one heap, a great way off, at Adam, the city that is beside Zarethan: and those that went down toward the Salt Sea were wholly cut off: and the people passed over right opposite Jericho.

And the priests that bore the ark of the covenant of the Lord stood firm on dry ground in the midst of Jordan, and all Israel passed over on dry ground, until all the nation were passed wholly over Jordan.

SIEGE AND CAPTURE OF JERICHO.
How the Walls of the City Fell Down.

And it came to pass, when Joshua was by Jericho, that he lifted up his eyes and looked, and, behold, there stood a man over against him with his sword drawn in his hand: and Joshua went to him, and said to him, "Art thou for us, or for our adversaries?"

And he said, "Nay; but as captain of the host of the Lord am I now come."

And Joshua fell on his face to the earth, and worshiped, and said to him, "What saith my Lord to his servant?" And the captain of the Lord's host said to Joshua, "Put off thy shoe from off thy foot; for the place whereon thou standest is holy."

And Joshua did so.

(Now Jericho was closely besieged by the children

of Israel: none went out, and none came in.) And the Lord said to Joshua, "See, I have given into thine hand Jericho, and the king thereof, and the mighty men of valor. And ye shall march around the city, all the men of war, going about the city once. Thus shalt thou do six days. And seven priests shall bear seven trumpets of rams' horns before the ark: and the seventh day ye shall march around the city seven times, and the priests shall blow the trumpets. And it shall be, that when they make a long blast with the ram's horn, and when ye hear the sound of the trumpet, all the people shall shout with a great shout; and the wall of the city shall fall down flat, and the people shall go up every man straight before him."

And Joshua the son of Nun called the priests, and said unto them, "Take up the ark of the covenant, and let seven priests bear seven trumpets of rams' horns before the ark of the Lord."

And they said unto the people, "Pass on, and march around the city, and let the armed men pass on before the ark of the Lord."

And it was so, that when Joshua had spoken unto the people, the seven priests bearing the seven trumpets of rams' horns before the Lord passed on, and blew the trumpets: and the ark of the covenant of the Lord followed them. And the armed men went before the priests that blew the trumpets, and the rear guard went after the ark, the priests blowing the trumpets as they went.

THE PLAIN OF JERICHO, LOOKING TOWARD THE JORDAN
FROM THE HILLS TO THE WEST

From a photograph taken by Prof. H. G. Mitchell
and used by his kind permission

A view of the Jordan plain, showing the desolate nature of the country

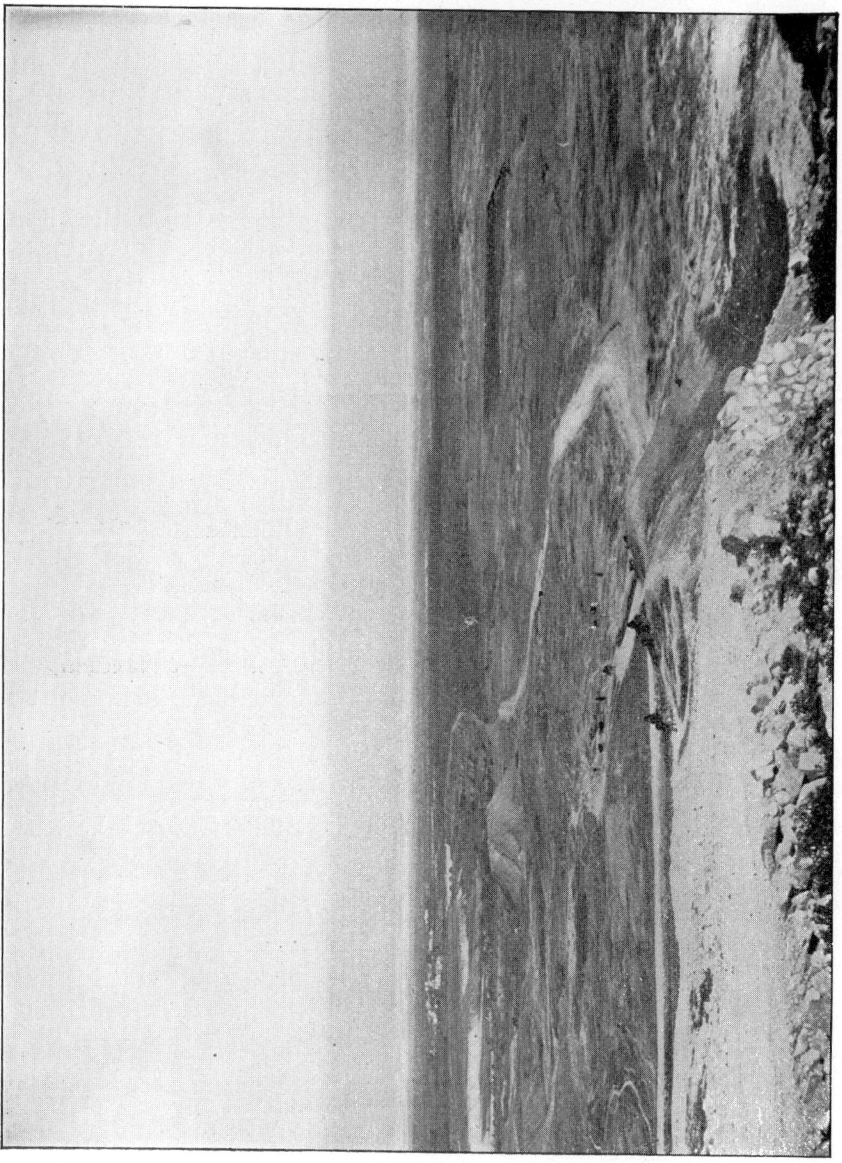

And Joshua commanded the people, saying, "Ye shall not shout, nor let your voice be heard, neither shall any word proceed out of your mouth, until the day I bid you shout; then shall ye shout."

So he caused the ark of the Lord to pass around the city, going about it once: and they came into the camp, and lodged in the camp.

And Joshua rose early in the morning, and the priests took up the ark of the Lord. And the seven priests bearing the seven trumpets of rams' horns before the ark of the Lord went on continually, and blew the trumpets: and the armed men went before them; and the rear guard came after the ark of the Lord, the priests blowing the trumpets as they went.

And the second day they marched around the city once, and returned into the camp: so they did six days. And it came to pass on the seventh day, that they rose early at the dawning of the day, and marched around the city after the same manner seven times. And it came to pass at the seventh time, when the priests blew the trumpets, Joshua said to the people, "Shout! for the Lord hath given you the city. And the city shall be devoted, even it and all that is therein, to the Lord: only Rahab shall live, she and all that are with her in the house, because she hid the messengers that we sent. And ye, be sure to keep yourselves from the devoted thing, lest when ye have devoted it, ye take of the devoted thing; so should ye make the camp of Israel accursed, and trouble it. But all the silver, and gold, and vessels of brass and iron, are holy unto the Lord: they shall come into the treasury of the Lord."

So the people shouted, and the priests blew the trumpets: and it came to pass, when the people heard the sound of the trumpet, that the people shouted with a great shout, and the wall fell down flat, so that the people went up into the city, every man straight before him, and they took the city. And they utterly destroyed all that was in the city, both man and woman, both young and old, and ox, and sheep, and ass, with the edge of the sword.

And Joshua said unto the two men that had spied out the land, "Go into Rahab's house, and bring out thence the woman, and all that she hath, as ye swore unto her." And the young men who were the spies went in, and brought out Rahab, and her father, and her mother, and her brethren, and all that she had, all her kindred also they brought out; and they set them without the camp of Israel.

And they burnt the city with fire, and all that was therein: only the silver, and the gold, and the vessels of brass and of iron, they put into the treasury of the house of the Lord.

But Rahab and her father's household, and all that she had, did Joshua save alive; and she dwelt in the midst of Israel, to this day; because she hid the messengers, which Joshua sent to spy out Jericho.

THE FALL OF JERICHO

Sound, sound for ever, Clarions of Thought!
When Joshua 'gainst the high-walled city fought,
He marched around it with his banners high.
His troops in serried order following nigh.
But not a sword was drawn, no shaft outsprang,
Only the trumpets the shrill onset rang.
At the first blast, smiled scornfully the king,
And at the second sneered, half wonderingly:
"Hop'st thou with noise my stronghold to break down?"
At the third round, the ark of old renown
Swept forward, still the trumpets sounding loud,
And then the troops with ensigns waving proud.
Stepped out upon the old walls children dark
With horns to mock the notes and hoot the ark.

At the fourth turn, braving the Israelites,
Women appeared upon the crenelated heights—
Those battlements embrowned with age and rust—
And hurled upon the Hebrews stones and dust,
And spun and sang when weary of the game.
At the fifth circuit came the blind and lame,
And with wild uproar clamorous and high
Railed at the clarion ringing to the sky.
At the sixth time, upon a tower's tall crest,
So high that there the eagle built his nest,
So hard that on it lightning lit in vain,
Appeared in merriment the king again:
"These Hebrew Jews musicians are, me-seems!"
He scoffed, loud laughing, "but they live on dreams."
The princes laughed, submissive to the king,
Laughed all the courtiers in their glittering ring,
And thence the laughter spread through all the town.
At the seventh blast—the city walls fell down.

—Victor Hugo.

THE ATTACK UPON AI.

The Story of a Rout and an Ambush. Defeat Turned to Victory.

(The spoil of the city of Jericho was "devoted," that is offered to the Lord, and could be the private property of no person. How the greed of one soldier got the better of him, the evil consequences, the execution of the guilty soldier for disobedience of military orders, and the subsequent victory of the Israelites are told in the following chapter.)

But the children of Israel committed a trespass in the devoted thing: for Achan, of the tribe of Judah, took of the devoted thing: and the anger of the Lord was kindled against the children of Israel.

And Joshua sent men from Jericho to Ai, which is beside Beth-aven, on the east side of Beth-el, and spoke unto them, saying, "Go up and spy out the land." And the men went up and spied out Ai.

And they returned to Joshua, and said unto him, "Let not all the people go up, but let about two or three thousand men go up and smite Ai; make not all the people to toil thither; for they are but few."

So there went up thither of the people about three thousand men: and they fled before the men of Ai. And the men of Ai smote of them about thirty and six men: and they chased them from before the gate even unto Shebarim, and smote them at the descent: and the hearts of the people melted, and became as water. And Joshua rent his clothes, and fell to the earth upon his face before the ark of the Lord until the evening, he and the elders of Israel; and they put dust upon their heads.

And Joshua said, "Alas, O Lord God, wherefore hast thou at all brought this people over Jordan, to deliver us into the hand of the Amorites, to cause us to perish? would that we had been content and dwelt beyond Jordan! O Lord, what shall I say, after Israel hath turned their backs before their enemies! For the Canaanites and all the inhabitants of the land shall hear of it, and shall surround us round, and cut off our name from the earth: and what wilt thou do for thy great name?"

And the Lord said unto Joshua, "Get thee up; wherefore art thou thus fallen upon thy face? Israel hath sinned; yea, they have even transgressed my covenant which I commanded them: yea, they have even taken of the devoted thing; and have also stolen, and lied also, and they have even put it among their own goods. Therefore the children of Israel cannot stand before their enemies, they turn their backs before their enemies, because they are become accursed: I will not be with you any more, except ye destroy the devoted thing from among you. Up, sanctify the people, and say, 'Sanctify yourselves against to-morrow: for thus saith the Lord, the God of Israel, There is a devoted thing in the midst of thee, O Israel: thou canst not stand before thine enemies, until ye take away the devoted thing from among you. In the morning therefore ye shall be brought near by your tribes: and it shall be, that the tribe which the Lord taketh shall come near by families; and the family which the Lord shall take shall come near by households; and the household which the Lord shall take shall come near man by man. And it shall be, that he that is taken with the devoted thing shall be burnt with fire, he and all that he hath: because he hath transgressed the covenant of the Lord, and because he hath wrought folly in Israel.'"

So Joshua rose up early in the morning, and brought Israel near by their tribes; and the tribe of Judah was taken: and he brought near the family of Judah; and he took the family of the Zerahites: and he brought near the family of the Zerahites man by man; and Zabdi was taken: and he brought near his household man by man; and Achan was taken. And Joshua said unto Achan, "My son, give, I pray thee, glory to the Lord, the God of Israel, and make confession to him; and tell me now what thou hast done; hide it not from me."

And Achan answered Joshua, and said, "Of a truth I have sinned against the Lord, the God of Israel, and thus and thus have I done: when I saw among the spoil a goodly Babylonish mantle, and two hundred shekels of silver, and a wedge of gold of fifty shekels weight, then I coveted them, and took them; and, behold, they are hid in the earth in the midst of my tent, and the silver under it."

So Joshua sent messengers, and they ran unto the tent; and, behold, it was hid in his tent, and the silver under it. And they took them from the midst of the tent, and brought them to Joshua, and to all the children of Israel; and they laid them down before the Lord. And Joshua, and all Israel with him, took Achan the son of Zerah, and the silver, and the mantle, and the wedge of gold, and his sons, and his daughters, and his oxen, and his asses, and his sheep, and his tent, and all that he had: and they brought them up unto the valley of Achor.

And Joshua said, "Why hast thou troubled us? the Lord shall trouble thee this day."

And all Israel stoned him with stones; and they burned them with fire, and stoned them with stones. And they raised over him a great heap of stones, to this day; and the Lord turned from the fierceness of his anger. Wherefore the name of that place was called, The valley of Achor (that is, troubling), unto this day.

And the Lord said unto Joshua, "Fear not, neither be thou dismayed: take all the people of war with thee, and arise, go up to Ai: see, I have given into thy hand the king of Ai, and his people, and his city, and his land: and thou shalt do to Ai and her king as thou didst unto Jericho and her king: only the spoil thereof, and the cattle thereof, shall ye take for a prey unto yourselves: set thee an ambush for the city behind it."

So Joshua arose, and all the people of war, to go up to Ai: and Joshua chose out thirty thousand men, the mighty men of valor, and sent them forth by night. And he commanded them, saying, "Behold, ye shall lie in ambush against the city, behind the city: go not very far from the city, but be ye all ready: and I, and all the people that are with me, will approach unto the city: and it shall come to pass, when they come out against us, as at the first, that we will flee before them; and they will come out after us, till we have drawn them away from the city; for they will say, 'They flee before us, as at the first'; so we will flee before them: and ye shall rise up from the ambush, and take possession of the city: for the Lord your God will deliver it into your hand. And it shall be, when ye have seized upon the city, that ye shall set the city on fire; according to the word of the Lord shall ye do: see, I have commanded you."

And Joshua sent them forth: and they went to the ambushment, and took their place between Beth-el and Ai, on the west side of Ai: but Joshua camped that night among the people.

And Joshua rose up early in the morning, and mustered the people, and went up, he and the elders of Israel, before the people to Ai. And all the people, even the men of war that were with him, went up, and drew nigh, and came before the city, to the north side of Ai: now there was a valley between him and Ai. And he took about five thousand men, and set them in ambush between Beth-el and Ai, on the west side of the city. So they set the people, even all the host that was on the north of the city, and their liers in wait that were on the west of the city; and Joshua went that night into the midst of the vale. And it came to pass, when the king of Ai saw it, that they hasted and rose up early, and the men of the city went out against Israel to battle, he and all his people, at the time appointed, before the valley; but he knew not that there was an ambush against him behind the city.

And Joshua and all Israel pretended that they were beaten before them, and fled by the way of the wilderness. And all the people that were in the city were called together to pursue after them: and they pursued after Joshua, and were drawn away from the city. And there was not a man left in Ai or Beth-el, that went not out after Israel: and they left the city open, and pursued after Israel. And the Lord said unto Joshua, "Stretch out the javelin that is in thy hand toward Ai; for I will give it into thine hand."

And Joshua stretched out the javelin that was in his hand toward the city. And the ambush arose quickly out of their place, and they ran as soon as he had stretched out his hand, and entered into the city, and took it; and they hasted and set the city on fire. And when the men of Ai looked behind them, they saw, and, behold, the smoke of the city ascended up to heaven, and they had no power to flee this way or that way: and the people that fled to the wilderness turned back upon the pursuers. And when Joshua and all Israel saw that the ambush had taken the city, and that the smoke of the city ascended, then they turned again and slew the men of Ai. And the others came forth out of the city against them; so they were in the midst of Israel, some on this side, and some on that side: and they smote them, so that they let none of them remain or escape.

And the king of Ai they took alive, and brought him to Joshua. And it came to pass, when Israel had made an end of slaying all the inhabitants of Ai in the field, in the wilderness wherein they pursued them, and they were all fallen by the edge of the sword, until they were consumed, that all Israel returned unto Ai, and smote it with the edge of the sword. And all that fell that day, both of men and women, were twelve thousand, even all the men of Ai. For Joshua drew not back his hand, wherewith he stretched out the javelin, until he had utterly destroyed all the inhabitants of Ai. Only the cattle and the spoil of that city Israel took for a prey to themselves, according to the word of the Lord which he commanded Joshua. So Joshua burnt Ai, and made it an heap for ever, even a desolation, unto this day.

THE SUBMISSION OF GIBEON.

How a Timid People Used a Successful Trick.

And it came to pass, when all the kings which were beyond Jordan, in the hill country, and in the lowland, and on all the shore of the great sea in front of Lebanon, heard of this, they gathered themselves together, to fight with Joshua and with Israel, with one accord.

But when the inhabitants of Gibeon heard what Joshua had done unto Jericho and to Ai, they were very cunning, and they pretended to be ambassadors, and took old sacks upon their asses, and wine skins, old and rent and bound up; and shoes old and patched upon their feet, and old garments upon them; and all the bread of their provision was dry and was become mouldy. And they went to Joshua to the camp at Gilgal, and said to him, and to the men of Israel, "We are come from a far country: now therefore make ye a covenant with us."

And the men of Israel said unto the Gibeonites, "Perhaps

ye dwell among us; and how shall we make a covenant with you?"

And they said to Joshua, "We are thy servants."

And Joshua said to them, "Who are ye? and from whence come ye?"

And they said unto him, "From a very far country thy servants are come because of the name of the Lord thy God: for we have heard the fame of him, and all that he did in Egypt, and all that he did to the two kings of the Amorites, that were beyond Jordan, to Sihon king of Heshbon, and to Og king of Bashan. And our elders and all the inhabitants of our country spoke to us, saying, 'Take provision in your hand for the journey, and go to meet them, and say unto them, We are your servants: and now make ye a covenant with us.' This bread we took hot for our provision out of our houses on the day we came forth to go to you; but now, behold, it is dry, and is become mouldy: and these wine skins, which we filled, were new; and, behold, they are rent: and these garments and our shoes are become old by reason of the very long journey."

And the men took of their provision, and asked not counsel at the mouth of the Lord.

And Joshua made peace with them, and made a covenant with them, to let them live: and the princes of the congregation swore unto them. And it came to pass at the end of three days after they had made a covenant with them, that they heard that they were their neighbors, and that they dwelt among them. And the children of Israel journeyed, and came to their cities on the third day. And the children of Israel smote them not, because the princes of the host had sworn unto them by the Lord, the God of Israel. And all the host murmured against the princes. But all the princes said unto all the host, "We have sworn unto them by the Lord, the God of Israel: now therefore we may not touch them. This we will do to them, and let them live; lest wrath be upon us, because of the oath which we swore unto them." And the princes said unto them, "Let them live: so they become hewers of wood and drawers of water to all the people;" as the princes had spoken unto them.

And Joshua called for them, and he spoke unto them, saying, "Wherefore have ye tricked us, saying, 'We are very far from you'; when ye dwell among us? Now therefore ye are cursed, and there shall never fail to be of you bondmen, both hewers of wood and drawers of water for the house of my God."

And they answered Joshua, and said, "Because it was certainly told thy servants how that the Lord thy God commanded his servant Moses to give you all the land, and to destroy all the inhabitants of the land from before you; therefore we were sore afraid for our lives because of you, and have done this thing. And now, behold, we are in thine hand: as it seemeth good and right unto thee to do to us, do."

And so did he to them, and delivered them out of the hand of the children of Israel, that they slew them not. And Joshua made them that day hewers of wood and drawers of water for the people, and for the altar

A PORTION OF THE RIDGE BY WHICH THE ROAD RAN EASTWARD
FROM UPPER BETH-HORON

From a photograph taken by Prof. H. G. Mitchell
and used by his kind permission

This road along the ridge was one of the important highways of the East. Throughout history we see hosts swarming up this avenue or swept down it in flight. Here Joshua fought his famous fight with the five kings. Here Judas Maccabæus won a great battle with the Syrians (see Tales of the Maccabees, Vol. III.). Joshua in his battle drove the Canaanites over the ridge and then cut them to pieces in the ravine on the other side

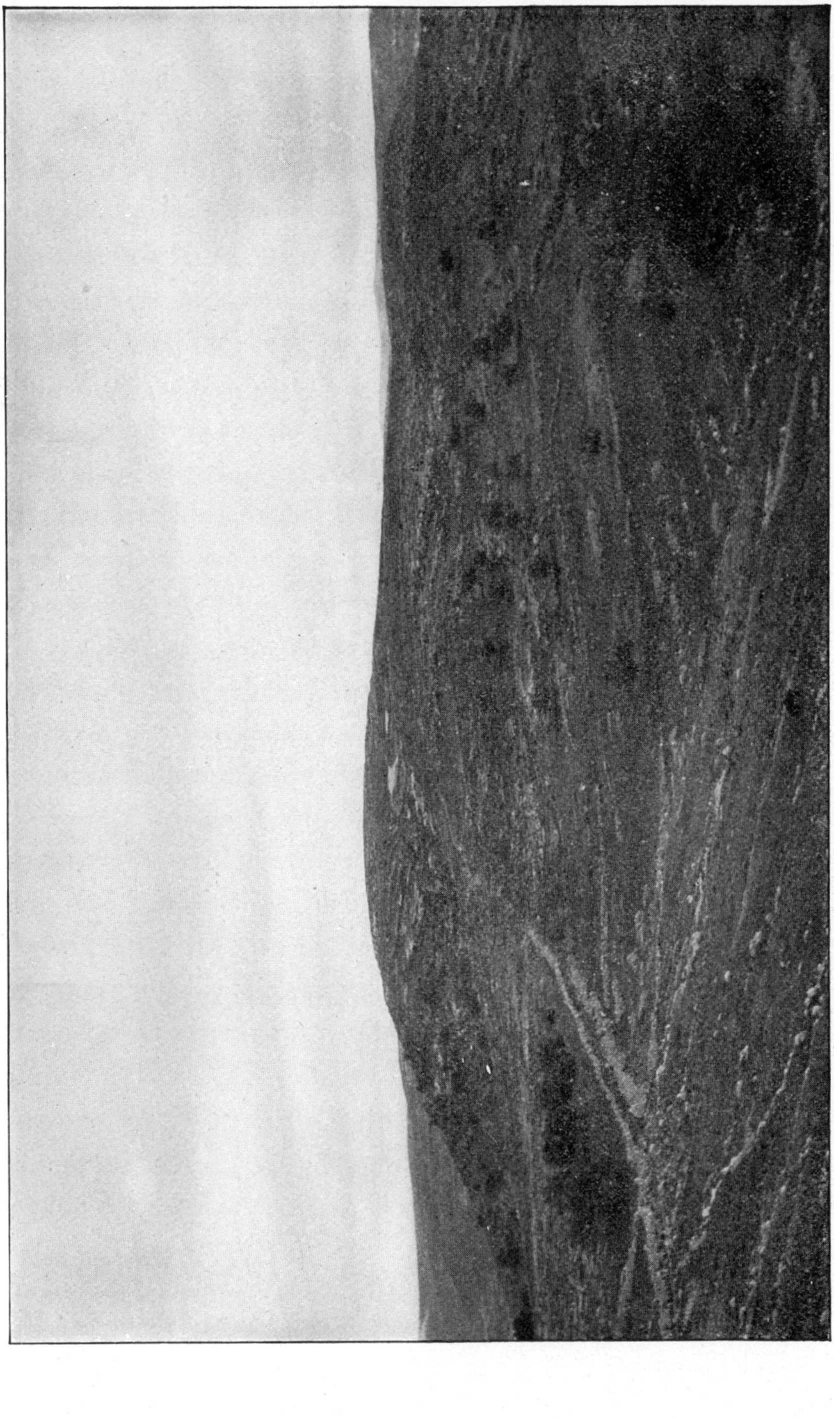

of the Lord, to this day, in the place which he should choose.

THE BATTLE WITH THE FIVE KINGS.
How Joshua Won a Great Fight.

Now it came to pass, when Adoni-zedek king of Jerusalem heard how Joshua had taken Ai, and had utterly destroyed it; as he had done to Jericho and her king, so he had done to Ai and her king; and how the inhabitants of Gibeon had made peace with Israel, and were among them; that they feared greatly, because Gibeon was a great city, as one of the royal cities, and because it was greater than Ai, and all the men thereof were mighty. Wherefore Adoni-zedek king of Jerusalem sent unto Hoham king of Hebron, and unto Piram king of Jarmuth, and unto Japhia king of Lachish, and unto Debir king of Eglon, saying, "Come up to me, and help me, and let us smite Gibeon: for it hath made peace with Joshua and with the children of Israel."

Therefore the five kings of the Amorites, the king of Jerusalem, the king of Hebron, the king of Jarmuth, the king of Lachish, the king of Eglon, gathered themselves together, and went up, they and all their hosts, and encamped against Gibeon, and made war against it. And the men of Gibeon sent unto Joshua to the camp to Gilgal, saying, "Desert not thy servants; come up to us quickly, and save us, and help us: for all the kings of the Amorites that dwell in the hill country are gathered together against us."

So Joshua went up from Gilgal, he, and all the people

of war with him, and all the mighty men of valor. And the Lord said to Joshua, "Fear them not: for I have delivered them into thine hands; there shall not a man of them stand before thee."

Joshua therefore came upon them suddenly; for he went up from Gilgal, marching all the night. And the Lord discomfited them before Israel, and he slew them with a great slaughter at Gibeon, and chased them by the way of the ascent to Beth-horon, and smote them to Azekah, and unto Makkedah. And it came to pass, as they fled from before Israel, while they were in the descent of Beth-horon, that the Lord cast down great hailstones from heaven upon them, and they died: they were more who died with the hailstones than they whom the children of Israel slew with the sword.

Then spoke Joshua to the Lord in the day when the Lord delivered up the Amorites before the children of Israel; and he said in the sight of Israel,—

"Sun, stand thou still upon Gibeon;
And thou, Moon, in the valley of Aijalon."
And the sun stood still, and the moon stayed,
Until the nation had avenged themselves of their enemies.

Is not this written in the book of Jashar? And the sun stayed in the midst of heaven, and hasted not to go down about a whole day. And there was no day like that before it or after it, that the Lord hearkened unto the voice of a man: for the Lord fought for Israel.

And these five kings fled, and hid themselves in the cave at Makkedah. And it was told Joshua, saying, "The five kings are found, hidden in the cave at Makkedah." And Joshua said, "Roll great stones unto the mouth of the cave, and set men by it to keep them: but stay not ye; pursue after your enemies, and smite the hindmost of them; suffer them not to enter into their cities: for the Lord your God hath delivered them into your hand."

And it came to pass, when Joshua and the children of Israel had made an end of slaying them with a very great slaughter, till they were consumed, and the remnant which remained of them had entered into the fortified cities, that all the people returned to the camp to Joshua at Makkedah in peace: none moved his tongue against any of the children of Israel. Then said Joshua, "Open the mouth of the cave, and bring forth those five kings to me out of the cave."

And they did so, and brought forth those five kings to him out of the cave, the king of Jerusalem, the king of Hebron, the king of Jarmuth, the king of Lachish, the king of Eglon. And it came to pass, when they brought forth those kings to Joshua, that Joshua called for all the men of Israel, and said to the chiefs of the men of war which went with him, "Come near, put your feet upon the necks of these kings."

And they came near, and put their feet upon the necks of them.

And Joshua said unto them, "Fear not, nor be dismayed; be strong and of good courage: for thus shall the Lord do to all your enemies against whom ye fight."

And afterward Joshua smote them and put them to death, and hung them on five trees: and they were hanging upon the trees until the evening. And it came to pass at the time of the going down of the sun, that Joshua commanded, and they took them down off the trees, and cast them into the cave wherein they had hidden themselves, and laid great stones on the mouth of the cave, to this very day.

THE LAST ADDRESSES OF JOSHUA TO THE PEOPLE.
Words of Warning and Advice.

And it came to pass after many days, when the Lord had given rest unto Israel from all their enemies round about, and Joshua was old; that Joshua called for all Israel, for their elders and for their heads, and for their judges and for their officers, and said to them, "I am old and well stricken in years: and we have seen all that the Lord your God hath done unto all these nations because of you; for the Lord your God, he it is that hath fought for you.

"Therefore be ye very courageous to keep and to do all that is written in the book of the law of Moses, that ye turn not aside therefrom to the right hand or to the left; that ye come not among these nations, these that remain among you; neither make mention of the name of their gods, nor cause to swear by them, neither serve them, nor bow down yourselves to them; but be loyal to the Lord your God, as ye have done unto this day.

AN OLD TOMB AT TIMNEH, CALLED THE TOMB OF JOSHUA

From a photograph of the Palestine Exploration Fund
and used by special permission

This is a good example of the rock-hewn tombs of Palestine. It is tradition only which calls it the resting place of the great captain

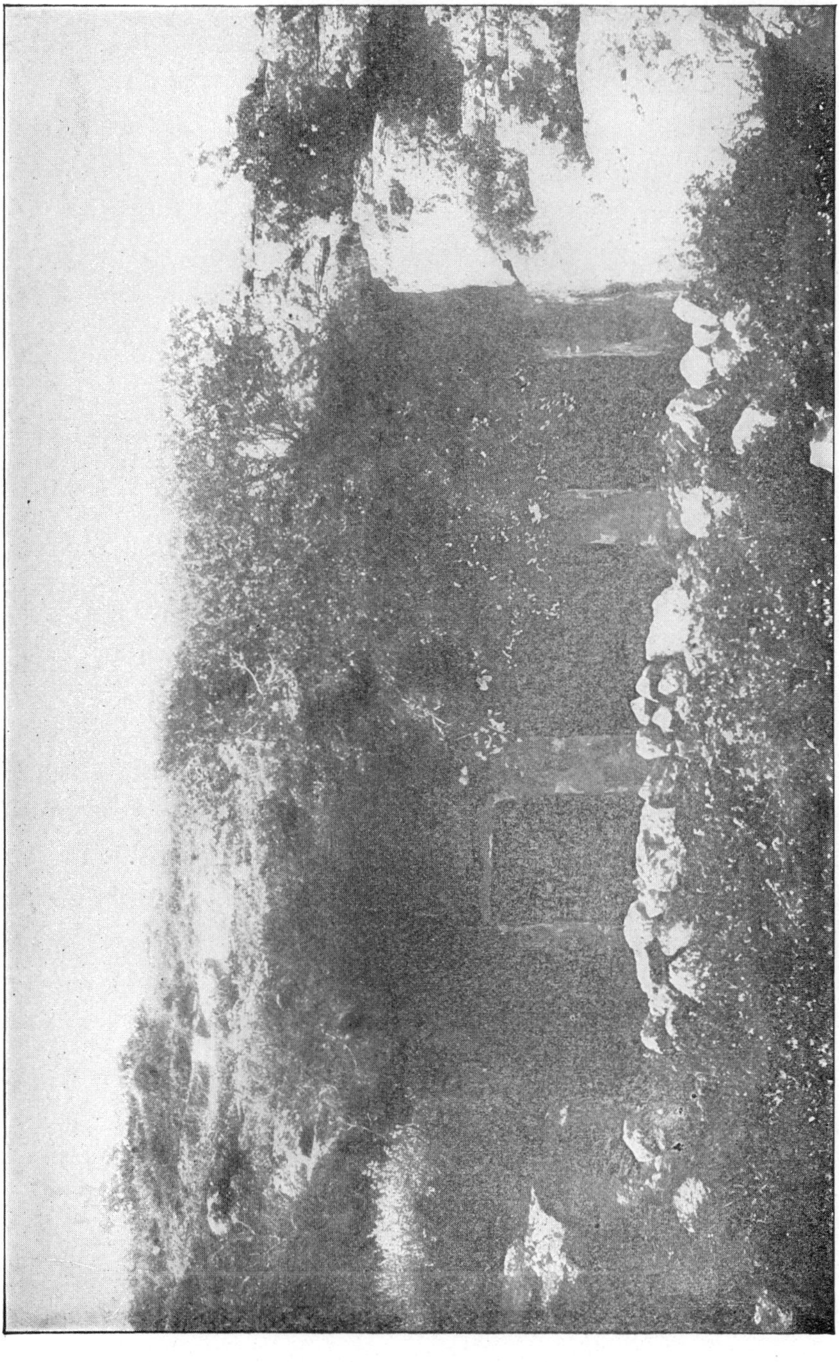

"For the Lord hath driven out from before you great nations and strong: but as for you, no man hath stood before you unto this day. One man of you shall chase a thousand; for the Lord your God, he it is that fighteth for you, as he spoke unto you. Take good heed therefore unto yourselves, that ye love the Lord your God."

And Joshua gathered all the tribes of Israel to Shechem, and called for the elders of Israel, and for their heads, and for their judges, and for their officers; and they presented themselves before God.

And Joshua said unto all the people, "Thus saith the Lord, the God of Israel, 'Fear the Lord, and serve him in sincerity and in truth; and put away the gods which your fathers served beyond the River, and in Egypt; and serve ye the Lord.' And if it seem evil to you to serve the Lord, choose you this day whom ye will serve; whether the gods which your fathers served that were beyond the River, or the gods of the Amorites, in whose land ye dwell: but as for me and my house, we will serve the Lord."

And the people answered and said, "Far be it from us that we should forsake the Lord, to serve other gods; for the Lord our God, he it is that brought us and our fathers up out of the land of Egypt, from the house of bondage, and that did those great signs in our sight, and preserved us in all the way wherein we went, and among all the peoples through the midst of whom we passed; and the Lord drove out from before us all the peoples, even the Amorites that dwelt in the land: therefore we also will serve the Lord; for he is our God."

And Joshua said unto the people, "Ye are not able to serve the Lord; for he is a holy God; he is a jealous God; he will not forgive your transgression nor your sins. If ye forsake the Lord, and serve foreign gods, then he will turn and do you evil, and consume you, after that he hath done you good."

And the people said unto Joshua, "Nay; but we will serve the Lord."

And Joshua said unto the people, "Ye are witnesses against yourselves that ye have chosen you the Lord, to serve him."

And they said, "We are witnesses."

THE DEATH OF JOSHUA.

The Great Captain Is Laid at Rest.

And after many years of fighting, and many victories, Joshua the son of Nun, the servant of the Lord, died, being an hundred and ten years old. And they buried him in the border of his inheritance in Timnath-serah, which is in the hill country of Ephraim, on the north of the mountain of Gaash. And Israel served the Lord all the days of Joshua, and all the days of the elders that outlived Joshua, and had known all the work of the Lord, that he had wrought for Israel.

The Judges

After the death of Joshua there followed a long period of unrest and fighting. The land was by no means conquered. Many times the Israelites were oppressed by the neighboring people, and all but wiped out of existence. But each time a hero arose who overthrew the oppressor, and became the leader or judge, as the office was called, of the people. These leaders were not all of the highest character, but they served to hold the nation together, and to preserve it from extinction, during this period of trouble and unrest.

EHUD

The Story of the Young Man Who Killed a King.

And the children of Israel again did that which was evil in the sight of the Lord: and the Lord strengthened Eglon the king of Moab against Israel, because they had done that which was evil in the sight of the Lord. And he gathered to him the children of Ammon and Amalek; and he went and smote Israel, and they possessed the city of palm trees (that is, Jericho). And the children of Israel served Eglon the king of Moab eighteen years. But when the children of Israel cried unto the Lord, the Lord raised them up a saviour, Ehud the son of Gera, the Benjamite, a left-handed man: and the children of Israel sent a present by him unto Eglon the king of Moab. And Ehud made him a sword which had two edges, of a cubit length; and he girded it under his raiment upon his right thigh. And he offered the present unto Eglon king of Moab: now Eglon was a very fat man. And when he had made an end of offering the present, he sent away the people that bore the present. But he himself turned back from the quarries that were by Gilgal, and said, "I have a secret errand unto thee, O king."

And he said, "Keep silence." And all that stood by him went out from him. And Ehud came to him; and he was sitting by himself alone in his summer room.

And Ehud said, "I have a message from God to thee." And he arose out of his seat.

And Ehud put forth his left hand, and took the sword from his right thigh, and thrust it into his body: and the haft also went in after the blade; and the fat closed upon the blade, for he drew not the sword out of his body; and it came out behind. Then Ehud went forth into the porch, and shut the doors of the room upon him, and locked them. Now when he was gone out, his servants came; and they saw, and, behold, the doors of the room were locked.

And they tarried till they were ashamed: and, behold, he opened not the doors of the room; therefore they took the key, and opened them: and, behold, their lord was fallen down dead on the earth.

And Ehud escaped while they tarried, and passed beyond the quarries, and escaped to Seirah.

And it came to pass, when he was come, that he blew a trumpet in the hill country of Ephraim, and the children of Israel went down with him from the hill country, and he before them. And he said unto them, "Follow after me: for the Lord hath delivered your enemies the Moabites into your hand."

And they went down after him, and took the fords of Jordan against the Moabites, and suffered not a man to pass over. And they smote of Moab at that time about ten thousand men, every strong man, and every man of valor; and there escaped not a man. So Moab was subdued that day under the hand of Israel. And the land had rest fourscore years.

A CAMP IN THE DESERT

The black tents of the Arabs on the desert sands

From a photograph belonging to Mr. S. E. Bridgman
and used by his kind permission

"The Midianites came up with their cattle and their tents, they came in as locusts for multitude; both they and their camels were without number: and they came into the land to destroy it." This is no doubt just the way in which the camps of the Midianites looked in the old days when they raided the farms of the Israelites

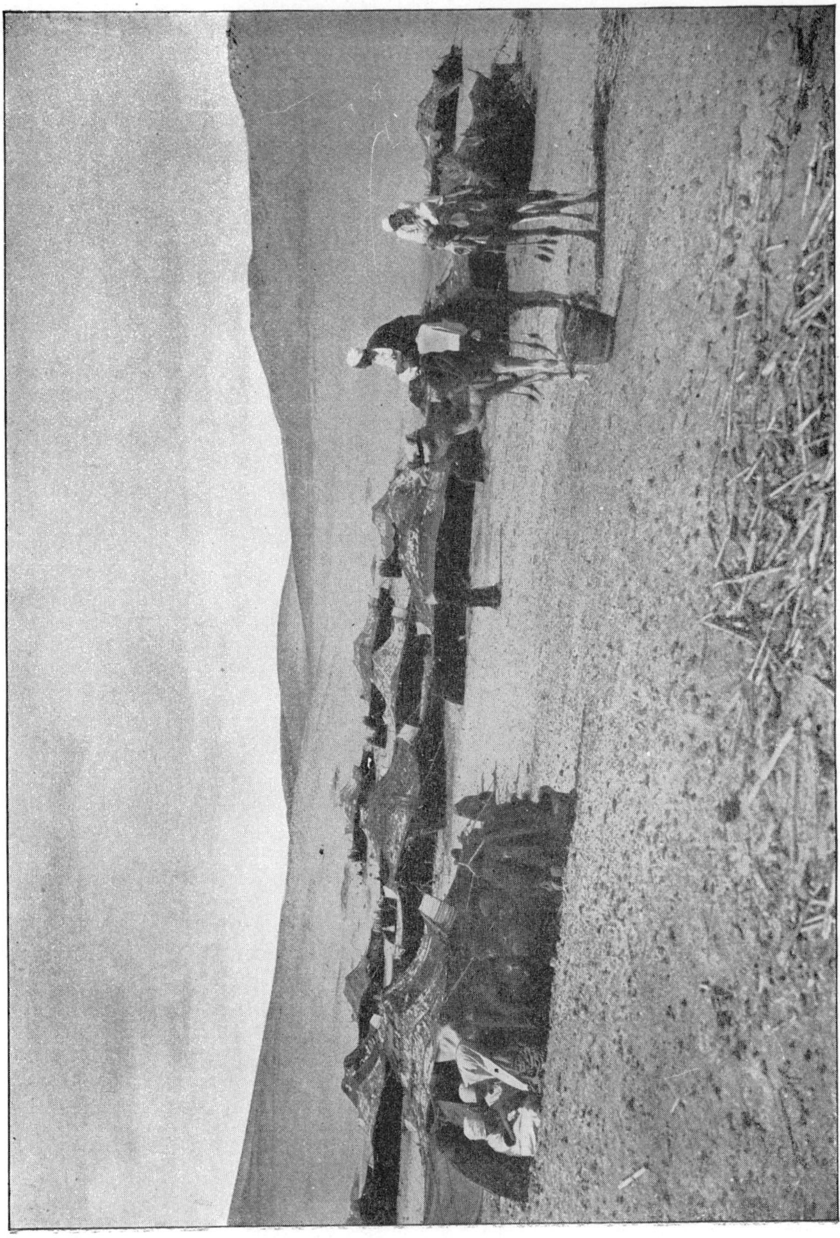

GIDEON

The Story of a Brave Man Who Freed His People from Oppression.

(There was a time when every year one of the tribes of the desert which lies south and east of Palestine raided the farms and pastures of the Israelites, plundering and burning, and carrying off the crops and herds.)

The Midianites came up with their cattle and their tents, they came in as locusts for multitude; both they and their camels were without number: and they came into the land to destroy it. And Israel was brought very low because of Midian; and the children of Israel cried unto the Lord.

And it came to pass, when the children of Israel cried unto the Lord because of Midian, that the Lord sent a prophet to the children of Israel: and he said unto them, "Thus saith the Lord, the God of Israel, 'I brought you up from Egypt, and brought you forth out of the house of bondage; and I delivered you out of the hand of the Egyptians, and out of the hand of all that oppressed you, and drove them out from before you, and gave you their land; and I said to you, I am the Lord your God; ye shall not fear the gods of the Amorites, in whose land ye dwell: but ye have not hearkened unto my voice.'"

And the angel of the Lord came, and sat under the

oak which was in Ophrah, which was on the land of Joash the Abiezrite: and his son Gideon was beating out wheat in the wine press, to hide it from the Midianites. And the angel of the Lord appeared to him, and said to him, "The Lord is with thee, thou mighty man of valor."

And Gideon said to him, "O my lord, if the Lord is with us, why then is all this befallen us? and where are all his wondrous works of which our fathers told us, saying, 'Did not the Lord bring us up from Egypt?' but now the Lord hath cast us off, and delivered us into the hand of Midian."

And the Lord looked upon him, and said, "Go in thy might, and save Israel from the hand of Midian: have not I sent thee?"

And he said to him, "O Lord, wherewith shall I save Israel? behold, my family is the poorest in Manasseh, and I am the least in my father's house."

And the Lord said unto him, "Surely I will be with thee, and thou shalt smite the Midianites as one man."

And he said unto him, "If now I have found grace in thy sight, then show me a sign that it is thou that talkest with me. Depart not hence, I pray thee, until I come to thee, and bring forth my present, and lay it before thee."

And he said, "I will tarry until thou come again."

And Gideon went in, and made ready a kid, and unleavened cakes of an ephah of meal: the flesh he put in a basket, and he put the broth in a pot, and brought it out to him under the oak, and presented it. And the angel of God said unto him, "Take the flesh and the unleavened

DESERT WARRIORS

Riding thus on their camels the hosts of Midian came out of the desert like locusts and swarmed over the fair fields of Palestine

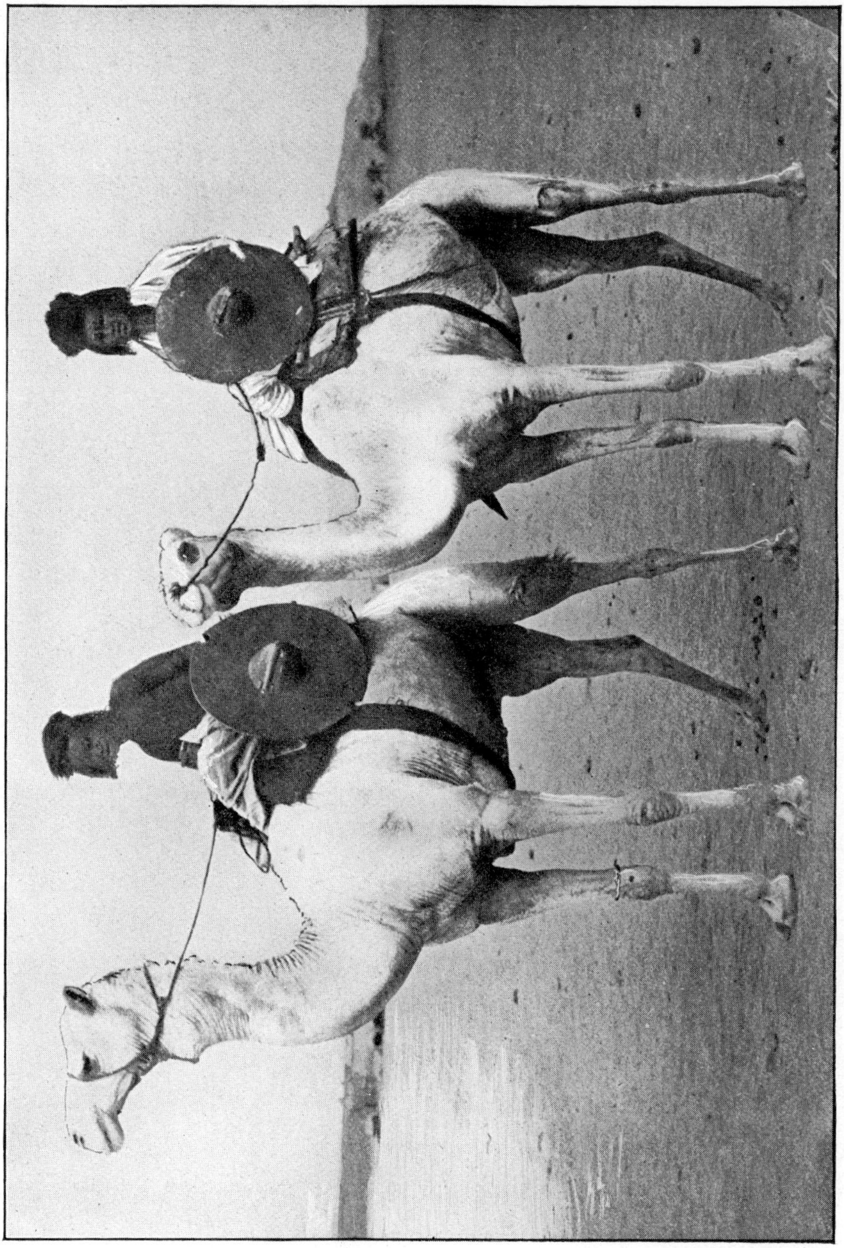

cakes, and lay them upon this rock, and pour out the broth."

And he did so. Then the angel of the Lord put forth the end of the staff that was in his hand, and touched the flesh and the unleavened cakes; and there went up fire out of the rock, and consumed the flesh and the unleavened cakes; and the angel of the Lord departed out of his sight. And Gideon saw that he was the angel of the Lord; and Gideon said, "Alas, O Lord God! because I have seen the angel of the Lord face to face."

And the Lord said unto him, "Peace be to thee; fear not: thou shalt not die."

Then Gideon built an altar there to the Lord, and called it "Jehovah is Peace": to this day it is yet in Ophrah of the Abiezrites.

And it came to pass the same night, that the Lord said to him, "Take thy father's bullock, and throw down the altar of Baal that thy father hath, and cut down the pillar that is by it: and build an altar to the Lord thy God upon the top of this stronghold, in the proper manner, and take a bullock, and offer a burnt offering with the wood of the pillar which thou shalt cut down." Then Gideon took ten men of his servants, and did as the Lord had spoken to him: and it came to pass, because he feared his father's household and the men of the city, so that he dared not do it by day, that he did it by night. And when the men of the city arose early in the morning, behold, the altar of Baal was broken down, and the pillar was cut down that was by it, and the bullock was offered upon the altar that was built. And they said one to another, "Who hath done this thing?" And when they inquired and asked, they said, "Gideon the son of Joash hath done this thing."

Then the men of the city said to Joash, "Bring out thy son, that he may die: because he hath broken down the altar of Baal, and because he hath cut down the pillar that was by it."

And Joash said to all that stood against him, "Will ye plead for Baal? or will ye save him? he that will plead for him, let him be put to death whilst it is yet morning: if he be a god, let him plead for himself, because one hath broken down his altar."

Therefore on that day he called him Jerubbaal, that is, "Let Baal plead."

How a Few Brave Men Saved the Nation.

Then all the Midianites and the Amalekites and the children of the east assembled themselves together; and they passed over, and camped in the valley of Jezreel. But the spirit of the Lord came upon Gideon; and he blew a trumpet; and the men of Abiezer were gathered together after him. And he sent messengers throughout all Manasseh; and they also were gathered together after him: and he sent messengers to Asher, and to Zebulun, and to Naphtali; and they came up to meet them. And Gideon said to God, "If thou wilt save Israel by mine hand, as thou hast spoken, behold, I will put a fleece of wool on the threshing-floor; if there be dew on the fleece only, and it be dry upon all the ground, then shall I know that thou wilt save Israel by mine hand, as thou hast spoken."

And it was so: for he rose up early on the morrow, and pressed the fleece together, and wrung the dew out of the fleece, a bowlful of water.

And Gideon said to God, "Let not thine anger be kindled against me, and I will speak but this once: let me prove, I pray thee, but this once with the fleece; let it now be dry only upon the fleece, and upon all the ground let there be dew."

And God did so that night: for it was dry upon the fleece only, and there was dew on all the ground.

Then Jerubbaal (which is another name for Gideon), and all the people that were with him, rose up early, and camped beside the spring of Harod: and the camp of Midian was on the north side of them, by the hill of Moreh, in the valley.

And the Lord said to Gideon, "The people that are with thee are too many for me to give the Midianites into their hand, lest Israel boast themselves against me, saying, 'Mine own hand hath saved me.' Now therefore, proclaim in the ears of the people, saying, 'Whosoever is fearful and trembling, let him return and depart from Mount Gilead.'"

And there returned of the people twenty and two thousand; and there remained ten thousand.

And the Lord said to Gideon, "The people are yet too many; bring them down unto the water, and I will try them for thee there: and it shall be, that of whom I say unto thee, 'These shall go with thee,' the same shall go with thee; and of whomsoever I say unto thee, 'These shall not go with thee,' the same shall not go."

So he brought down the people unto the water: and the Lord said unto Gideon, "Every one that lappeth of the water with his tongue, as a dog lappeth, him shalt thou set by himself; likewise every one that boweth down upon his knees to drink."

And the number of them that lapped, putting their hand to their mouth, was three hundred men: but all the rest of the people bowed down upon their knees to drink water.

And the Lord said unto Gideon, "By the three hundred men that lapped will I save you, and deliver the Midianites into thine hand: and let all the people go every man to his place."

So the people took victuals in their hand, and their trumpets: and he sent all the men of Israel every man to his tent, but retained the three hundred men: and the camp of Midian was beneath him in the valley.

And it came to pass the same night, that the Lord said to him, "Arise, get thee down into the camp; for I have delivered it into thine hand. But if thou fear to go down, go thou with Purah thy servant down to the camp: and thou shalt hear what they say; and afterward shall thine hands be strengthened to go down into the camp."

Then went he down with Purah his servant to the outermost part of the armed men that were in the camp. And the Midianites and the Amalekites and all the children of

THE PLAIN OF ESDRAELON

From a photograph belonging to Prof. H. G. Mitchell
and used by his kind permission

The plain of Esdraelon or Jezreel is one of the famous battle fields of the world's history. Lying in the heart of Palestine, the great highways of commerce come down through the hills and cross its level fields. Through it runs the little river Kishon. On the banks of this stream the hosts of Sisera were routed (see Tales of Brave Women, Vol. III.). Here Gideon and his three hundred men swept before them the hordes of Midian in the panic of the night attack. Here began the battle between Saul and the Philistines which ended in the death of the king, whose force had been pushed back to the height of Gilboa (see The Great Kings in this volume). Here King Josiah was mortally wounded in his fatal fight with the armies of Egypt (see The Story of a Divided Kingdom, Vol. III.). Through its fertile fields in all ages of history the armies of the great kingdoms of the East have marched to battle and conquest

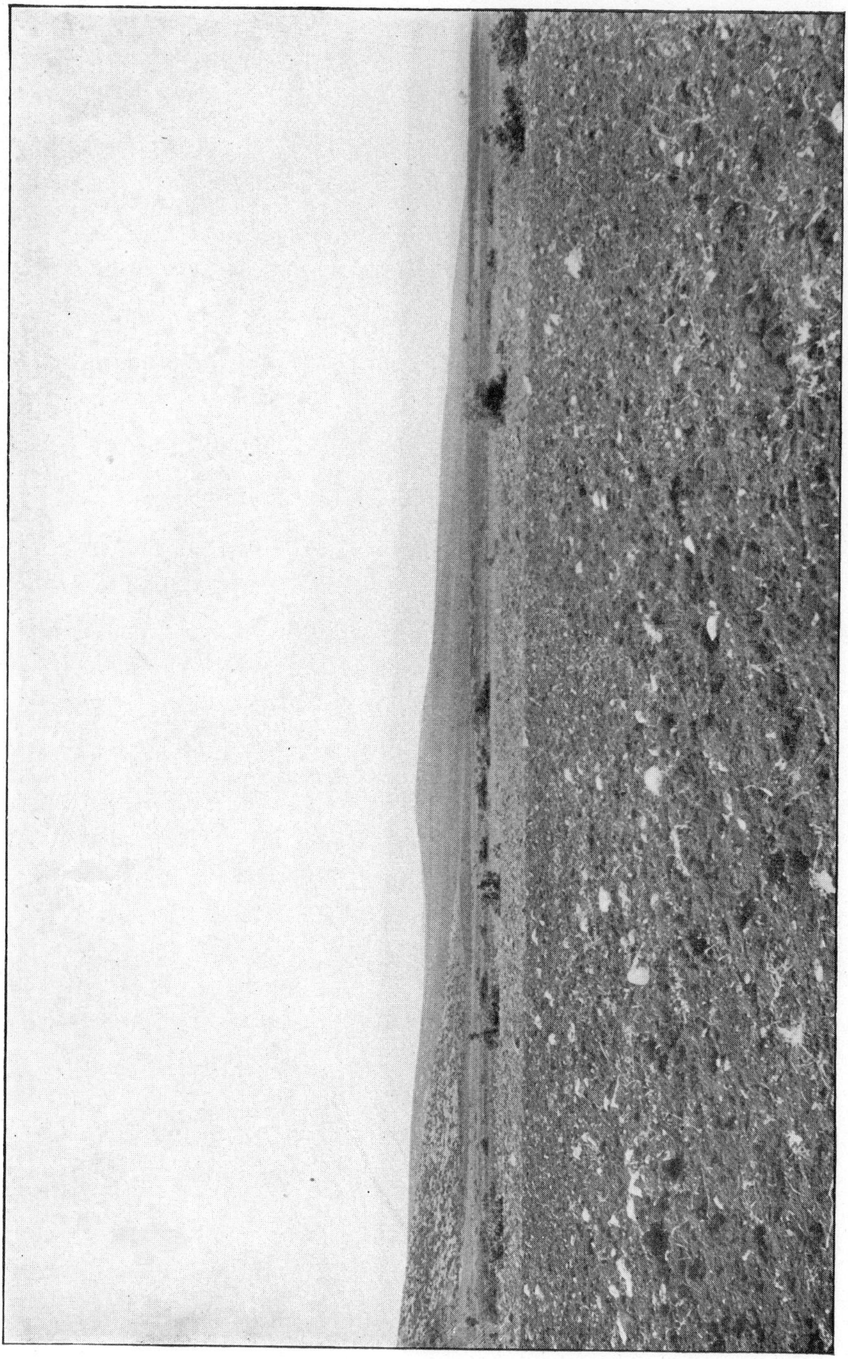

the east lay along in the valley like locusts for multitude; and their camels were without number, as the sand which is upon the sea shore for multitude. And when Gideon was come, behold, there was a man that told a dream to his fellow, and said, "Behold, I dreamed a dream, and, lo, a cake of barley bread tumbled into the camp of Midian, and came to the tent, and smote it that it fell, and turned it upside down, that the tent lay flat."

And his fellow answered and said, "This is nothing else save the sword of Gideon the son of Joash, a man of Israel: into his hand God hath delivered Midian, and all the host."

And when Gideon heard the telling of the dream, and the interpretation thereof, he worshiped; and returned into the camp of Israel, and said, "Arise; for the Lord hath delivered into your hand the host of Midian."

And he divided the three hundred men into three companies, and he put into the hands of all of them trumpets, and empty pitchers, with torches within the pitchers. And he said to them, "Look on me, and do likewise: and, behold, when I come to the outermost part of the camp, it shall be that, as I do, so shall ye do. When I blow the trumpet, I and all that are with me, then blow ye the trumpets also on every side of all the camp, and say,—

"'For the Lord and for Gideon.'"

So Gideon, and the hundred men that were with him, came unto the outermost part of the camp in the beginning of the middle watch, when they had but newly set the watch: and they blew the trumpets, and broke in pieces the pitchers that were in their hands. And the three companies blew the trumpets, and broke the pitchers, and held the torches in their left hands, and the trumpets in their right hands to blow wherewith: and they cried, "The sword of the Lord and of Gideon."

And they stood every man in his place round about the camp: and all the host ran; and they shouted, and put them to flight. And they blew the three hundred trumpets, and the Lord set every man's sword against his fellow, and against all the host: and the host fled in confusion. And the men of Israel were gathered together out of Naphtali, and out of Asher, and out of all Manasseh, and pursued after Midian. And Gideon sent messengers throughout all the hill country of Ephraim, saying, "Come down against Midian, and hold the fords as far as the fords of Jordan." So all the men of Ephraim were gathered together, and held the fords as far as the fords of Jordan. And they took the two princes of Midian, Oreb and Zeeb; and they slew Oreb at the rock of Oreb, and Zeeb they slew at the wine press of Zeeb, and pursued Midian: and they brought the heads of Oreb and Zeeb to Gideon beyond Jordan.

Then the men of Israel said unto Gideon, "Rule thou over us, both thou, and thy son, and thy son's son also: for thou hast saved us out of the hand of Midian."

And Gideon said unto them, "I will not rule over you, neither shall my son rule over you: the Lord shall rule over you."

So Midian was subdued before the children of Israel, and they lifted up their heads no more. And the land had rest forty years in the days of Gideon.

And Gideon the son of Joash died in a good old age, and was buried in the sepulcher of Joash his father, in Ophrah of the Abiezrites.

ABIMELECH

The Story of the Sons of Gideon, and the Evil Which Befell Them.

ABIMELECH SEIZES THE LEADERSHIP.

(This is the first of the bloody conflicts for leadership in Hebrew history, so common after the kingdom was established. Abimelech, the son of Gideon, whose mother was a woman of Shechem and a servant, killed all the other children but Jotham, and died himself in battle after a brief period of supremacy.)

And Abimelech the son of Jerubbaal went to Shechem to his mother's brethren, and spoke with them, and with all the family of the house of his mother's father, saying, "Speak, I pray you, in the ears of all the men of Shechem, 'Which is better for you, that all the sons of Jerubbaal, who are threescore and ten persons, rule over you, or that one rule over you? remember also that I am your bone and your flesh.'"

And his mother's brethren spoke of him in the ears of all the men of Shechem all these words: and their hearts inclined to follow Abimelech; for they said, "He is our brother." And they gave him threescore and ten pieces of silver, wherewith Abimelech hired vain and light fellows, who followed him. And he went unto his father's house at Ophrah, and slew his brethren the sons of Jerubbaal, being threescore and ten persons, upon one stone: but Jotham the youngest son of Jerubbaal was left; for he hid himself.

AN OLD FABLE.

(This is one of the earliest of those stories called fables in which animals or trees or other things not living are represented as speaking and acting like living persons. Such stories were usually told to teach some lesson.)

And all the men of Shechem assembled themselves together, and all the house of Millo, and went and made Abimelech king, by the oak of the pillar that was in Shechem. And when they told it to Jotham, he went and stood in the top of mount Gerizim, and lifted up his voice, and cried, and said unto them, "Hearken unto me, ye men of Shechem, that God may hearken unto you. The trees went forth on a time to anoint a king over them; and they said unto the olive tree, 'Reign thou over us.' But the olive tree said unto them, 'Should I leave my fatness, wherewith by me they honor God and man, and go to wave to and fro over the trees?' And the trees said to the fig tree, 'Come thou, and reign over us.' But the fig tree said unto them, 'Should I leave my sweetness, and my good fruit, and go to wave to and fro over the trees?' And the trees said to the vine, 'Come thou, and reign over us.' And the vine said unto them, 'Should I leave my wine, which cheereth God and man, and go to wave to and fro over the trees?' Then said all the trees to the bramble, 'Come thou, and reign over us.' And the bramble said to the trees, 'If in truth ye anoint me king over you, then come and put your trust in my shadow: and if not, let fire come out of the bramble, and devour the cedars of Lebanon.'

"Now therefore, if ye have dealt truly and uprightly, in that ye have made Abimelech king, and if ye have dealt well with Jerubbaal and his house, and have done to him according to the deserving of his hands; (for my father fought for you, and adventured his life, and delivered you out of the hand of Midian: and ye are risen up against my father's house this day, and have slain his sons, threescore and ten persons, upon one stone, and have made Abimelech, the son of his maid-servant, king over the men of Shechem, because he is your brother;) if ye then have dealt truly and uprightly with Jerubbaal and with his house this day, then rejoice ye in Abimelech, and let him also rejoice in you: but if not, let fire come out from Abimelech, and devour the men of Shechem, and the house of Millo; and let fire come out from the men of Shechem, and from the house of Millo, and devour Abimelech." And Jotham ran away, and fled, for fear of Abimelech his brother.

THE FATE OF ABIMELECH.

After Several Years of Uneasy Rule Abimelech Met His Fate at the Hands of His Enemies.

And it was told Abimelech that all the men of the tower of Shechem were gathered together. And Abimelech went up to mount Zalmon, he and all the people that were

SHECHEM

In the time of the Judges, Shechem was known as the City of Abimelech. The people of the town first made him king and then revolted against him. Afterward he captured the city and utterly destroyed it

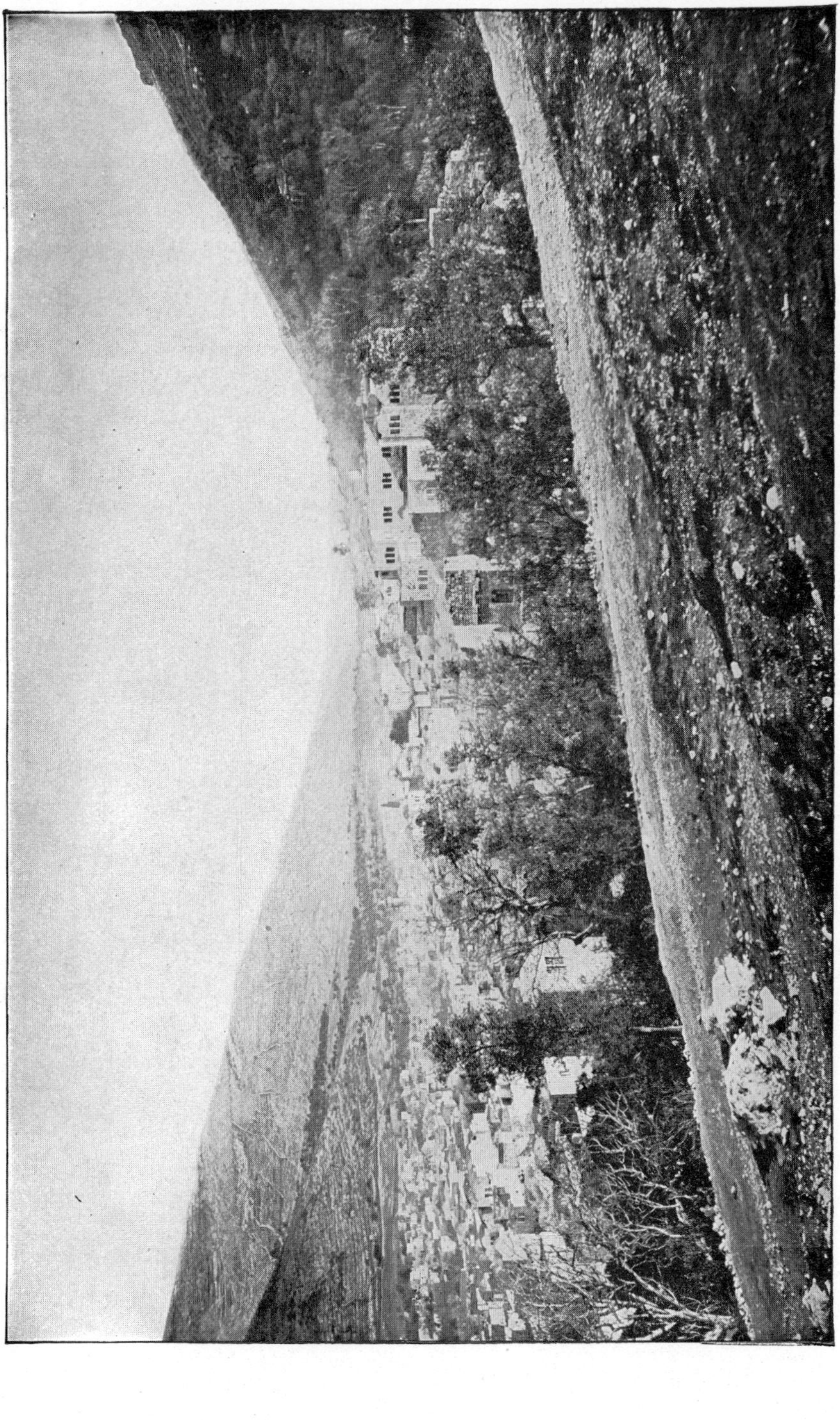

with him; and Abimelech took an axe in his hand, and cut down a bough from the trees, and took it up, and laid it on his shoulder: and he said to the people that were with him, "What ye have seen me do, make haste, and do as I have done."

And all the people likewise cut down every man his bough, and followed Abimelech, and put them about the tower, and set the hold on fire upon them; so that all the men of the tower of Shechem died also, about a thousand men and women.

Then went Abimelech to Thebez, and encamped against Thebez, and took it. But there was a strong tower within the city, and thither fled all the men and women, and all they of the city, and shut themselves in, and went up to the roof of the tower. And Abimelech came unto the tower, and fought against it, and went close under the door of the tower to burn it with fire. And a certain woman cast an upper millstone upon Abimelech's head, and broke his skull. Then he called hastily unto the young man his armor-bearer, and said unto him, "Draw thy sword, and kill me, that men say not of me, 'A woman slew him.'"

And his young man thrust him through, and he died. And when the men of Israel saw that Abimelech was dead, they departed every man unto his place.

SAMUEL

*The Story of a Man Who Began to Do Right When He
Was a Boy, and Who Never Departed from
the Way in Which He Began.*

(Samuel is one of the finest characters in the Old Testament. In the midst of evil times, and in contact with evil men, he never departed from the strict way of truth and righteousness and service to God. Samuel was fortunate in having an excellent mother. She dedicated her son to God, and gave him very early to the service of God. She loved him very much, and no doubt missed him very much from the home. Every year she went to see him, and brought him a little coat which she had made.

"But Samuel ministered before the Lord, being a child. Moreover his mother made him a little robe, and brought it to him from year to year, when she came up with her husband to offer the yearly sacrifice.")

HOW SAMUEL LEARNED TO OBEY THE VOICE OF GOD.

And the child Samuel ministered to the Lord before Eli. And the word of the Lord was precious in those days; there was no open vision. And it came to pass at that time, when Eli was laid down in his place (now his eyes had begun to grow dim, so that he could not see), and the lamp of God was not yet gone out, and Samuel was laid down to sleep, in the temple of the Lord, where the

SOURCES OF THE JORDAN. THE ANCIENT DAN

Dan was a city on the northern boundary of Palestine, and Beer-sheba was a city on the southern boundary, so there came to be a national saying "from Dan to Beer-sheba," to indicate the whole kingdom. "And all Israel from Dan even to Beer-sheba knew that Samuel was established to be a prophet of the Lord." The picture is taken near the supposed site of the ancient city at the point where a great spring bursting forth forms the principal source of the Jordan river

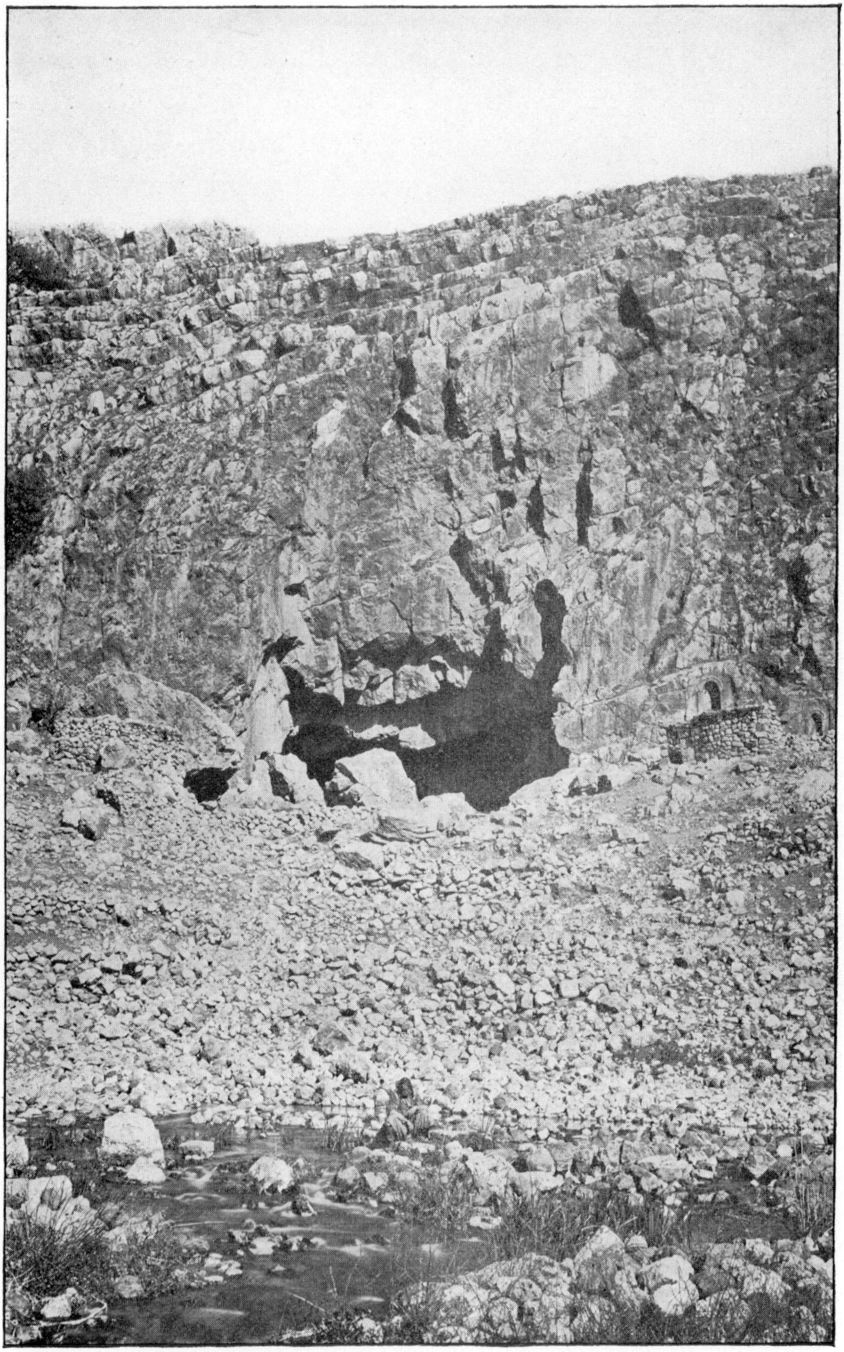

ark of God was; that the Lord called Samuel: and he said, "Here am I."

And he ran to Eli, and said, "Here am I; for thou calledst me."

And he said, "I called not; lie down again."

And he went and lay down. And the Lord called yet again, "Samuel."

And Samuel arose and went to Eli, and said, "Here am I; for thou calledst me."

And he answered, "I called not, my son; lie down again."

Now Samuel did not yet know the Lord, neither was the word of the Lord yet revealed to him. And the Lord called Samuel again the third time. And he arose and went to Eli, and said, "Here am I; for thou calledst me."

And Eli perceived that the Lord had called the child. Therefore Eli said to Samuel, "Go, lie down: and it shall be, if he call thee, that thou shalt say, 'Speak, Lord; for thy servant heareth.'"

So Samuel went and lay down in his place. And the Lord came, and stood, and called as at other times, "Samuel, Samuel."

Then Samuel said, "Speak; for thy servant heareth."

And the Lord said, "Behold, I will do a thing in Israel, at which both the ears of every one that heareth it shall tingle. In that day I will perform against Eli all that I have spoken concerning his house, from the beginning even unto the end. For I have told him that I will judge his house for ever, for the iniquity which he knew, because his sons did bring a curse upon themselves, and he restrained them not. And therefore I have sworn unto the house of Eli, that the iniquity of Eli's house shall not be purged with sacrifice nor offering for ever."

And Samuel lay until the morning, and opened the doors of the house of the Lord. And Samuel feared to show Eli the vision. Then Eli called Samuel, and said, "Samuel, my son."

And he said, "Here am I."

And he said, "What is the thing that the Lord hath spoken unto thee? I pray thee hide it not from me: God do so to thee, and more also, if thou hide anything from me of all the things that he spoke unto thee."

And Samuel told him every word, and hid nothing from him. And he said, "It is the Lord: let him do what seemeth him good."

And Samuel grew, and the Lord was with him, and let none of his words fall to the ground. And all Israel from Dan even to Beer-sheba knew that Samuel was established to be a prophet of the Lord.

HOW THE WICKEDNESS OF THE LEADERS BROUGHT SORE DEFEAT UPON ISRAEL AND HOW ELI DIED WHEN HE HEARD THE NEWS.

Now Israel went out against the Philistines to battle, and camped beside Eben-ezer: and the Philistines camped in Aphek. And the Philistines put themselves in array against Israel: and when they joined battle, Israel was

THE RUINS OF SHILOH (SEILUN), FROM THE NORTHEAST

Used by special permission of the Palestine Exploration Fund

The mound is covered with foundations, heaps of stones, and walls
"And there ran a man of Benjamin out of the army, and came to Shiloh the same day with his clothes rent, and with earth upon his head." Shiloh was one of the principal sanctuaries of Israel throughout the time of the Judges. Here the ark was kept, and here Eli was living when the man of Benjamin came out of the fatal fight to tell Eli that his sons were slain and the Ark of God was taken by the Philistines

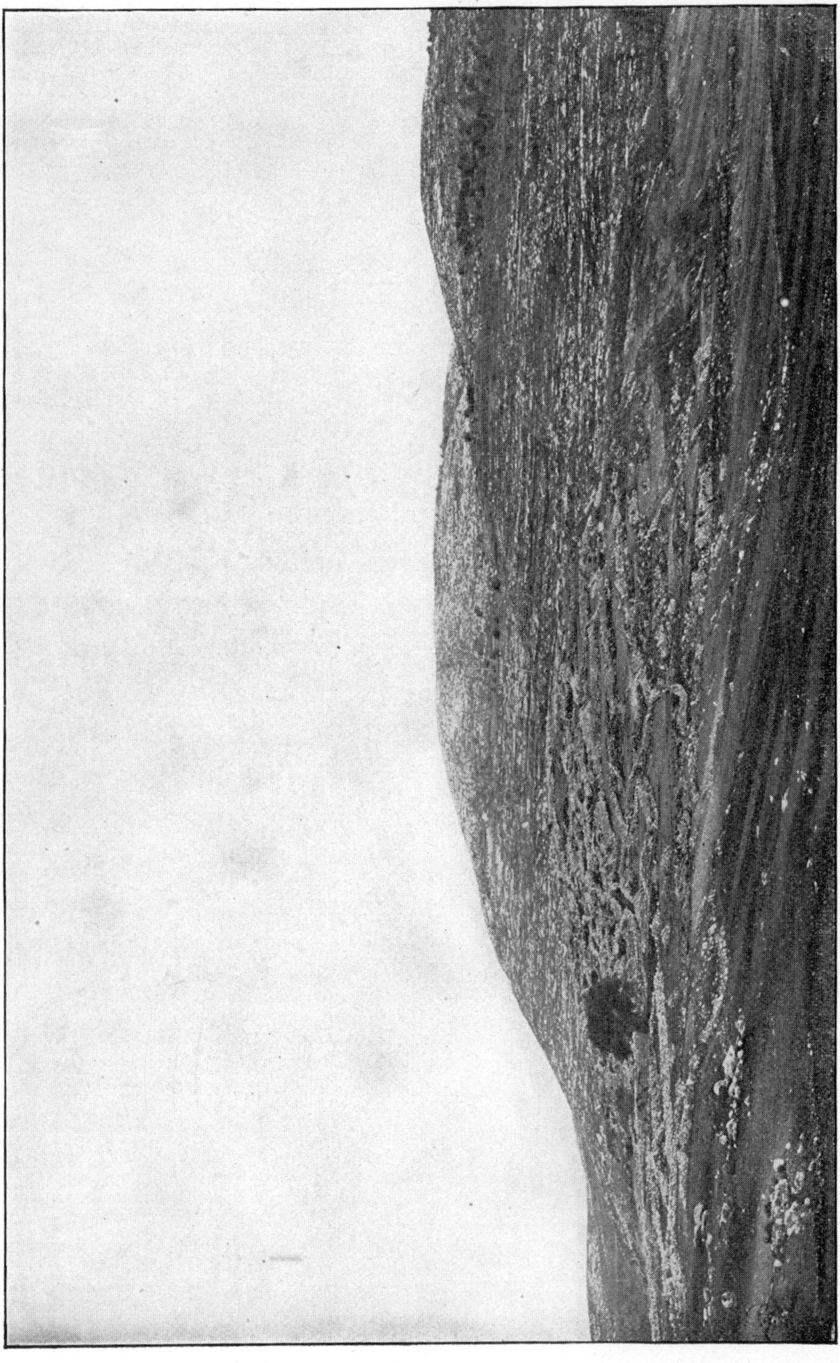

smitten before the Philistines: and they slew of the army in the field about four thousand men.

And when the people were come into the camp, the elders of Israel said, "Wherefore hath the Lord smitten us to-day before the Philistines? Let us fetch the ark of the covenant of the Lord out of Shiloh unto us, that it may come among us, and save us out of the hand of our enemies."

So the people sent to Shiloh, and they brought from thence the ark of the covenant of the Lord of hosts, which sitteth upon the cherubim: and the two sons of Eli, Hophni and Phinehas, were there with the ark of the covenant of God. And when the ark of the covenant of the Lord came into the camp, all Israel shouted with a great shout, so that the earth rang again. And when the Philistines heard the noise of the shout, they said, "What meaneth the noise of this great shout in the camp of the Hebrews?"

And they understood that the ark of the Lord was come into the camp. And the Philistines were afraid, for they said, "God is come into the camp." And they said, "Woe unto us! for there hath not been such a thing heretofore. Woe unto us! who shall deliver us out of the hand of these mighty gods? these are the gods that smote the Egyptians with all manner of plagues in the wilderness. Be strong, and quit yourselves like men, O ye Philistines, that ye be not servants unto the Hebrews, as they have been to you: quit yourselves like men, and fight."

And the Philistines fought, and Israel was smitten, and they fled every man to his tent: and there was a very great slaughter; for there fell of Israel thirty thousand footmen. And the ark of God was taken; and the two sons of Eli, Hophni and Phinehas, were slain. And there ran a man of Benjamin out of the army, and came to Shiloh the same day with his clothes rent, and with earth upon his head. And when he came, lo, Eli sat upon his seat by the wayside watching: for his heart trembled for the ark of God. And when the man came into the city, and told it, all the city cried out. And when Eli heard the noise of the crying, he said, "What meaneth the noise of this tumult?"

And the man hasted, and came and told Eli. Now Eli was ninety and eight years old; and his eyes were set, that he could not see.

And the man said unto Eli, "I am he that came out of the army, and I fled to-day out of the army."

And he said, "How went the matter, my son?"

And he that brought the tidings answered and said, "Israel is fled before the Philistines, and there hath been also a great slaughter among the people, and thy two sons also, Hophni and Phinehas, are dead, and the ark of God is taken."

And it came to pass, when he made mention of the ark of God, that he fell from off his seat backward by the side of the gate, and his neck broke, and he died: for he was an old man, and heavy. And he had judged Israel forty years.

The Great Kings

After the judges came the kings. There were many kings in Israel's history, but the first three were really the greatest. Saul was the founder of the kingdom, a mighty king in spite of his faults. David made the nation great because he was great himself. Solomon by his wisdom and skill raised Israel to such wealth and splendor as it never had before nor after.

SAUL

The Story of the Farmer Who Became King.

(Samuel was the last and the best of the Judges of Israel. He conquered the Philistines, and for many years the land had peace. He was a "circuit judge," going from district to district. As he grew old he attempted to put his sons in his place, but they were not like their father. They took bribes and did that which was evil. Then the people demanded a king. How Samuel at first resisted, but at last yielded and anointed Saul as king, is told in the following story.)

THE PEOPLE DEMAND A KING TO RULE OVER THEM.

Samuel Warns Them of the Dangers of a Kingdom.

After a great victory over the Philistines, Samuel took a stone, and set it between Mizpah and Shen, and called the name of it Eben-ezer (that is, the stone of help), saying, "Hitherto hath the Lord helped us."

So the Philistines were subdued, and they came no more within the border of Israel: and the hand of the Lord was against the Philistines all the days of Samuel.

And Samuel judged Israel all the days of his life. And he went from year to year in circuit to Beth-el, and Gilgal, and Mizpah; and he judged Israel in all those places. And his return was to Ramah, for there was his house; and there he judged Israel: and he built there an altar unto the Lord.

And it came to pass, when Samuel was old, that he made his sons judges over Israel. Now the name of his firstborn was Joel; and the name of his second, Abijah: they were judges in Beer-sheba. And his sons walked not in his ways, but turned aside after money, and took bribes, and perverted judgment.

Then all the elders of Israel gathered themselves together, and came to Samuel unto Ramah: and they said to him, "Behold, thou art old, and thy sons walk not in thy ways: now make us a king to judge us like all the nations."

But the thing displeased Samuel, when they said, "Give us a king to judge us."

And Samuel prayed unto the Lord. And the Lord said unto Samuel, "Hearken unto the voice of the people in all that they say unto thee: for they have not rejected thee, but they have rejected me, that I should not be king over them. According to all the works which they have done since the day that I brought them up out of Egypt even to this day, in that they have forsaken me, and served other gods, so do they also to thee. Now therefore hearken to their voice: howbeit thou shalt protest solemnly to them, and shalt show them the manner of the king that shall reign over them."

And Samuel told all the words of the Lord unto the people that asked of him a king. And he said, "This will be the manner of the king that shall reign over you: he will take your sons, and appoint them unto him, for his chariots, and to be his horsemen; and they shall run before his chariots: and he will appoint them for captains of thousands, and captains of fifties; and he will set some to plow his ground, and to reap his harvest, and to make his instruments of war, and the instruments of his chariots. And he will take your daughters to be confectionaries, and to be cooks, and to be bakers. And he will take your fields, and your vineyards, and your oliveyards, even the best of them, and give them to his servants. And he will take the tenth of your seed, and of your vineyards, and give to his officers, and to his servants. And he will take your menservants, and your maidservants, and your goodliest young men, and your asses, and put them to his work. He will take the tenth of your flocks: and ye shall be his servants. And ye shall cry out in that day because of your king which ye shall have chosen you; and the Lord will not answer you in that day."

But the people refused to hearken to the voice of Samuel; and they said, "Nay; but we will have a king over us; that we also may be like all the nations; and that our king may judge us, and go out before us, and fight our battles."

And Samuel heard all the words of the people, and he repeated them in the ears of the Lord. And the Lord said to Samuel, "Hearken to their voice, and make them a king."

And Samuel said to the men of Israel, "Go ye every man unto his city."

THE TALL SON OF KISH IS CHOSEN.
Saul Is Secretly Anointed by Samuel to Be King.

Now there was a man of Benjamin, whose name was Kish, a Benjamite, a mighty man of valor. And he had a son whose name was Saul, a young man and a goodly: and there was not among the children of Israel a goodlier person than he: from his shoulders and upward he was higher than any of the people. And the asses of Kish Saul's father were lost. And Kish said to Saul his son, "Take now one of the servants with thee, and arise, go seek the asses."

And he passed through the hill country of Ephraim, but they found them not: and he passed through the land of the Benjamites, but they found them not. When they were come to the land of Zuph, Saul said to his servant that was with him, "Come and let us return; lest my father stop caring for the asses, and be anxious for us."

And he said to him, "Behold now, there is in this city a man of God, and he is a man who is held in honor; all that he saith cometh surely to pass: now let us go thither; peradventure he can tell us concerning our journey whereon we go."

Then said Saul to his servant, "But, behold, if we go, what shall we bring the man? for the bread is spent in our vessels, and there is not a present to bring to the man of God: what have we?" And the servant answered Saul again, and said, "Behold, I have in my hand the fourth part of a shekel of silver: that will I give to the man of God, to tell us our way."

Then said Saul to his servant, "Well said; come, let us go."

So they went unto the city where the man of God was. As they went up the ascent to the city, they found young maidens going out to draw water, and said to them, "Is the seer here?"

And they answered them and said, "He is; behold, he is before thee: make haste now, for he is come to-day into the city; for the people have a sacrifice to-day in the high place: as soon as ye are come into the city, ye shall straightway find him, before he goes up to the high place to eat: for the people will not eat until he come, because he doth bless the sacrifice; and afterwards those eat who are bidden. Now therefore get you up; for at this time ye shall find him."

And they went up to the city; and as they came within the city, behold, Samuel came out toward them to go up to the high place.

Now the Lord had revealed to Samuel a day before Saul came, saying, "To-morrow about this time I will send thee a man out of the land of Benjamin, and thou shalt anoint him to be prince over my people Israel, and he shall save my people out of the hand of the Philistines: for I have looked upon my people, because their cry is come unto me."

And when Samuel saw Saul, the Lord said to him, "Behold the man of whom I spoke to thee! this same shall have authority over my people."

Then Saul drew near to Samuel in the gate, and said, "Tell me, I pray thee, where the seer's house is."

And Samuel answered Saul, and said, "I am the seer; go up before me unto the high place, for ye shall eat with me to-day: and in the morning I will let thee go, and will tell all that is in thine heart. And as for thine asses that were lost three days ago, set not thy mind on them; for they are found. And for whom is all that is desirable in Israel? Is it not for thee, and for all thy father's house?"

And Saul answered and said, "Am not I a Benjamite, of the smallest of the tribes of Israel? and my family the least of all the families of the tribe of Benjamin? wherefore then speakest thou to me after this manner?"

And Samuel took Saul and his servant and brought them into the guest chamber, and made them sit in the chiefest place among those who were bidden, who were about thirty persons. And Samuel said to the cook, "Bring the portion which I gave thee, of which I said to thee, 'Set it by thee.'"

And the cook took up the shoulder, and that which was upon it, and set it before Saul. And Samuel said, "Behold that which hath been reserved! set it before thee and eat; because to the appointed time hath it been kept for thee, for I said, 'I have invited the people.'"

So Saul did eat with Samuel that day. And when they were come down from the high place into the city, he communed with Saul upon the housetop.

And they arose early: and it came to pass about the dawning of the day, that Samuel called to Saul on the housetop, saying, "Up, that I may send thee away."

And Saul arose, and they went out both of them, he

THE ANCIENT MIZPAH, LOOKING FROM THE SOUTH

It is situated on a high hill to the northwest of Jerusalem

From a photograph taken by Prof. H. G. Mitchell
and used by his kind permission

There were many places in Palestine called Mizpah, "watch tower," but it seems probable that the location shown in the picture was the site of Samuel's home

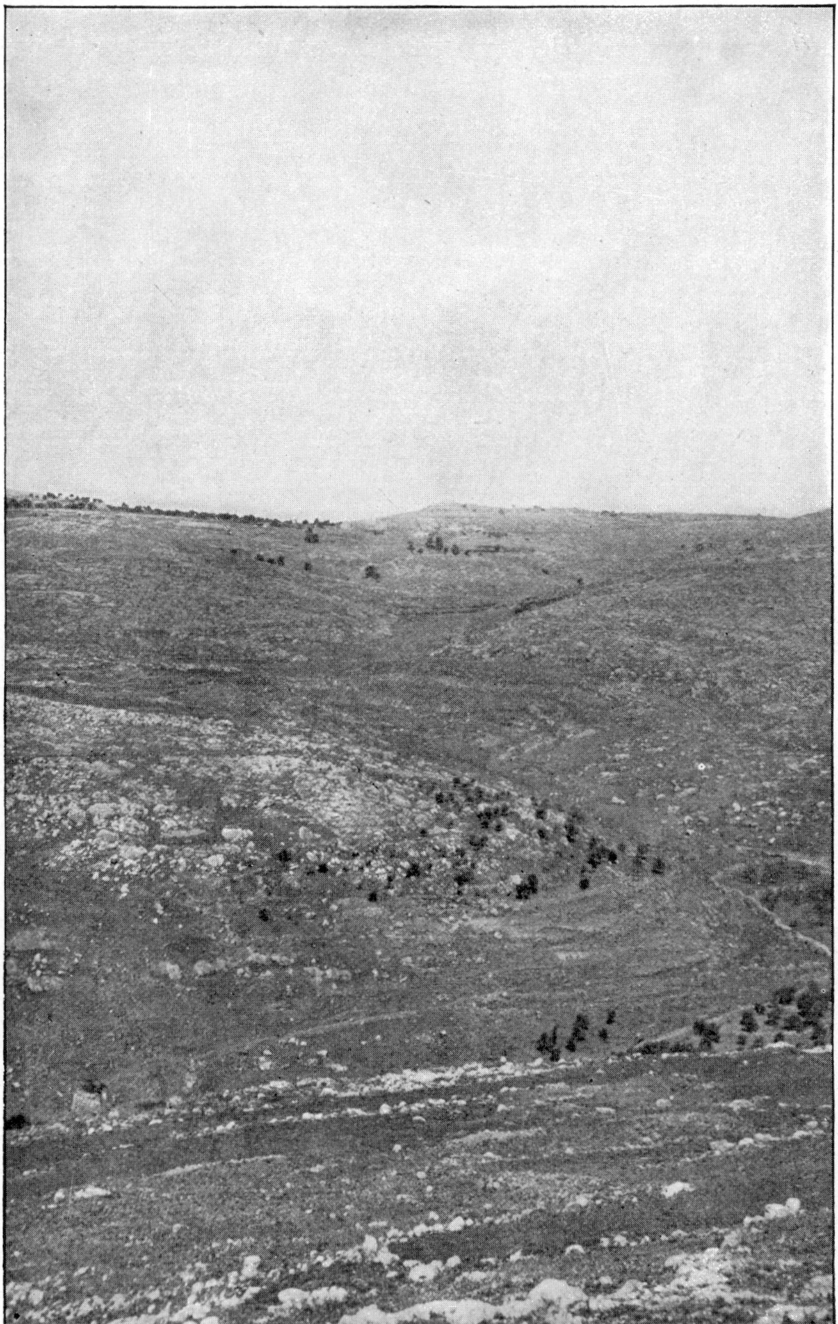

and Samuel, abroad. As they were going down at the end of the city, Samuel said to Saul, "Bid the servant pass on before us" (and he passed on), "but stand thou still that I may cause thee to hear the word of God."

Then Samuel took the vial of oil, and poured it upon his head, and kissed him, and said, "Is it not that the Lord hath anointed thee to be prince over his inheritance?" And Saul departed from Samuel.

And when Saul reached home his uncle said to him and to his servant, "Whither went ye?" And he said, "To seek the asses: and when we saw that they were not found, we came to Samuel."

And Saul's uncle said, "Tell me, I pray thee, what Samuel said to you." And Saul said to his uncle, "He told us plainly that the asses were found." But concerning the matter of the kingdom, whereof Samuel spoke, he told him not.

SAUL IS PUBLICLY PROCLAIMED KING.

"God Save the King!"

And Samuel called the people together to the Lord to Mizpah; and he said to the children of Israel, "Thus saith the Lord, the God of Israel, I brought up Israel out of Egypt, and I delivered you out of the hand of the Egyptians, and out of the hand of all the kingdoms that oppressed you: but ye have this day rejected your God, who himself saveth you out of all your calamities and your distresses; and ye have said to him, 'Nay, but set a king over us.' Now therefore present yourselves before the Lord by your tribes, and by your thousands."

So Samuel brought all the tribes of Israel near, and the tribe of Benjamin was chosen. And he brought the tribe of Benjamin near by their families, and the family of the Matrites was chosen: and Saul the son of Kish was chosen; but when they sought him, he could not be found. Therefore they asked of the Lord further, "Is the man yet come hither?"

And the Lord answered, "Behold, he hath hid himself in the camp."

And they ran and fetched him thence; and when he stood among the people, he was higher than any of the people from his shoulders and upward. And Samuel said to all the people, "See ye him whom the Lord hath chosen, that there is none like him among all the people?"

And all the people shouted, and said,—

"God save the king!"

Then Samuel told the people the manner of the kingdom, and wrote it in a book, and laid it up before the Lord. And Samuel sent all the people away, every man to his house. And Saul also went to his house to Gibeah; and there went with him the host, whose hearts God had touched.

But certain worthless fellows said, "How shall this man save us?"

And they despised him, and brought him no present. But he held his peace.

SAUL IS TRIED AND IS NOT FOUND WANTING.
The First Battle of the New King.

Then Nahash the Ammonite came up, and encamped against Jabesh-gilead: and all the men of Jabesh said to Nahash, "Make a covenant with us, and we will serve thee."

And Nahash the Ammonite said unto them, "On this condition will I make it with you, that all your right eyes be put out; and I will lay it for a reproach upon all Israel."

And the elders of Jabesh said to him, "Give us seven days' respite, that we may send messengers to all the borders of Israel: and then, if there be none to save us, we will come out to thee."

Then came the messengers to Gibeah of Saul, and spoke these words in the ears of the people: and all the people lifted up their voice, and wept. And, behold, Saul came following the oxen out of the field; and Saul said, "What aileth the people that they weep?"

And they told him the words of the men of Jabesh. And the spirit of God came mightily upon Saul when he heard those words, and his anger was kindled greatly. And he took a yoke of oxen, and cut them in pieces, and sent them throughout all the borders of Israel by the hand of messengers, saying, "Whosoever cometh not forth after Saul and after Samuel, so shall it be done to his oxen."

And the dread of the Lord fell on the people, and they came out as one man. And he numbered them in Bezek; and the children of Israel were three hundred thousand, and the men of Judah thirty thousand. And they said to the messengers that came, "Thus shall ye say unto the men of Jabesh-gilead, 'To-morrow, by the time the sun is hot, ye shall have deliverance.' "

And the messengers came and told the men of Jabesh; and they were glad. Therefore the men of Jabesh said, "To-morrow we will come out unto you, and ye shall do with us all that seemeth good unto you."

And it was so on the morrow, that Saul put the people in three companies; and they came into the midst of the camp in the morning watch, and smote the Ammonites until the heat of day: and it came to pass, that they which remained were scattered, so that two of them were not left together.

And the people said to Samuel, "Who is he that said, 'Shall Saul reign over us?' bring the men, that we may put them to death."

And Saul said, "There shall not a man be put to death this day: for to-day the Lord hath wrought deliverance in Israel."

SAUL THE WARRIOR.
Battles and Victories.

Saul was thirty years old when he began to reign; and he reigned two years over Israel. And Saul chose him three thousand men of Israel; whereof two thousand were with Saul in Michmash and in the mount of Beth-el, and a thousand were with Jonathan in Gibeah of Benjamin: and the rest of the people he sent every man to his tent. And Jonathan smote the garrison of the Philistines that was in Geba, and the Philistines heard of it. And Saul blew the trumpet throughout all the land, saying, "Let the Hebrews hear." And all Israel heard that Saul had smitten the garrison of the Philistines, and that Israel also was held in abomination by the Philistines. And the people were gathered together after Saul to Gilgal.

And the Philistines assembled themselves together to fight with Israel, thirty thousand chariots, and six thousand horsemen, and people as the sand which is on the sea shore in multitude: and they came up and pitched in Michmash, eastward of Beth-aven. When the men of Israel saw that they were in a strait (for the people were distressed), then the people hid themselves in caves, and in thickets, and in rocks, and in holds, and in pits. Now some of the Hebrews had gone over Jordan to the land of Gad and Gilead; but as for Saul, he was yet in Gilgal, and all the people followed him trembling.

And he tarried seven days, according to the set time that Samuel had appointed: but Samuel came not to Gilgal; and the people were scattered from him. And Saul said, "Bring hither the burnt offering to me, and the peace offerings." And he offered the burnt offering. And it came to pass that, as soon as he had made an end of offering the burnt offering, behold, Samuel came; and Saul went out to meet him, that he might salute him. And Samuel said, "What hast thou done?" And Saul said, "Because I saw that the people were scattered from me, and that thou camest not within the days appointed, and that the Philistines assembled themselves together at Michmash; therefore said I, 'Now will the Philistines come down upon me to Gilgal, and I have not intreated the favor of the Lord': I forced myself therefore to do it, and offered the burnt offering."

And Samuel said to Saul, "Thou hast done foolishly: thou hast not kept the commandment of the Lord thy God, which he commanded thee: for now would the Lord have established thy kingdom upon Israel forever. But now thy kingdom shall not continue: the Lord hath sought him a man after his own heart, and the Lord hath appointed him to be prince over his people, because thou hast not kept that which the Lord commanded thee."

And Samuel arose, and went up from Gilgal to Gibeah of Benjamin. And Saul numbered the people that were present with him, about six hundred men. And Saul, and Jonathan his son, and the people that were present with them, abode in Geba of Benjamin: but the Philistines encamped in Michmash. And bands of the Philistines came out and ravaged the country all about.

Now there was no blacksmith found throughout all the land of Israel: for the Philistines said, "There shall be no blacksmith, lest the Hebrews make them swords or spears": but all the Israelites went down to the Philistines, to sharpen their axes and ploughshares and other tools.

So it came to pass in the day of battle, that there was neither sword nor spear found in the hand of any of the people that were with Saul and Jonathan; except in the hands of Saul and Jonathan his son. And the garrison of the Philistines went out unto the pass of Michmash.

Now it fell upon a day, that Jonathan the son of Saul

THE VALLEY OF AIJALON

"Throughout history we see hosts swarming up this avenue or swept down it in flight. Joshua drove the Canaanites down this valley. Down Aijalon the early men of Ephraim and Benjamin raided the Philistines. Up Aijalon the Philistines swarmed to the very heart of Israel's territory at Michmash, disarmed the Israelites, and forced them to come down the vale to get their tools sharpened, so that the mouth of the vale was called the 'Valley of the Smiths,' even till after the Exile. Down Aijalon Saul and Jonathan beat the Philistines from Michmash."
—*George Adam Smith*

David also fought in Aijalon, and in 66 A. D., a Roman army suffered a terrible defeat in the valley

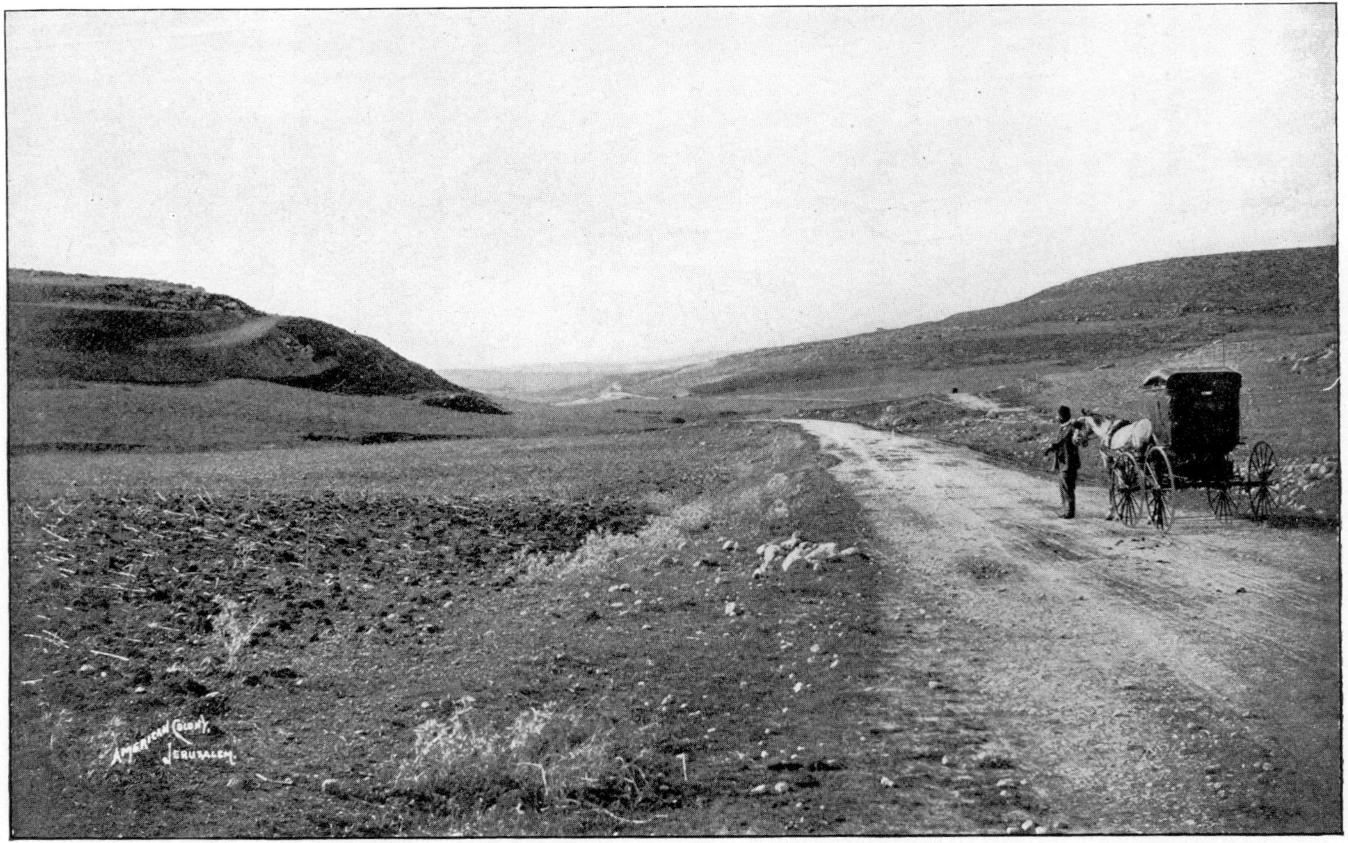
American Colony,
Jerusalem.

said unto the young man who bore his armor, "Come and let us go over to the Philistines' garrison, that is on yonder side."

But he told not his father. And Saul abode in the uttermost part of Gibeah under the pomegranate tree which is in Migron: and the people that were with him were about six hundred men. And the people knew not that Jonathan was gone. And between the passes, by which Jonathan sought to go over unto the Philistines' garrison, there was a rocky crag on the one side, and a rocky crag on the other side. The one crag rose up on the north in front of Michmash, and the other on the south in front of Geba. And Jonathan said to the young man that bore his armor, "Come and let us go over unto the garrison of the Philistines: it may be that the Lord will work for us: for there is no reason why the Lord cannot save by many or by few."

And his armorbearer said to him, "Do all that is in thine heart: turn thee, behold I am with thee according to thy wish." Then said Jonathan, "Behold, we will pass over to the men, and we will show ourselves to them. If they say thus unto us, 'Tarry until we come to you'; then we will stand still in our place, and will not go up to them. But if they say thus, 'Come up to us'; then we will go up: for the Lord hath delivered them into our hand: and this shall be the sign to us."

And both of them showed themselves to the garrison of the Philistines: and the Philistines said, "Behold, the Hebrews come forth out of the holes where they had hid themselves." And the men of the garrison answered Jonathan and his armorbearer, and said, "Come up to us, and we will show you something."

And Jonathan said to his armorbearer, "Come up after me: for the Lord hath delivered them into the hand of Israel."

And Jonathan climbed up upon his hands and upon his feet, and his armorbearer after him: and they fell before Jonathan; and his armorbearer slew them after him. And that first slaughter, which Jonathan and his armorbearer made, was about twenty men, within an acre of land. And there was a trembling in the camp, in the field, and among all the people. And the watchmen of Saul in Gibeah of Benjamin looked; and, behold, the multitude melted away, and they went hither and thither.

Then said Saul to the people that were with him, "Number now, and see who is gone from us."

And when they had numbered, behold, Jonathan and his armorbearer were not there. And Saul said to Ahijah, "Bring hither the ark of God."

For the ark of God was there at that time with the children of Israel. And it came to pass, while Saul talked unto the priest, that the tumult that was in the camp of the Philistines went on and increased: and Saul said to the priest, "Withdraw thine hand."

And Saul and all the people that were with him were gathered together, and came to the battle: and, behold, every man's sword was against his fellow, and there was a very great rout. Now the Hebrews that were with the

Philistines as beforetime, which went up with them into the camp from the country round about; even they also turned to be with the Israelites that were with Saul and Jonathan. Likewise all the men of Israel which had hid themselves in the hill country of Ephraim, when they heard that the Philistines fled, even they also followed hard after them in the battle.

So the Lord saved Israel that day: and the battle passed over by Beth-aven. And the men of Israel were distressed that day: but Saul commanded the people, saying, "Cursed be the man that eateth any food until it be evening, and I be avenged on mine enemies." So none of the people tasted food. And all the people came into the forest; and there was honey upon the ground. And when the people were come unto the forest, behold, the honey dropped: but no man ate any; for the people feared the oath. But Jonathan heard not when his father charged the people with the oath: wherefore he put forth the end of the rod that was in his hand, and dipped it in the honeycomb, and ate it; and he was strengthened. Then said one of the people, "Thy father straitly charged the people with an oath, saying, "Cursed be the man that eateth food this day."

And the people were faint. Then said Jonathan, "My father hath troubled the land: see, I pray you, how I have been strengthened, because I tasted a little of this honey. How much more, if the people had eaten freely to-day of the spoil of their enemies which they found? for now hath there been no great slaughter among the Philistines."

And they smote of the Philistines that day from Michmash to Aijalon: and the people were very faint. And the people flew upon the spoil, and took sheep, and oxen, and calves, and slew them on the ground: and the people did eat them with the blood. Then they told Saul, saying, "Behold, the people sin against the Lord, in that they eat with the blood." And he said, "Ye have dealt treacherously: roll a great stone to me this day."

And Saul said, "Disperse yourselves among the people, and say to them, 'Bring me hither every man his ox, and every man his sheep, and slay them here, and eat; and sin not against the Lord in eating with the blood.'"

And all the people brought every man his ox with him that night, and slew them there. And Saul built an altar unto the Lord: the same was the first altar that he built to the Lord.

And Saul said, "Let us go down after the Philistines by night, and fight them until the morning light, and let us not leave a man of them."

And they said, "Do whatsoever seemeth good unto thee." Then said the priest, "Let us draw near hither to God."

And Saul asked counsel of God, "Shall I go down after the Philistines? wilt thou deliver them into the hand of Israel?"

But he answered him not that day. And Saul said, "Draw nigh hither, all ye chiefs of the people: and know and see wherein this sin hath been this day. For as the Lord liveth, who saveth Israel, though it be in Jonathan my son, he shall surely die." But there was not a man among all the people that answered him.

Then said he unto all Israel, "Be ye on one side, and I and Jonathan my son will be on the other side."

And the people said to Saul, "Do what seemeth good to thee."

Therefore Saul said to the Lord, the God of Israel, "Show the right."

And Jonathan and Saul were chosen by lot: but the people escaped.

And Saul said, "Cast lots between me and Jonathan my son." And Jonathan was chosen.

Then Saul said to Jonathan, "Tell me what thou hast done."

And Jonathan told him, and said, "I did certainly taste a little honey with the end of the rod that was in mine hand; and, lo, I must die."

And Saul said, "God do so and more also: for thou shalt surely die, Jonathan."

And the people said to Saul, "Shall Jonathan die, who hath wrought this great salvation in Israel? God forbid: as the Lord liveth, there shall not one hair of his head fall to the ground; for he hath wrought with God this day."

So the people rescued Jonathan, that he died not. Then Saul went up from following the Philistines: and the Philistines went to their own place.

Now when Saul had taken the kingdom over Israel, he fought against all his enemies on every side, against Moab, and against the children of Ammon, and against Edom, and against the kings of Zobah, and against the Philistines: and whithersoever he went he defeated them.

THE DISOBEDIENCE OF SAUL.
"To Obey Is Better than Sacrifice."

And Samuel said to Saul, "The Lord sent me to anoint thee to be king over his people, over Israel: now therefore hearken thou to the voice of the words of the Lord. Thus saith the Lord of hosts, 'I have marked that which Amalek did to Israel, how he set himself against him in the way, when he came up out of Egypt. Now go and smite Amalek, and utterly destroy all that they have, and spare them not; but slay both man and woman, infant and suckling, ox and sheep, camel and ass.'"

And Saul summoned the people, and numbered them in Telaim, two hundred thousand footmen, and ten thousand men of Judah. And Saul came to the city of Amalek, and laid wait in the valley. And Saul said unto the Kenites, "Go, depart, get you down from among the Amalekites, lest I destroy you with them: for ye showed kindness to all the children of Israel, when they came up out of Egypt."

So the Kenites departed from among the Amalekites, and Saul smote the Amalekites and defeated them. And he took Agag the king of the Amalekites alive, and utterly destroyed all the people with the edge of the sword. But Saul and the people spared Agag, and the best of the sheep, and of the oxen, and of the fatlings, and the lambs, and all that was good, and would not utterly destroy them:

RUINS OF A ROMAN BRIDGE AT BETH-SHAN, OVER WHICH THE ROAD TO GADARA PASSED

Used by special permission of the Palestine Exploration Fund

After the battle of Gilboa the bodies of Saul and his sons were found on the field by the Philistines and carried to the town of Beth-shan and fastened to the wall. But the men of Jabesh-Gilead heard of this indignity to the dead, and making a night march removed the bodies

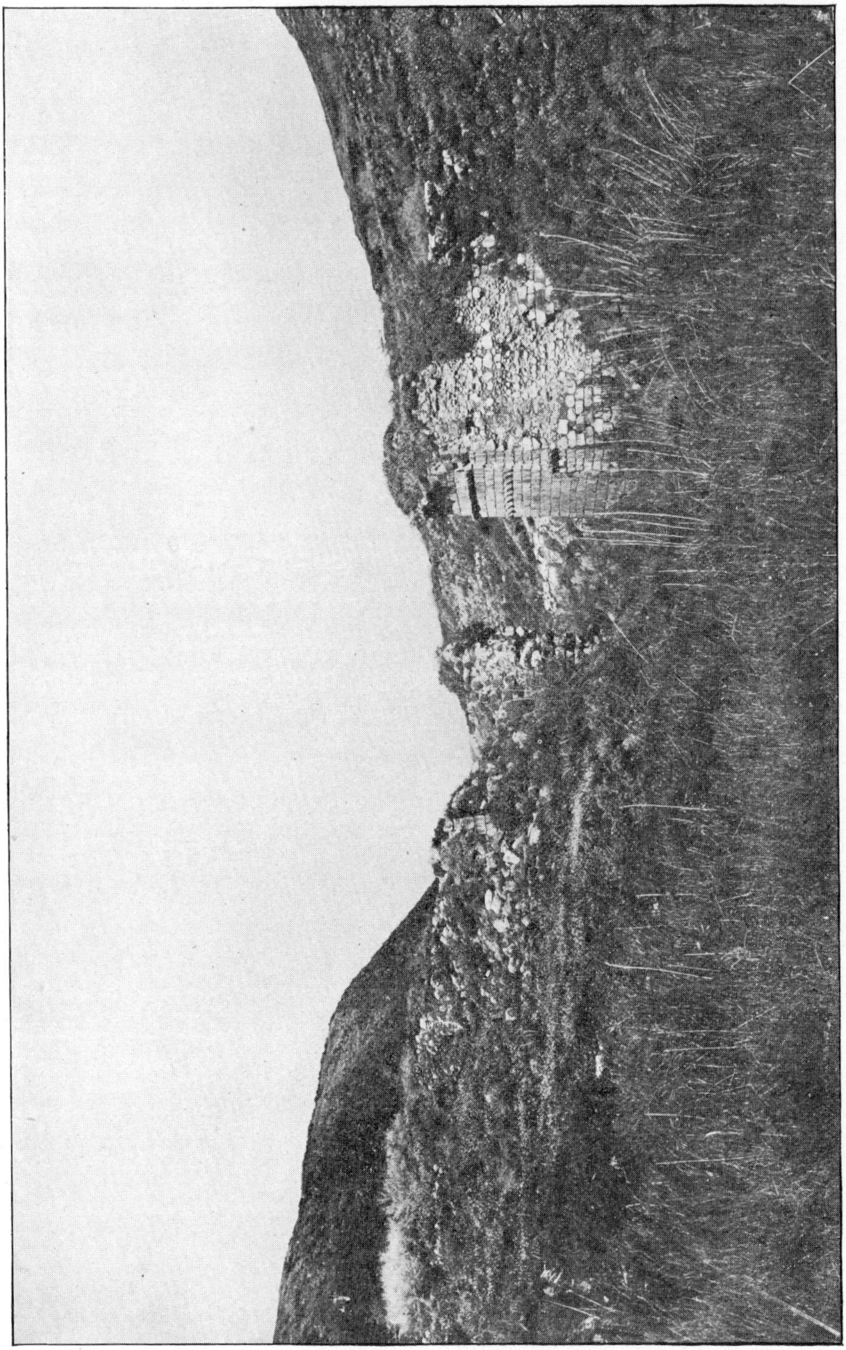

but everything that was useless and refuse, that they destroyed utterly.

Then came the word of the Lord unto Samuel, saying, "It repenteth me that I have set up Saul to be king: for he is turned back from following me, and hath not performed my commandments."

And Samuel was wroth; and he cried to the Lord all night. And Samuel rose early to meet Saul in the morning; and it was told Samuel, saying, "Saul came to Carmel, and, behold, he set him up a monument, and is gone about, and passed on, and gone down to Gilgal." And Samuel came to Saul: and Saul said to him, "Blessed be thou of the Lord: I have performed the commandment of the Lord."

And Samuel said, "What meaneth then this bleating of the sheep in mine ears, and the lowing of the oxen which I hear?"

And Saul said, "They have brought them from the Amalekites: for the people spared the best of the sheep and of the oxen, to sacrifice to the Lord thy God; and the rest we have utterly destroyed."

Then Samuel said to Saul, "Stay, and I will tell thee what the Lord hath said to me this night."

And he said unto him, "Say on."

And Samuel said, "Though thou wast little in thine own sight, wast thou not made the head of the tribes of Israel? And the Lord anointed thee king over Israel; and the Lord sent thee on a journey, and said, 'Go and utterly destroy the sinners the Amalekites, and fight against them until they be consumed.' Wherefore then didst thou not obey the voice of the Lord, but didst fly upon the spoil, and didst that which was evil in the sight of the Lord?"

And Saul said unto Samuel, "Yea, I have obeyed the voice of the Lord, and have gone the way which the Lord sent me, and have brought Agag the king of Amalek, and have utterly destroyed the Amalekites. But the people took of the spoil, sheep and oxen, the chief of the devoted things, to sacrifice unto the Lord thy God in Gilgal."

And Samuel said, "Hath the Lord as great delight in burnt offerings and sacrifices, as in obeying the voice of the Lord? Behold,—

"To obey is better than sacrifice, and to hearken than the fat of rams."

"For rebellion is as the sin of witchcraft, and stubbornness is as idolatry and image worship. Because thou hast rejected the word of the Lord, he hath also rejected thee from being king."

And Saul said to Samuel, "I have sinned: for I have transgressed the commandment of the Lord, and thy words: because I feared the people, and obeyed their voice. Now therefore, I pray thee, pardon my sin, and turn again with me, that I may worship the Lord."

And Samuel said to Saul, "I will not return with thee: for thou hast rejected the word of the Lord, and the Lord hath rejected thee from being king over Israel."

And as Samuel turned about to go away, he laid hold upon the skirt of his robe, and it rent. And Samuel said to him, "The Lord hath rent the kingdom of Israel from thee this day, and hath given it to a neighbor of thine, that is better than thou. And also the Strength of Israel will not lie nor repent: for he is not a man, that he should repent."

Then he said, "I have sinned: yet honor me now, I pray thee, before the elders of my people, and before Israel; and turn again with me, that I may worship the Lord thy God."

So Samuel turned again after Saul; and Saul worshiped the Lord.

Then said Samuel, "Bring ye hither to me Agag the king of the Amalekites." And Agag came unto him cheerfully. And Agag said, "Surely the bitterness of death is past."

And Samuel said, "As thy sword hath made women childless, so shall thy mother be childless among women."

And Samuel hewed Agag in pieces before the Lord in Gilgal.

Then Samuel went to Ramah; and Saul went up to his house to Gibeah of Saul. And Samuel came no more to see Saul until the day of his death; for Samuel mourned for Saul: and the Lord repented that he had made Saul king over Israel.

THE DOWNFALL OF THE KING.

"God is Departed from Me."

(For some time after this Saul continued to be king over Israel, but he had many troubles. These troubles made him sad and despondent, so that often the people thought him insane. At last war broke out again with the fierce and powerful Philistines, who lived on the plains to the west of the hill-country which was the home of the Israelites. Saul was very much discouraged at the beginning of this war. The story of what he did, and how he died at last like a hero on the battle-field, is as follows.)

Now Samuel was dead, and all Israel had lamented him, and buried him in Ramah, even in his own city. And Saul had put away those that had familiar spirits, and the wizards, out of the land. And the Philistines gathered themselves together, and came and camped in Shunem: and Saul gathered all Israel together, and they camped in Gilboa. And when Saul saw the host of the Philistines, he was afraid, and his heart trembled greatly. And when Saul inquired of the Lord, the Lord answered him not.

Then said Saul to his servants, "Seek me a woman that hath a familiar spirit, that I may go to her, and inquire of her."

And his servants said to him, "Behold, there is a woman that hath a familiar spirit at En-dor."

And Saul disguised himself and put on other raiment, and went, he and two men with him, and they came to the woman by night: and he said, "Divine unto me, I pray thee, by the familiar spirit, and bring me up whomsoever I shall name unto thee."

And the woman said unto him, "Behold, thou knowest what Saul hath done, how he hath cut off those that have familiar spirits, and the wizards, out of the land: where-

EN-DOR

This was where the great king came at night, in despair, to consult the woman " with the familiar spirit "

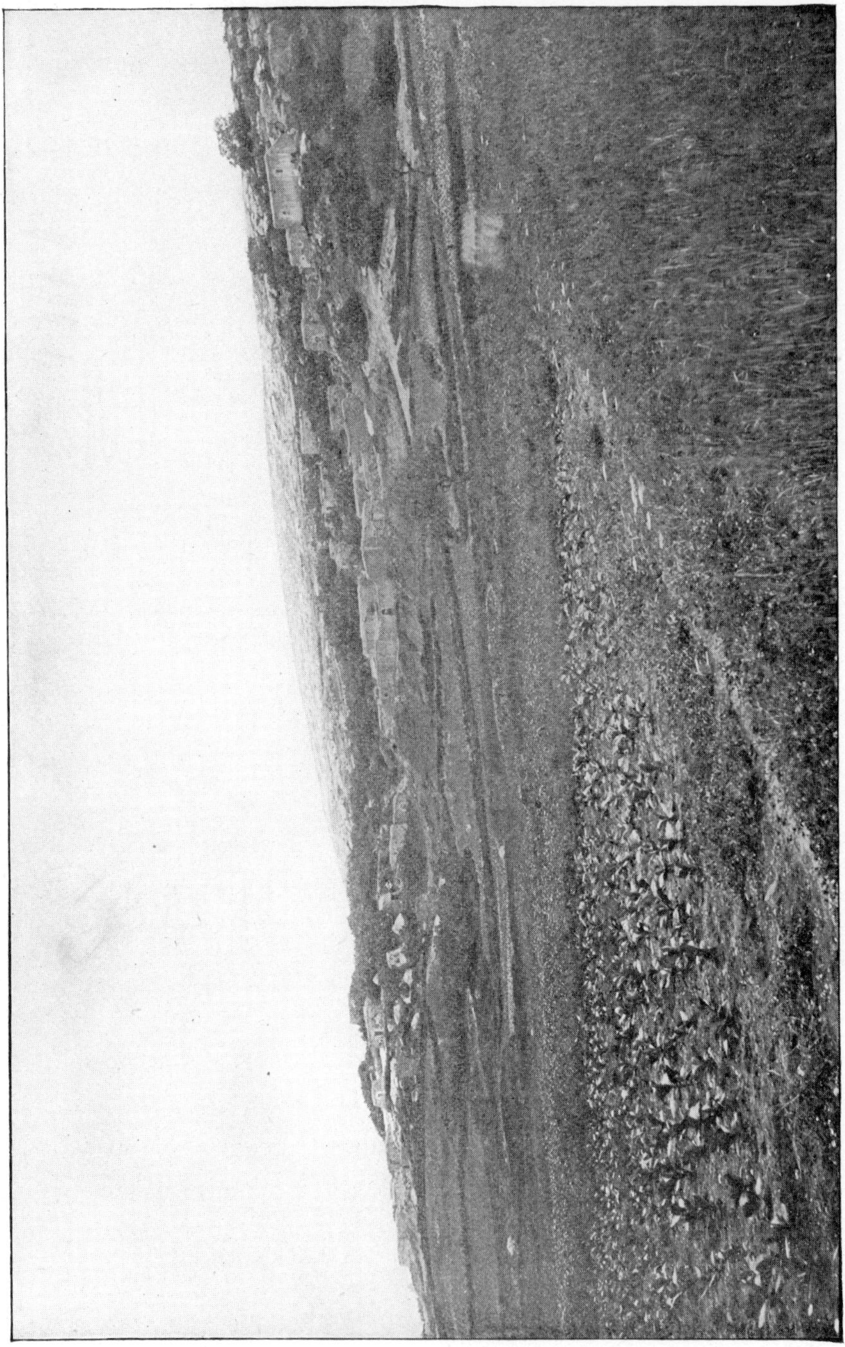

fore then layest thou a snare for my life, to cause me to die?"

And Saul swore to her by the Lord, saying, "As the Lord liveth, there shall no punishment happen to thee for this thing."

Then said the woman, "Whom shall I bring up unto thee?"

And he said, "Bring me up Samuel."

And when the woman saw Samuel, she cried with a loud voice: and the woman spoke to Saul, saying, "Why hast thou deceived me? for thou art Saul."

And the king said to her, "Be not afraid: for what seest thou?"

And the woman said to Saul, "I see one like a god coming up out of the earth."

And he said unto her, "What form is he of?"

And she said, "An old man cometh up; and he is covered with a robe."

And Saul perceived that it was Samuel, and he bowed with his face to the ground, and did obeisance. And Samuel said to Saul, "Why hast thou disquieted me, to bring me up?"

And Saul answered, "I am sore distressed; for the Philistines make war against me, and God is departed from me, and answereth me no more, neither by prophets, nor by dreams: therefore I have called thee, that thou mayest make known to me what I shall do."

And Samuel said, "Wherefore dost thou ask of me, seeing the Lord is departed from thee, and is become thine adversary? And the Lord hath done unto thee as he spoke by me: and the Lord hath rent the kingdom out of thine hand, and given it to thy neighbor, even to David. Because thou obeyedst not the voice of the Lord, and didst not execute his fierce wrath upon Amalek, therefore hath the Lord done this thing unto thee this day. Moreover the Lord will deliver Israel also with thee into the hand of the Philistines: and to-morrow shalt thou and thy sons be with me: the Lord shall deliver the host of Israel also into the hand of the Philistines."

Then Saul fell straightway his full length upon the earth, and was sore afraid, because of the words of Samuel; and there was no strength in him; for he had eaten no food all the day, nor all the night.

THE FATAL FIELD OF GILBOA.

The Tide of Battle Rolls Over King Saul and His Sons.

Now the Philistines fought against Israel: and the men of Israel fled from before the Philistines, and fell down slain in Mount Gilboa. And the Philistines followed hard upon Saul, and upon his sons; and the Philistines slew Jonathan, and Abinadab, and Malchi-shua, the sons of Saul. And the battle went sore against Saul, and the archers overtook him; and he was greatly distressed by reason of the archers.

Then said Saul to his armorbearer, "Draw thy sword, and thrust me through therewith; lest the Philistines come and thrust me through, and maltreat me."

But his armorbearer would not; for he was sore afraid. Therefore Saul took his sword and fell upon it.

And when his armorbearer saw that Saul was dead, he likewise fell upon his sword, and died with him. So Saul died, and his three sons, and his armorbearer, and all his men, that same day together. And when the men of Israel that were on the other side of the valley, and they that were beyond Jordan, saw that the men of Israel fled, and that Saul and his sons were dead, they forsook the cities, and fled; and the Philistines came and dwelt in them.

And it came to pass on the morrow, when the Philistines came to strip the slain, that they found Saul and his three sons fallen in Mount Gilboa. And they cut off his head, and stripped off his armor, and sent into the land of the Philistines round about, to carry the tidings unto the house of their idols, and to the people. And they put his armor in the house of the god Ashtaroth: and they fastened his body to the wall of Beth-shan. And when the inhabitants of Jabesh-gilead heard what the Philistines had done to Saul, all the valiant men arose, and went all night, and took the body of Saul and the bodies of his sons from the wall of Beth-shan; and they came to Jabesh, and burnt them there. And they took their bones and buried them under the tamarisk tree in Jabesh, and fasted seven days.

DAVID

The Story of the Shepherd Boy Who Became King.

THE SHEPHERD LAD OF BETHLEHEM.

Samuel Secretly Anoints David as the Future King of Israel.

(After Samuel had said to Saul that God wanted no king who would not do exactly as he said, he himself became very sad, because he loved Saul.)

But the Lord said to Samuel, "How long wilt thou mourn for Saul, seeing I have rejected him from being king over Israel? fill thine horn with oil, and go, I will send thee to Jesse the Beth-lehemite: for I have provided me a king among his sons."

And Samuel said, "How can I go? if Saul hear it, he will kill me."

And the Lord said, "Take an heifer with thee, and say, 'I am come to sacrifice to the Lord.' And call Jesse to the sacrifice, and I will show thee what thou shalt do: and thou shalt anoint to me him whom I name to thee."

And Samuel did that which the Lord spoke, and came to Beth-lehem. And the elders of the city came to meet him trembling, and said, "Comest thou peaceably?"

And he said, "Peaceably: I am come to sacrifice to the Lord: sanctify yourselves, and come with me to the sacri-

DAVID

This is the head of the great statue of David in Florence, carved by the most famous of all sculptors, Michael Angelo. The story is that the great sculptor took a piece of marble partly spoiled by another man, and carved this wonderful statue out of it. The statue shows the young shepherd with his sling, ready for the conflict with the giant

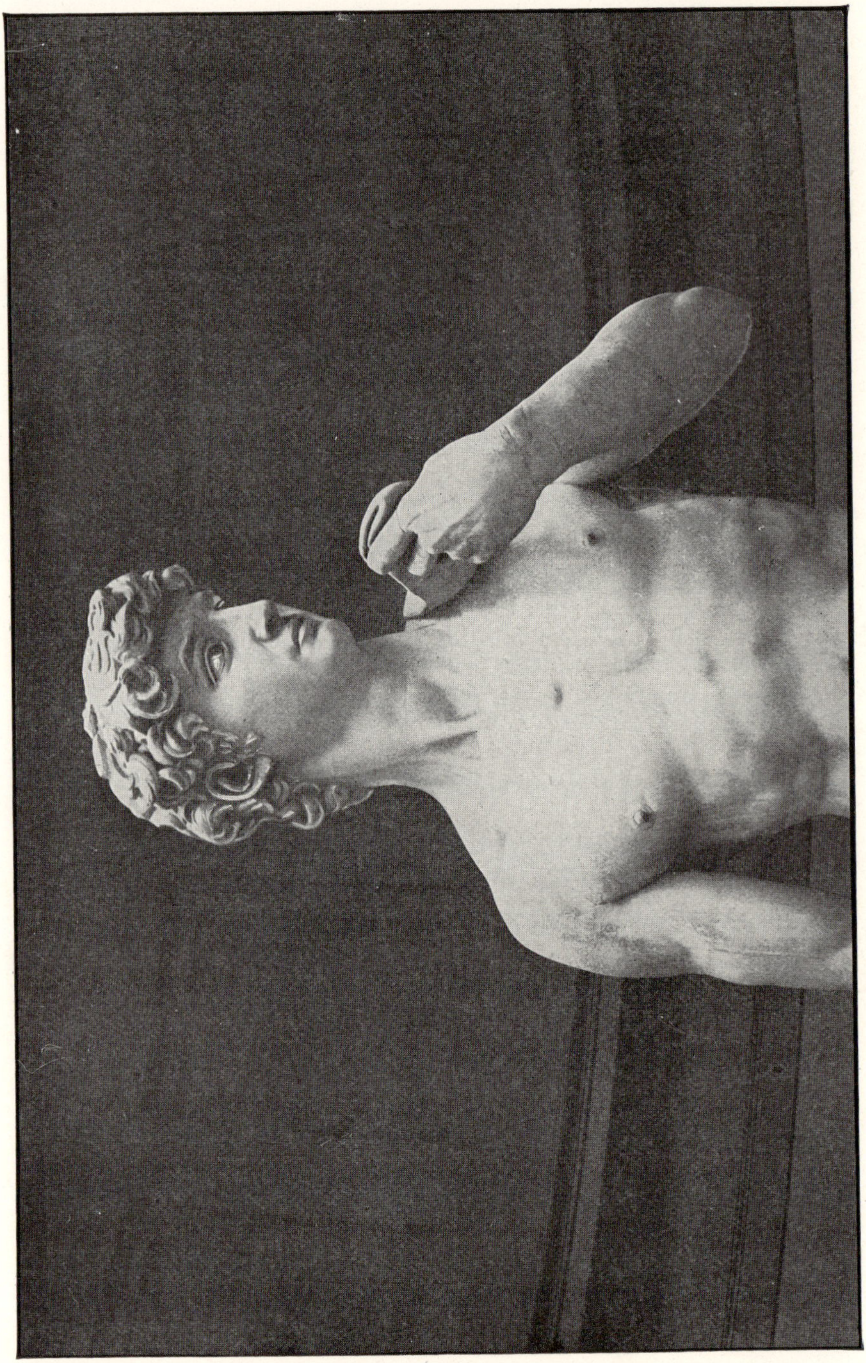

fice." And he sanctified Jesse and his sons, and called them to the sacrifice.

And it came to pass, when they were come, that he looked on Eliab, and said, "Surely the Lord's anointed is before him."

But the Lord said unto Samuel, "Look not on his countenance, or on the height of his stature; because I have rejected him: for the Lord seeth not as man seeth; for man looketh on the outward appearance, but the Lord looketh on the heart."

Then Jesse called Abinadab, and made him pass before Samuel. And he said, "Neither hath the Lord chosen this."

Then Jesse made Shammah to pass by. And he said, "Neither hath the Lord chosen this."

And Jesse made seven of his sons to pass before Samuel. And Samuel said unto Jesse, "The Lord hath not chosen these."

And Samuel said unto Jesse, "Are here all thy children?"

And he said, "There remaineth yet the youngest, and, behold, he keepeth the sheep."

And Samuel said unto Jesse, "Send and fetch him: for we will not sit down till he come hither."

And he sent, and brought him in. Now he was ruddy, and withal of a beautiful countenance, and goodly to look upon. And the Lord said, "Arise, anoint him; for this is he."

Then Samuel took the horn of oil, and anointed him

in the midst of his brethren: and the spirit of the Lord came mightily upon David from that day forward. So Samuel rose up, and went to Ramah.

DAVID AND GOLIATH.
How a Giant Was Killed by a Stone from a Shepherd's Sling.

Now the Philistines gathered together their armies to battle. And Saul and the men of Israel were gathered together, and camped in the vale of Elah, and set the battle in array against the Philistines. And the Philistines stood on the mountain on the one side, and Israel stood on the mountain on the other side: and there was a valley between them.

And there went out a champion out of the camp of the Philistines, named Goliath, of Gath, whose height was six cubits and a span. And he had an helmet of brass upon his head, and he was clad with a coat of mail; and the weight of the coat was five thousand shekels of brass. And he had greaves of brass upon his legs, and a javelin of brass between his shoulders. And the staff of his spear was like a weaver's beam; and his spear's head weighed six hundred shekels of iron: and his shieldbearer went before him. And he stood and cried to the armies of Israel, and said to them, "Why are ye come out to set your battle in array? am not I a Philistine, and ye servants to Saul? choose you a man for you, and let him come down to me. If he be able to fight with me, and kill me, then will we be your servants: but if I prevail against him, and kill him, then shall ye be our servants, and serve us."

SCENE OF THE FIGHT BETWEEN DAVID AND GOLIATH IN THE VALLEY OF ELAH

Copyright by Underwood & Underwood
and used by special permission

"It is the very battlefield for those ancient foes. Israel in one of the gateways to her mountain land; the Philistines on the low hills they so often overran; and between them the great valley. The Philistines were probably on the hill of Sochoh

"Sochoh is a strong position isolated from the rest of the ridge, and it keeps open the line of retreat down the valley. Saul's army was probably not immediately opposite, but a little way up on the slopes of the incoming Wady el Jindy, and so placed that the Philistines, in attacking it, must cross not only the level land and the main stream, but one of the two other streams as well, and must also climb the slopes for some distance. Both positions were thus very strong, and this fact perhaps explains the long hesitation of the armies in face of each other, even though the Philistines had the advantage of Goliath. The Israelite position certainly looks the stronger. It is interesting, too, that from its rear the narrow pass goes right up to the interior of the land near Bethlehem; so that the shepherd boy, whom the story represents as being sent by his father for news of the battle, would have almost twelve miles to cover between his father's house and the camp"

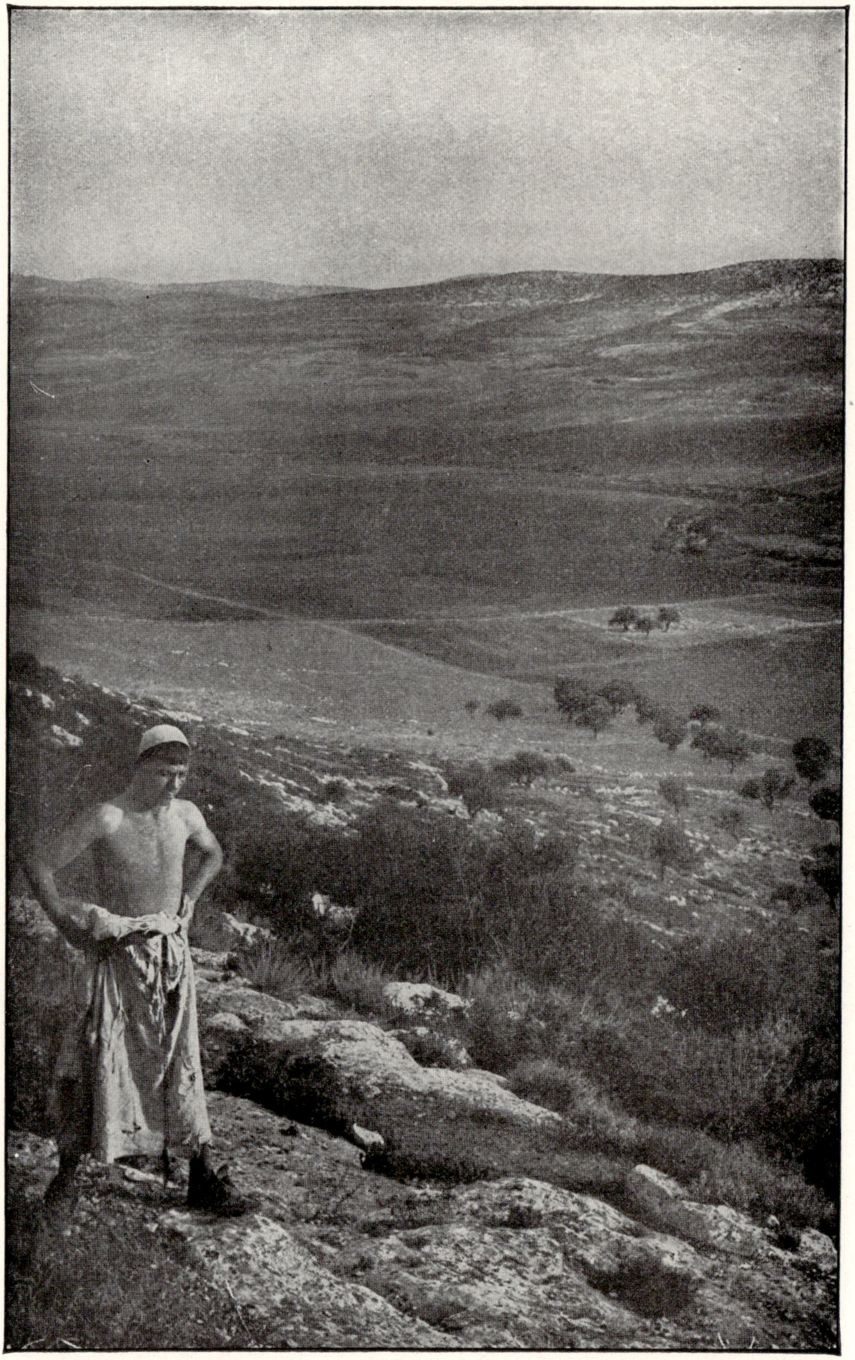

And the Philistine said, "I defy the armies of Israel this day; give me a man, that we may fight together."

And when Saul and all Israel heard those words of the Philistine, they were dismayed, and greatly afraid.

Now David was the son of that Ephrathite of Bethlehem-judah, whose name was Jesse; and he had eight sons: and the man was an old man in the days of Saul. And the three eldest sons of Jesse had gone after Saul to the battle: and the names of his three sons that went to the battle were Eliab the firstborn, and next unto him Abinadab, and the third Shammah. And David was the youngest: and the three eldest followed Saul.

And Jesse said to David his son, "Take now for thy brethren an ephah of this parched corn, and these ten loaves, and carry them quickly to the camp to thy brethren; and bring these ten cheeses unto the captain of their thousand; and look how thy brethren fare, and bring back some token of their welfare."

Now Saul, and they, and all the men of Israel, were in the vale of Elah, fighting with the Philistines. And David rose up early in the morning, and left the sheep with a keeper, and took the presents and went, as Jesse had commanded him; and he came to the barricade of wagons, as the host which was going forth to the fight shouted for the battle. And Israel and the Philistines put the battle in array, army against army. And David left the presents he had brought in the hand of the keeper of the baggage, and ran to the army, and came and saluted his brethren. And as he talked with them, behold, there came up the champion, the Philistine of Gath, Goliath by name, out of the ranks of the Philistines, and spoke as before: and David heard him. And all the men of Israel, when they saw the man, fled from him, and were sore afraid. And the men of Israel said, "Have ye seen this man that is come up? surely to defy Israel is he come up. and it shall be that the man who killeth him, the king will enrich him with great riches, and will give him his daughter in marriage, and make his father's house free in Israel."

And David spoke to the men that stood by him, saying, "What shall be done to the man that killeth this Philistine, and taketh away the reproach from Israel? for who is this Philistine, that he should defy the armies of the living God?"

And the people answered him after this manner, saying, "So shall it be done to the man that killeth him."

And Eliab his eldest brother heard when he spoke unto the men; and Eliab's anger was kindled against David, and he said, "Why art thou come down? and with whom hast thou left those few sheep in the wilderness? I know thy pride, and the naughtiness of thine heart; for thou art come down that thou mightest see the battle."

And David said, "What have I done now? I have only asked a question."

And he turned away from him toward another, and spoke after the same manner: and the people answered him again in the same way. And when the words were heard which David spoke, they rehearsed them before Saul; and he sent for him. And David said to Saul. "Let no man's heart fail because of him; thy servant will go and fight with this Philistine."

And Saul said to David, "Thou art not able to go against this Philistine to fight with him: for thou art but a youth, and he a man of war from his youth."

And David said to Saul, "Thy servant kept his father's sheep; and when there came a lion, or a bear, and took a lamb out of the flock, I went out after him, and smote him, and delivered it out of his mouth: and when he arose against me, I caught him by his beard, and smote him, and slew him. Thy servant smote both the lion and the bear: and this Philistine shall be as one of them, seeing he hath defied the armies of the living God." And David said, "The Lord that delivered me out of the paw of the lion, and out of the paw of the bear, he will deliver me out of the hand of this Philistine."

And Saul said to David, "Go, and the Lord shall be with thee."

And Saul clad David with his own garments, and he put an helmet of brass upon his head, and he clad him with a coat of mail. And David girded on his sword. But David said to Saul, "I cannot go with these; for I have not proved them."

And David put them off him. And he took his staff in his hand, and chose him five smooth stones out of the brook, and put them in the shepherd's bag which he had, and his sling was in his hand: and he drew near to the Philistine. And the Philistine came on and drew near to David; and the man that bore the shield went before him. And when the Philistine looked about, and saw David, he despised him: for he was but a youth, and ruddy, and of a fair countenance. And the Philistine said to David, "Am I a dog, that thou comest to me with staves?"

And the Philistine cursed David by his gods. And the Philistine said to David, "Come to me, and I will give thy flesh unto the fowls of the air, and to the beasts of the field."

Then said David to the Philistine, "Thou comest to me with a sword, and with a spear, and with a javelin: but I come to thee in the name of the Lord of hosts, the God of the armies of Israel, whom thou hast defied. This day will the Lord deliver thee into mine hand; and I will smite thee, and take thine head from off thee; and I will give the carcases of the host of the Philistines this day to the fowls of the air, and to the wild beasts of the earth; that all the earth may know that there is a God in Israel: and that all this host may know that the Lord saveth not with sword and spear: for the battle is the Lord's, and he will give you into our hand."

And it came to pass, when the Philistine arose, and came and drew nigh to meet David, that David hastened, and ran toward the army to meet the Philistine. And David put his hand in his bag, and took thence a stone, and slung it, and smote the Philistine in his forehead; and the stone sank into his forehead, and he fell upon his face to the earth. So David prevailed over the Philistine with a sling and with a stone, and smote the Philistine, and slew him; but there was no sword in the hand of David. Then

David ran, and stood over the Philistine, and took his sword and drew it out of its sheath, and slew him, and cut off his head therewith. And when the Philistines saw that their champion was dead, they fled. And the men of Israel and of Judah arose, and shouted, and pursued the Philistines, to the gates of Ekron. And the wounded of the Philistines fell down by the way. And the children of Israel returned from chasing after the Philistines, and they plundered their camp. And David took the head of the Philistine, and brought it to Jerusalem; but he put his armor in his tent.

And when Saul saw David go forth against the Philistine, he said unto Abner, the captain of the host, "Abner, whose son is this youth?"

And Abner said, "As thy soul liveth, O king, I cannot tell."

And the king said, "Inquire thou whose son the stripling is."

And as David returned from the slaughter of the Philistine, Abner took him, and brought him before Saul with the head of the Philistine in his hand. And Saul said to him, "Whose son art thou, young man?"

And David answered, "I am the son of thy servant Jesse the Beth-lehemite."

And it came to pass, when he had made an end of speaking unto Saul, that the soul of Jonathan was knit with the soul of David, and Jonathan loved him as his own soul.

And Saul took him that day, and would let him go no more home to his father's house. Then Jonathan and

David made a covenant, because he loved him as his own soul. And Jonathan stripped himself of the robe that was upon him, and gave it to David, and his apparel, even to his sword, and to his bow, and to his girdle. And David went out whithersoever Saul sent him, and behaved himself wisely: and Saul set him over the men of war, and it was good in the sight of all the people, and also in the sight of Saul's servants.

SAUL AND DAVID

Deep was the furrow in the royal brow,
When David's hand, lightly as vernal gales
Rippling the brook of Kedron, skimm'd the lyre:
He sung of Jacob's youngest born,—the child
Of his old age,—sold to the Ishmaelite;
His exaltation to the second power
In Pharaoh's realm; his brethren thither sent;
Suppliant they stood before his face, well known,
Unknowing,—till Joseph fell upon the neck
Of Benjamin, his mother's son, and wept.
Unconsciously the warlike shepherd paused;
But when he saw, down the yet quivering string,
The tear-drop trembling glide, abash'd, he check'd,
Indignant at himself, the bursting flood,
And, with a sweep impetuous, struck the chords:
From side to side his hands transversely glance,
Like lightning 'thwart a stormy sea; his voice
Arises 'mid the clang, and straightway calms
Th' harmonious tempest, to a solemn swell
Majestical, triumphant; for he sings
Of Arad's mighty host by Israel's arm
Subdued; of Israel through the desert led
He sings; of him who was their leader, call'd
By God himself, from keeping Jethro's flock,
To be a ruler o'er the chosen race.
Kindles the eye of Saul; his arm is poised,—
Harmless the javelin quivers in the wall.

THE JEALOUSY OF SAUL.

How Saul Was Jealous of David and Hated Him, and How Jonathan Loved Him.

And it came to pass as they came, when David returned from the slaughter of the Philistine, that the women came out of all the cities of Israel, singing and dancing, to meet King Saul, with timbrels, with joy, and with instruments of music. And the women sang one to another in their play, and said,—

"Saul hath slain his thousands,
And David his ten thousands."

And Saul was very wroth, and this saying displeased him; and he said, "They have ascribed unto David ten thousands, and to me they have ascribed but thousands: and what can he have more but the kingdom?"

And Saul eyed David jealously from that day and forward.

And it came to pass on the morrow, that an evil spirit from God came mightily upon Saul, and he raved in the midst of the house: and David played upon his harp, as he did day by day: and Saul had his spear in his hand. And Saul cast the spear; for he said, "I will smite David even to the wall."

And David escaped from his presence twice. And Saul was afraid of David, because the Lord was with him, and was departed from Saul. Therefore Saul removed him from him, and made him his captain over a thousand; and he went out and came in before the people. And David behaved himself wisely in all his ways; and the Lord was

THE VALLEY OF THE KIDRON, IN THE WILDERNESS OF JUDÆA

The building on the left is the convent of Mar Saba

Used by special permission of the Palestine Exploration Fund

The "Wilderness of Judæa" is a wonderful place. Much of it is not a wilderness at all in our understanding of the term. It is, on its western edge at least, just a wild pasture land. But it was a very wild, desolate, and solitary place. The shepherd who kept his flocks there was in danger from the wild beasts and from raids of fierce robbers. Below the pasture land it is wilderness indeed. The land breaks off abruptly and falls in crag and precipice down to the very shores of the Dead Sea. "You cannot live in Judæa without being daily aware of the presence of the awful deep which bounds it on the east. From Beth-lehem and other points you look down into that deep, and you feel Judæa rising from it about you almost as a sailor feels his narrow deck"

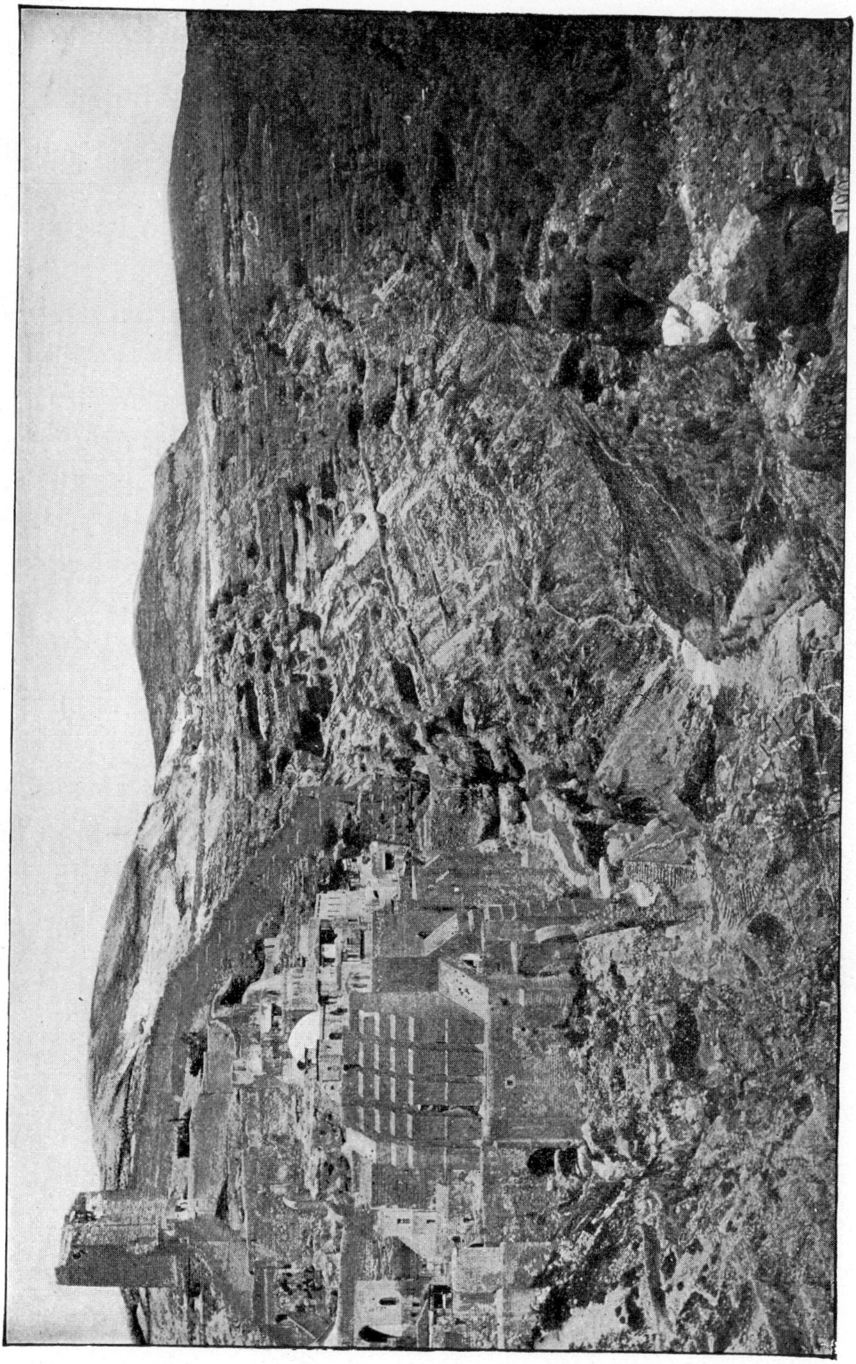

with him. And when Saul saw that he behaved himself very wisely, he stood in awe of him. But all Israel and Judah loved David; for he went out and came in before them.

And Saul spoke to Jonathan his son, and to all his servants, that they should slay David. But Jonathan Saul's son delighted much in David. And Jonathan told David, saying, "Saul my father seeketh to slay thee: now therefore, I pray thee, take heed to thyself in the morning, and abide in a secret place, and hide thyself: and I will go out and stand beside my father in the field where thou art, and I will talk with my father of thee; and if I see aught, I will tell thee."

And Jonathan spoke good of David unto Saul his father, and said unto him, "Let not the king sin against his servant, against David; because he hath not sinned against thee, and because his works have been very good toward thee; for he put his life in his hand, and smote the Philistine, and the Lord wrought a great victory for all Israel: thou sawest it, and didst rejoice: wherefore then wilt thou sin against innocent blood, to slay David without a cause?"

And Saul hearkened unto the voice of Jonathan: and Saul swore, "As the Lord liveth, he shall not be put to death."

And Jonathan called David, and Jonathan showed him all those things. And Jonathan brought David to Saul, and he was in his presence, as before.

And there was war again: and David went out, and fought with the Philistines, and slew them with a great slaughter; and they fled before him. And an evil spirit from the Lord was upon Saul, as he sat in his house with his spear in his hand; and David played upon his harp. And Saul sought to smite David even to the wall with the spear; but he slipped away out of Saul's presence, and he struck the spear into the wall: and David fled, and escaped that night.

And David came and said to Jonathan, "What have I done? what is mine iniquity? and what is my sin before thy father, that he seeketh my life?"

And he said, "God forbid; thou shalt not die: behold, my father doeth nothing either great or small, but that he discloseth it unto me: and why should my father hide this thing from me? it is not so."

And David swore moreover, and said, "Thy father knoweth well that I have found grace in thine eyes; and he saith, 'Let not Jonathan know this, lest he be grieved': but truly as the Lord liveth, and as thy soul liveth, there is but a step between me and death."

Then said Jonathan to David, "Whatsoever thy soul desireth, I will even do it for thee."

And David said to Jonathan, "Behold, to-morrow is the new moon, and I should not fail to sit with the king at meat: but let me go, that I may hide myself in the field until the third day at even. If thy father miss me at all, then say, 'David earnestly asked leave of me that he might run to Beth-lehem his city: for it is the yearly sacrifice there for all the family.' If he say thus, 'It is well'; thy servant shall have peace: but if he be wroth, then know that evil is determined by him. Therefore deal kindly with thy servant; for thou hast brought thy servant into a covenant of the Lord with thee: but if there be in me iniquity, slay me thyself; for why shouldest thou bring me to thy father?"

And Jonathan said, "Far be it from thee: for if I should at all know that evil were determined by my father to come upon thee, then would not I tell it thee?"

Then said David to Jonathan, "Who shall tell me if perchance thy father answer thee roughly?"

And Jonathan said to David, "Come and let us go out into the field." And they went out both of them into the field.

And Jonathan said to David, "The Lord, the God of Israel, be witness; when I have sounded my father about this time to-morrow, or the third day, behold, if there be good toward David, shall I not then send unto thee, and disclose it unto thee? The Lord do so to Jonathan, and more also, should it please my father to do thee evil, if I disclose it not unto thee, and send thee away, that thou mayest go in peace: and the Lord be with thee, as he hath been with my father. And thou shalt not only while yet I live show me the kindness of the Lord, that I die not: but also thou shalt not cut off thy kindness from my house for ever: no, not when the Lord hath cut off the enemies of David every one from the face of the earth."

So Jonathan made a covenant with David.

And Jonathan caused David to swear again, for the love that he had to him: for he loved him as he loved his own soul. Then Jonathan said to him, "To-morrow is the feast of the new moon: and thou shalt be missed, because thy seat will be empty. And when thou hast stayed three days, thou shalt go down quickly, and come to the place where thou didst hide thyself before. And I will shoot three arrows, as though I shot at a mark. And, behold, I will send the lad, saying, 'Go, find the arrows.' If I say to the lad, 'Behold, the arrows are on this side of thee: take them,' then come; for there is peace to thee and no hurt, as the Lord liveth. But if I say thus to the boy, 'Behold, the arrows are beyond thee': go thy way; for the Lord hath sent thee away. And as touching the matter which thou and I have spoken of, behold, the Lord is between thee and me for ever."

So David hid himself in the field: and when the feast of the new moon was come, the king sat down to eat. And the king sat upon his seat, as at other times, even upon the seat by the wall; and Jonathan stood up, and Abner sat by Saul's side: but David's place was empty. Nevertheless Saul spoke not anything that day: for he thought, "Something hath befallen him." And it came to pass on the morrow after the new moon, which was the second day, that David's place was empty: and Saul said to Jonathan his son, "Wherefore cometh not the son of Jesse to meat, neither yesterday, nor to-day?"

And Jonathan answered Saul, "David earnestly asked leave of me to go to Beth-lehem: and he said, 'Let me go, I pray thee; for our family hath a sacrifice in the city; and my brother, he hath commanded me to be there: and

RUINS OF THE FORTRESS OF MASSADA, WILDERNESS OF JUDÆA

This is another picture of a portion of the "Wilderness of Judæa." It is easy to see how David, who was thoroughly familiar with the country, could hide himself and his men safely from pursuit during the time in which he was an outlaw and a fugitive from the king

This fortress was the scene of a terrible siege and massacre in 70 A. D., after the fall of Jerusalem. About a thousand men, women, and children fled to this place. The Romans followed and in spite of almost insurmountable difficulties besieged the place. Driven to the last extremity, the defenders killed the women and children and then themselves. Only two women and five children survived

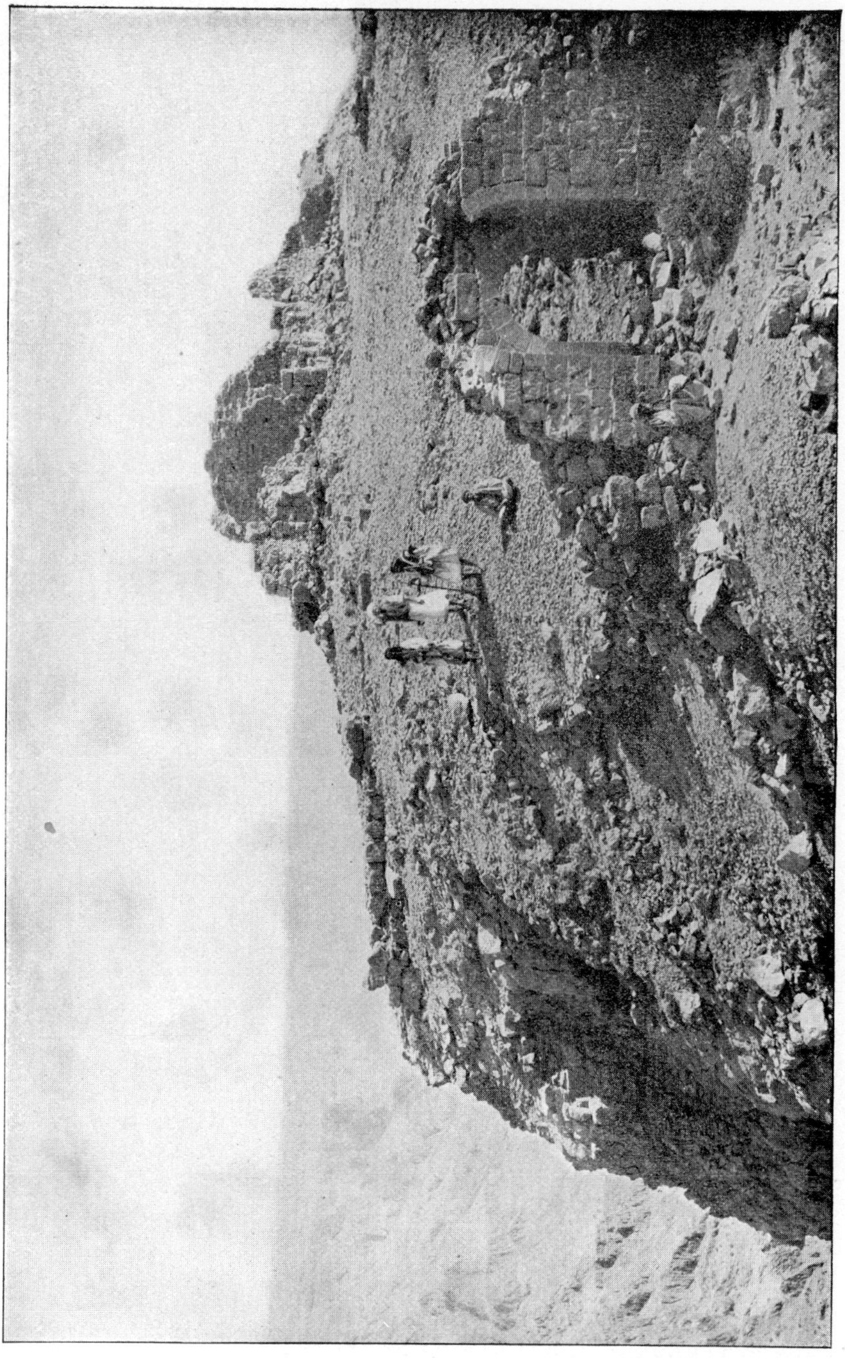

now, if I have found favor in thine eyes, let me get away, I pray thee, and see my brethren.' Therefore he is not come unto the king's table."

Then Saul's anger was kindled against Jonathan, and he said, "Do not I know that thou hast chosen the son of Jesse to thine own shame? For as long as the son of Jesse liveth upon the ground, thou shalt not be stablished, nor thy kingdom. Wherefore now send and fetch him unto me, for he shall surely die."

And Jonathan answered Saul his father, and said to him, "Wherefore should he be put to death? what hath he done?"

And Saul cast his spear at him to smite him: whereby Jonathan knew that it was determined of his father to put David to death. So Jonathan arose from the table in fierce anger, and did eat no meat the second day of the month: for he was grieved for David, because his father had done him shame.

And it came to pass in the morning, that Jonathan went out into the field at the time appointed with David, and a little lad with him. And he said to his lad, "Run, find now the arrows which I shoot."

And as the lad ran, he shot an arrow beyond him. And when the lad was come to the place of the arrow which Jonathan had shot, Jonathan cried after the lad, and said, "Is not the arrow beyond thee?"

And Jonathan cried after the lad, "Make speed, haste, stay not."

And Jonathan's lad gathered up the arrows, and came

to his master. But the lad knew not anything: only Jonathan and David knew the matter. And Jonathan gave his weapons to his lad, and said unto him, "Go, carry them to the city."

And as soon as the lad was gone, David arose out of his hiding place, and fell on his face to the ground, and bowed himself three times: and they kissed one another, and wept one with another. And Jonathan said to David, "Go in peace, forasmuch as we have sworn both of us in the name of the Lord, saying, 'The Lord shall be between me and thee, and between my family and thy family, for ever.'"

And he arose and departed: and Jonathan went into the city.

DAVID AN OUTLAW.

How He Showed Mercy to His Enemy.

(After this David became a fugitive from the king, who pursued him and tried to kill him. David gathered a band of followers and for a time lived as an outlaw, hiding in caves, plundering farms, living from hand to mouth. Several times he had the king in his power, but each time he allowed him to escape. This is the story of one of these adventures.)

And the Ziphites came to Saul to Gibeah, saying, "Doth not David hide himself in the hill of Hachilah, which is before the desert?"

Then Saul arose, and went down to the wilderness of Ziph, having three thousand chosen men of Israel with him, to seek David in the wilderness of Ziph. And Saul encamped in the hill of Hachilah, which is before the desert. But David abode in the wilderness, and he saw that Saul came after him into the wilderness. David therefore sent out spies, and understood that Saul was certainly come. And David arose, and came to the place where Saul had encamped: and David beheld the place where Saul lay, and Abner the son of Ner, the captain of his host: and Saul lay within the barricade of the wagons, and the people were encamped round about him. Then said David, "Who will go down with me to Saul to the camp?"

And Abishai said, "I will go down with thee."

So David and Abishai came to the people by night: and, behold, Saul lay sleeping within the barricade of the wagons, with his spear stuck in the ground at his head: and Abner and the people lay round about him. Then said Abishai to David, "God hath delivered up thine enemy into thine hand this day: now therefore let me smite him, I pray thee, with the spear to the earth at one stroke, and I will not need to smite him the second time."

And David said to Abishai, "Destroy him not: for who can put forth his hand against the Lord's anointed, and be guiltless?"

And David said, "As the Lord liveth, the Lord shall smite him; or his day shall come to die; or he shall go down into the battle, and perish. The Lord forbid that I should put forth mine hand against the Lord's anointed: but now take, I pray thee, the spear that is at his head, and the jar of water, and let us go."

So David took the spear and the jar of water from Saul's

head; and they went away, and no man saw it, nor knew it, neither did any awake: for they were all asleep; because a deep sleep from the Lord was fallen upon them. Then David went over to the other side, and stood on the top of the mountain afar off; a great space being between them: and David cried to the people, and to Abner the son of Ner, saying, "Answerest thou not, Abner?"

Then Abner answered and said, "Who art thou that criest to the king?"

And David said to Abner, "Art not thou a valiant man? and who is like to thee in Israel? wherefore then hast thou not kept watch over thy lord the king? for there came one of the people in to destroy the king thy lord. This thing is not good that thou hast done. As the Lord liveth, ye are worthy to die, because ye have not kept watch over your lord, the Lord's anointed. And now, see where the king's spear is, and the jar of water that was at his head."

And Saul knew David's voice, and said, "Is this thy voice, my son David?"

And David said, "It is my voice, my lord, O king."

And he said, "Wherefore doth my lord pursue after his servant? for what have I done? or what evil is in mine hand? Now therefore, I pray thee, let my lord the king hear the words of his servant. If it be the Lord that hath stirred thee up against me, let him accept an offering: but if it be the children of men, cursed be they before the Lord; for they have driven me out this day that I should not cleave to the inheritance of the Lord, saying, 'Go,

A SHEPHERD NEAR DAVID'S HOUSE LEADING HIS FLOCK OVER
THE JUDEAN HILLS

Copyright by Underwood & Underwood
and used by special permission

The principal business and the greatest interest of the people in the hill country of Judea was connected with the flocks

"If, as we have seen, the prevailing character of Judæa be pastoral, with husbandry only incidental to her life, it is not surprising that the forms which have impressed both her history and her religion upon the world should be those of the pastoral habit. Her origin; more than once her freedom and power of political recuperation; more than once her prophecy; her images of God, and her sweetest poetry of the spiritual life, have been derived from this source. It is the stateliest shepherds of all time whom the dawn of history reveals upon her fields—men not sprung from her own remote conditions, nor confined to them, but moving across the world in converse with great empires, and bringing down from heaven truths sublime and universal to wed with the simple habits of her life. These were the patriarchs of the nation. The founder of its one dynasty, and the first of its literary prophets, were also taken from following the flocks. The king and every true leader of men was called a shepherd. Jehovah was the Shepherd of His people, and they the sheep of His pasture. It was in Judæa that Christ called Himself the Good Shepherd, as it was in Judæa also that, taking the other great feature of her life, He said He was the True Vine"

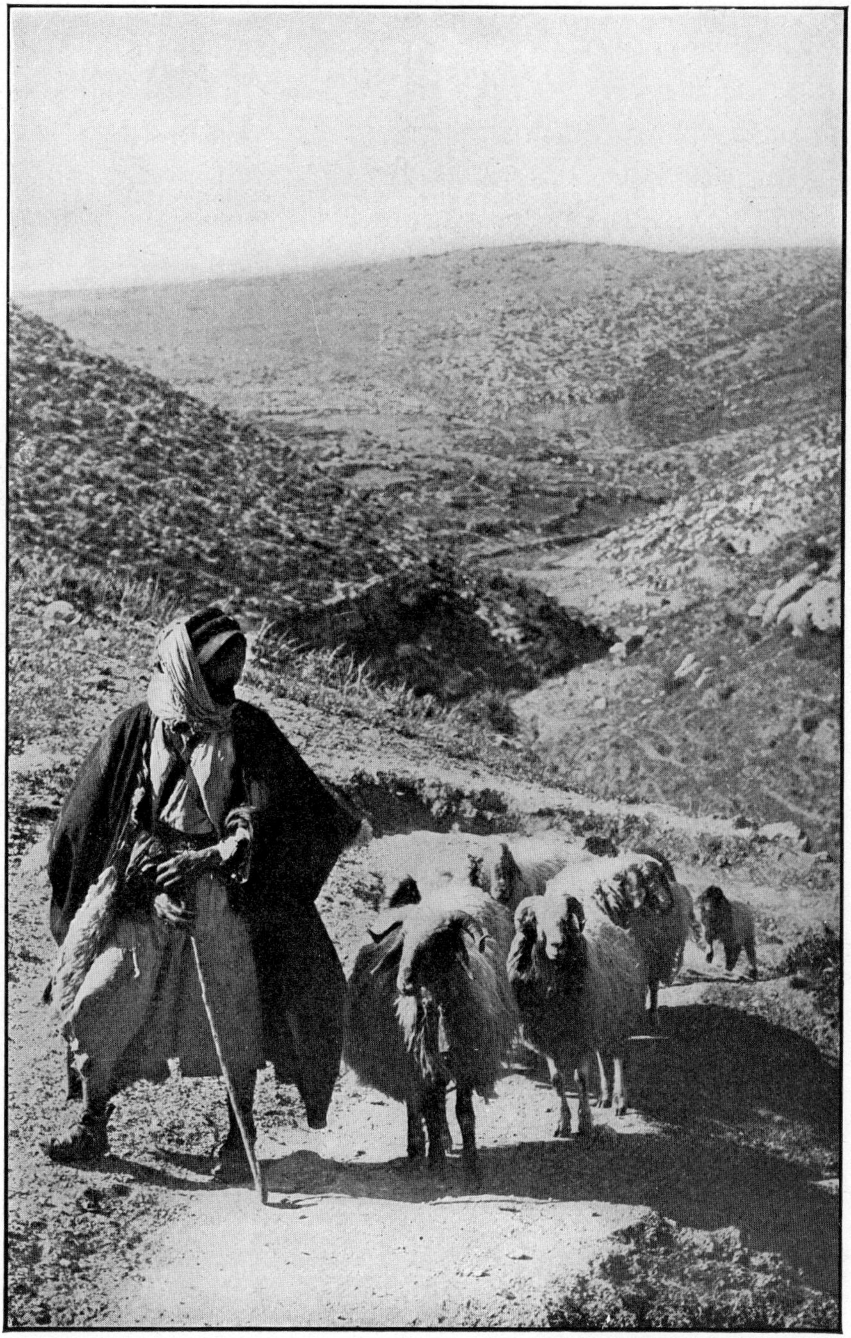

serve other gods.' Now therefore, let not my blood fall to the earth away from the presence of the Lord: for the king of Israel is come out to seek a flea, as when one doth hunt a partridge in the mountains."

Then said Saul, "I have sinned: return, my son David: for I will no more do thee harm, because my life was precious in thine eyes this day: behold, I have played the fool, and have erred exceedingly."

And David answered and said, "Behold the spear, O king! let then one of the young men come over and fetch it. And the Lord shall render to every man his righteousness and his faithfulness: because the Lord delivered thee into my hand to-day, and I would not put forth mine hand against the Lord's anointed. And, behold, as thy life was very precious this day in mine eyes, so let my life be precious in the eyes of the Lord, and let him deliver me out of all tribulation."

Then Saul said to David, "Blessed be thou, my son David: thou shalt both do mightily, and shalt surely prevail."

So David went his way, and Saul returned to his place.

SAUL'S PURSUIT OF DAVID.

How David a Second Time Spared the King's Life.

(Day after day Saul pursued David. First, some one would report David at a certain point, then he would be seen at another. But every time, by forced marches, hiding in caves by day, and stealing out by night, the bold outlaw escaped his foe. Once Saul entered the very cave where David and his faithful men were hiding in the shadows. Again Saul was in David's power. Again his men wished him to kill the king, but David refused, and spared the king's life.)

And David abode in the wilderness in the strongholds, and remained in the hill country in the wilderness of Ziph. And Saul sought him every day, but God delivered him not into his hand.

And David saw that Saul was come out to seek his life: and David was in the wilderness of Ziph in the wood. And Jonathan Saul's son arose, and went to David into the wood, and strengthened his hand in God. And he said unto him, "Fear not: for the hand of Saul my father shall not find thee; and thou shalt be king over Israel, and I shall be next unto thee; and that also Saul my father knoweth."

And they two made a covenant before the Lord: and David abode in the wood, and Jonathan went to his house.

Then came up the Ziphites to Saul to Gibeah, saying, "Doth not David hide himself with us in the strongholds in the wood, in the hill of Hachilah, which is on the south of the desert? Now therefore, O king, come down, according to all the desire of thy soul to come down; and our part shall be to deliver him up into the king's hand."

And Saul said, "Blessed be ye of the Lord; for ye have had compassion on me. Go, I pray you, make yet more sure, and know and see his place where his haunt is, and who hath seen him there: for it is told me that he dealeth very subtilly. See therefore, and take knowledge of all the lurking places where he hideth himself, and come ye again to me of a certainty, and I will go with you: and it shall come to pass, if he be in the land, that I will search him out among all the thousands of Judah."

And they arose, and went to Ziph before Saul: but David and his men were in the wilderness of Maon. And Saul and his men went to seek him. And they told David: wherefore he came down to the rock, and abode in the wilderness of Maon. And when Saul heard that, he pursued after David in the wilderness of Maon.

And Saul went on this side of the mountain, and David and his men on the other side of the mountain: and David made haste to get away for fear of Saul; for Saul and his men compassed David and his men round about to take them. But there came a messenger to Saul, saying, "Haste thee, and come; for the Philistines have made a raid upon the land."

So Saul returned from pursuing after David.

And it came to pass, when Saul was returned from following the Philistines, that it was told him, saying, "Behold, David is in the wilderness of En-gedi."

Then Saul took three thousand chosen men out of all Israel, and went to seek David and his men upon the rocks of the wild goats.

And he came to the sheepcotes by the way, where was a cave; and Saul went in.

Now David and his men were abiding in the innermost parts of the cave. And the men of David said unto him, "Behold, the day of which the Lord said unto thee, 'Behold, I will deliver thine enemy into thine hand, and thou shalt do to him as it shall seem good unto thee.'"

Then David arose, and cut off the skirt of Saul's robe privily. And it came to pass afterward, that David's heart smote him, because he had cut off Saul's skirt.

And he said unto his men, "The Lord forbid that I should do this thing unto my lord, the Lord's anointed, to put forth mine hand against him, seeing he is the Lord's anointed."

So David checked his men with these words, and suffered them not to rise against Saul. And Saul rose up out of the cave, and went on his way.

David also arose afterward, and went out of the cave, and cried after Saul, saying, "My lord the king!"

And when Saul looked behind him, David bowed with his face to the earth, and did obeisance.

And David said to Saul, "Wherefore hearkenest thou to men's words, saying, 'Behold, David seeketh thy hurt'? Behold, this day thine eyes have seen how that the Lord had delivered thee to-day into mine hand in the cave: and some bade me kill thee: but mine eye spared thee; and I said, 'I will not put forth mine hand against my lord; for he is the Lord's anointed.'

"Moreover, my father, see, yea, see the skirt of thy robe in my hand: for in that I cut off the skirt of thy robe, and killed thee not, know thou and see that there is neither evil nor transgression in mine hand, and I have not sinned against thee, though thou huntest after my soul to take it.

"The Lord judge between me and thee, and the Lord avenge me of thee: but mine hand shall not be upon thee."

STREET OF JERUSALEM

"The Joppa Gate" in the center

This is a characteristic scene in Jerusalem, the bazaars in the area outside, the camels and donkeys with their burdens, and the traffic going in and out of the city. "In an aperture of the western wall of Jerusalem hang the 'oaken valves' called the Beth-lehem or Joppa Gate. The area outside is one of the notable places of the city. Long before David coveted Zion there was a citadel there. When at last the son of Jesse ousted the Jebusites, and began to build, the site of the citadel became the northwest corner of the wall, defended by a tower much more imposing than the old one. The location of the gate, however, was not disturbed, for the reason, most likely, that the roads which met and merged in front of it could not well be transferred to another spot, while the area outside had become a recognized market place. In Solomon's day there was a great traffic at this locality, shared in by traders from Egypt and the rich dealers from Tyre and Sidon."— *Lew Wallace in "Ben-Hur"*

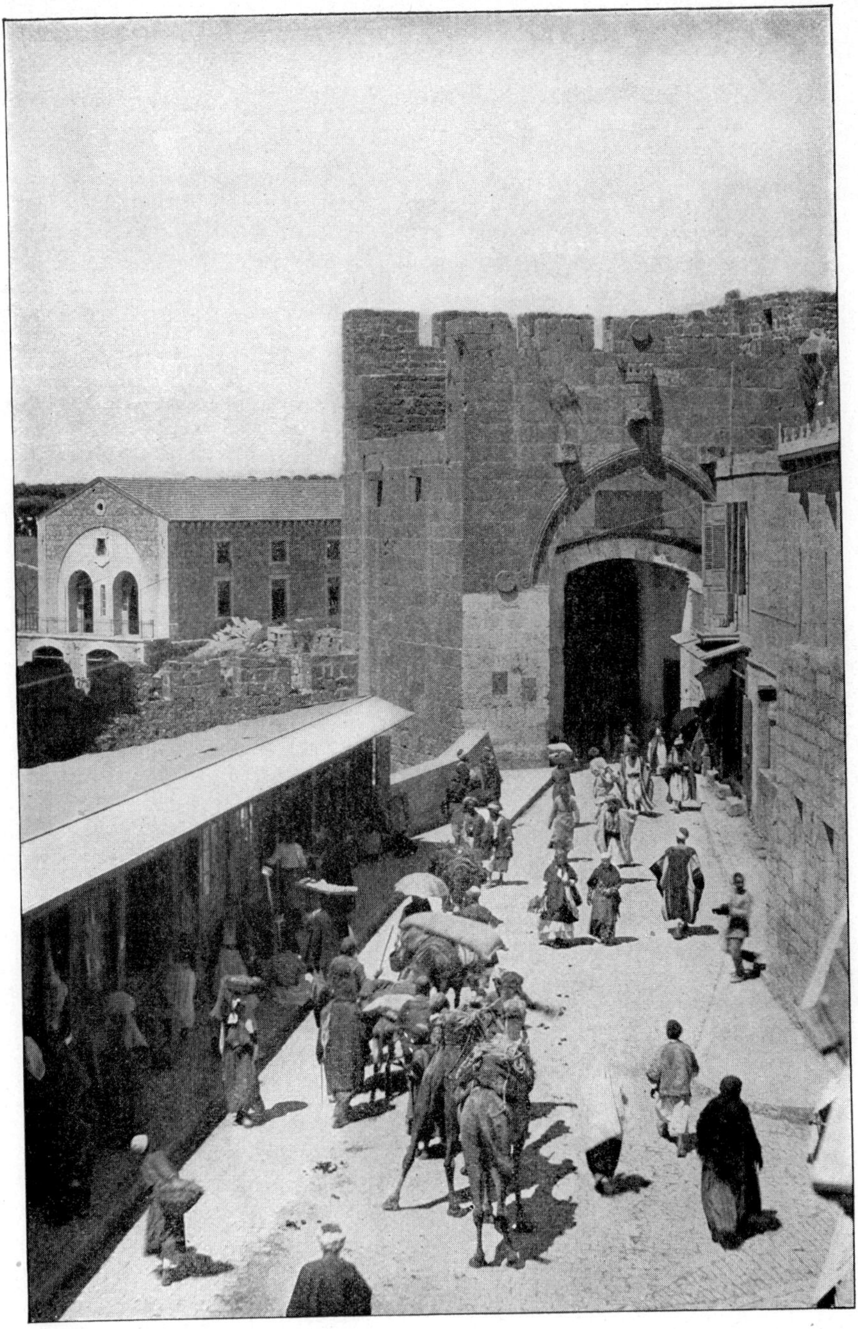

And it came to pass, when David had made an end of speaking these words unto Saul, that Saul said, "Is this thy voice, my son David?" And Saul lifted up his voice, and wept.

And he said to David, "Thou art more righteous than I: for thou hast rewarded me good, whereas I have rewarded thee evil.

"And thou hast showed this day how that thou hast dealt well with me: forasmuch as when the Lord had delivered me into thine hand, thou killedst me not.

"For if a man find his enemy, will he let him go well away? wherefore the Lord reward thee good for that thou hast done unto me this day.

"And now, behold, I know well that thou shalt surely be king, and that the kingdom of Israel shall be established in thine hand.

"Swear now therefore unto me by the Lord, that thou wilt not cut off my seed after me, and that thou wilt not destroy my name out of my father's house."

And David swore unto Saul. And Saul went home; but David and his men went up to the stronghold.

ONE OF DAVID'S ADVENTURES IN THE WILDERNESS.

How the Sheep Master of Maon Refused to Pay Tribute.

(While David was roaming about the country followed by a company of men as young and gallant as himself, much as Robin Hood roamed about the forests of England, he had many adventures, some of them chivalrous and some of which he was perhaps afterward, when he became king, just a little ashamed. This is the story of one of these adventures.)

There was a man in Maon whose possessions were in Carmel; and the man was very rich, and he had three thousand sheep, and a thousand goats: and he was shearing his sheep in Carmel.

Now the name of the man was Nabal (the Fool); and the name of his wife Abigail: and the woman was of good understanding, and of a beautiful countenance: but the man was churlish and evil in his doings; and he was of the house of Caleb.

And David heard in the wilderness that Nabal sheared his sheep. And David sent ten young men, and David said unto the young men, "Get you up to Carmel, and go to Nabal, and greet him in my name: and thus shall ye say, 'All hail! Peace be both unto thee, and peace be to thine house, and peace be unto all that thou hast. And now I have heard that thou hast shearers: thy shepherds have now been with us, and we did them no hurt, neither was there aught missing unto them, all the while they were in Carmel. Ask thy young men, and they will tell thee: wherefore let the young men find favor in thine eyes, for we come in a good day: give, I pray thee, whatsoever cometh to thine hand, unto thy servants, and to thy son David.'"

And when David's young men came, they spoke to Nabal according to all those words in the name of David, and ceased.

And Nabal answered David's servants, and said, "Who is David? and who is the son of Jesse? there are many servants nowadays that break away every man from his master. Shall I then take my bread, and my water, and my flesh that I have killed for my shearers, and give it unto men of whom I know not whence they be?"

So David's young men turned on their way, and went back, and came and told him according to all these words.

And David said unto his men, "Gird ye on every man his sword." And they girded on every man his sword; and David also girded on his sword: and there went up after David about four hundred men; and two hundred remained in the camp.

But one of the young men told Abigail, Nabal's wife, saying, "Behold, David sent messengers out of the wilderness to salute our master; and he flew upon them. But the men were very good unto us, and we were not hurt, neither missed we anything, as long as we were with them, when we were in the fields: they were a wall unto us both by night and by day, all the while we were with them keeping the sheep. Now therefore consider what thou wilt do; for evil is determined against our master, and against all his house: for he is such a worthless fellow that one cannot speak to him."

Then Abigail made haste, and took two hundred loaves, and two bottles of wine, and five sheep ready dressed, and five measures of parched corn, and an hundred clusters of raisins, and two hundred cakes of figs, and laid them on asses.

And she said unto her young men, "Go on before me; behold, I come after you."

But she told not her husband Nabal. And it was so,

as she rode on her ass, and came down by the covert of the mountain, that, behold, David and his men came down against her; and she met them.

Now David had said, "Surely in vain have I kept all that this fellow hath in the wilderness, so that nothing was missed of all that pertained unto him: and he hath returned me evil for good. God do so unto the enemies of David, and more also, if I leave of all that pertain to him by the morning light so much as one man child."

And when Abigail saw David, she hasted, and lighted off her ass, and fell before David on her face, and bowed herself to the ground. And she fell at his feet, and said, "Upon me, my lord, upon me be the iniquity: and let thine handmaid, I pray thee, speak in thine ears, and hear thou the words of thine handmaid. Let not my lord, I pray thee, regard this worthless fellow, even Nabal: for as his name is, so is he; Nabal [the Fool] is his name, and folly is with him: but I thine handmaid saw not the young men of my lord, whom thou didst send.

"Now therefore, my lord, as the Lord liveth, and as thy soul liveth, seeing the Lord hath withholden thee from blood-guiltiness, and from avenging thyself with thine own hand, now therefore let thine enemies, and them that seek evil to my lord, be as Nabal. And now this present which thy servant hath brought unto my lord, let it be given unto the young men that follow my lord.

"Forgive, I pray thee, the trespass of thine handmaid: for the Lord will certainly make my lord a sure house, because my lord fighteth the battles of the Lord; and evil

JERUSALEM, LOOKING UP THROUGH THE VALLEY OF HINNOM

It is said that continual fires were kept burning in the valley of Hinnom for the destruction of the refuse from the city. It was here, too, that the human sacrifices to the god Molech took place, where the victims were made "to pass through the fire"

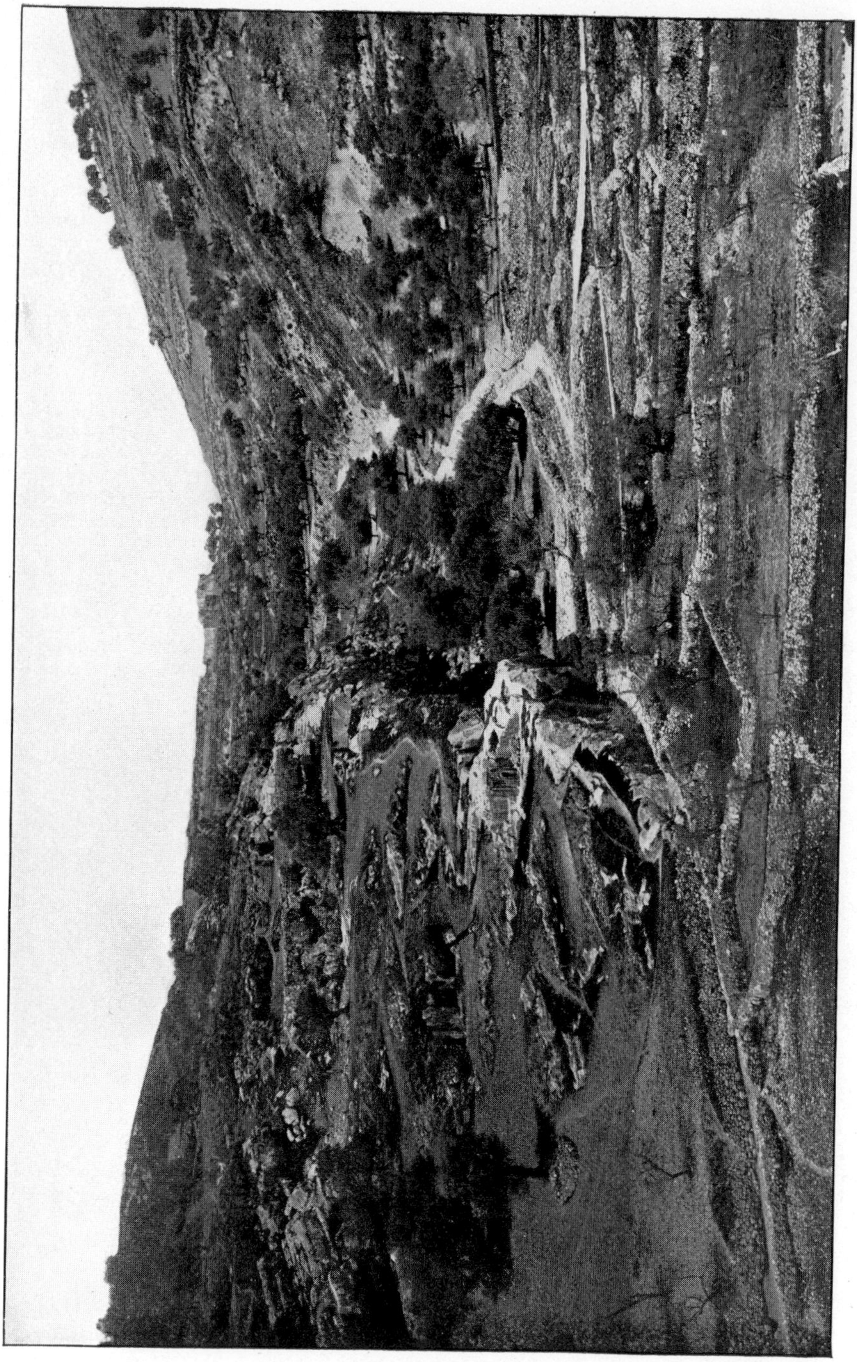

shall not be found in thee all thy days. And though man be risen up to pursue thee, and to seek thy soul, yet the soul of my lord shall be bound in the bundle of life with the Lord thy God; and the souls of thine enemies, them shall he sling out, as from the hollow of a sling.

"And it shall come to pass, when the Lord shall have done to my lord according to all the good that he hath spoken concerning thee, and shall have appointed thee prince over Israel; that this shall be no grief unto thee, nor offense of heart unto my lord, either that thou hast shed blood causeless, or that my lord hath avenged himself: and when the Lord shall have dealt well with my lord, then remember thine handmaid."

And David said to Abigail, "Blessed be the Lord, the God of Israel, which sent thee this day to meet me: and blessed be thy wisdom, and blessed be thou, which hast kept me this day from bloodguiltiness, and from avenging myself with mine own hand. For in very deed, as the Lord, the God of Israel, liveth, which hath withholden me from hurting thee, except thou hadst hasted and come to meet me, surely there had not been left unto Nabal by the morning light so much as one man child."

So David received of her hand that which she had brought him: and he said unto her, "Go up in peace to thine house; see, I have hearkened to thy voice, and have accepted thy person."

And Abigail came to Nabal; and, behold, he held a feast in his house, like the feast of a king; and Nabal's heart was merry within him, for he was very drunken: wherefore she told him nothing, less or more, until the morning light.

And it came to pass in the morning, when the wine was gone out of Nabal, that his wife told him these things, and his heart died within him, and he became as a stone.

And it came to pass about ten days after, that the Lord smote Nabal, that he died.

And when David heard that Nabal was dead, he said, "Blessed be the Lord, that hath pleaded the cause of my reproach from the hand of Nabal, and hath kept back his servant from evil: and the evil-doing of Nabal hath the Lord returned upon his own head."

And David sent and spoke concerning Abigail, to take her to him to wife. And when the servants of David were come to Abigail to Carmel, they spoke unto her, saying, "David hath sent us unto thee, to take thee to him to wife."

And she arose, and bowed herself with her face to the earth, and said, "Behold, thine handmaid is a servant to wash the feet of the servants of my lord."

And Abigail hasted, and arose, and rode upon an ass, with five damsels of hers that followed her; and she went after the messengers of David, and became his wife.

DAVID BECOMES KING.

The Lament for Saul and Jonathan. After Long Waiting the Throne is Gained.

(At last came that fatal battle with the Philistines in the hills and, when the sun set, Saul and his three sons lay dead upon the field.)

And it came to pass after the death of Saul, on the

third day, that, behold, a man came out of the camp from Saul with his clothes rent, and earth upon his head: and when he came to David, he fell to the earth, and did obeisance. And David said to him, "From whence comest thou?" And he said unto him, "Out of the camp of Israel am I escaped."

And David said to him, "How went the day? I pray thee, tell me."

And he answered, "The people are fled from the battle, and many of the people also are fallen and dead; and Saul and Jonathan his son are dead also."

And David said to the young man that told him, "How knowest thou that Saul and Jonathan his son are dead?"

And the young man that told him said, "As I happened by chance upon Mount Gilboa, behold, Saul leaned upon his spear; and, lo, the chariots and the horsemen followed hard after him. And when he looked behind him, he saw me, and called unto me. And I answered, 'Here am I.'

"And he said unto me, 'Who art thou?'

"And I answered him, 'I am an Amalekite.'

"And he said to me, 'Stand, I pray thee, beside me, and slay me, for anguish hath taken hold of me; because my life is yet whole in me.' So I stood beside him, and slew him, because I was sure that he could not live after he was fallen: and I took the crown that was upon his head, and the bracelet that was on his arm, and have brought them hither unto my lord."

Then David took hold of his clothes, and rent them;

and likewise all the men that were with him: and they mourned, and wept, and fasted until even, for Saul, and for Jonathan his son, and for the people of the Lord, and for the house of Israel; because they were fallen by the sword. And David said to the young man that told him, "Whence art thou?"

And he answered, "I am the son of a stranger, an Amalekite."

And David said to him, "Why wast thou not afraid to put forth thine hand to destroy the Lord's anointed?"

And David called one of the young men and said, "Go near, and fall upon him." And he smote him that he died.

And David said to him, "Thy blood be upon thy head; for thy mouth hath testified against thee, saying, 'I have slain the Lord's anointed.'"

And David lamented with this lamentation over Saul and over Jonathan his son: and he bade them teach the children of Judah the song of the bow.

The Song of the Bow.

Thy glory, O Israel, is slain upon thy high places!
How are the mighty fallen!
Tell it not in Gath,
Publish it not in the streets of Ashkelon;
Lest the daughters of the Philistines rejoice,
Lest the daughters of our enemies triumph.
Ye mountains of Gilboa,
Let there be no dew nor rain upon you, neither fields of
    offerings:
For there the shield of the mighty was vilely cast away,

"DAVID STREET" IN JERUSALEM

From a picture taken by Prof. Lyon and used by his kind permission

This narrow, busy street in Jerusalem still bears the name of the great king who scaled the heights and took the citadel from the Jebusites so long ago

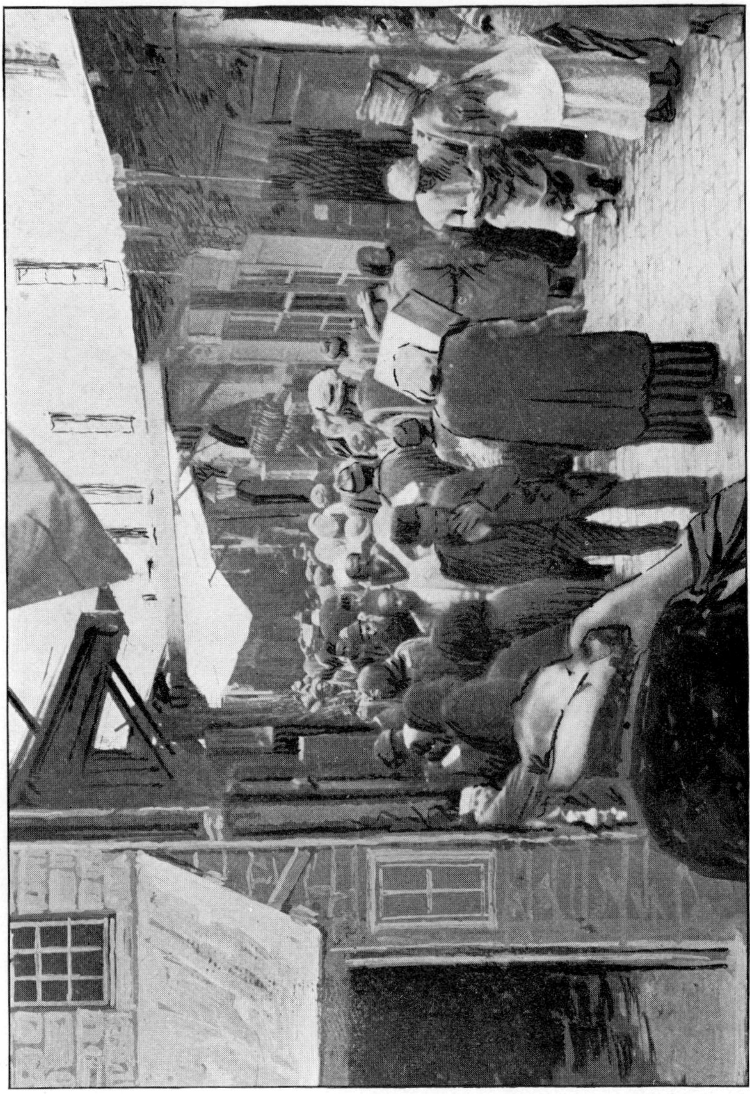

The shield of Saul, not anointed with oil.
From the blood of the slain, from the fat of the mighty,
The bow of Jonathan turned not back,
And the sword of Saul returned not empty.
Saul and Jonathan were lovely and pleasant in their lives,
And in their death they were not divided:
They were swifter than eagles,
They were stronger than lions.
Ye daughters of Israel, weep over Saul,
Who clothed you in scarlet delicately,
Who put ornaments of gold upon your apparel.
How are the mighty fallen in the midst of the battle!
Jonathan is slain upon thy high places.
I am distressed for thee, my brother Jonathan:
Very pleasant hast thou been unto me:
Thy love to me was wonderful,
Passing the love of women.
How are the mighty fallen,
And the weapons of war perished!

And they told David, saying, "The men of Jabesh-gilead were they that buried Saul." And David sent messengers unto the men of Jabesh-gilead, and said to them, "Blessed be ye of the Lord, that ye have showed this kindness to your lord, even to Saul, and have buried him. And now the Lord show kindness and truth unto you: and I also will requite you this kindness, because ye have done this thing. Now therefore let your hands be strong, and be ye valiant: for Saul your lord is dead, and also the house of Judah have anointed me king over them."

Then came all the tribes of Israel to David unto Hebron,

and spoke, saying, "Behold, we are thy bone and thy flesh. In times past, when Saul was king over us, it was thou that didst lead out and bring in Israel: and the Lord said to thee, 'Thou shalt feed my people Israel, and thou shalt be prince over Israel.'"

So all the elders of Israel came to the king to Hebron; and King David made a covenant with them in Hebron before the Lord: and they anointed David king over Israel.

David was thirty years old when he began to reign, and he reigned forty years.

AN EVIL DEED.
How a Brave Prophet Rebuked a King.

(David once did a very evil deed. He wished to have as his wife the wife of another man, named Uriah, a very brave soldier in the royal army. David caused this soldier to be placed in a very dangerous place in the battle, where he knew he would be killed. The prophet told the king a story to show him how wicked he was. Then the eyes of the king were opened to his sin, and he repented, but the child which had been born to him died.)

And it came to pass in the morning, that David wrote a letter to Joab, and sent it by the hand of Uriah. And he wrote in the letter, saying, "Set ye Uriah in the forefront of the hottest battle, and retire ye from him, that he may be smitten, and die."

And it came to pass, when Joab kept watch upon the city, that he assigned Uriah unto the place where he knew that valiant men were. And the men of the city went out, and fought with Joab: and there fell some of the people, even of the servants of David; and Uriah the Hittite died also. Then Joab sent and told David all the things concerning the war; and he charged the messenger, saying, "When thou hast made an end of telling all the things concerning the war to the king, it shall be that, if the king's wrath arise, and he say unto thee, 'Wherefore went ye so nigh unto the city to fight? knew ye not that they would shoot from the wall? why went ye so near the wall?' then shalt thou say, 'Thy servant Uriah the Hittite is dead also.'"

So the messenger went, and came and showed David all that Joab had sent him for. And the messenger said to David, "The men prevailed against us, and came out unto us into the field, and we were upon them even unto the entering of the gate. And the archers shot at thy servants from off the wall; and some of the king's servants are dead, and thy servant Uriah the Hittite is dead also."

Then David said to the messenger, "Thus shalt thou say unto Joab, 'Let not this thing displease thee, for the sword devoureth one as well as another: make thy battle more strong against the city, and overthrow it': and encourage thou him."

And when the wife of Uriah heard that Uriah her husband was dead, she made lamentation for her husband. And when the mourning was past, David sent and took her home to his house, and she became his wife, and a child was born to them. But the thing that David had done displeased the Lord.

And the Lord sent Nathan to David. And he came

to him, and said to him, "There were two men in one city; the one rich, and the other poor. The rich man had exceeding many flocks and herds: but the poor man had nothing save one little ewe lamb, which he had bought and nourished up: and it grew up together with him, and with his children; it did eat of his own morsel of food, and drank of his own cup, and lay in his bosom, and was unto him as a daughter. And there came a traveler to the rich man, and he spared to take of his own flock and of his own herd, to dress for the wayfaring man that was come to him, but took the poor man's lamb, and dressed it for the man that was come to him."

And David's anger was greatly kindled against the man; and he said to Nathan, "As the Lord liveth, the man that hath done this is worthy to die: and he shall restore the lamb fourfold, because he did this thing, and because he had no pity."

And Nathan said to David,—

"Thou art the man!"

"Thus saith the Lord, the God of Israel, I anointed thee king over Israel, and I delivered thee out of the hand of Saul; and if that had been too little, I would have added unto thee such and such things. Wherefore hast thou despised the word of the Lord, to do that which is evil in his sight? thou hast smitten Uriah the Hittite with the sword, and hast taken his wife to be thy wife, and hast slain him with the sword of the children of Ammon. Now therefore, the sword shall never depart from thine house;

RUINS OF RABBATH AMMON
An important city in Moab, taken by David

Used by special permission of the Palestine Exploration Fund

It was during the long siege of this city that Uriah the Hittite, whose wife David wished as his own, was killed. The army of Joab, David's general, encamped about the city and finally by the capture of the springs which supplied water to the people the strong walled place fell. Joab sent for David, so that he was on the ground when the last assault was made and the city was taken. Very rich spoil fell into the hands of the victors

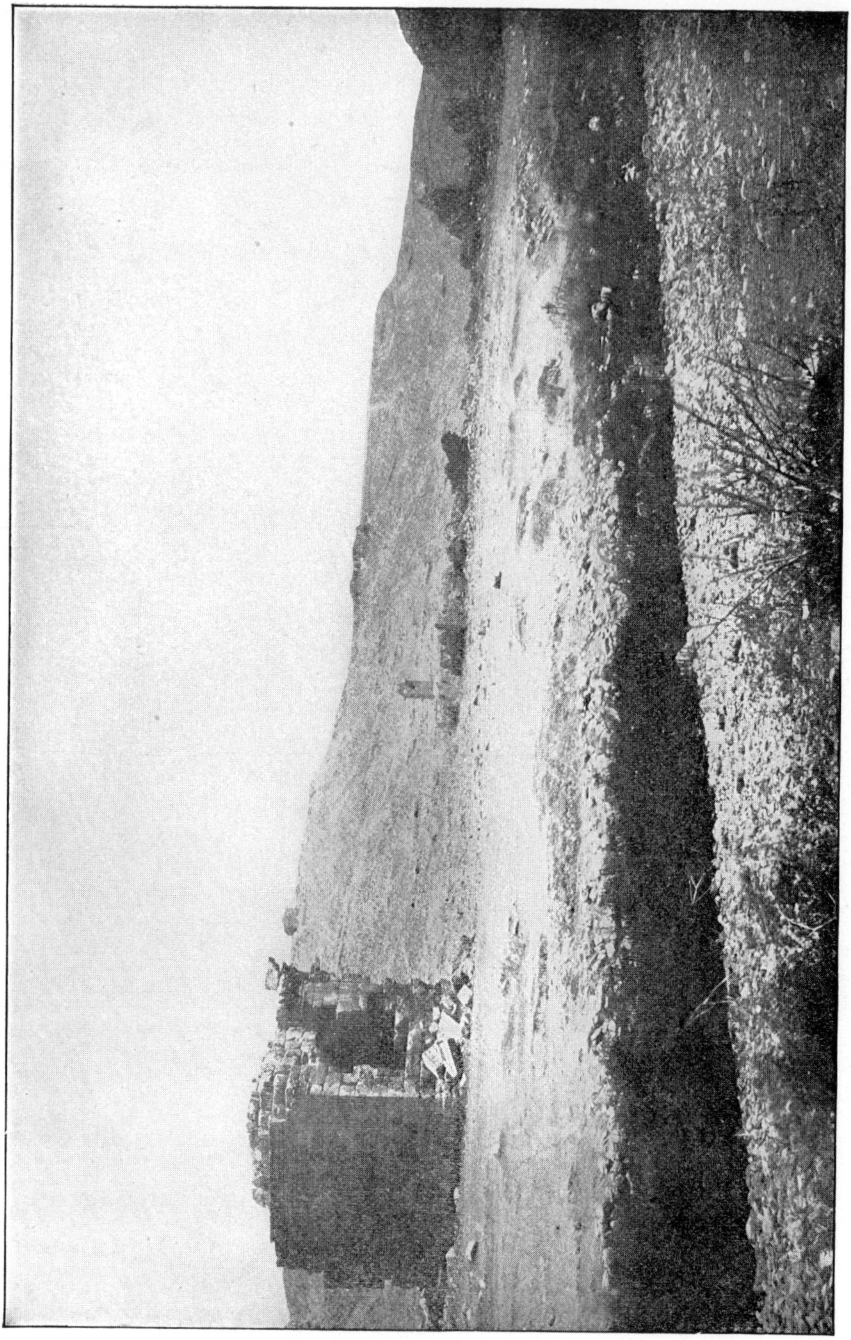

because thou hast despised me, and hast taken the wife of Uriah the Hittite to be thy wife."

And David said to Nathan, "I have sinned against the Lord."

And Nathan said to David, "The Lord also hath put away thy sin; thou shalt not die. Howbeit, because by this deed thou hast given great occasion to the enemies of the Lord to blaspheme, the child also that is born unto thee shall surely die."

And Nathan departed to his house.

And the child which had been born to David was very sick. David therefore besought God for the child; and David fasted, and went in, and lay all night upon the earth. And the elders of his house arose, and stood beside him, to raise him up from the earth: but he would not, neither did he eat with them. And it came to pass on the seventh day, that the child died. And the servants of David feared to tell him that the child was dead: for they said, "Behold, while the child was yet alive, we spoke unto him, and he hearkened not to our voice: what will he then do if we tell him that the child is dead?"

But when David saw that his servants whispered together, David perceived that the child was dead: and David said to his servants, "Is the child dead?"

And they said, "He is dead."

Then David arose from the earth, and washed, and anointed himself, and changed his apparel; and he came into the house of the Lord, and worshiped: then he came to his own house; and when he required they set food before him, and he ate. Then said his servants to him, "What thing is this that thou hast done? thou didst fast and weep for the child, while it was alive; but when the child was dead, thou didst rise and eat."

And he said, "While the child was yet alive, I fasted and wept: for I said 'Who knoweth whether the Lord will not be gracious to me, that the child may live?' But now he is dead, wherefore should I fast? can I bring him back again? I shall go to him, but he shall not return to me."

CAVE OF ADULLAM

David and his three captains bold
Kept ambush once within a hold.
It was in Adullam's cave,
Nigh which no water they could have,
Nor spring nor running brook was near
To quench the thirst that parched them there.
Then David, King of Israel,
Straight bethought him of a well,
Which stood beside the city gate
At Bethlehem; where, before his state
Of kingly dignity, he had
Oft drunk his fill, a shepherd lad;
But now his fierce Philistine foe
Encamped before it he does know.
Yet ne'er the less, with heat opprest,
Those three bold captains he addrest;
And wished that one to him would bring
Some water from his native spring.
His valiant captains instantly
To execute his will did fly.
The mighty three the ranks broke through
Of armed foes, and water drew
For David, their beloved king,
At his own sweet native spring.
Back through their armed foes they haste,
With the hard-earned treasure graced.
But when the good king David found
What they had done, he on the ground
The water poured. "Because," said he,
"That it was at the jeopardy
Of your three lives this thing ye did,
That I should drink it, God forbid."

—*Charles Lamb.*

A KNIGHTLY DEED.

David and His Three Brave Captains. How They Brought the Water for Which He Longed and How He Would Not Drink It.

There were three valiant captains in David's army. These three went down, and came to David in the harvest time to the cave of Adullam; and the troop of the Philistines were encamped in the valley of Rephaim.

And David was then in the stronghold, and the garrison of the Philistines was then in Beth-lehem. And David longed, and said, "Oh that one would give me water to drink of the well of Beth-lehem, which is by the gate!"

And the three mighty men broke through the host of the Philistines, and drew water out of the well of Beth-lehem, that was by the gate, and took it, and brought it to David: but he would not drink thereof, but poured it out to the Lord.

And he said, "Be it far from me, O Lord, that I should do this: shall I drink the blood of the men that went in jeopardy of their lives?" therefore he would not drink it.

These things did the three mighty men.

HOW DAVID BOUGHT A THRESHING-FLOOR FOR AN ALTAR.

"Neither Will I Offer Burnt Offerings Unto the Lord My God of That Which Cost Me Nothing."

And David said unto the Lord, "I have sinned greatly in that I have done: but now, O Lord, put away, I beseech thee, the iniquity of thy servant; for I have done very foolishly."

A PALESTINE THRESHING FLOOR, WITH CATTLE TREADING OUT THE GRAIN

From a photograph belonging to Dr. W. J. Moulton
and used by his kind permission

This was the method, still in use, whereby during all the times of the Bible the farmer in Palestine threshed out his grain. It was then thrown up by forks and the wind blew away the chaff. A level place for a threshing floor was much prized. It was such a floor that David bought of Araunah as a suitable place to build an altar

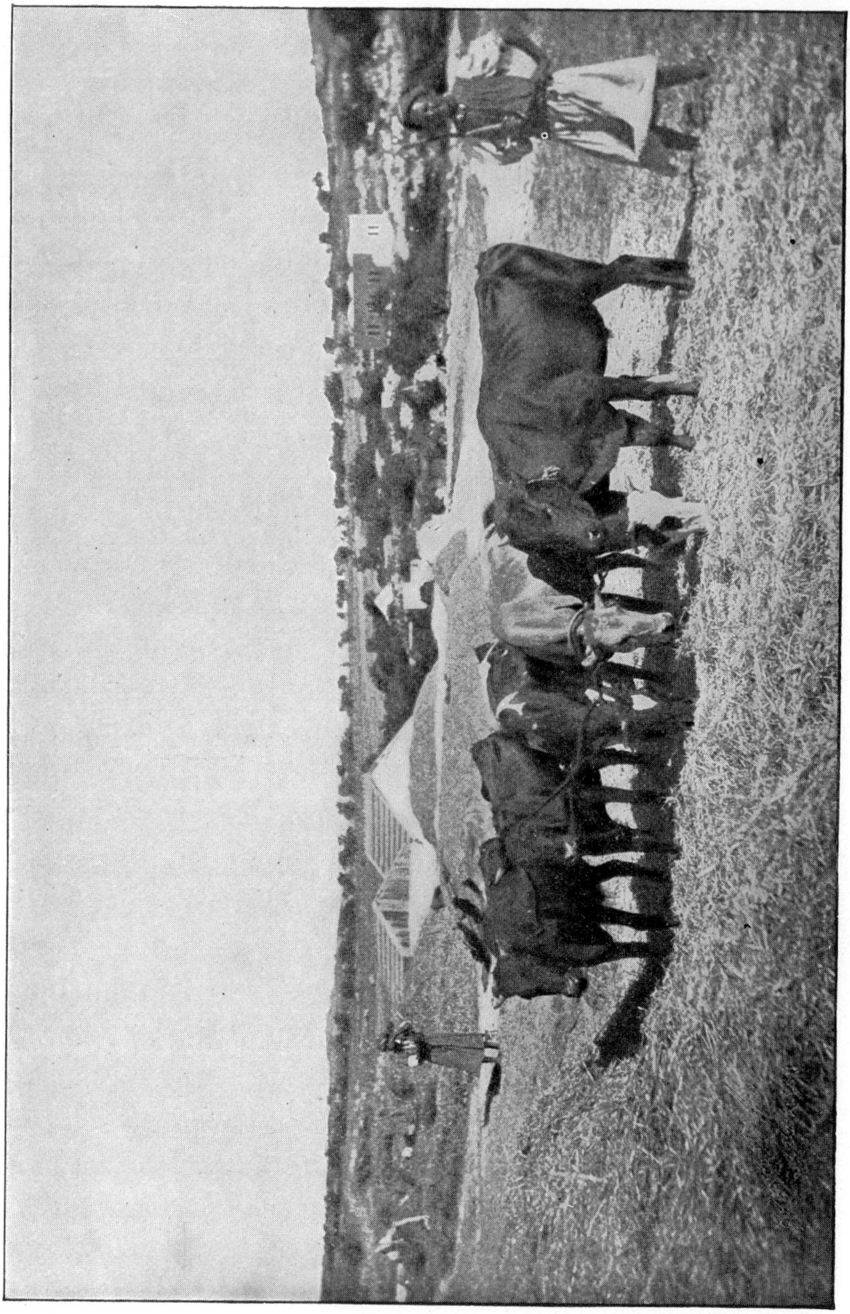

And when David rose up in the morning, the word of the Lord came to the prophet Gad, David's seer, saying, "Go and speak to David, 'Thus saith the Lord: I offer thee three things; choose thee one of them, that I may do it unto thee.'"

So Gad came to David, and told him, and said unto him, "Shall seven years of famine come unto thee in thy land? or wilt thou flee three months before thy foes while they pursue thee? or shall there be three days' pestilence in thy land? now advise thee, and consider what answer I shall return to him that sent me."

And David said unto Gad, "I am in a great strait: let us fall now into the hand of the Lord; for his mercies are great: and let me not fall into the hand of man."

So the Lord sent a pestilence upon Israel from the morning even to the time appointed: and there died of the people from Dan even to Beer-sheba seventy thousand men.

And when the angel stretched out his hand toward Jerusalem to destroy it, the Lord repented him of the evil, and said to the angel that destroyed the people, "It is enough; now stay thine hand."

And the angel of the Lord was by the threshing-floor of Araunah the Jebusite. And David spoke unto the Lord when he saw the angel that smote the people, and said, "Lo, I have sinned, and I have done perversely: but these sheep, my people, what have they done? let thine hand, I pray thee, be against me, and against my father's house."

And Gad came that day to David, and said unto him, "Go up, rear an altar unto the Lord in the threshing-floor of Araunah the Jebusite."

And David went up according to the saying of Gad, as the Lord commanded. And Araunah looked forth, and saw the king and his servants coming on toward him: and Araunah went out, and bowed himself before the king with his face to the ground.

And Araunah said, "Wherefore is my lord the king come to his servant?"

And David said, "To buy the threshing-floor of thee, to build an altar unto the Lord, that the plague may be stayed from the people."

And Araunah said unto David, "Let my lord the king take and offer up what seemeth good unto him: behold, the oxen for the burnt offering, and the threshing instruments and the furniture of the oxen for the wood: all this, O king, doth Araunah give unto the king."

And Araunah said unto the king, "The Lord thy God accept thee."

And the king said unto Araunah, "Nay; but I will verily buy it of thee at a price: neither will I offer burnt offerings unto the Lord my God which cost me nothing."

So David bought the threshing-floor and the oxen for fifty shekels of silver.

And David built there an altar unto the Lord, and offered burnt offerings and peace offerings. So the Lord was intreated for the land, and the plague was stayed from Israel.

THE REBELLION OF ABSALOM.

How an Evil Son Met His Fate in the Branches of an Oak.

(David had much trouble and many wars during his reign, but the rebellion of his own son Absalom brought more grief to him than anything else. For a time the rebellion was successful, and David was driven from his own palace. Then the tide turned and Absalom was defeated and slain in a great battle. The strange way in which Absalom met his death, and how David mourned for his son, are told in the following story.)

And David numbered the people that were with him, and set captains of thousands and captains of hundreds over them. And David sent forth the people, a third part under the hand of Joab, and a third part under the hand of Abishai the son of Zeruiah, Joab's brother, and a third part under the hand of Ittai the Gittite. And the king said to the people, "I will surely go forth with you myself also."

But the people said, "Thou shalt not go forth: for if we flee away, they will not care for us; neither if half of us die, will they care for us: but thou art worth ten thousand of us: therefore now it is better that thou be ready to succor us out of the city."

And the king said to them, "What seemeth to you best I will do."

And the king stood by the gate side, and all the people went out by hundreds and by thousands. And the king commanded Joab and Abishai and Ittai, saying, "Deal gently for my sake with the young man, even with Absalom."

And all the people heard when the king gave all the captains charge concerning Absalom. So the people went out into the field against Israel: and the battle was in the forest of Ephraim. And the people of Israel were smitten there before the servants of David, and there was a great slaughter there that day of twenty thousand men. For the battle was there spread over the face of all the country: and the forest devoured more people that day than the sword devoured. And Absalom chanced to meet the servants of David. And Absalom rode upon his mule, and the mule went under the thick boughs of a great oak, and his head caught hold of the oak, and he was taken up between the heaven and the earth; and the mule that was under him went on. And a certain man saw it and told Joab, and said, "Behold, I saw Absalom hanging in an oak."

And Joab said to the man that told him, "And, behold, thou sawest it, and why didst thou not smite him there to the ground? and I would have given thee ten pieces of silver and a girdle."

And the man said to Joab, "Though I should receive a thousand pieces of silver in mine hand, yet would I not put forth mine hand against the king's son: for in our hearing the king charged thee and Abishai and Ittai, saying, 'Beware that none touch the young man Absalom.' Otherwise if I had dealt falsely against his life (and there is no matter hid from the king), then thou thyself wouldest have stood aloof."

Then said Joab, "I may not tarry thus with thee."

And he took three darts in his hand, and thrust them

JERUSALEM, FROM THE WELL OF EN-ROGEL

"Leaving Jerusalem by St. Stephen's Gate and walking down the valley of Jehoshaphat, by the dry bed of the Kidron, you meet at length the deep rugged valley of Hinnom, skirting the city in a semi-circular form on the southern and western sides. At the junction of these two valleys stands a low, vaulted stone building — this is the well of En-Rogel"

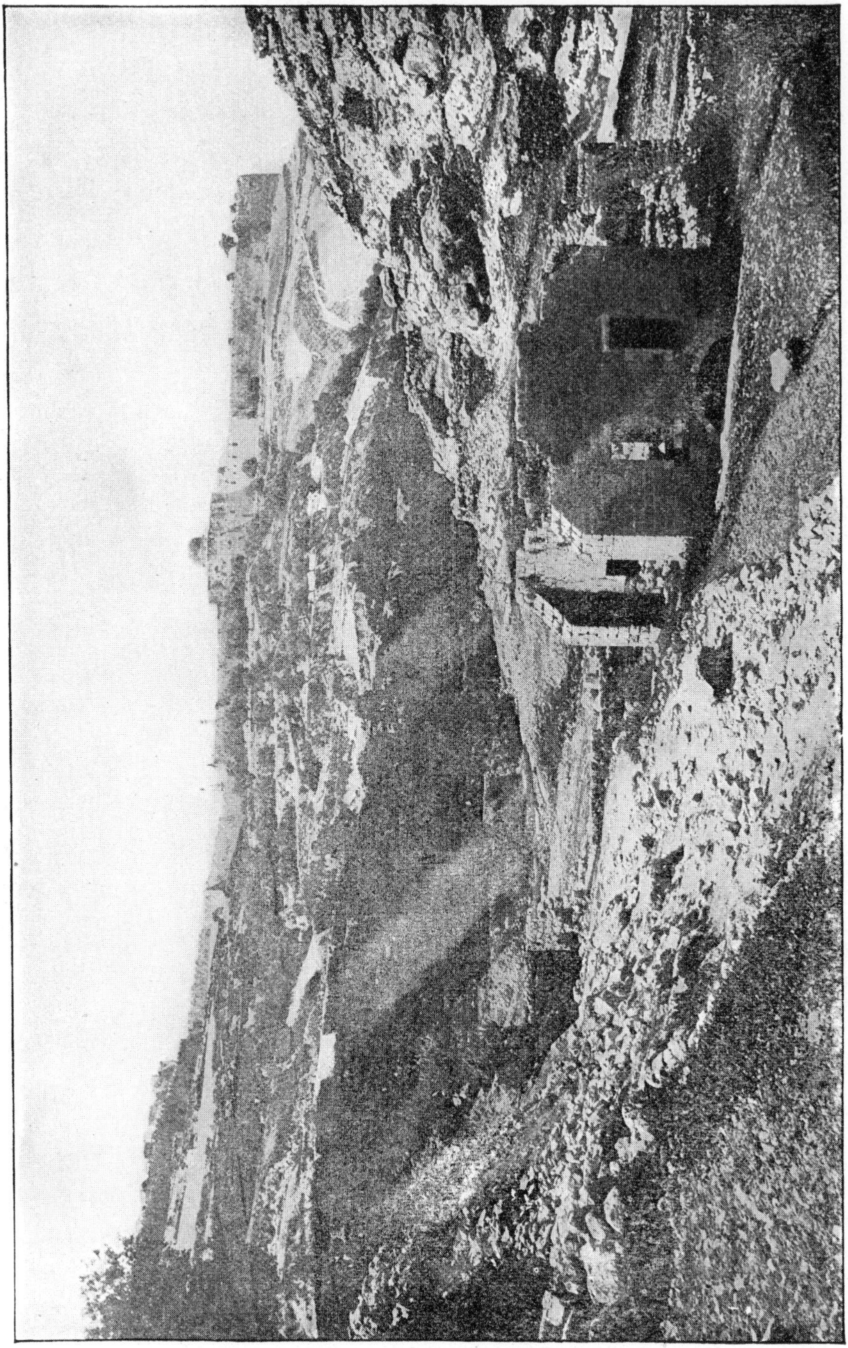

through the heart of Absalom, while he was yet alive in the midst of the oak. And ten young men that bore Joab's armor came up and smote Absalom, and slew him. And Joab blew the trumpet, and the people returned from pursuing after Israel: for Joab held back the people. And they took Absalom and cast him into the great pit in the forest, and raised over him a very great heap of stones: and all Israel fled every one to his tent.

Then said Ahimaaz the son of Zadok, "Let me now run, and bear the king tidings, how that the Lord hath avenged him of his enemies."

And Joab said to him, "Thou shalt not be the bearer of tidings this day, but thou shalt bear tidings another day: but this day thou shalt bear no tidings, because the king's son is dead."

Then said Joab to the Cushite, "Go tell the king what thou hast seen."

And the Cushite bowed himself unto Joab, and ran. Then said Ahimaaz the son of Zadok yet again to Joab, "But come what may, let me, I pray thee, also run after the Cushite."

And Joab said, "Wherefore wilt thou run, my son, seeing that thou wilt have no reward for the tidings?"

"But come what may," said he, "I will run."

And he said unto him, "Run."

Then Ahimaaz ran by the way of the Plain, and outran the Cushite.

Now David sat between the two gates: and the watchman went up to the roof of the gate unto the wall, and lifted up his eyes, and looked, and, behold, a man running alone. And the watchman cried, and told the king. And the king said, "If he be alone, there is tidings in his mouth."

And he came apace, and drew near. And the watchman saw another man running: and the watchman called unto the porter, and said, "Behold, another man running alone."

And the king said, "He also bringeth tidings."

And the watchman said, "I think the running of the foremost is like the running of Ahimaaz the son of Zadok."

And the king said, "He is a good man, and cometh with good tidings."

And Ahimaaz called, and said unto the king, "All is well."

And he bowed himself before the king with his face to the earth, and said, "Blessed be the Lord thy God, who hath delivered up the men that lifted up their hand against my lord the king."

And the king said, "Is it well with the young man Absalom?"

And Ahimaaz answered, "When Joab sent the king's servant, even me thy servant, I saw a great tumult, but I knew not what it was."

And the king said, "Turn aside, and stand here."

And he turned aside, and stood still. And, behold, the Cushite came; and the Cushite said, "Tidings for my lord the king: for the Lord hath avenged thee this day of all them that rose up against thee."

ANCIENT TOMBS NEAR JERUSALEM

From a photograph belonging to Dr. W. J. Moulton
and used by his kind permission

Many of the kings of Judah were buried in these rock tombs. "Every family who could afford it had their tomb hewn out of the rock, with niches for the reception of many bodies"

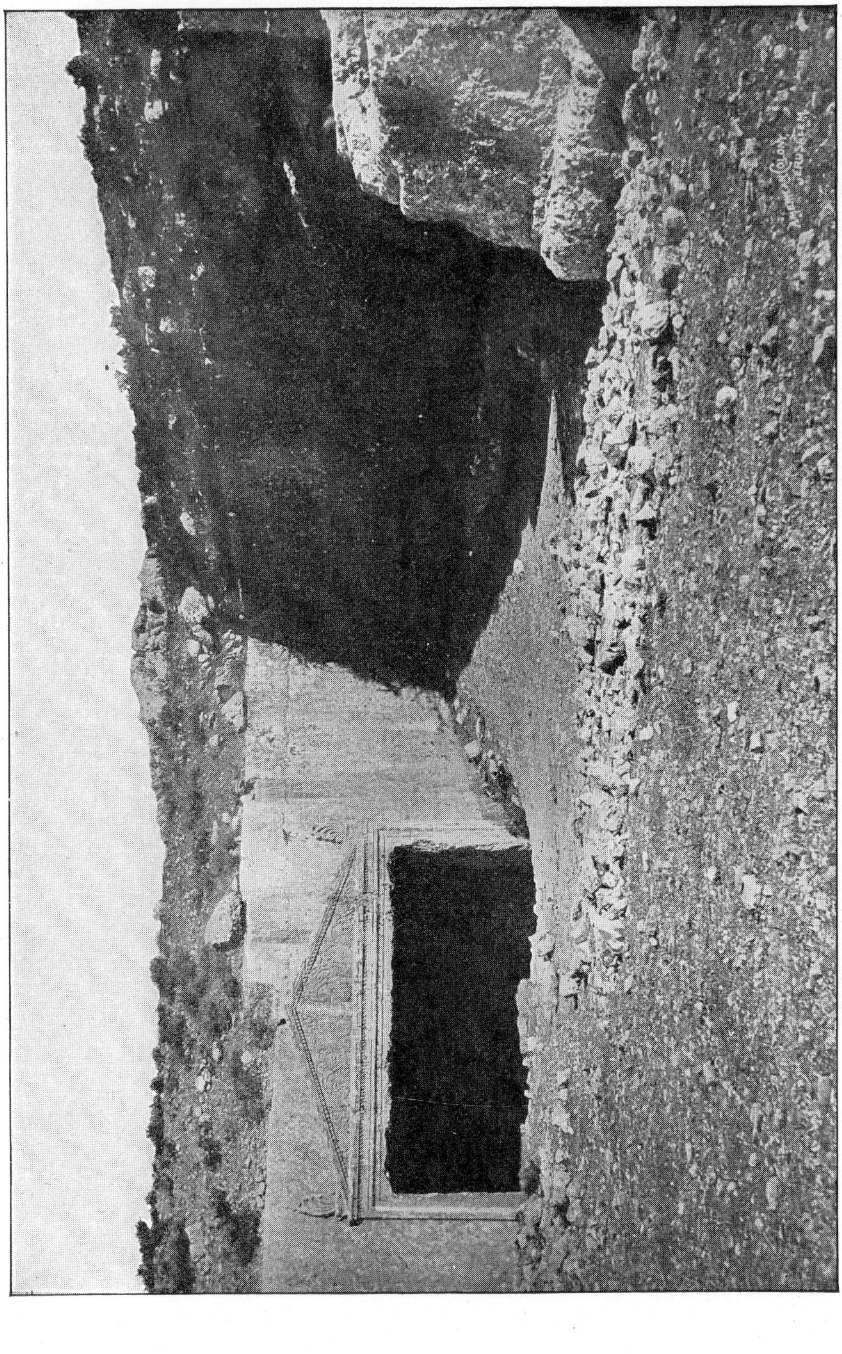

And the king said unto the Cushite, "Is it well with the young man Absalom?"

And the Cushite answered, "The enemies of my lord the king, and all that rise up against thee to do thee hurt, be as that young man is."

And the king was much moved, and went up to the chamber over the gate, and wept: and as he went, thus he said, "O my son Absalom, my son, my son Absalom! would God I had died for thee, O Absalom, my son, my son!"

THE PASSING OF DAVID.

"I Go the Way of All the Earth."

Now the days of David drew nigh that he should die; and he charged Solomon his son, saying, "I go the way of all the earth: be thou strong therefore, and show thyself a man; and keep the charge of the Lord thy God, to walk in his ways, to keep his statutes, and his commandments, and his judgments, and his testimonies, according to that which is written in the law of Moses, that thou mayest prosper in all that thou doest, and whithersoever thou turnest thyself: that the Lord may establish his word which he spoke concerning me, saying, 'If thy children take heed to their way, to walk before me in truth with all their heart and with all their soul, there shall not fail thee a man on the throne of Israel.'"

And David died, and his son Solomon reigned in his stead.

SOLOMON

The Story of the Wisest and Greatest King Israel Ever Had.

(After some opposition on the part of the other sons of David, Solomon was established on the throne.)

THE DREAM OF SOLOMON.
He Makes a Wise Choice.

And the king went to Gibeon to sacrifice there; for that was the great high place: a thousand burnt offerings did Solomon offer upon that altar. In Gibeon the Lord appeared to Solomon in a dream by night: and God said, "Ask what I shall give thee."

And Solomon said, "Thou hast showed unto thy servant David my father great kindness, according as he walked before thee in truth, and in righteousness, and in uprightness of heart with thee; and thou hast kept for him this great kindness, that thou hast given him a son to sit on his throne, as it is this day. And now, O Lord my God, thou hast made thy servant king instead of David my father: and I am but a little child; I know not how to go out or come in. And thy servant is in the midst of thy people which thou hast chosen, a great people, that cannot be numbered nor counted for multitude. Give thy servant therefore an understanding heart to judge thy

A CEDAR OF LEBANON

From a photograph belonging to the Public Library of Springfield, Mass.,
and used by special permission

This is the largest of the "Cedars of Lebanon" now standing. It measures forty feet in circumference near the roots. These great trees grow in abundance upon the Lebanon range, and cedar wood was very much used in Bible times. Solomon's temple had beams of cedar, David's palace was built of it, and one of Solomon's palaces was called the house of the forest of Lebanon

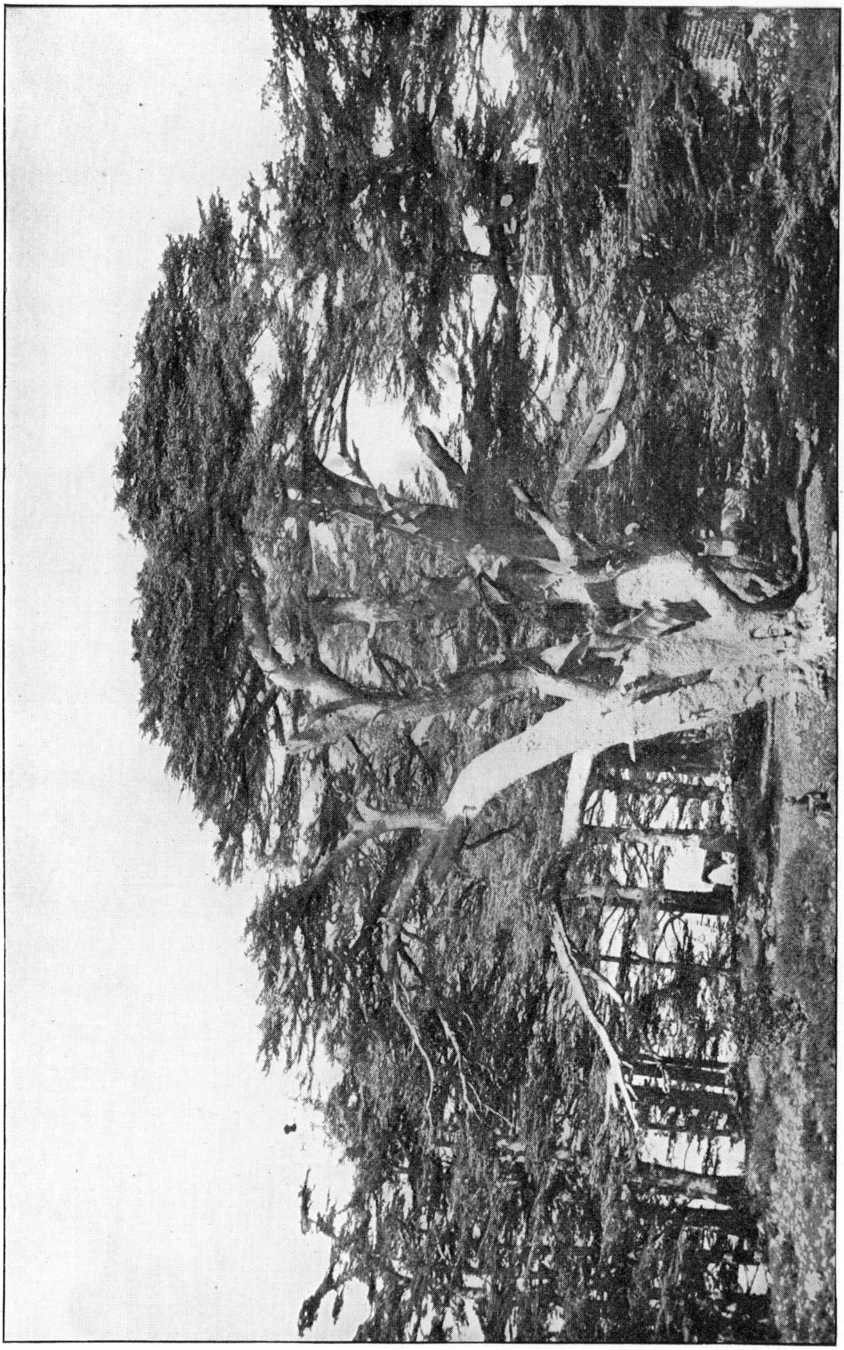

people, that I may discern between good and evil; for who is able to judge this thy great people?"

And the speech pleased the Lord, that Solomon had asked this thing. And God said unto him, "Because thou hast asked this thing, and hast not asked for thyself long life; neither hast asked riches for thyself, nor hast asked the life of thine enemies; but hast asked for thyself understanding to discern judgment; behold, I have done according to thy word: lo, I have given thee a wise and an understanding heart; so that there hath been none like thee before thee, neither after thee shall any arise like unto thee. And I have also given thee that which thou hast not asked, both riches and honor, so that there shall not be any among the kings like to thee, all thy days. And if thou wilt walk in my ways, to keep my statutes and my commandments, as thy father David did walk, then I will lengthen thy days."

And Solomon awoke, and, behold, it was a dream: and he came to Jerusalem, and stood before the ark of the covenant of the Lord, and offered up burnt offerings, and offered peace offerings, and made a feast to all his servants.

LORD OF THE LANDS.

The Prosperity and the Wisdom of Solomon.

And Solomon ruled over all the kingdoms from the River Euphrates to the land of the Philistines, and to the border of Egypt: they brought presents, and served Solomon all the days of his life. And Solomon's provision for one day was thirty measures of fine flour, and threescore measures of meal; ten fat oxen, and twenty oxen out of the pastures, and an hundred sheep, beside harts, and gazelles, and roebucks, and fatted fowl. For he had dominion over all the region on this side the River Euphrates, from Tiphsah even to Gaza, over all the kings on this side the River Euphrates: and he had peace on all sides round about him. And Judah and Israel dwelt safely, every man under his vine and under his fig tree, from Dan even to Beer-sheba, all the days of Solomon. And Solomon had forty thousand stalls of horses for his chariots, and twelve thousand horsemen. And those officers provided victual for King Solomon, and for all that came unto King Solomon's table, every man in his month: they let nothing be lacking. Barley also and straw for the horses and swift steeds brought they to the place where the officers were, every man according to his charge.

And God gave Solomon wisdom and understanding exceeding much, and largeness of heart, even as the sand that is on the sea shore.

And Solomon's wisdom excelled the wisdom of all the children of the east, and all the wisdom of Egypt. For he was wiser than all men; and his fame was in all the nations round about. And he spoke three thousand proverbs: and his songs were a thousand and five. And he spoke of trees, from the cedar that is in Lebanon even unto the hyssop that springeth out of the wall: he spoke also of beasts, and of fowl, and of creeping things, and of fishes. And there came of all peoples to hear the wisdom of Solomon, from all kings of the earth, which had heard of his wisdom.

THE TREATY WITH KING HIRAM.
Cedars of Lebanon and Stones from the Quarries for the Temple.

And Hiram king of Tyre sent his servants to Solomon; for he had heard that they had anointed him king instead of his father: for Hiram was ever a lover of David. And Solomon sent to Hiram, saying, "Thou knowest how David my father could not build an house for the name of the Lord his God for the wars which were about him on every side, until the Lord put his enemies under his feet. But now the Lord my God hath given me rest on every side; there is neither adversary, nor evil happening. And, behold, I purpose to build an house for the name of the Lord my God, as the Lord spoke to David my father, saying, 'Thy son, whom I will set upon thy throne in thy room, he shall build the house for my name.' Now therefore command thou that they hew me cedar trees out of Lebanon; and my servants shall be with thy servants; and I will give thee hire for thy servants according to all that thou shalt say: for thou knowest that there is not among us any that has skill to hew timber like unto the Zidonians."

And it came to pass, when Hiram heard the words of Solomon, that he rejoiced greatly, and said, "Blessed be the Lord this day, who hath given unto David a wise son over this great people."

And Hiram sent to Solomon, saying, "I have heard the message which thou hast sent to me: I will do all thy desire concerning timber of cedar, and concerning timber of fir. My servants shall bring them down from Lebanon to the sea: and I will make them into rafts to go by sea to the place that thou shalt appoint me, and will cause them to be broken up there, and thou shalt receive them: and thou shalt accomplish my desire, in giving food for my household."

So Hiram gave Solomon timber of cedar and timber of fir according to all his desire. And Solomon gave Hiram twenty thousand measures of wheat for food to his household, and twenty measures of pure oil: thus gave Solomon to Hiram year by year. And the Lord gave Solomon wisdom, as he promised him; and there was peace between Hiram and Solomon; and they two made a league together.

And King Solomon raised a levy out of all Israel; and the levy was thirty thousand men. And he sent them to Lebanon, ten thousand a month by turns: a month they were in Lebanon, and two months at home: and Adoniram was over the levy. And Solomon had three score and ten thousand that bore burdens, and fourscore thousand that were hewers in the mountains; besides Solomon's chief officers that were over the work, three thousand and three hundred, which were overseers of the people that wrought in the work. And the king commanded, and they hewed out great stones, costly stones, to lay the foundation of the house with wrought stone. And Solomon's builders

THE LEBANON RANGE AND A GROVE OF CEDARS

The grand mountain range called Lebanon, "white," from the snow which lies for seven months on its summits, is very often mentioned in the Old Testament. The highest summits are from five thousand five hundred to seven thousand feet

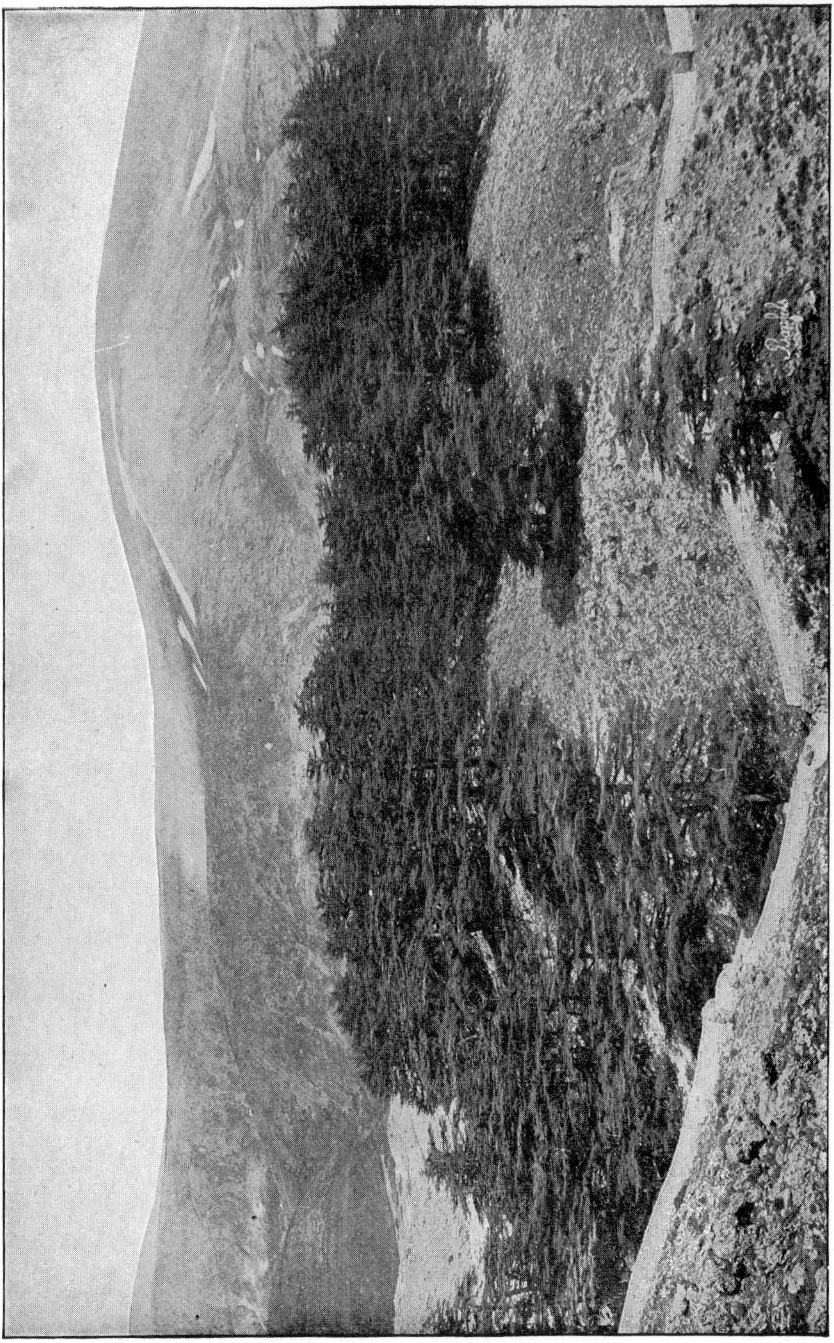

and Hiram's builders did fashion them, and prepared the timber and the stones to build the house.

SOLOMON'S TEMPLE.
The House of the Lord Is Built.

Then Solomon began to build the house of the Lord at Jerusalem in Mount Moriah, where the Lord appeared to David his father, which he made ready in the place that David had appointed, in the threshing-floor of Araunah the Jebusite.

And he began to build in the second day of the second month, in the fourth year of his reign. Now these are the foundations which Solomon laid for the building of the house of God. The length by cubits after the first measure was threescore cubits, and the breadth twenty cubits. And the porch that was before the house, the length of it, according to the breadth of the house, was twenty cubits, and the height an hundred and twenty: and he overlaid it within with pure gold.

And the greater house he ceiled with fir tree, which he overlaid with fine gold, and wrought thereon palm trees and chains. And he adorned the house with precious stones for beauty: and the gold was gold of Parvaim. He overlaid also the house, the beams, the thresholds, and the walls thereof, and the doors thereof, with gold; and graved cherubim on the walls.

And he made the most holy house; the length thereof, according to the breadth of the house, was twenty cubits, and the breadth thereof twenty cubits: and he overlaid it with fine gold, amounting to six hundred talents. And the weight of the nails was fifty shekels of gold. And he overlaid the upper chambers with gold. And in the most holy house he made two cherubim of image work; and they overlaid them with gold. And the wings of the cherubim were twenty cubits long: the wing of the one cherub was five cubits, reaching to the wall of the house; and the other wing was likewise five cubits, reaching to the wing of the other cherub. And the wing of the other cherub was five cubits, reaching to the wall of the house: and the other wing was five cubits also, joining to the wing of the other cherub. The wings of these cherubim spread themselves forth twenty cubits: and they stood on their feet, and their faces were toward the house.

And he made the veil of blue, and purple, and crimson, and fine linen, and wrought cherubim thereon. Also he made before the house two pillars of thirty and five cubits high, and the capital that was on the top of each of them was five cubits. And he made chains in the oracle, and put them on the tops of the pillars; and he made an hundred pomegranates, and put them on the chains. And he set up the pillars before the temple, one on the right hand, and the other on the left; and called the name of that on the right hand Jachin, and the name of that on the left Boaz.

Moreover he made an altar of brass, twenty cubits the length thereof, and twenty cubits the breadth thereof, and ten cubits the height thereof. Also he made the molten sea of ten cubits from brim to brim, round in compass, and

THE MOSQUE OF OMAR AND THE ANCIENT TEMPLE AREA

In the background is the Mosque of El Akoa and beyond are the Judæan hills, to the south and southeast

Used by special permission of the Detroit Photograph Company

The Mohammedan Mosque of Omar now stands upon the old temple area. It is a handsome octagonal building, standing on a platform near the center of the area, from which it is elevated by several steps. It is said to have been built in 636 by the Caliph Omar. In 1099, when the Crusaders captured Jerusalem, ten thousand Arabs were massacred in this enclosure. In 1187 the Moslems, under Saladin, again took the city, and the mosque has been one of their most sacred places ever since

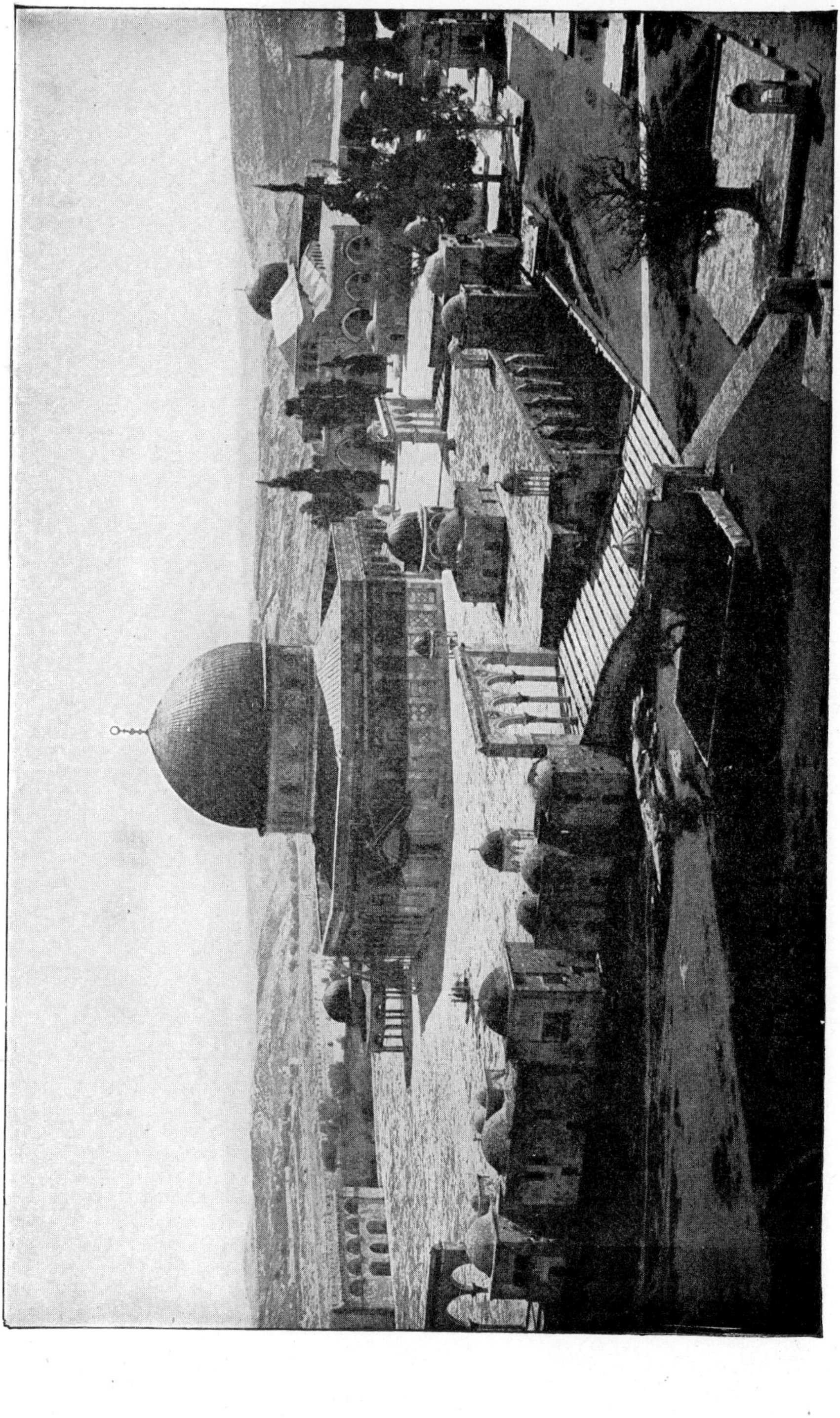

the height thereof was five cubits; and a line of thirty cubits compassed it round about. And under it were the images of oxen, which did compass it round about, for ten cubits, compassing the sea round about. The oxen were in two rows, cast when it was cast. It stood upon twelve oxen, three looking toward the north, and three looking toward the west, and three looking toward the south, and three looking toward the east: and the sea was set upon them above, and all their hinder parts were inward. And it was an handbreadth thick; and the brim thereof was wrought like the brim of a cup, like the flower of a lily: it received and held three thousand baths.

He made also ten lavers, and put five on the right hand, and five on the left, to wash in them; such things as belonged to the burnt offering they washed in them: but the sea was for the priests to wash in.

And he made the ten candlesticks of gold according to the ordinance concerning them; and he set them in the temple, five on the right hand, and five on the left.

He made also ten tables, and placed them in the temple, five on the right side, and five on the left. And he made an hundred basins of gold.

Furthermore he made the court of the priests, and the great court, and doors for the court, and overlaid the doors of them with brass. And he set the sea on the right side of the house eastward, toward the south. And King Solomon made the two pillars, and the bowls, and the two capitals which were on the top of the pillars; and the two networks to cover the two bowls of the capitals that were on the top of the pillars; and the four hundred pomegranates for the two networks; two rows of pomegranates for each network, to cover the two bowls of the capitals that were upon the pillars. He made also the bases, and the lavers made he upon the bases; one sea, and the twelve oxen under it. The pots also, and the shovels, and the flesh-hooks, and all the vessels thereof, did King Solomon make for the house of the Lord of bright brass. In the plain of Jordan did the king cast them, in the clay ground between Succoth and Zeredah. Thus Solomon made all these vessels in great abundance: for the weight of the brass could not be found out.

And Solomon made all the vessels that were in the house of God, the golden altar also, and the tables whereon was the showbread; and the candlesticks with their lamps, that they should burn according to the ordinance before the oracle, of pure gold; and the flowers, and the lamps, and the tongs, of gold, and that perfect gold; and the snuffers, and the basins, and the spoons, and the firepans, of pure gold: and as for the entry of the house, the inner doors thereof for the most holy place, and the doors of the house, to wit, of the temple, were of gold.

Thus all the work that Solomon wrought for the house of the Lord was finished. And Solomon brought in the things that David his father had dedicated; even the silver, and the gold, and all the vessels, and put them in the treasuries of the house of God.

INTERIOR OF THE MOSQUE OF OMAR

Used by special permission of the Detroit Photograph Company

The center of the mosque is occupied by the top of the natural rock, shown in the foreground. It is possible that the great altar of Solomon's temple was at this place

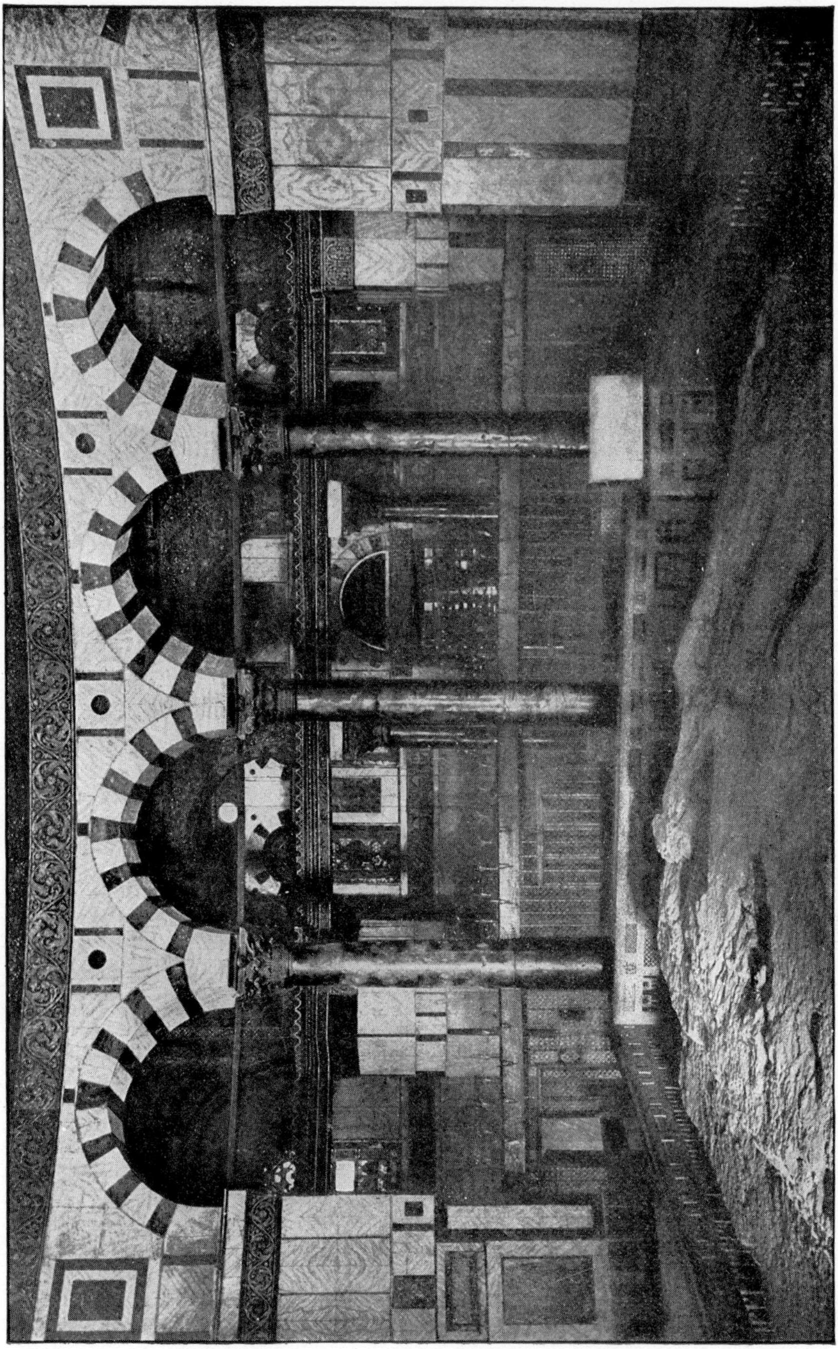

SOLOMON'S PALACE.
Costly and Beautiful.

And Solomon was building his own house thirteen years, and he finished all his house. For he built the house of the forest of Lebanon; the length thereof was an hundred cubits, and the breadth thereof fifty cubits, and the height thereof thirty cubits, upon four rows of cedar pillars, with cedar beams upon the pillars. And it was covered with cedar above over the forty and five beams, that were upon the pillars; fifteen in a row. And there were three rows of latticed windows. And he made the porch of pillars; the length thereof was fifty cubits, and the breadth thereof thirty cubits; and a porch before them; and pillars and thick beams before them. And he made the porch of the throne where he was to judge, even the porch of judgment: and it was covered with cedar from floor to floor. And his house where he was to dwell, the other court within the porch, was of the like work.

He made also an house for Pharaoh's daughter (whom Solomon had taken to wife), like unto this porch. All these were of costly stones, even of hewn stone, according to measure, sawed with saws, within and without, even from the foundation unto the coping, and so on the outside unto the great court. And the foundation was of costly stones, even great stones, stones of ten cubits, and stones of eight cubits. And above were costly stones, even hewn stone, according to measure, and cedar wood. And the great court round about had three rows of hewn stone, and a row of cedar beams; like the inner court of the house of the Lord, and the porch of the house.

THE DEDICATION OF THE TEMPLE.
The Great Assembly and Sacrifice.

Then Solomon assembled the elders of Israel, and all the heads of the tribes, the princes of the fathers' houses of the children of Israel, unto King Solomon in Jerusalem, to bring up the ark of the covenant of the Lord out of the city of David, which is Zion. And they brought up the ark of the Lord, and the tent of meeting, and all the holy vessels that were in the Tent.

And King Solomon and all the congregation of Israel, that were assembled unto him, were with him before the ark, sacrificing sheep and oxen, that could not be told nor numbered for multitude. And the priests brought in the ark of the covenant of the Lord unto its place, into the oracle of the house, to the most holy place. There was nothing in the ark save the two tables of stone which Moses put there at Horeb, when the Lord made a covenant with the children of Israel, when they came out of the land of Egypt. And it came to pass, when the priests were come out of the holy place, that the cloud filled the house of the Lord, so that the priests could not stand to minister by reason of the cloud: for the glory of the Lord filled the house of the Lord.

Then spoke Solomon, "The Lord hath said that he would dwell in the thick darkness. I have surely built thee an house of habitation, a place for thee to dwell in for ever."

And the king turned his face about, and blessed all the congregation of Israel: and all the congregation of Israel stood. And he said, "Blessed be the Lord, the God of Israel, which spoke with his mouth unto David my father, and hath with his hand fulfilled it, saying, 'Since the day that I brought forth my people Israel out of Egypt, I chose no city out of all the tribes of Israel to build an house, that my name might be there; but I chose David to be over my people Israel.' Now it was in the heart of David my father to build an house for the name of the Lord, the God of Israel. But the Lord said unto David my father, 'Whereas it was in thine heart to build an house for my name, thou didst well that it was in thine heart: nevertheless thou shalt not build the house; but thy son, he shall build the house for my name.' And the Lord hath established his word that he spoke; for I am risen up in the place of David my father, and sit on the throne of Israel, as the Lord promised, and have built the house for the name of the Lord, the God of Israel. And there have I set a place for the ark, wherein is the covenant of the Lord, which he made with our fathers, when he brought them out of the land of Egypt."

The Prayer of the King.

And Solomon stood before the altar of the Lord in the presence of all the congregation of Israel, and spread forth his hands toward heaven: and he said, "O Lord, the God of Israel, there is no God like thee, in heaven above, or on earth beneath; who keepest covenant and mercy with thy servants, that walk before thee with all their heart: who hast kept with thy servant David my father that which thou didst promise him: yea, thou hast spoken with thy mouth, and hast fulfilled it with thine hand, as it is this day.

"Now therefore, O Lord, the God of Israel, keep with thy servant David my father that which thou hast promised him, saying, 'There shall not fail thee a man in my sight to sit on the throne of Israel; if only thy children take heed to their way, to walk before me as thou hast walked before me.' Now therefore, O God of Israel, let thy word, I pray thee, be verified, which thou hast spoken unto thy servant David my father. But will God in very deed dwell on the earth? behold, heaven and the heaven of heavens cannot contain thee; how much less this house that I have builded!

"Yet have thou respect unto the prayer of thy servant, and to his supplication, O Lord my God, to hearken unto the cry and to the prayer which thy servant prayeth before thee this day: that thine eyes may be open toward this house night and day, even toward the place whereof thou hast said, 'My name shall be there': to hearken unto the prayer which thy servant shall pray toward this place. And hearken thou to the supplication of thy servant, and of thy people Israel, when they shall pray toward this place: yea, hear thou in heaven thy dwelling place; and when thou hearest, forgive.

"If a man sin against his neighbor, and an oath be laid upon him to cause him to swear, and he come and swear

JERUSALEM, FROM THE MOUNT OF OLIVES

From an old photograph in the possession of the Springfield Public Library
and used by kind permission

The view of Jerusalem from the Mount of Olives in the days of the city's glory, was one of splendor. Of this view in the time of Christ a writer says, referring especially to the temple, "In the setting even more than the rising sun, must the vast proportions, the symmetry, and the sparkling sheen of this mass of snowy marble and gold have stood out gloriously"

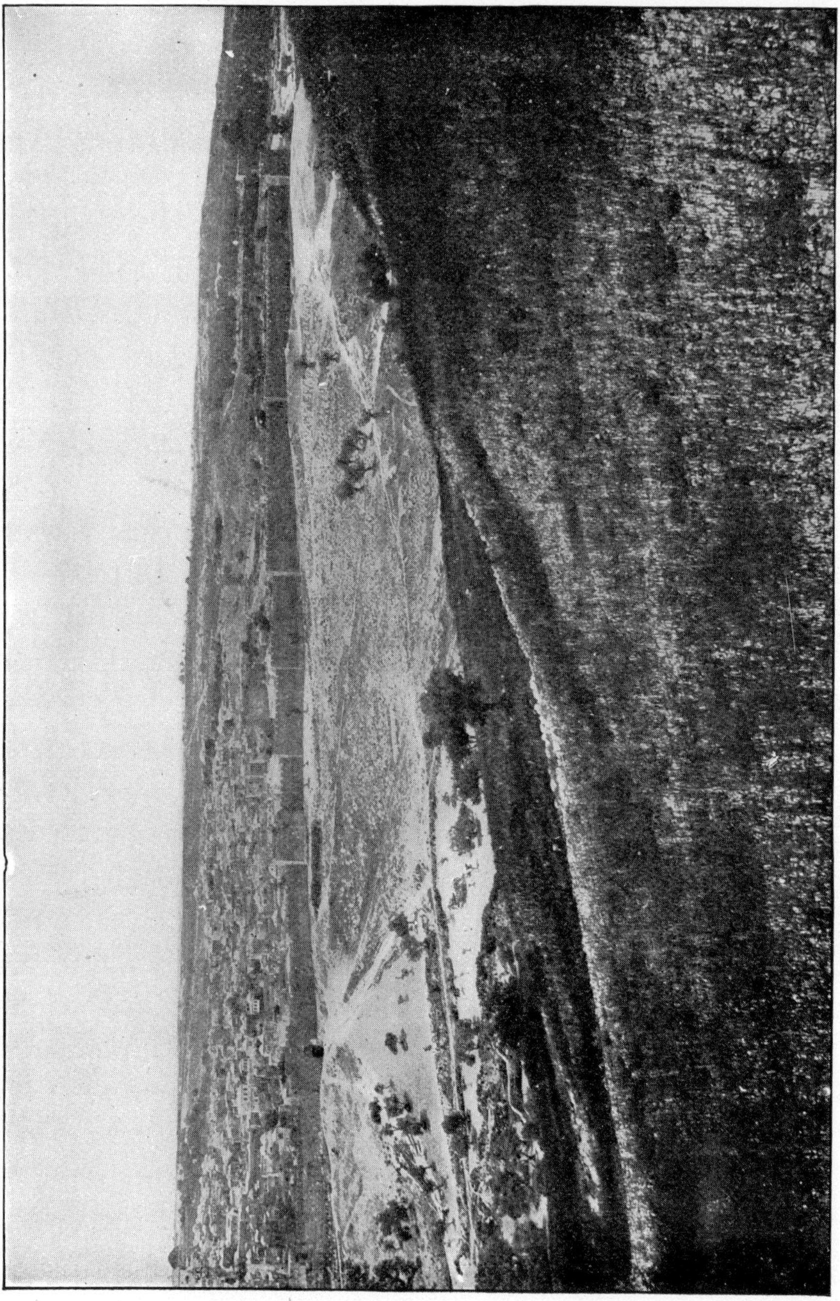

before thine altar in this house: then hear thou in heaven, and do, and judge thy servants, condemning the wicked, to bring his way upon his own head; and justifying the righteous, to give him according to his righteousness.

"When thy people Israel be smitten down before the enemy, because they have sinned against thee; if they turn again to thee, and confess thy name, and pray and make supplication unto thee in this house: then hear thou in heaven, and forgive the sin of thy people Israel, and bring them again unto the land which thou gavest unto their fathers. When heaven is shut up, and there is no rain, because they have sinned against thee; if they pray toward this place, and confess thy name, and turn from their sin, when thou dost afflict them: then hear thou in heaven, and forgive the sin of thy servants, and of thy people Israel, when thou teachest them the good way wherein they should walk; and send rain upon thy land, which thou hast given to thy people for an inheritance.

"If there be in the land famine, if there be pestilence, if there be blasting or mildew, locust or caterpillar; if their enemy besiege them in the land of their cities; whatsoever plague, whatsoever sickness there be; what prayer and supplication soever be made by any man, or by all thy people Israel, which shall know every man the plague of his own heart, and spread forth his hands toward this house: then hear thou in heaven thy dwelling place, and forgive, and do, and render unto every man according to all his ways, whose heart thou knowest (for thou, even thou only, knowest the hearts of all the children of men);

that they may fear thee all the days that they live in the land which thou gavest unto our fathers.

"Moreover concerning the stranger, that is not of thy people Israel, when he shall come out of a far country for thy name's sake (for they shall hear of thy great name, and of thy mighty hand, and of thy stretched out arm); when he shall come and pray toward this house: hear thou in heaven thy dwelling place, and do according to all that the stranger calleth to thee for; that all the peoples of the earth may know thy name, to fear thee, as doth thy people Israel, and that they may know that this house which I have built is called by thy name.

"If thy people go out to battle against their enemy, by whatsoever way thou shalt send them, and they pray unto the Lord toward the city which thou hast chosen, and toward the house which I have built for thy name: then hear thou in heaven their prayer and their supplication, and maintain their cause.

"If they sin against thee (for there is no man that sinneth not), and thou be angry with them, and deliver them to the enemy, so that they carry them away captive unto the land of the enemy, far off or near; yet if they shall bethink themselves in the land whither they are carried captive, and turn again, and make supplication unto thee in the land of them that carried them captive, saying, 'We have sinned, and have done perversely, we have dealt wickedly'; if they return unto thee with all their heart and with all their soul in the land of their enemies, which carried them captive, and pray unto thee toward their land, which thou gavest unto their fathers, the city which thou hast chosen, and the house which I have built for thy name: then hear thou their prayer and their supplication in heaven thy dwelling place, and maintain their cause; and forgive thy people which have sinned against thee, and all their transgressions wherein they have transgressed against thee; and give them compassion before those who carried them captive, that they may have compassion on them: for they be thy people, and thine inheritance, which thou broughtest forth out of Egypt, from the midst of the furnace of iron: that thine eyes may be open to the supplication of thy servant, and unto the supplication of thy people Israel, to hearken unto them whensoever they cry unto thee. For thou didst separate them from among all the peoples of the earth, to be thine inheritance, as thou hast spoken by Moses thy servant, when thou broughtest our fathers out of Egypt, O Lord God."

And it was so, that when Solomon had made an end of praying all this prayer and supplication unto the Lord, he arose from before the altar of the Lord, from kneeling on his knees with his hands spread forth toward heaven. And he stood, and blessed all the congregation of Israel with a loud voice, saying, "Blessed be the Lord, that hath given rest unto his people Israel, according to all that he promised: there hath not failed one word of all his good promise, which he promised by Moses his servant. The Lord our God be with us, as he was with our fathers: let him not leave us nor forsake us: that he may incline our hearts unto him, to walk in all his ways, and keep his commandments, and his statutes, and his judgments, which he commanded our fathers. And let these my words, wherewith I have made supplication before the Lord, be nigh unto the Lord our God day and night, that he maintain the cause of his servant, and the cause of his people Israel, as every day shall require: that all the peoples of the earth may know that the Lord, he is God; there is none else. Let your heart therefore be perfect with the Lord our God, to walk in his statutes, and to keep his commandments, as at this day."

And the king, and all Israel with him, offered sacrifice before the Lord. And Solomon offered for the sacrifice of peace offerings, which he offered unto the Lord, two and twenty thousand oxen, and an hundred and twenty thousand sheep. So the king and all the children of Israel dedicated the house of the Lord.

A ROYAL PILGRIMAGE.
The Visit of the Queen of Sheba.

And when the queen of Sheba heard of the fame of Solomon concerning the name of the Lord, she came to prove him with hard questions. And she came to Jerusalem with a very great caravan, with camels that bore spices, and very much gold, and precious stones: and when she was come to Solomon, she communed with him of all that was in her heart. And Solomon told her all her questions: there was not anything hid from the king which he told her not. And when the queen of Sheba had seen all the wisdom of Solomon, and the house that he had built,

JERUSALEM, FROM THE CITADEL, LOOKING TOWARD THE
MOUNT OF OLIVES

From a picture in the possession of the Forbes Library
and used by kind permission

This view reverses the position of the spectator in the previous picture.
Looking from the citadel, the slope of the Mount of Olives rises in the east

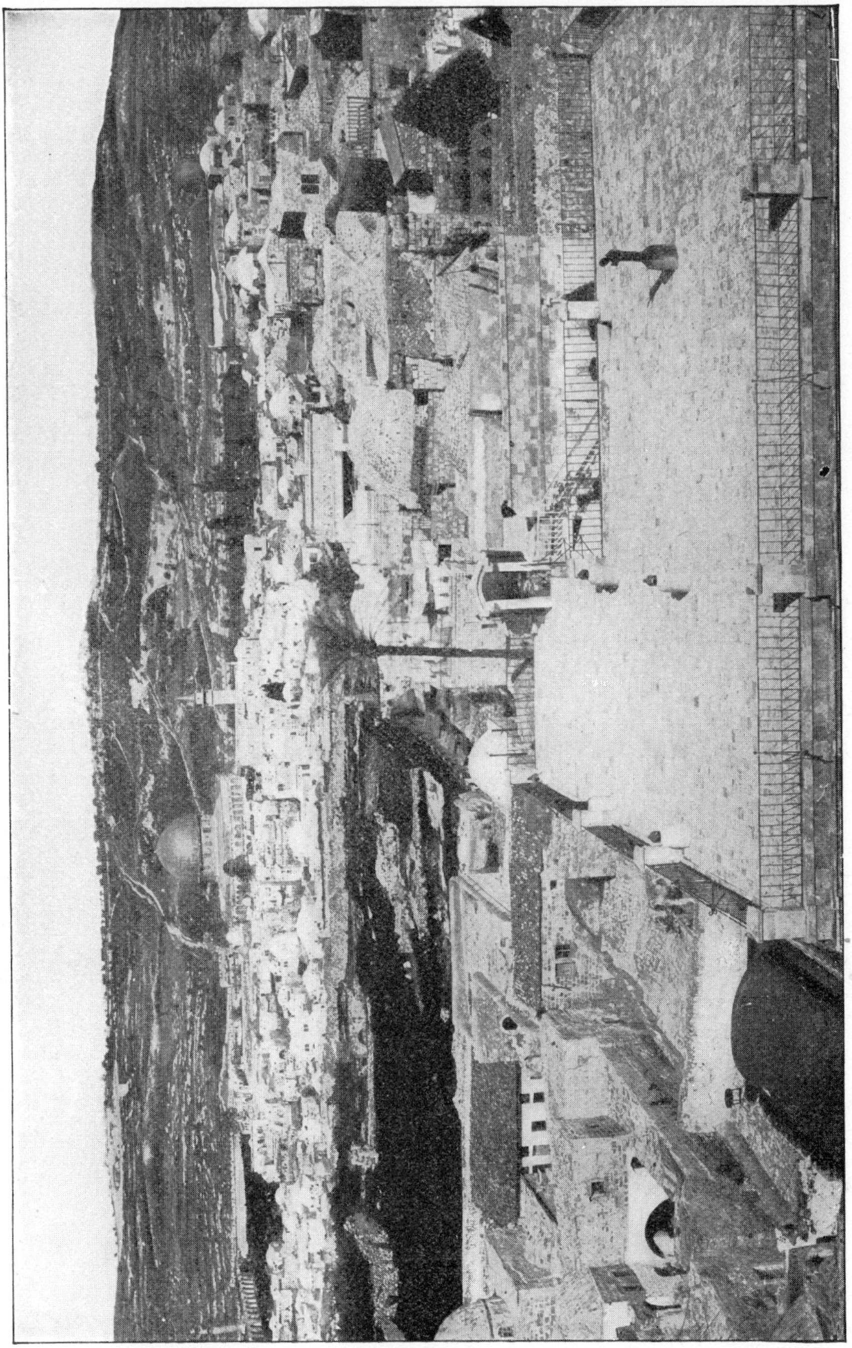

and the meat of his table and the seating of his servants, and the attendance of his ministers, and their apparel, and his cupbearers, and his ascent by which he went up unto the house of the Lord; there was no more spirit in her.

And she said to the king, "It was a true report that I heard in mine own land of thine acts, and of thy wisdom. Howbeit I believed not the words, until I came, and mine eyes had seen it: and, behold, the half was not told me: thy wisdom and prosperity exceedeth the fame which I heard. Happy are thy men, happy are these thy servants, which stand continually before thee, and that hear thy wisdom. Blessed be the Lord thy God, which delighted in thee, to set thee on the throne of Israel: because the Lord loved Israel for ever, therefore made he thee king, to do judgment and justice."

And she gave the king an hundred and twenty talents of gold, and of spices very great store, and precious stones: there came no more such abundance of spices as these which the queen of Sheba gave to King Solomon.

And King Solomon gave to the queen of Sheba all her desire, whatsoever she asked, beside that which Solomon gave her of his royal bounty. So she turned, and went to her own land, she and her servants.

THE GREATNESS OF SOLOMON'S EMPIRE.
Gold and Ivory Brought by Ship and Caravan.

(For forty years Solomon reigned in Jerusalem, and during nearly all this time the land was peaceful and prosperous. The empire of Solomon was greater in extent than the territory ruled over by any king which came after him. At last the great king died and was buried in Jerusalem, the city which his father had made the capital.)

And King Solomon made a navy of ships in Eziongeber, which is beside Elath, at the head of the Red Sea, in the land of Edom. And Hiram sent in the navy his servants, sailors that had knowledge of the sea, with the servants of Solomon. And they came to Ophir, and fetched from thence gold, four hundred and twenty talents, and brought it to King Solomon.

And the navy also of Hiram, that brought gold from Ophir, brought in from Ophir great plenty of almug trees and precious stones. And the king made of the almug trees pillars for the house of the Lord, and for the king's house, harps also and psalteries for the singers: there came no such almug trees, nor were seen, unto this day.

Now the weight of gold that came to Solomon in one year was six hundred threescore and six talents of gold, beside that which the traders brought, and the traffic of the merchants, and of all the kings of the mingled people, and of the governors of the country. And King Solomon made two hundred bucklers of beaten gold: six hundred shekels of gold went to one buckler. And he made three hundred shields of beaten gold; three pounds of gold went to one shield: and the king put them in the house of the forest of Lebanon.

Moreover the king made a great throne of ivory, and overlaid it with the finest gold. There were six steps to the throne, and the top of the throne was round behind:

and there were arms on either side of the seat, and two lions standing beside the arms. And twelve lions stood there on the one side and on the other upon the six steps: there was not the like made in any kingdom. And all King Solomon's drinking vessels were of gold, and all the vessels of the house of the forest of Lebanon were of pure gold: none were of silver; it was nothing accounted of in the days of Solomon.

For the king had at sea a navy of Tarshish with the navy of Hiram: once every three years came the navy of Tarshish, bringing gold, and silver, ivory, and apes, and peacocks.

So King Solomon exceeded all the kings of the earth in riches and in wisdom. And all the earth sought the presence of Solomon, to hear his wisdom, which God had put in his heart. And they brought every man his present, vessels of silver, and vessels of gold, and raiment, and armor, and spices, horses, and mules, a rate year by year.

And Solomon gathered together chariots and horsemen: and he had a thousand and four hundred chariots, and twelve thousand horsemen, which he bestowed in the chariot cities, and with the king at Jerusalem. And the king made silver to be in Jerusalem as stones, and cedars made he to be as the sycamore trees that are in the lowland, for abundance.

NOTES

NOTES.

ABRAHAM. HIS JOURNEYS.

Ur of the Chaldees was an ancient city on the great plain of Babylon.

Haran. A city lying far to the north of Ur, northeast of Palestine, on the road from the east to the Mediterranean coast.

Canaan, Palestine, the *Land of Israel,* are all names which have been used at different times for the same country. Canaan is the oldest Biblical name. It means "the lowlands" near the Mediterranean, but was used for the whole country.

Shechem. A city in the middle of Canaan, in a valley between two mountains, Ebal and Gerizim.

Oak of Mamre. The name suggests an oak that was connected with a sacred place. Its exact site is not known, but it must be somewhere near Hebron.

Beth-el was a sacred place, in later times very important. It is on the great road north and south, about twelve miles north of Jerusalem. *Ai* was about two miles east, in the head of a valley which falls rapidly toward the Jordan.

The South was used as the name of the country to the south of Canaan, as we use "the South" and "the West" to mean sections of our own country.

DIVISION OF THE LAND.

Plain of the Jordan. The river Jordan runs through a deep valley, which broadens out in its southern part into a plain. It was warm, rich and fertile. Here were situated the cities of Sodom and Gomorrah.

Zoar. One of the cities of the Plain of the Jordan, perhaps on higher ground than the others.

Hebron, near which the oaks of Mamre were, lies about twenty miles south of Jerusalem. It was from very early time regarded as a sacred city. It is still a town of considerable size.

The Fight of the Five Kings.

The five kings were from Babylonia and the mountain country of Elam beyond Babylonia. As the story stands, the king of Elam had conquered Babylonia and the land of Canaan. After a time, part of the land of Canaan revolted, and he came, with his Babylonian allies, to punish the rebellious Canaanites.

Slime pits. Pits of bitumen, a black, sometimes sticky mineral, which is found in the valley of Jordan.

Dan. A town in the north of Palestine. The story makes Abraham's chase of the kings extend all the length of the land afterwards held by the Hebrews.

Hobah. A town north of Damascus, not mentioned elsewhere in the Bible.

Damascus. A very old city, northeast of Palestine. It is situated in a beautiful spot, watered by two rivers, and has been the starting point of caravans for the east, west, and south since long before the days of Abraham.

Melchizedek. King of Salem. Salem was probably Jerusalem. Melchizedek was, like many other ancient kings, also the chief priest of his city. As such, it was right that he should bless the returning chief in war.

A Covenant between God and Abraham.

Euphrates. The greatest river of western Asia. It rises in the mountains of Armenia and flows to the Persian gulf. The Bible often calls it simply "the Great River."

Beer-sheba. The farthest town to the south in Palestine. "From Dan to Beer-sheba" was used to mean all the land from the north to the south.

EN ROGEL, FROM THE SOUTH
From a photograph taken by Prof. H. G. Mitchell
and used by his kind permission

A nearer view of the famous old well outside the walls of Jerusalem

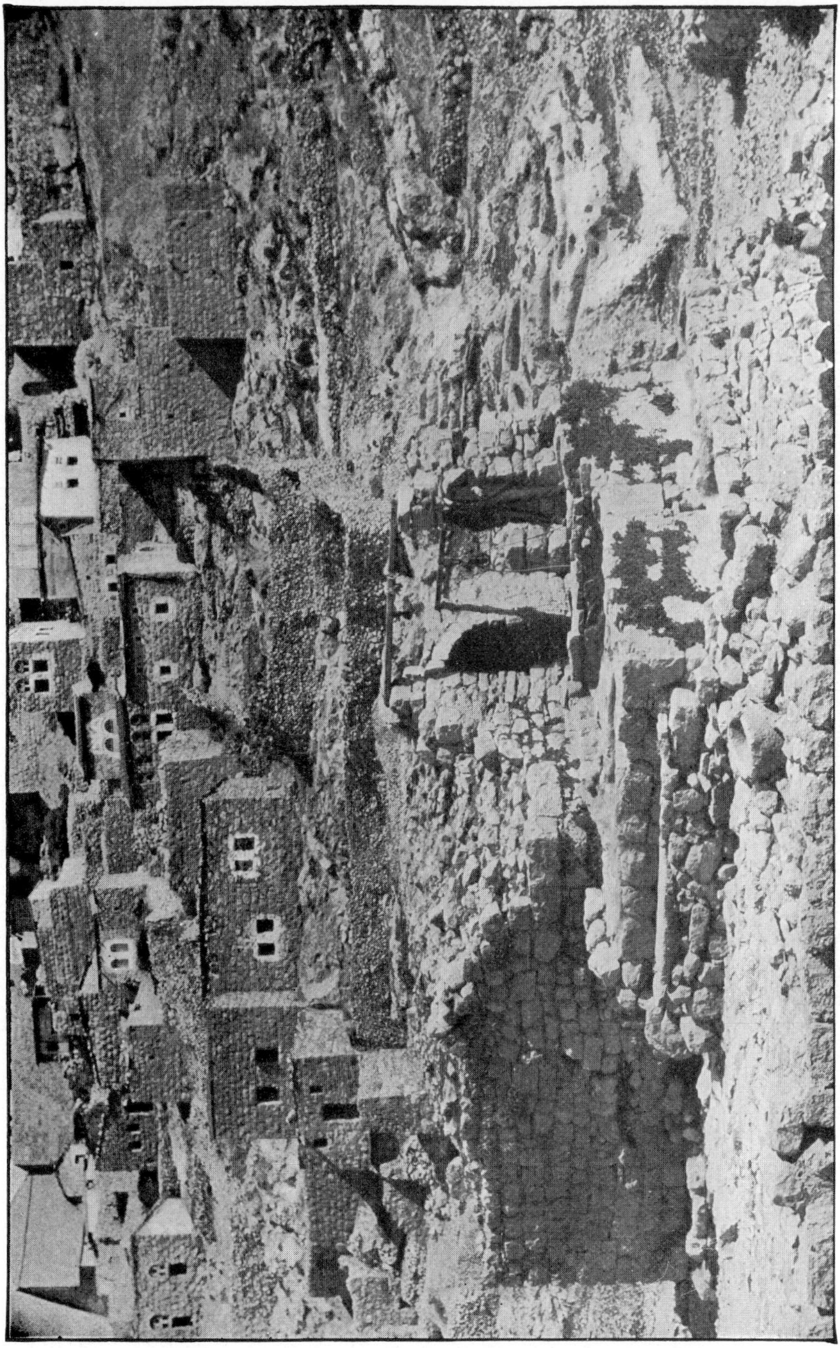

NOTES

Wilderness of Paran. The half desert country lying south of Palestine.

TESTING OF ABRAHAM.

Land of Moriah. An unknown region. The Jews later supposed that Isaac was sacrificed on the hill at Jerusalem on which Solomon built the temple, but the Bible itself does not affirm it.

Sacrifices were offered on bare rocks or on altars built of stone or earth. At first they were a way of expressing fellowship with God. The people ate part of an offering, and the rest of it was burnt, to symbolize that it was God's share. Later the offering was something given to God. This last is the idea in the story of the sacrifice of Isaac.

DEATH AND BURIAL OF SARAH.

Hittites and *children of Heth* mean the Hittites, one of the tribes of peoples in Palestine before the arrival of the Hebrews. There was a great Hittite empire north of Palestine.

Shekel. An amount of money; in early times not a coin but a weight of money. In this story Abraham "weighed" the silver.

ISAAC AND REBEKAH.

Mesopotamia means "between the rivers," the wide land far east between the Euphrates and the Tigris.

Cave of Machpelah. In early times caves were often used as burial places. The present inhabitants of Hebron believe the cave of Machpelah is under a building in their city.

JACOB.

Pottage. A sort of stew of lentils, a vegetable like beans.

Birthright. In many parts of the world, the oldest child has, by his birth, the right of becoming the head of the family at the death of his father, with sometimes other rights and responsibilities.

Paddan-aram or *Padan-aram*. "The country of Syria," lying northeast of Palestine, between Damascus and the river Euphrates.

Pillars of stone. Standing stones and heaps of stones were often set up at places held sacred. Oil was poured on such stones as an offering to God, or to express the idea that the places were holy. Such sacred places are found in almost all lands, and were very common in Palestine. The stones are still sometimes found standing.

Jegar-sahadutha and *Galeed* both mean "heap of witness," one in the language of Canaan, the other in that of Mesopotamia.

Jabbok. A stream flowing into the Jordan from the east.

Peniel. "Face of God." Sometimes spelled Penuel.

Seir. A section of country southeast of Palestine. It is high and rocky, sometimes called Mt. Seir.

Succoth, "booths." Its site is not known.

Allon-bacuth, "the oak of weeping"

JOSEPH.

Dothan. About ten miles north of Samaria. A story about Elisha is also located at Dothan. *Tales of Old Judea, 148.*

Caravan. A train of camels or horses. In the East people traveled together in caravans for protection against robbers.

Egypt. A land where civilization is very ancient. All through the Old Testament times it was a powerful kingdom. Its king was called, in the early stories of the Bible, the Pharaoh.

Divining cup. The custom of divining, that is, discovering hidden secrets by magic, was widespread in the ancient world. Sometimes cups of sacred water were used, and a special cup might be thought to have special value for divination.

Goshen. A section in the northeast of Egypt, next to the Isthmus of Suez.

Rameses. A city in the land of Goshen. "The land of Rameses" is the country about this city.

Embalming was a custom in Egypt. These people thought that their life in the next world depended on keeping the body from decay; so they filled the body with certain chemicals which kept it from the natural decay. The preserved body is called a mummy.

JOSHUA.

Shittim. A place on the east of the Jordan. The site is not known.

Jerusalem, Hebron, Jarmuth, Lachish, and *Eglon* are all in the southern part of Palestine, in what was later the kingdom of Judah.

Book of Jashar. A collection of poems of ancient heroes, from which also the beautiful lament of David over Saul is taken. *Hero Tales, 426.*

THE JUDGES.

Hill country of Ephraim. The mountain ridge in the central part of Palestine, which belonged to the tribe of Ephraim.

Summer room. A room built on the flat top of a house, to get the cool breezes in the hot summer days.

Philistines. A people who, like the Hebrews, migrated into the land of the Canaanites. They occupied the land along the coast of the Mediterranean. For a long time they were stronger in war than the Hebrews, and ruled over them. This name "Palestine" comes from "Philistine."

Beating out wheat in the wine press. Ordinarily in the East, wheat is threshed by being trodden out with oxen on a bare, hard piece of ground. It is usually in a prominent place, to get the wind for winnowing, and so could be easily seen by the enemy. The wine press furnished a small, flat place where the little wheat they had could be threshed in secret.

Angel of the Lord. Any messenger from God, sometimes thought of in early times as being God himself in the form of a man.

Ophrah. A place in northern central Palestine, site not known.

Baal and Asherah. The Baals were the gods of the Canaanites. Each locality had its Baal (Lord), with an altar and a stone pillar, on some prominent place (the "high places" of the Bible). The asherah was a sacred tree or post standing near the stone pillar.

Jezreel. A beautifully situated town in northern central Palestine.

Pitchers. Jars in which were hidden torches. When the jars were broken with a crash, the torches suddenly flamed out in the darkness, and the noise and the unexpected light made a panic in the Midianite army.

SAUL.

Mizpah. A town on the east of Jordan. Probably the same place that is mentioned in the story of Jacob.

Ramah, "hill." A common name of places in Palestine.

Vial. A vessel in which was carried a sacred oil. A common way to honor a guest was to pour a little oil on his head. Kings and priests were set apart for their office by anointing with oil.

Jabesh. A city east of the Jordan. The people of the city did not forget the good deed of Saul. Many years later, when Saul was defeated and killed, brave men from this city traveled all night, took his body from the battlefield, and gave it an honorable funeral at Jabesh.

JERUSALEM, FROM THE NORTHEAST

Used by special permission of the Detroit Photograph Company

The view is taken from Mount Scopus, the northward extension of the Mount of Olives. The valley between is the head of the Kidron

This fine picture gives a distinct view of the modern city with its walls and towers, and the valley which lies between

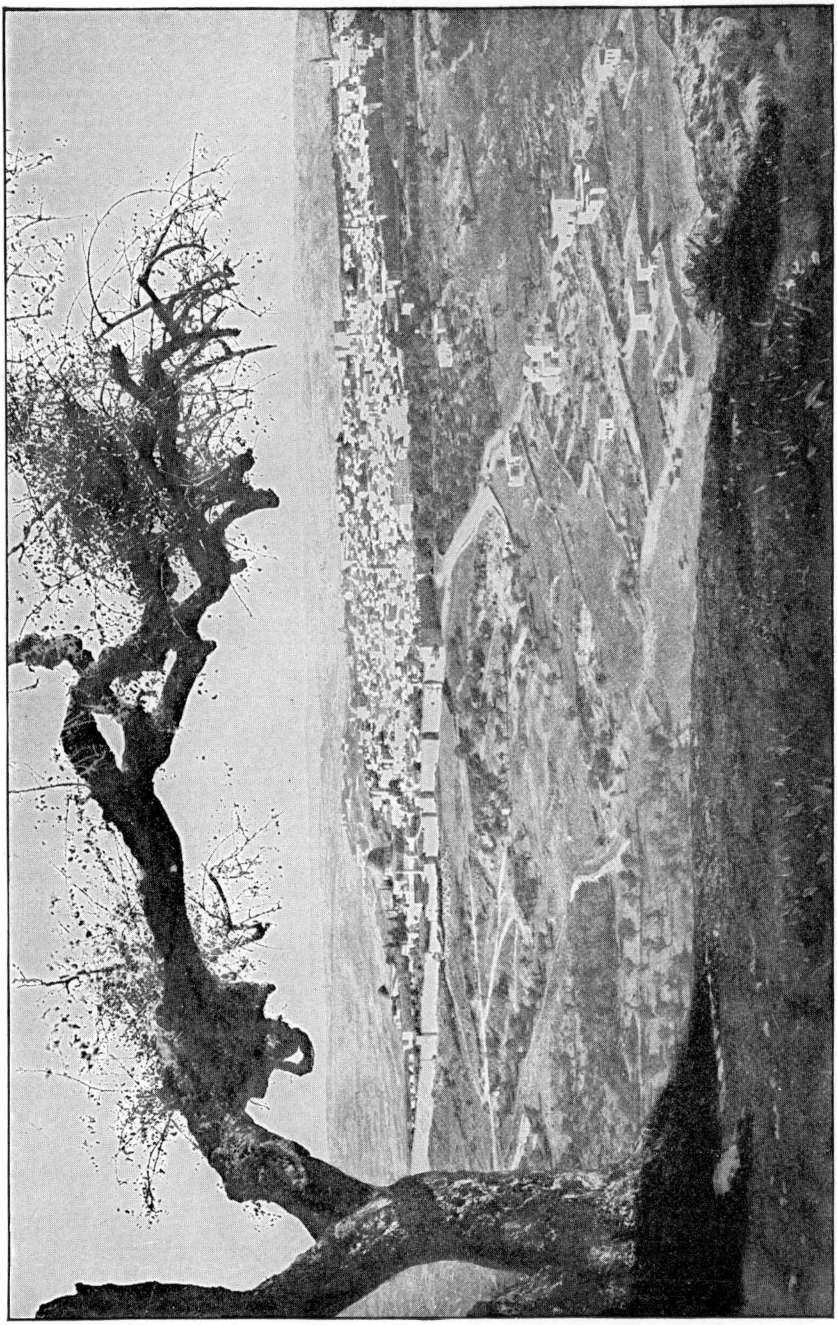

Ammonites. A people who lived on the east of the Jordan, with whom the Hebrews had made war.

Michmash. A small town about seven miles north of Jerusalem, on the edge of a deep ravine going down toward the Jordan.

Eating with the blood. The blood was not eaten by the Hebrews. They thought of it as the seat of life, and, since life belonged to God, man ought not to eat it.

Familiar Spirit. "Familiar" is here connected with "family," household. It means a spirit which is ready to serve one, like one of his servants. The woman with a "familiar spirit" was a "medium," who was supposed to be able to summon spirits.

DAVID.

Cubit. See *Weights and Measures. Span.* The half of a cubit, about nine inches.

Gath. A Philistine city on the plain west of the hills of Judæa.

Armor. The helmet of brass was not uncommon. The "coat of mail" was a close-fitting cloak, covered with brass scales, so as to allow free movement. The greaves were coverings for the shins and the knees. The armor of the Bible times was much simpler than that in Europe in the middle ages.

SOLOMON.

Tyre. A city on the coast of the Mediterranean, north of Palestine, for a long time the center of much commerce between Egypt, Asia, Greece, and the lands farther west. Its inhabitants were Phœnicians.

Zidon, like Tyre, a Phœnician coast city, rich and commercial.

Sheba. A land in southern Arabia, which got wealth by trading between Egypt and the countries on the Mediterranean, and the distant south and east.

Ophir. A land about which there have been many opinions. Some have thought it in East Africa, some in the far east—India or the Malay Peninsula,—some in Southeast Arabia. Perhaps the last opinion is as probable as any.

Almug. A wood evidently valued for its rarity and beauty. What the wood was is not known, nor where it came from.

Ezion-Geber. A town at the head of the Eastern gulf, now called the Gulf of Akabah, of the Red Sea. In ancient times it was a port of commerce, but now there is no trade anywhere on this gulf.

Red Sea. Between Egypt and Arabia. In the time of Solomon there was commerce on it with Southern Arabia, Eastern Africa, and perhaps with countries still farther away. Part of Solomon's wealth came from his share in this commerce.

TABLE OF MEASURES.

	Palm.	Span.	Cubit.	Value in Inches.
Palm.	1		.	3
Span.	3	1		9
Cubit.	6	2	1	18

WEIGHTS.

A shekel. The English equivalent of this weight is not known. It varied at different times in the history of Israel. According to our estimate a shekel was about .3 of an avoirdupois ounce. Probably the earliest standard of weight was a grain of wheat and the early Babylonian shekel was equal to 180 grains of wheat. According to this estimate the weight of Goliath's coat of brass was about 90 pounds and the weight of his spearhead about 10 pounds.

A mina. A weight equal to 60 shekels.

A talent. A weight equal to 60 minas.

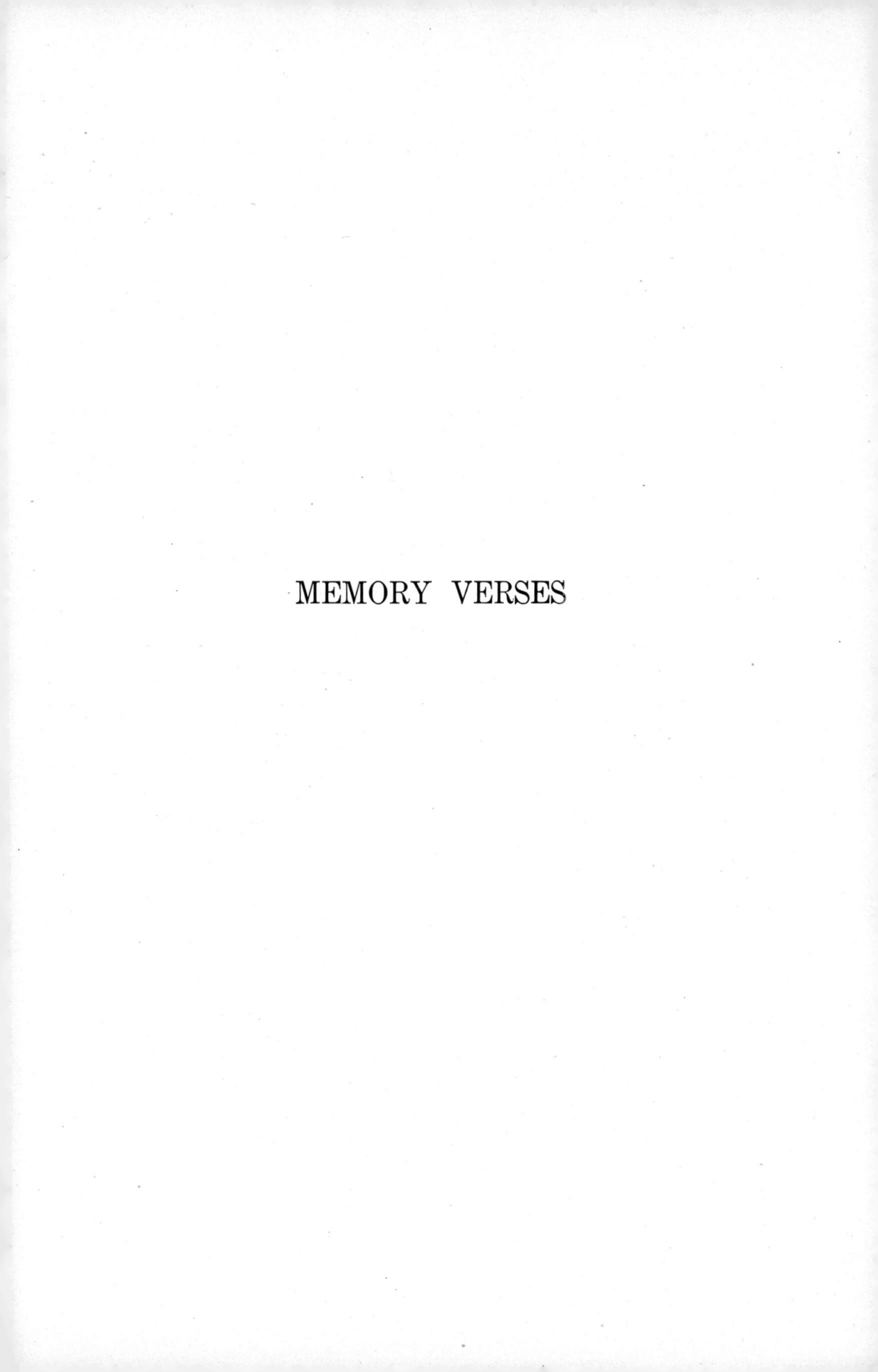

MEMORY VERSES

MEMORY VERSES.

One for Each Week of the Year.

Lord, thou hast been our dwelling place in all generations. Before the mountains were brought forth, or ever thou hadst formed the earth and the world, even from everlasting to everlasting, thou art God.—*Psalms 90:1,2.*

If God be for us, who can be against us?—*Romans 8:31.*

Wherefore take unto you the whole armor of God, that ye may be able to withstand in the evil day, and, having done all, to stand.—*Ephesians 6:13.*

Fight the good fight of faith, lay hold on eternal life, whereunto thou art also called, and hast professed a good profession before many witnesses.—*I Timothy 6:12.*

Lift up your heads, O ye gates; and be ye lift up, ye everlasting doors; and the King of glory shall come in. —*Psalms 24:7.*

The Lord reigneth, let the earth rejoice; let the multitude of isles be glad thereof.—*Psalms 97:1.*

The Lord is my strength and my shield.—*Psalms 28:7.*

Only be thou strong and very courageous.—*Joshua 1:7.*

The Lord is my strength and song, and he is become my salvation; he is my God, and I will prepare him an habitation; my father's God, and I will exalt him.—*Exodus 15:2.*

Brethren, I count not myself to have apprehended: but this one thing I do, forgetting those things which are behind, and reaching forth unto those things which are before, I press toward the mark for the prize of the high calling of God in Christ Jesus.—*Philippians 3:13, 14.*

Finally, my brethren, be strong in the Lord, and in the power of his might.—*Ephesians 6:10.*

Then said Jesus unto his disciples, "If any man will come after me, let him deny himself, and take up his cross and follow me."—*Matthew 16:24.*

Know ye not that they which run in a race run all, but one receiveth the prize? So run, that ye may obtain.—*I Corinthians 9:24.*

He that findeth his life, shall lose it: and he that loseth his life for my sake, shall find it.—*Matthew 10:39.*

For I reckon that the sufferings of this present time are not worthy to be compared with the glory which shall be revealed in us.—*Romans 8:18.*

The night is far spent, the day is at hand: let us therefore cast off the works of darkness, and let us put on the armor of light.—*Romans 13:12.*

He that is not with me is against me: and he that gathereth not with me scattereth.—*Luke 11:23.*

We will rejoice in thy salvation, and in the name of God we will set up our banners.—*Psalms 20:5.*

His banner over me was love.—*Song of Solomon 2:4.*

And every man that striveth for the mastery is temperate in all things. Now they do it to obtain a corruptible crown; but we an incorruptible.—*I Corinthians 9:25.*

Watch ye, stand fast in the faith, quit you like men, be strong.—*I Corinthians 16:13.*

Whosoever will be chief among you, let him be your servant.—*Matthew 20:27.*

For the kingdom of God is not in word but in power.—*I Corinthians 4:20.*

Give unto the Lord, ye kindreds of the people, give unto the Lord glory and strength.—*I Chronicles 16:28.*

The Lord is my rock, and my fortress, and my deliverer. —*II Samuel 22:2.*

I will say of the Lord, he is my refuge and my fortress: my God; in him will I trust.—*Psalms 91:2.*

I therefore so run, not as uncertainly; so fight I, not as one that beateth the air: but I keep under my body, and bring it into subjection.—*I Corinthians 9:26, 27.*

Who through faith subdued kingdoms, wrought righteousness, obtained promises, stopped the mouths of lions, quenched the violence of fire, escaped the edge of the sword, out of weakness were made strong, waxed valiant in fight, turned to flight the armies of the aliens.—*Hebrews 11: 33, 34.*

Thou therefore endure hardness, as a good soldier of Jesus Christ.—*II Timothy 2:3.*

Be thou faithful unto death, and I will give thee the crown of life.—*Revelations 2:10.*

Walk worthily of God, who calleth you unto his kingdom and glory.—*I Thessalonians 2:12.*

Hold fast the profession of our faith without wavering; for he is faithful that promised.—*Hebrews 10:23.*

Put on the whole armor of God, that ye may be able to stand against the wiles of the devil.—*Ephesians 6:11.*

I can do all things through Christ who strengtheneth me.—*Philippians 4:13.*

Blessed are those servants, whom the Lord, when he cometh, shall find watching.—*Luke 12:37.*

Take ye heed, watch and pray.—*Mark 13:33.*

He that taketh not his cross, and followeth after me, is not worthy of me.—*Matthew 10:38.*

Blessed be the Lord God, the God of Israel, who only doeth wondrous things. And blessed be his glorious name forever: and let the whole earth be filled with his glory.—*Psalms 72:18, 19.*

He that is slow to anger is better than the mighty; and he that ruleth his spirit than he that taketh a city.—*Proverbs 16:32.*

Wherefore, seeing we also are compassed about with so great a cloud of witnesses, let us lay aside every weight, and the sin which doth so easily beset us, and let us run with patience the race that is set before us.—*Hebrews 12:1*.

Let the heavens be glad, and let the earth rejoice, and let men say among the nations, the Lord reigneth.—*I Chronicles 16:31*.

Sing unto the Lord a new song, and his praise from the end of the earth, ye that go down to the sea, and all that is therein; the isles, and the inhabitants thereof.—*Isaiah 42:10*.

Save thy people, and bless thine inheritance: feed them also, and lift them up for ever.—*Psalms 28:9*.

Give us help from trouble; for vain is the help of man.—*Psalms 60:11*.

And ye shall know the truth, and the truth shall make you free.—*John 8:32*.

Stand fast therefore in the liberty wherewith Christ hath made us free, and be not entangled again with the yoke of bondage.—*Galatians 5:1*.

But the salvation of the righteous is of the Lord: he is their strength in the time of trouble.—*Psalms 37:39*.

The Lord is my strength and song, and is become my salvation.—*Psalms 118:14*.

He giveth power to the faint: and to them that have no might he increaseth strength.—*Isaiah 40:29*.

Who shall separate us from the love of Christ? Shall tribulation, or distress, or persecution, or famine, or nakedness, or sword? Nay, in all these things we are more than conquerors through him that loved us.—*Romans 8:35, 37.*

Fear not, little flock, for it is your Father's good pleasure to give you the kingdom.—*Luke 12:32.*

I have fought a good fight, I have finished my course, I have kept the faith.—*II Timothy 4:7.*